Praise for the second edition of *A Concise Introduction to*

"This edition expands on the current knowledge of the Canadian health care system from a mental health perspective lens. It provides a comprehensive overview of mental health across the lifespan applicable to all health care providers. It is an indispensable resource for students, consumers, policy-makers, and academics who want to develop their knowledge and understanding of mental health in Canada. This edition can be used as a stand-alone text or a relevant resource for those teaching in the area of mental health."
—Robert J. Meadus, PhD, RN, School of Nursing, Memorial University

"The authors have created an important resource for professionals and students alike in the mental health field, who will find this unique and well-written text comprehensive and appealing. As we further embrace a multi-disciplinary approach for addressing the complexities experienced by people with mental health disorders and their families, this text proves essential for understanding mental health and mental illness from multiple perspectives. It is truly outstanding."
—Michèle Preyde, PhD, Department of Family Relations and Applied Nutrition, University of Guelph

# A CONCISE INTRODUCTION
# TO MENTAL HEALTH
# IN CANADA

# A CONCISE INTRODUCTION TO MENTAL HEALTH IN CANADA

## Second Edition

Elliot M. Goldner, Emily Jenkins, and Dan Bilsker

Canadian Scholars' Press
Toronto

A Concise Introduction to Mental Health in Canada, Second Edition
By Elliot M. Goldner, Emily Jenkins, and Dan Bilsker

First published in 2016 by
**Canadian Scholars' Press Inc.**
425 Adelaide Street West, Suite 200
Toronto, Ontario
M5V 3C1
**www.cspi.org**

**Library and Archives Canada Cataloguing in Publication**

Goldner, Elliot M. (Elliot Michael), 1953-, author
    A concise introduction to mental health in Canada / Elliot Goldner,
Emily Jenkins, and Dan Bilsker.—Second edition.

Includes bibliographical references and index.
Issued in print and electronic formats.
ISBN 978-1-55130-906-4 (paperback).—ISBN 978-1-55130-907-1 (pdf).—
ISBN 978-1-55130-908-8 (epub)

    1. Mental health—Canada.  I. Jenkins, Emily K., author  II. Bilsker, Daniel, author  III. Title.

RA790.7.C3G65 2016          362.20971          C2016-902618-3          C2016-902619-1

Text design by Brad Horning
Cover design by Gord Robertson
Cover image by iStock/Nikolaev

Printed and bound in Canada by Webcom.

Canada

MIX
Paper from
responsible sources
FSC
www.fsc.org    FSC® C004071

# CONTENTS

Foreword
  Louise Bradley, President and CEO,
  Mental Health Commission of Canada ............................................................. ix

Preface ......................................................................................................... xi

**Chapter 1**
What Is Mental Health? ........................................................................... 1

**Chapter 2**
Biological Foundations of Mental Health ............................................ 23

**Chapter 3**
Mental Health Examined through the Social Sciences ......................... 47

**Chapter 4**
The Spectrum of Mental Health Problems ........................................... 73

**Chapter 5**
Substance Use, Dependence, and Addictive Behaviour ....................... 95

**Chapter 6**
Stigma, Discrimination, and Mental Health in the Workplace .......... 123

**Chapter 7**
Mental Health and Illness among Children and Youth ..................... 143

**Chapter 8**
Sex, Gender, and Sexuality ................................................................. 169

**Chapter 9**
Culture, Ethnicity, and Mental Health .............................................. 189

**Chapter 10**
Mental Health and Illness in Older Adults ........................................ 209

**Chapter 11**
Responding to Mental Health Crisis, Emergency, and Disaster .........................233

**Chapter 12**
Treatment for Mental Disorders and Substance Use Disorder ...........................253

**Chapter 13**
Mental Health Services in Canada......................................................................279

**Chapter 14**
Mental Health Professions and Practices............................................................299

**Chapter 15**
Mental Health and Substance Use:
Opportunities to Improve Population and Public Health ..................................319

Copyright Acknowledgements...........................................................................343

Index...............................................................................................................349

# FOREWORD

My career in mental health began as a registered nurse in Corner Brook, Newfoundland. But my first encounter with the system was more than a decade before that—when I was admitted to psychiatric care as a troubled youth.

I credit much of my success, both personally and professionally, to the extraordinary care I received during those crucial formative years. I have no doubt that my path would have taken a vastly different turn had I not received early intervention and supports. My own experience has fuelled my passion for mental health, and I believe we are making great strides in the direction of compassionate care, recovery-oriented practices, and innovative treatments.

In order to understand mental health, as a student, a care provider, or the family member of a person with lived experience, this book offers an excellent and insightful starting place. It is written with an eye to uncovering the social, biological, cultural, and spiritual facets of mental health—and the authors skilfully articulate the ever-growing base of knowledge that informs our understanding of the topic.

Like any complex subject, mental health is best examined from all sides. The approach taken by the authors is innovative: it marries viewpoints from across disciplinary backgrounds and incorporates the expertise of both junior and senior professors in the field. This is an example of the kind of innovation championed by the Mental Health Commission of Canada (MHCC).

Since the writing of the first edition of this volume, new findings and developments have enriched our field of knowledge. In the last 10 years alone, Canada has developed a leading Mental Health Strategy. Even more importantly, we are seeing the recommendations laid out in that strategy grow and bear fruit. For example, Canadian workplaces are embracing practices that promote mental health and wellness among their employees. This is both socially responsible and financially prudent, given that mental illness costs the Canadian economy some $51 billion each year. It is also an essential part of addressing the residual stigma that clings to mental health problems and illnesses. These inroads are particularly promising within our first-responder communities, where the incidence of post-traumatic stress disorder—among other mental health concerns—is disproportionately high.

While this progress points to a positive trajectory, we can't escape the fact that, today, in Canada, 10 people will die by suicide. The same is true for tomorrow. And the day after that. This is a statistic that has remained stubbornly unchanged since the writing of the first edition of this book.

For me, this statistic isn't just a number. It's a very personal reminder of the unique brand of grief and devastation left in the wake of a suicide. At the age of 36, my closest friend took her own life. This tragedy reinforced my belief that we must take more action—as a society—to save these precious lives.

In particular, we know that at-risk populations such as Indigenous peoples must be empowered to heal their communities. We must walk alongside First Nations leaders, embracing our cultural humility, as they address decades of intergenerational trauma and the legacy of residential schools.

Thankfully, as our understanding of mental health grows, so do our innovative practices. We are seeing success with game-changers such as Housing First, which gives individuals living with mental health problems and illnesses the dignity of a safe place to live *first*, and, once they are settled, offers appropriate treatments and supports. We are also seeing tremendous success with the uptake of Mental Health First Aid. As of this writing, more than 170,000 Canadians have been trained to recognize the early signs and symptoms of a mental health crisis and are equipped to offer support until professional help can be engaged.

Beyond this, we are seeing compelling discoveries in neurosciences related to brain development and function. At the same time, epidemiological studies are painting a more complete picture of the prevalence of mental illness. It is, in fact, even more common than previously believed. These discoveries are emerging alongside promising practices ranging from new psychoactive substances to the benefits of music therapy for patients living with dementia.

Yet, as our understanding of mental health grows, so do our many questions. To find answers, we must work together—not just as a nation, but on a global scale—to exchange and adapt the innovative ideas that are improving lives in countries around the world. I am proud to say that the MHCC is leading a number of homegrown initiatives that are gaining global attention, some of which are highlighted in this book.

While the authors rightly characterize their work as a "concise introduction to mental health in Canada," they should also take great pride in the depth and breadth of their writing. Given the dynamic nature of mental health, this second edition adds tremendous value with its up-to-date insights.

While this book is ideal for students, practitioners, and people living with mental illness, it deserves a much broader audience. Truly addressing the mental health needs of Canadians requires a commitment across jurisdictions, from all levels of government, and beyond. There is also a clear role for the business community to play, from social enterprises to promoting mental wellness at work.

This book is a treasure trove of information, and every page is stamped with the authors' wisdom, compassion, and desire for transformational change. While I wish this resource had been available to me as a young nurse in Corner Brook, I know it will greatly benefit today's emerging leaders.

—Louise Bradley, President and CEO,
Mental Health Commission of Canada

# PREFACE

Since the initial publication of our textbook in 2011, there have been some noteworthy changes in the mental health and illness landscape both in Canada and internationally. The revised Diagnostic and Statistical Manual of Mental Disorders (Version 5) was published and accompanied by significant reflection and critique regarding the diagnostic process. We continue to witness dramatic shifts in our understandings of mental health and illness. Research and technological advancements over the last several decades have contributed to new medications and treatment options that have altered the experiences of people with mental disorders. Deinstitutionalization and the emergence of the Recovery Model have changed the way that people with mental illnesses are supported and provide new hope for individuals to live meaningful and fulfilling lives within the community. A focus on mental *health* (as opposed to mental *illness*) has continued to gain momentum within the population and public health field, resulting in a new focus on mental health promotion and illness prevention with the goal of improving the health and well-being of our societies.

Despite these advancements, the Canadian mental health care system remains fragmented and under-resourced, and widespread stigma continues to permeate the lives of individuals experiencing mental illness. In this second edition of our textbook, we continue our mission to bring these issues to the forefront of awareness and motivate readers to become agents of change.

This second edition of *A Concise Introduction to Mental Health in Canada* represents a unique contribution to the mental health literature. It incorporates a broad range of perspectives to explore mental health and illness in Canada "from synapse to society." This second edition includes important updates to terminology, highlights new insights in the mental health field, and presents more recent scientific data. Careful attention was made to craft a reader-friendly book that includes timely and relevant "real world" examples of mental health issues, success stories, and thought-provoking insights. As in our last edition, we have included a self-help tool kit which offers readers evidence-based strategies and skills to promote and maintain their own mental health and well-being.

The writing of the first edition of this book involved an unusual collaboration between faculty members and graduate students, each from distinct disciplinary backgrounds. As we write this second edition, we find ourselves in different roles, but we continue to bring a diversity of perspective and disciplinary foundation, allowing for a truly interdisciplinary book. We believe that this partnership enhances the quality and relevance of this text for readers.

We hope that this book provides readers with a foundational knowledge of mental health and illness in Canada and inspires the mental health leaders of tomorrow. We hope that readers will enjoy this book as much as we enjoyed writing it.

## Acknowledgements

In addition to the encouragement and support we received from our families and friends, we want to thank a number of individuals and organizations for their help and advice. First, we wish to thank Jessica Palma, who is one of the authors of the first edition of this book. We have retained many ideas and sections that originated in the first edition and therefore Jessica is an important contributor. We also wish to thank a number of colleagues who generously devoted their time to review our initial manuscript and gave us invaluable recommendations. In this regard, we wish to thank: Roger Bland, Martha Donnelly, Benedikt Fischer, David Gardner, Marlee Groening, John Higenbottam, Elsabeth Jensen, Joy Johnson, Marina Morrow, Charlotte Ross, and Victoria Smye. We want to thank the students enrolled at Simon Fraser University who used the first edition of the textbook and who responded to our request to provide their recommendations to strengthen the second edition. Some students also submitted original photographs and images that have been used and these are each credited individually. A special thanks to Alexa Geddes, Solomon McKenzie, and Emily Wilson for helping us to update references and make various alterations and improvements to the manuscript while preparing the final version for publication.

# Chapter 1

# WHAT IS MENTAL HEALTH?

The mind is its own place, and in itself
Can make Heaven of Hell, and a Hell of Heaven.
                              —John Milton (English poet and civil servant)

## Introduction

Let us imagine that you and a good friend agree to try to make a determination of each other's mental health, choosing one of the following five ratings. How might you go about doing so?

In general, would you say your mental health is:[1]

EXCELLENT     VERY GOOD     GOOD     FAIR     POOR

Unfortunately, you won't be able to rely on a blood test, brain scan, or other measurement. No laboratory test or physiological measure has been discovered that can produce a rating of a person's overall mental health, despite the strong links that exist between mental states and the physiological function of various organs of the body. Although changes in heart rate and respiration, and alterations in levels of hormones and nervous system activity may occur with anxiety, depression, or other mental states, they are too non-specific to be used for diagnosis. Possibly, laboratory measures, brain imaging techniques, or other technological tools will be developed to assist with determinations of overall mental health in the future. At present, we must rely on observations, historical information, and inference, i.e., applying logical reasoning to draw conclusions.

In order to help you make an accurate rating, you might want to have a good definition of mental health. However, the World Health Organization (WHO) states that no single definition of mental health is widely accepted; cultural differences and competing professional theories may lead to the adoption of different definitions of mental health in various contexts and cultures. For the most part, good mental health is now regarded as not only the absence of mental disorders, emotional problems, or distress, but also the presence of factors such as the ability to enjoy oneself and the capacity to participate meaningfully in daily life. A reasonable definition of mental health is given below.

> **Mental Health** can be defined as "a state of emotional and psychological well-being in which an individual is able to use his or her cognitive and emotional capabilities, function in society, and meet the ordinary demands of everyday life." (WHO, 2010a)

As noted in the Canadian Senate's Standing Committee on Social Affairs, Science and Technology report on mental health[2] (Kirby & Keon, 2004), "Mental health [infers] various capacities including the ability to: understand oneself and one's life; relate to other people and respond to one's environment; experience pleasure and enjoyment; handle stress and withstand discomfort; evaluate challenges and problems; pursue goals and interests; and, explore choices and make decisions."

The Senate report also noted that good mental health is associated with positive self-esteem, happiness, interest in life, work satisfaction, mastery and sense of coherence, and enables individuals to realize their potential and contribute to society. Mental health has been found to be strongly correlated with quality of life (i.e., an individual's overall sense of well-being, satisfaction, and fulfillment in life) (WHO, 2010a). This correlation is also present among individuals with major physical health problems; thus, a person may have a serious physical illness that causes disability, but be likely to maintain a high quality of life if his or her mental health is good. At the population level, good mental health is associated with good physical health, economic productivity, and greater social cohesion and stability (WHO, 2010a). Consequently, actions that successfully improve the overall mental health of the population are likely to be accompanied by other important benefits to society.

In considering your friend's mental health, you note that she seems calm and comfortable and is breathing softly at a steady rate. Her body posture is relaxed and she has a broad smile and an easily evoked laugh. Are these indicators of good mental health? Yes, they are! When health care professionals undertake an examination of an individual's mental health, they generally begin by simply observing the person's overall behaviour, psychomotor activity, speech, and general demeanour.

However, the observation that someone appears to be calm and relaxed is not enough to assume good mental health. If a careful evaluation of a person's mental health is called for, health care professionals may undertake a **mental status examination**, which involves a series of observations, structured questions, and tests of concentration, memory, and other mental functions. For example, a frequently used component of the mental status examination is to ask the person being interviewed to subtract seven from the number 100, then subtract seven from the answer, then subtract seven once again, and to continue doing so (as a mental exercise without paper or pencil). This is meant to test a number of functions, including the person's ability to concentrate on a task, use certain memory functions, and apply arithmetic calculation. Properly done, a mental status examination will take into account an individual's cultural and educational background and examine a wide range of mental activity, including a person's capacity to think clearly, express emotions, and make rational judgments.

More detailed and rigorous approaches to assess mental function have been developed in the form of psychological testing. Thousands of psychological tests have been created, evaluating a range of mental abilities, personality traits, and individual characteristics. Many have been designed to test specific functions, such as short-term memory in those who have experienced brain injury or disease; others examine broad mental functions, such as intelligence or personality, and these are typically designed for specific groups, such as children or adults within a designated age range.

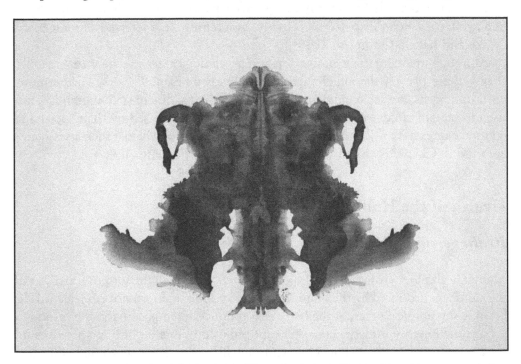

**Figure 1.1:** This is the first ink blot in the Rorschach test. The test involves presentation of 10 ink blots (the same 10 are used in all tests) to the subject, who is asked to describe what the images appear to be. The person who administers the test observes various facets of the response and makes interpretations based on the way the subject describes the images. In the past, this was a popular test to examine mental function. However, in recent decades, it has fallen into disfavour, and it is now considered by some critics to be a manifestation of pseudo-science.

*Source:* zmeel/iStockphoto

But even rigorous mental status examination or detailed psychological testing may be insufficient to provide a meaningful picture of a person's mental health. A cross-sectional view (i.e., examining only one brief point in time) is often inadequate to provide a valid understanding because a person's mental health must be considered over a span of time, taking into account the fluctuations that occur in various facets of his or her mental life. Some features of our mental lives may fluctuate markedly, including mood states and more transient emotions, such as happiness, sadness, fear, hopefulness, and hopelessness. One "snapshot" may not provide an accurate view of the larger landscape that can be found over time. Transient states of mind across the lifespan may be influenced profoundly by various factors, including one's environment, the existence or absence of stressors, the occurrence of significant life events, and substance use, including consumption of alcohol and other substances that are used frequently in some sectors of the Canadian population. For example, recent studies of youth in Canada have identified a sub-population of teens who use marijuana daily (Boak et al., 2013); when this pattern occurs on awakening, it is referred to by teens as "wake and bake" (Quintero, 2009).

Although mental status examination and psychological testing are valuable tools, they will not provide the full picture of an individual's mental health. Furthermore, anthropologists and sociologists have questioned the validity of such methods when used in certain circumstances, arguing that they may be biased by their social and cultural context. We will return to the important question of whether such assessments are valid in Chapter 4, when we discuss the diagnosis of mental illness.

# Health of the Human Mind

## *Brain versus Mind*

Mental health literally means "health of the *mind*." Although the various functions of the mind are produced by the brain, the mind and the brain are not equivalent. The brain is the physical organ of the body that produces mental activity; the mind is a set of functions and experiences resulting from a combination of brain activity and the environment in which it operates. Cultural, historical, and educational influences play a large role in shaping the mind. The brain has been compared to computer hardware; in contrast, the mind has been compared to the overall function of the computer with various software programs operating. Whereas the brain is an actual physical object, the mind is a *construct*, that is to say, a concept for which there is not a single observable referent and which cannot be directly observed. We develop constructs in order to organize our thoughts and ideas and attach meaning to our internal and external environments. The mind is an example of a construct that is used by many of us to make sense of our experiences. Other examples of constructs are intelligence, love, and fear.

There are multiple influences on the development of the human mind, as depicted in Figure 1.2. Although biological factors, such as genetic and neurophysiological characteristics, play an important role, many social, psychological, and environmental elements also play large roles in shaping mental health. This combination of factors operates at both the level of the individual and at the level of entire populations. The factors depicted as concentric circles in Figure 1.2 do not work in isolation; they interact with each other. For example, a stable political and economic environment will present conditions in which society can prosper and flourish, allowing families to provide healthy environments for their children's growth and development. In contrast, unstable political and economic environments, such as those that might accompany times of war, can create havoc, leading to loss and separation of family members, emotional suffering, and food shortages. This social disorder can have a negative impact on our emotional lives, with particularly detrimental consequences for children, who are still developing their unique mental and physical health characteristics.

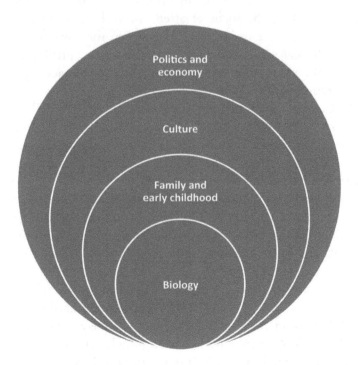

**Figure 1.2:** Multiple factors influence mental health and mental illness. It is difficult to keep these many factors in mind when seeking to understand mental health issues. There is a tendency to decrease these many to one or two groups of factors and create a "reductionistic" explanation. In this book, we seek to help the reader adopt a multi-layered understanding of mental health and mental illness.

## *Pendulum Swings: Physical Science and Social Sciences*

In recent history, mental health has often been viewed from one of two contrasting perspectives. One is the perspective of the physical sciences, such as biology, chemistry, physics, and neuroscience. From this perspective, there is an emphasis on the function of the brain, neurotransmitters, and endocrine system (e.g., hormones, such as adrenaline, estrogen, and testosterone), and on factors that may affect the function of these biological systems, such as genetic influences and use of pharmaceutical agents.

The other perspective focuses on factors identified by the social sciences, including the disciplines of anthropology, criminology, economics, geography, history, political science, psychology, and sociology. These factors encompass the effects of family life, culture, society, and political and economic environments (see Figure 1.2).

During different eras, one or the other of these two perspectives has dominated. For example, in the 19th century, scientists tended to hold a biological perspective, and explained mental health in terms of brain function. At the time, it was thought that a better understanding of mental health could be derived through study of the brain's intricate structure and function. However, by the middle of the 20th century, social and psychological explanations of human behaviour and mental function dominated, thus shifting the focus of attention and scientific exploration away from the physical sciences. Later in the 20th century, there was a strong resurgence of interest in biological explanations of mental function, precipitated by exciting discoveries about the actions of neurotransmitters and the impact of pharmacological substances on brain function (Scheid & Brown, 2010).

These shifts back and forth between the two perspectives have been described as pendulum swings. These swings occur, in part, because of reductionistic thinking, that is, a tendency to analyze problems in simplistic terms while ignoring relevant knowledge outside of a narrow view. One of the reasons pendulum swings occur is that reductionistic thinking is very common; in fact, we all have a tendency to think in this way and it requires substantial effort to apply more complex ways of conceptualizing the world around us. Lawrence Kohlberg and other scientists have found that children are likely to use reductionistic thinking and reasoning, whereas some adolescents and adults develop more complex approaches to problem solving (Kohlberg, Levine, & Hewer, 1983).

Mental health and mental illness are complex topics and, consequently, reductionistic explanations are likely to create misunderstanding. Let us consider the example of depression. As mentioned above, there was a pendulum swing toward biological explanations of mental health during the latter half of the 20th century, and, when a physician made a diagnosis of depression, it was common practice for the doctor to explain to the patient that "depression is a chemical imbalance of the brain." However, this biological explanation is inadequate because there are so many different factors associated with depression. As well as biological antecedents, there are many other precipitants for depression, such as difficulties in relationships, loss of loved ones, loneliness, difficulties at work, and economic strain.

Therefore, the simplistic explanation that "depression is caused by a chemical imbalance of the brain" is erroneous and does not reflect the many factors that may trigger depressive conditions. However, some might argue that defining depression as a neurochemical imbalance is describing the ultimate physical manifestation that may be reached through various pathways. Even if this were so, we maintain that a description of depression as a chemical imbalance of the brain is an inapt simplification. It risks narrowing our treatment options to include only the prescription of medication or other biological treatment to alter the brain's chemistry. Although the use of medications or other somatic treatments may offer benefits to many people with depression, it is important to recognize the benefits of non-biological approaches to the treatment of depression and other mental health problems. Throughout this book, we include examples of a wide range of approaches, going "from synapse to society," in our discussions of mental health.

One of the goals of this book is to help you, the reader, strengthen your ability to utilize multiple frameworks and theories simultaneously when you seek to understand mental health. To help you build this capacity, we have integrated and melded streams of knowledge that have emerged from a wide variety of disciplinary and intellectual traditions. This book provides an overview of many topics, often providing only basic introductory information; therefore, further studies and readings are encouraged. At the end of each chapter, you will find the following features: Glossary (these terms appear in boldface where they first appear in the text); Critical Thinking Questions; Recommended Readings; and Recommended Websites. These are meant to assist you as you continue to expand your knowledge beyond the covers of this book.

## A Historical View of Mental Health in Canada

In addition to the definition of "mental health" provided earlier in the chapter, the term is often used to refer to the entire field of mental health, including the various efforts by societies to address mental health and mental illness. This includes a wide range of formal and informal services and supports, such as counselling and psychotherapy services provided by a wide range of health care professionals, emergency and hospital-based psychiatric treatment services, social services for people with mental health problems, and initiatives aimed at promoting good mental health instituted by governments and non-profit agencies. In this section, we examine societal approaches to mental health from a historical perspective and consider the evolution of mental health practices in Canada.

### *Traditional Mental Health and Spiritual Practices*

Long before this land was known as Canada, First Nations, Inuit, and Metis people developed practices that addressed mental and spiritual health. We have only limited knowledge of these traditional practices. It is important to keep in mind that Canada's indigenous population comprises many hundreds of different nations, each with their own practices and traditions. Practices have been passed down through many generations by oral tradition, and some persist to this day. Traditional practices that are relevant to mental health and spirituality among Canada's Indigenous peoples include ritual chants, ceremonial dances, drumming, ritual journeys, communal sweats, and other spiritual rites (Kirmayer & Valaskakis, 2009; McCormick, 2009).

**Figure 1.3:** Sweat lodge in Saint Norbert, Manitoba

*Source*: GetStock/Judy Waytiuk

An example is the sweat lodge ritual, which is still regularly practised by First Nations people in many parts of Canada. As a purification ceremony, it can be performed by itself or in combination with other ceremonial activities. Generally, the ritual involves the careful selection of a site for the sweat lodge, which is then created by first digging a fire pit in which specially chosen rocks are heated. A dome is then built to encompass the fire pit and form the lodge, often constructed of saplings that are then covered with layers of blankets or other materials. For some, the dome represents the womb of Mother Earth. Once built, the sweat lodge is used by a group of people for the purposes of purification and improvement of their mental and spiritual health. What is it like to go through the sweat lodge ritual? Many people describe a meditative response in which one's senses seem to be tuned differently, invoked by the communal experience and the sensory effects of the intense heat from the rocks. Those who complete a sweat lodge ritual often describe emerging with a new perspective on important issues or problems they have been encountering. Throughout the world, many rituals and practices have been developed for the purpose of promoting spiritual and mental well-being. Often these exist within religious contexts and include communal or individual prayer and meditation.

## *Treatment of Mental Illness in Canada*

Since the migration of European settlers to North America and the establishment of the nation of Canada, the societal approach to mental health has focused on the treatment of individuals considered to be "mentally ill." At the time of Confederation, it was presumed that mental illnesses were caused by physical disease or damage to the brain, although the specific structures or problems could not be identified. Medical scientists devoted their efforts to finding brain abnormalities but their efforts were generally unsuccessful. Abnormal brain structure could rarely be identified, even in people with severe mental illnesses.

Without an understanding of the causes of mental illness, scientists and physicians were challenged to devise appropriate treatments. Following European examples, residential asylums were established. These were large hospital-like facilities in which the mentally ill were "treated" (Scheid & Brown, 2010). Typically, hundreds or thousands of individuals were housed together in institutional settings where they were tended to by physicians, nurses, and orderlies. The stated purposes of the residential asylums was to provide safe settings for physical and spiritual care and to shield individuals from the harm and peril that commonly befell people with mental illnesses. However, a contrary view ascribes less humanitarian motivations for asylum development. This view asserts that members of society were concerned primarily with the segregation of those with mental illness and did not want the discomfort of eccentric behaviour in their midst. Whatever motivations may have been in play within Canadian society, a policy of institutionalization led to the proliferation of these large asylums, also known as psychiatric hospitals, across the country beginning in the mid- to late 1800s and continuing until the 1960s. Over the first century of Canada's nationhood, there were few treatments that effectively reduced the suffering of people affected by severe mental illness. Historical accounts of Canadian asylums indicate that many tended to be custodial (i.e., providing protective supervision) rather than caring. Many people who were admitted to these institutions ended up as inmates for decades of their lives, removed from friends, family, and society, living out a bleak existence, and often never emerging (Austin & Boyd, 2010; Chow & Priebe, 2013). Due to this situation,

> institutions experienced severe overcrowding and had little more than food, clothing, pleasant surroundings, and perhaps some means of employment and exercise to offer. Limited resources made life in institutions difficult. Although a medical superintendent usually directed an institution, overcrowded wards, and few resources created rowdy, dangerous, and unbearable situations. (Austin & Boyd, 2010)

In addition, "provincial mental hospitals became extremely overcrowded, and in too many instances, individual treatment was unavailable, with the exception of some radical treatments (lobotomy) and whatever psychoactive drugs were available in different eras" (Davidson, Blankstein, Flett, & Neil, 2014).

Current wisdom indicates that there is a relatively small group of individuals who do appear to need long-term residential care because the seriousness of their symptoms or degree of disability exceeds even the most intensive community services and supports. However, such individuals are best served in smaller facilities that are more home-like and less institutional in their design and approach. Most people, even those with relatively severe mental disorders, can be supported in community settings (Vázquez-Bourgon, Salvador-Carulla, & Vázquez-Barquero, 2012).

**Figure 1.4:** Building K of the historic Mimico Lunatic Asylum of the 1880s has been renovated by Humber College in Toronto.

*Source:* GetStock/Charline Xia

## *Increased Use and Acceptance of Psychotherapy*

By the 1950s, while many people with mental illnesses were being placed in large residential asylums, a new development in psychiatry began to have a substantial impact. Psychoanalysis, a form of treatment developed by the Viennese psychiatrist Sigmund Freud in the early 1900s, had become popular in North America as a treatment for less severe and more common mental health problems (Scheid & Brown, 2010). Psychoanalysis was based on a complicated set of theories developed by Freud that postulated the existence of deep-seated emotional conflicts that people had not realized were the cause of their problems. Psychoanalytic treatment consisted of frequent sessions in which *psychoanalysts* probed into the inner thoughts and conflicts of their patients, who stretched out on the couch and agreed to share their every thought. Psychoanalytic treatment, which could continue for months or even years, aimed to help patients resolve long-standing emotional difficulties. Freud's imaginative theories and ideas captured the interest of artists, writers, and playwrights, who popularized psychoanalysis as a way to explore the depths of the human psyche.

**Figure 1.5:** Sigmund Freud

*Source:* GetStock/topham Picture Point

With the advent of psychoanalysis, a new era of psychotherapy (i.e., talking therapy) had begun. It became commonly accepted that the average person was likely to experience emotional problems and might benefit from a course of psychotherapy. Previously, psychiatric or psychological treatment was thought to be something required only by individuals who had severe mental problems.

With the spread of interest in psychotherapy in the mid-20th century, there was a large swing away from the biological ideas that had been dominant. Psychosocial ideas and theories became more prevalent, resulting in a generation of psychiatrists, psychologists, and other mental health practitioners who distanced themselves from the physical sciences. However, although this pendulum swing was extreme, it was to be brief. The dominance of psychosocial ideas was overthrown by a rapid succession of discoveries leading to the production of medications that could reduce symptoms of mental illness, including psychosis, depression, and anxiety. The latter half of the 20th century was primarily an era of psychopharmacology, in which chemists, psychiatrists, and pharmaceutical companies worked in tandem to produce a panoply of medications to treat mental illness.

## *Deinstitutionalization of People with Severe Mental Illnesses*

The trend of institutionalizing people with severe mental illnesses had continued to increase until the 1960s, when the number of psychiatric beds peaked (see Figure 1.6, summarizing Quebec data, as an example). Concern regarding the dismal conditions of some psychiatric hospitals buoyed a large family-led movement in support for the policy of **deinstitutionalization**, that is, plans by the government to decrease the use of psychiatric hospitals and replace them with community-based treatment. The push from families, coupled with the optimism that accompanied the introduction of antipsychotic medication, led Canada to begin the process of closing its institutions. Figure 1.6 also illustrates the profound downsizing of psychiatric hospitals that had proceeded unabated over previous decades. It demonstrates that, despite an increase

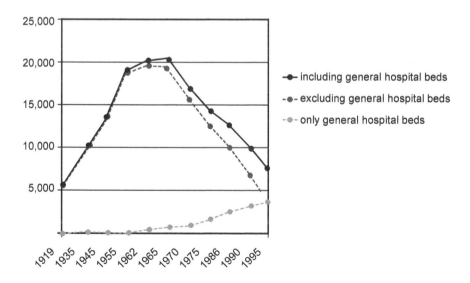

**Figure 1.6:** Psychiatric beds in Quebec, 1919–1995

*Source:* Lesage, A.D., Morissette, R., Fortier, L., Reinharz, D., & Contandriopoulos, A-P. (2000). Downsizing psychiatric hospitals: Needs for care and services of current and discharged long-stay inpatients. *Canadian Journal of Psychiatry*, 45(6), 526–531.

in the number of general hospital beds available for psychiatric treatment, the total number of psychiatric beds has plummeted.

Deinstitutionalization resulted in the need to develop adequate services for people with severe mental illness in community settings through support for the parents as caregivers, placements in group homes, placements in home shares, supports for independent living, and other services to have individuals included in their communities. Yet, the creation of community-based services and supports has proven to be a difficult and largely unmet challenge as a result of fiscal restraints, competing demands for health budget dollars, and broad social factors. Despite intentions to replace institutional care with community support, funds were often "poached" and diverted to other domains of health care. A system of community-based services and supports that could replace institutional care for people with mental illness in Canada has not been adequately developed (Sealy, 2012).

In recent years, there has been profound concern regarding the abysmal health status of people with severe mental illness and the high proportion of mental illness in the growing homeless populations of Canada's cities (Frankish, Hwang, & Quantz, 2005; Krausz et al., 2013; Martens, 2001).

Such concern has been intensified by evidence of an influx of the mentally ill to jails and the justice system in general, and the high rates of violent criminal victimization of people affected by mental illness (Canadian Mental Health Association, 2005; Vancouver Police Department, 2008). This movement of individuals with mental disorders into jails and other institutions, such as hospital emergency departments, is described as **transinstitutionalization** and is considered to be the consequence of inadequate community-based services and supports for individuals who require them (Prins, 2011; Testa, 2015).

## Mental Health of Canadians

In efforts to examine the mental health of the Canadian population, Statistics Canada asked a representative sample of the population to assess its own mental health and posed the question that appears at the beginning of this chapter (Statistics Canada, 2015):

In general, would you say your mental health is:

EXCELLENT     VERY GOOD     GOOD     FAIR     POOR

As part of a national survey undertaken by Statistics Canada in 2013–2014, approximately 65,000 people 12 years of age or older responded to the question above. Can you guess the proportion of people who rated their mental health as very good or excellent? What proportion rated their mental health as fair or poor?

Figure 1.7 shows a summary of the survey findings. The findings of the Statistics Canada survey provide useful information about the distribution of mental health and illness across the general population in Canada. It is encouraging to find that 71.6 percent of the surveyed population aged 12 and over rated their own mental health as either very good or excellent. It is notable, however, that approximately 6.2 percent of the general population rated their own mental health as fair or poor. Return to the exercise at the beginning of this chapter in which you and your friend were rating each other's mental health. How do your ratings compare with the general population in Canada?

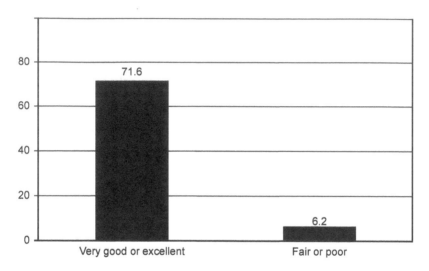

**Figure 1.7:** Self-rated mental health (percentage of population), Canada, 2013–2014

*Source:* Statistics Canada. (2015). Table 105-0592—*Health indicator profile, annual estimates, by age group and sex, Canada, provinces, territories, health regions (2013–2014 boundaries) and peer groups, occasional*, CANSIM (database). Retrieved from http://www5.statcan.gc.ca/cansim/a26?lang=eng&retrLang=eng&id=1050592&&pattern=&stByVal=1&p1=1&p2=31&tabMode=dataTable&csid=

## Epidemiology and Mental Health

The type of survey described above is an example of studies done in the field of **epidemiology**, defined as the study of the distribution of health and illness within populations. Epidemiological studies provide essential information about factors contributing to health and disease, including causation and risk factors, and lead to the development of clinical treatments and public health interventions.

There are a few important terms in epidemiology that you should know in order to understand the findings of epidemiological studies. These terms are used to provide information about health and illness within a population. **Prevalence** is one such term. It is defined as the proportion of individuals in a population who have a particular health condition. Prevalence may be measured at any one point in time (point prevalence) or over a period of time, often one year (one-year prevalence). For example, the 2012

Canadian Community Health Survey (CCHS), undertaken by Statistics Canada, reported the one-year prevalence of mood disorder, which includes forms of depression and bipolar disorder, in Canadian adults to be 5.4 percent (Statistics Canada, 2012a). This means that more than 5 in 100 adults were estimated to have suffered from a mood disorder at some time over the course of one year. Similarly, the same survey found that generalized anxiety disorder (a common form of anxiety disorder) had a one-year prevalence of 2.6 percent, and reported that the one-year prevalence of substance use disorder was 4.4 percent. Findings of the survey regarding lifetime prevalence were as follows: mood disorders 12.6 percent, generalized anxiety disorder 8.7 percent, and substance use disorder 21.6 percent. However, it is generally agreed that lifetime prevalence rates, which are based on reports by individuals as to whether they have ever had symptoms of specific illnesses in their lifetime, are gross underestimates (i.e., they are reported to be much lower than they are in reality). This is most likely due to our imperfect memories and our tendency to forget various events, particularly undesirable ones. In fact, prospective surveys (i.e., ones that gather information beginning at a point in time and go forward) have been found to produce prevalence rates of mental disorders that are twice as high as those gathered in retrospective surveys (i.e., ones that gather information about the past) (Moffit et al., 2010). Therefore, true lifetime prevalence rates are likely much higher than those reported in the 2012 CCHS.

The term **"incidence"** refers to the proportion of people who have a *new case* of the condition being studied. The prevalence rate is higher than the incidence rate because prevalence includes both new and existing cases.

**Years Lived with Disability (YLD)** represents the number of years of life that have been accompanied by a disability due to a disease or injury. YLD is estimated by multiplying the number of incident (new) cases of an illness in a population by the average duration of the condition and a weight factor that reflects the average degree of disability caused by the condition. Of the many different injuries and illnesses that exist, the illness that is estimated to be responsible for the greatest number of YLD worldwide is *depression* (Health Canada, 2002). This is because depression affects a very large proportion of the population, tends to begin relatively early in life, often recurs or persists, and tends to interfere with the capacity for individuals to function in many realms of their lives.

**Years of Life Lost (YLL)** is a measure of the number of years of life lost due to premature mortality (death) in the population. It is calculated by multiplying the number of deaths by the estimated number of years of life lost (determined by subtracting the age of death from the average life expectancy). In Nunavut, one of Canada's northern territories, suicide is responsible for more YLL than any other cause of death (Statistics Canada, 2012b). Once again, one of the reasons for the high rate is that the suicides often occur relatively early in life and are thus responsible for the loss of many years of expected longevity. A critical question that needs to be addressed is how to best reduce rates of suicide that are so high in Nunavut and other northern territories in Canada, and we will return to this question in Chapter 11.

An important population health measure is **Disability Adjusted Life Years (DALY)**. It is created by combining the years lived with disability (YLD) and the years of life lost (YLL) and, consequently, provides a pooled measure of disability and premature mortality. DALYs have been used extensively by the WHO and by other public health scientists in order to estimate the **burden of disease** caused by various illnesses and injuries (Murray & Lopez, 1996). In a series of well-known studies, the WHO estimated that depression is currently the third leading contributor to the burden of disease worldwide (lower respiratory infections and diarrheal diseases are the only illnesses that cause more disease worldwide). In high income-countries, including Canada, depression is estimated by the WHO to be *the* leading contributor to the burden of disease (WHO, 2010b). As well as depression, other mental health problems contribute significantly to the burden of disease. Both alcohol use disorders and self-inflicted injuries are among the top 20 contributors to burden of disease worldwide.

## *An Estimate of Mental Health Epidemiology in Canada*

A research project undertaken for the Mental Health Commission of Canada estimated the prevalence rates of mental disorders in Canada in 2011 and projected forward in time to estimate expected rates in the year 2041. The project utilized data that had been collected by Statistics Canada and in other surveys to create the best possible epidemiological estimates (Smetanin et al., 2013). Figure 1.8 shows that, in 2011, the one-year prevalence of mental disorders was estimated to be about 20 percent. This means that, in 2011, one in five people would have had some form of mental disorder, such as depression, anxiety disorder, schizophrenia, substance use disorder, or dementia. By modelling the expected growth of the population and expected change in demographics (such as the proportion of young and elderly people), the project was also able to estimate the one-year prevalence of the population in the year 2041 and projected that it would be slightly higher than in 2011. The projected increase was due to the expected increase in the size of the population of older adults and, consequently, an increased prevalence of dementia expected to occur by 2041.

The project also estimated that, by the time Canadians reach the age of 40, approximately 50 percent will have or will have had a mental disorder. If people reach the age of 90, approximately 65 percent of men and 70 percent of women will have had a mental disorder. The high rate of mental disorders in the population may surprise you. These estimates indicate that, during their lives, most Canadians will have a mental disorder. Of course, in many instances, individuals will have relatively short-lasting problems that are mild and moderate in nature. However, many others will have long-lasting or recurring problems that may cause substantial suffering or disability. Figure 1.9 shows the estimated one-year prevalence of mental disorder in Canadians aged 9 years and older for both males (on the left side of the figure) and females (on the right side of the figure).

Males and females show a similar pattern, with prevalence rates of mental disorder rising relatively high in the teenage years and in early adulthood. Prevalence rates then drop in people in their forties, fifties, and sixties and then rise again among individuals

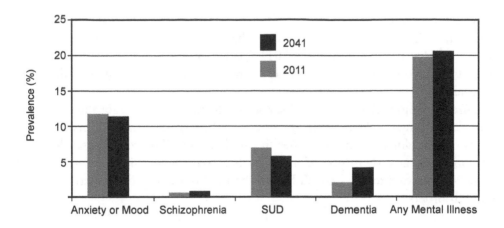

**Figure 1.8:** Estimated 12-month prevalence of specific mental illnesses in Canada

*Source:* Mental Health Commission of Canada. (2013). Making the case for investing in mental health in Canada, p. 10. Retrieved from www.mentalhealthcommission.ca/English/system/files/private/document/Investing_in_Mental_Health_FINAL_Version_ENG.pdf

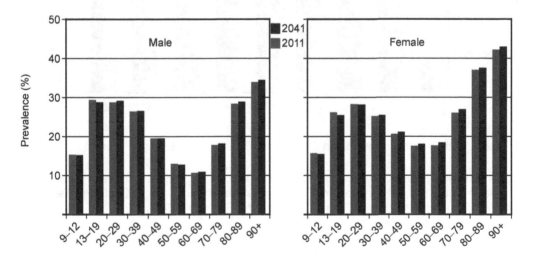

**Figure 1.9:** Estimated 12-month prevalence of any mental illness in Canada for select years 2011 to 2041

*Source:* Mental Health Commission of Canada. (2013). Making the case for investing in mental health in Canada, p. 8. Retrieved from www.mentalhealthcommission.ca/English/system/files/private/document/Investing_in_Mental_Health_FINAL_Version_ENG.pdf

living into their seventies, eighties, nineties, and above. The high rate of mental disorders among people in the older age groups is due primarily to the incidence of dementia, a mental disorder that most often begins later in life and which becomes increasingly prevalent as people age.

Overall, estimated rates of mental disorders in males and females were found to be similar, with rates among females somewhat higher than males (20.9 percent of females and 18.7 percent of males) in 2011. In Chapter 8 we discuss potential reasons why girls and women may have a higher overall prevalence rate of mental disorders than males.

Figure 1.10 shows that, when we look across the lifespan at the absolute numbers of people with mental disorders in any one year, the largest number of people are in their twenties. Unlike many other health problems and illnesses, mental disorders commonly emerge early in people's lives. As discussed above, this is one of the main factors contributing to the high YLD and the high burden of disease attributed to mental disorders.

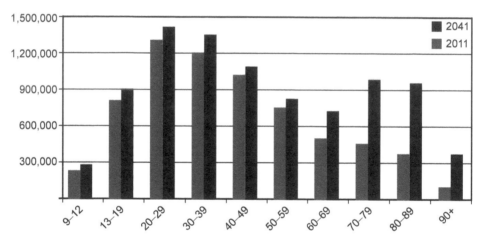

**Figure 1.10:** Number of people in Canada with mental illness by age group

*Source:* Mental Health Commission of Canada. (2013). Making the case for investing in mental health in Canada, p. 9. Retrieved from www.mentalhealthcommission.ca/English/system/files/private/document/Investing_in_Mental_Health_FINAL_Version_ENG.pdf

## Conclusion

We started the chapter by asking the question "What is mental health?" It turns out that the answer is not straightforward. However, there is general agreement that mental health is not only the absence of mental disorders, but also the ability to enjoy and participate meaningfully in daily life. Mental health refers to the health of the "mind," a construct that includes the brain as well as the environment in which the brain functions.

There is a rich history in Canada of approaches taken to address mental health. A prominent change over the past century has been a movement away from the institutionalization of people with severe mental health problems to approaches that emphasize community-based services and supports. Epidemiological methods have provided useful measures to understand the distribution of mental health and illness throughout the population.

In the following two chapters we will examine various factors that contribute to the mental health of people in Canada by applying, first, a physical sciences perspective and, second, the perspective of the social sciences.

## Notes

1. This question was asked in a survey of approximately 65,000 Canadians undertaken by Statistics Canada (Statistics Canada, 2015). We include the findings of this survey question later in this chapter.
2. Chaired by Michael J. Kirby, the Canadian Senate's Standing Committee on Social Affairs, Science and Technology undertook an extensive study of mental health and illness in Canada and published a multi-volume report that produced a series of provocative findings and detailed recommendations. The study led to the formation, in 2008, of the Mental Health Commission of Canada, a national, non-profit organization funded by the Government of Canada to focus national attention on mental health issues and to work to improve the health and social outcomes of people living with mental illness. The Commission has been endorsed by all levels of government and operates at arm's length from them.

## Glossary

**burden of disease:** The impact of a health problem in an area measured by financial cost, mortality, morbidity, or other indicators.

**deinstitutionalization:** Plans by governments to decrease the use of psychiatric hospitals and replace them with community-based treatment.

**Disability Adjusted Life Years (DALY):** A combined measure of disability and premature mortality. Calculated by adding years lived with disability and years of life lost.

**epidemiology:** The study of the distribution of health and illness of populations.

**incidence:** The proportion of people who have a new case of the condition being studied.

**mental health:** A state of emotional and psychological well-being in which an individual is able to use his or her cognitive and emotional capabilities, function in society, and meet the ordinary demands of everyday life.

**mental status examination:** A series of observations, structured questions, and tests undertaken by a health care professional to evaluate a person's mental health.

**prevalence:** The proportion of individuals in a population who have a particular health condition.

**transinstitutionalization:** The process by which individuals who historically would have been detained inside mental health institutions are instead being transferred into detention by other state institutions (e.g., criminal justice system, general hospitals).

**Years of Life Lost (YLL):** A measure of the number of years of life lost due to premature mortality (death) in the population.

**Years Lived with Disability (YLD):** The number of years of life accompanied by disability due to a disease or injury.

## Critical Thinking Questions

1. How has mental health been defined by the WHO?
2. What is the difference between the brain and the mind?
3. How has the history of mental health shaped our current understanding of mental health in Canada?
4. Define deinstitutionalization and explain how it has impacted services for those with mental illness.
5. What are some of the key terms that can be used to understand the findings of epidemiological studies?

## Recommended Readings

Goffman, E. (1961). *Asylums: Essays on the Social Situation of Mental Patients and Other Inmates.* New York: Doubleday.

Moran, J.E., & Wright, D. (2008). *Mental Health and Canadian Society: Historical Perspectives.* Montreal & Kingston: McGill-Queen's University Press.

Streiner, D.L., & Norman, G.R. (2009). PDQ Epidemiology. PMPH-USA.

Torrey, E.F., & Miller, J. (2001). *Invisible Plague: The Rise of Mental Illness from 1750 to the Present.* Toronto: Scholarly Book Services Inc.

Zimmerman, M. (2013). *Interview Guide for Evaluating DSM-5 Psychiatric Disorders & the Mental Status Examination.* Philadelphia: Psych Products Press.

## Recommended Websites

The History of Madness in Canada. http://historyofmadness.ca/

The Mental Health Commission of Canada. www.mentalhealthcommission.ca/english/pages/default.aspx

Network for Aboriginal Mental Health Research. www.namhr.ca/index.php

The World Health Organization—Mental Health. www.who.int/mental_health/en/

The World Mental Health Survey Initiative. www.hcp.med.harvard.edu/wmh/

# References

Austin, W., & Boyd, M.A. (2010). *Psychiatric and mental health nursing for Canadian practice.* Philadelphia: Lippincott Williams & Wilkins.

Boak, A., Hamilton, H.A., Adlaf, E.M., & Mann, R.E. (2013). Drug use among Ontario students, 1977–2013: Detailed OSDUHS findings. *CAMH research document series no. 36.* Toronto: Centre for Addiction and Mental Health.

Canadian Mental Health Association. (2005). Criminalization of mental illness. Retrieved from www.cmha.bc.ca/files/2-criminalization.pdf

Chow, W.S., & Priebe, S. (2013). Understanding psychiatric institutionalization: A conceptual review. *BMC Psychiatry,* 13(169). doi: 10.1186/1471-244X-13-169

Davidson, G., Blankstein, K., Flett, G., & Neil, J. (2014). *Abnormal psychology* (5th Canadian ed.). Etobicoke, ON: Wiley.

Frankish, C., Hwang, S., & Quantz, D. (2005). Homelessness and health in Canada: Research lessons and priorities. *Canadian Journal of Public Health/Revue canadienne de Santé publique,* 96(2), S23–S29.

Health Canada. (2002). A report on mental illnesses in Canada. Ottawa: Health Canada.

Kirby, M.J.L., & Keon, W.J. (2004). Mental health, mental illness and addiction: Overview of policies and programs in Canada. The Standing Senate Committee on Social Affairs, Science and Technology. Retrieved from www.parl.gc.ca/38/1/parlbus/commbus/senate/com-e/soci-e/rep-e/report1/repintnov04vol1-e.pdf

Kirmayer, L.J., & Valaskakis, G.G. (Eds.). (2009). *Healing traditions: The mental health of Aboriginal peoples in Canada.* Vancouver: University of British Columbia Press.

Kohlberg, L., Levine, C., & Hewer, A. (1983). *Moral stages: A current formulation and a response to critics.* Basel, NY: Karger.

Krausz, R.M., Clarkson, A.F., Strehlau, V., Torchalla, I., Li, K., & Schuetz, C.G. (2013). Mental disorder, service use, and barriers to care among 500 homeless people in 3 different urban settings. *Social Psychiatry and Psychiatric Epidemiology,* 48(8), 1235–1243. doi: 10.1007/s00127-012-0649-8

Martens, W.H.J. (2001). A review of physical and mental health in homeless persons. *Public Health Reviews,* 29(1), 13–33.

McCormick, R.M. (2009). First Nations counsellor training in British Columbia: Strengthening the circle. *Canadian Journal of Community Mental Health,* 16(2), 91–99.

Moffitt, T.E., Caspi, A., Taylor, A., Kokaua, J., Milne, B.J., Polanczyk, G., & Poulton, R. (2010). How common are common mental disorders? Evidence that lifetime prevalence rates are doubled by prospective *versus* retrospective ascertainment. *Psychological Medicine,* 40(6), 899–909.

Murray, C.J.L., & Lopez, A.D. (1996). The global burden of disease: A comprehensive assessment of mortality and disability from disease, injuries, and risk factors in 1990 and projected to 2020. World Health Organization. Cambridge: Harvard School of Public Health.

Prins, S.J. (2011). Does transinstitutionalization explain the overrepresentation of people with serious mental illnesses in the criminal justice system? *Community Mental Health Journal*, 47(6), 716–722.

Quintero, G. (2009). Controlled release: A cultural analysis of collegiate polydrug use. *Journal of Psychoactive Drugs*, 41(1), 39–47. doi: 10.1080/02791072.2009.10400673

Scheid, T.L., & Brown, T.N. (2010). *A handbook for the study of mental health: Social contexts, theories, and systems* (illustrated ed.). Cambridge: Cambridge University Press.

Sealy, P.A. (2012). The impact of the process of deinstitutionalization of mental health services in Canada: An increase in accessing of health professionals for mental health concerns. *Social Work in Public Health*, 27(3), 229–237.

Smetanin, P., Stiff, D., Briante, C. Adair, C.E., Ahmad, S., & Khan, M. (2013). Making the case for investing in mental health in Canada. Retrieved from www.mentalhealthcommission.ca/English/document/5210/making-case-investing-mental-health-canada-backgrounder-key-facts

Statistics Canada. (2012a). Mental and substance use disorders in Canada. Ottawa: Statistics Canada. Retrieved from www.statcan.gc.ca/pub/82-624-x/2013001/article/11855-eng.pdf

Statistics Canada. (2012b). Table t102-0705-0—Potential years of life lost, by selected causes of death (ICD-10) and sex, five-year average, Canada and Inuit regions, every 5 years, CANSIM (database). Retrieved from http://www5.statcan.gc.ca/cansim/a26?lang=eng&retrLang=eng&id=1020705&pattern=potential+years+of+life+lost%2C+by+selected+causes+of+death&tabMode=dataTable&srchLan=-1&p1=1&p2=1

Statistics Canada. (2015). Canadian Community Health Survey: Annual component (CCHS). Retrieved from www23.statcan.gc.ca/imdb/p2SV.pl?Function=getSurvey&db=imdb&adm=8&dis=2&SDDS=3226&lang=en

Testa, M. (2015). Imprisonment of the mentally ill: A call for diversion to the community mental health system. *Albany Government Law Review*, 8, 405–438.

Vancouver Police Department. (2008). Lost in transition: How a lack of capacity in the mental health system is failing Vancouver's mentally ill and draining police resources. Retrieved from ftp.vancouver.ca/police/Whatsnew/transition.htm

Vázquez-Bourgon, J., Salvador-Carulla, L., & Vázquez-Barquero, J.L. (2012). Community alternatives to acute inpatient care for severe psychiatric patients. *Actas Españolas de Psiquiatría*, 40(6), 323–332.

World Health Organization. (2010a). Mental health and development: Targeting people with mental health conditions as a vulnerable group. Retrieved from apps.who.int/iris/bitstream/10665/44257/1/9789241563949_eng.pdf

World Health Organization. (2010b). Mental health: Depression. Retrieved from www.who.int/mental_health/management/depression/en/

# Chapter 2

# BIOLOGICAL FOUNDATIONS
# OF MENTAL HEALTH

The hypothalamus is one of the most important parts of the brain, involved in many kinds of motivation, among other functions. The hypothalamus controls the 'Four F's': fighting, fleeing, feeding, and mating.

—Karl Pribram (neuroscientist and neurosurgeon)

## Introduction

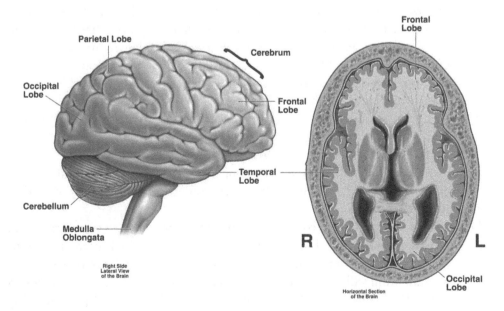

**Figure 2.1:** Even the world's most impressive man-made technological achievements cannot begin to compare to the brain's astounding capacity.

*Source*: GetStock/Nucleus Medical Art Inc.

Healthy functioning of the brain is, of course, an important component of good mental health. The structural and electrochemical function of the brain is so highly sophisticated and advanced that the world's most impressive man-made technological achievements cannot begin to compare to its astounding features. The average brain consists of about 100 billion (100,000,000,000) **neurons** or cells (Williams & Herrup, 1988). Even more difficult to fathom is the number of interconnections among these neurons. Since each individual neuron may be connected to 10,000 others (Eysenck & Keane, 2015) the number of connections is so immense that it defies imagination and is thought to be similar to the number of elementary particles that exist in the entire universe!

To add to the astounding number of interconnections among neurons, the electrical impulses that fire rapidly through this enormous web of connections do so in parallel, and they are modulated by the secretion of neurotransmitters, chemical messengers that regulate electrical transmission by their release and uptake into the microscopic spaces, or synapses, present between the neurons. Neuroscience researchers have mapped the existence of a group of neurotransmitters with varying chemical composition, some of which tend to promote the transmission of electrical impulses across the synapse whereas others may inhibit neurotransmission. The most abundant neurotransmitter in the brain is glutamate, which is excitatory, whereas the chief inhibitory neurotransmitter is GABA (gamma-amino-butyric acid). Other neurotransmitters include monoamines, such as norepinephrine, dopamine, and serotonin, and these appear to play important roles in regulation of mood and emotion. Various types of receptors have been identified that are responsive to the neurotransmitter molecules released into the synapses, and it has been found that certain drugs have an influence on these and can modulate neurotransmission in particular areas of the brain. Psychoactive drugs such as cocaine, opioids, and marijuana appear to exert their effects in this way. Similarly, antidepressant and antipsychotic medications that are prescribed to patients are thought to exert their therapeutic effects through the modulation of neurotransmitters at these receptor sites. Some receptors have been found to become less responsive (i.e., "downregulated") when they are repeatedly exposed to high levels of neurotransmitters. Such changes in the responsiveness of receptors are thought be one of the mechanisms that occur in the development of certain mental disorders and addictive behaviours.

Neuroscientists have also discovered an important process that occurs in the brain during human development. The enormous number of potential interconnections among the fetal brain's neuronal network is gradually consolidated over time, creating a smaller (but still vast) number of interconnections through a child's growth development. This can be thought of as an intrinsic, self-generated programming of the brain's circuitry and may constitute the neuronal basis of learning. Recent research indicates that adolescence is an important time in neurodevelopment with an expansion and then contraction of excitatory synaptic connections in the brain (Lee et al., 2014).

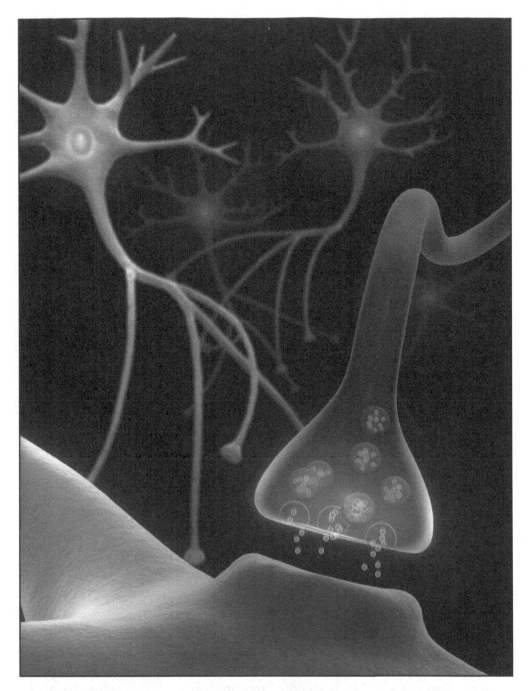

Figure 2.2: Neurotransmitters, the brain's "chemical messengers," are released into synapse and taken up by a receptor.

*Source*: Xiaofeng Luo/iStockphoto

It is truly astounding that each one of us walks around with the equivalent of a supercomputer inside our skull. The human brain is so advanced that our top scientists and engineers are humbled at the task of understanding its simplest functions and features (Markram, 2006).

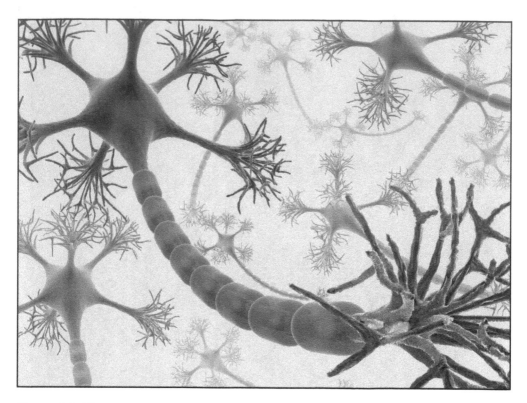

**Figure 2.3:** The average brain consists of 100 *billion* (100,000,000,000) neurons.

*Source:* ktsimage/iStockphoto

Through centuries of study, recently accelerated by advancements in neuroanatomical, neurophysiological, and neurosurgical technologies, scientists have pieced together a rudimentary understanding of brain function. Particular regions of the brain have been matched to specific functions. For example, areas of the brain that are involved in vision, speech, motor movements, bodily sensations, memory, sleep and wakefulness, emotion, appetite, balance, and breathing have been identified. Furthermore, pathways that connect different areas of the brain through bundles of nerve fibres have been mapped, suggesting a number of areas that network with each other during some of these functions. However, it is clear that a picture of brain function in which different regions constitute the seat of specific functions is a simplistic one. Brain functions involve multiple regions working in synchrony (Perez

Velazquez & Wennberg, 2009; von der Malsburg, Phillips, & Singer, 2010). The mind relies on complex brain activity and interposes historical experience, imbued with cultural meaning, and fuelled with knowledge gained through a lifetime and accumulated through human history.

---

**Box 2.1: The BRAIN Initiative**

The BRAIN (Brain Research through Advancing Innovative Neurotechnologies) Initiative is a large and ambitious research project that, since 2013, has received many millions of dollars in funding from the US government as a presidential initiative. It involves researchers from more than 125 institutions in the US and collaboration with researchers in other countries (including Canada). Its goal is to make substantial strides forward in uncovering the mysteries of brain disorders such as schizophrenia, autism, Alzheimer's disease, depression, and traumatic brain injury. It is hoped that the BRAIN Initiative will develop and apply new technologies that will enable researchers to produce dynamic images of the brain; show how individual brain cells and complex neural circuits process thought, language, and emotion; shed light on the complex links between brain function and behaviour; and examine potential new treatment technologies and interventions. Current projects include proposals to develop ultrasound methods for measuring brain activity and the use of deep brain stimulation to treat traumatic brain injuries.

---

In this chapter, we discuss a number of the prominent functions of the brain and features of mental activity. We also point to some of the key structures and functions that are relevant to mental health and illness.

## Brain Functions and Mental Activity

### *Wakefulness/Arousal*

Our minds function in different states of arousal, ranging from deep stages of sleep to highly stimulated wakefulness and arousal. An area known as the reticular formation, located deep in the core of the brain in the areas known as the brainstem and midbrain, plays an important role in the regulation of sleep, wakefulness, and arousal. However, many brain areas appear to work in complex interaction to regulate these states. The healthy mind has a regular pattern of sleep and wakefulness, whereas injury or disease can result in disturbances in these states, including a prolonged loss of consciousness, known as a coma. We commonly alter our state of arousal through the use of substances that cause either stimulation or sedation. The use of coffee, tea, or other caffeine-containing drinks to stimulate arousal has become prominent in many societies and cultures.

---

**Box 2.2: Caffeine Drinks**

Drinks containing caffeine, such as coffee, tea, and cola-flavoured soda pop, stimulate areas of the brain, such as the reticular formation, involved in arousal and wakefulness (Boutrel & Koob, 2004). The resulting feelings of increased alertness and heightened energy are responsible for the popularity and widespread use of these beverages. It is estimated that more than 75 percent of adults in Canada ingest caffeine on any given day (Statistics Canada, 2008), and it is likely that the majority would have great difficulty stopping. Does this mean that the vast majority of Canadians are addicted to caffeine? We will examine this question in more depth in Chapter 5, where we address substance use and addiction. Did you know that the original ingredients of Coca-Cola included cocaine (Coca is the name of the plant from which cocaine is derived)? Cocaine was removed from the Coca-Cola recipe in 1903 after it became apparent that cocaine was causing many health problems. However, the beverage had become so popular that the original name was kept.

---

**Figure 2.4:** It is estimated that more than 75 percent of adults in Canada ingest caffeine every day.

*Source:* Nicky Gordon/iStockphoto

Other substances, such as alcohol, opiates, and various sedatives, commonly diminish alertness and arousal and may induce sleep. Mental activity during sleep remains largely mysterious, and although a number of theories about the language and meaning of dreams have been proposed, they remain unconfirmed.

## *Regulation of Physiological Activity*

Another set of functions that involve brain areas in the brainstem and midbrain regulate rhythmic physiological activities such as breathing and heart rate. These functions occur mostly without our awareness. Yet, changes in our overall state of mind may have a profound impact on these rhythms. For example, an intense state of fear will generally result in a marked increase in one's heart rate and breathing pattern, whereas feelings of deep relaxation and comfort may decrease heart rate and slow the pace of respiration. Numerous experimental studies have demonstrated that individuals who are accomplished at meditative and yogic practices are able to reliably induce such changes in physiological activity (Delmonte, 1984; Kothari, Bordia, & Gupta, 1973; Wallace, 1970).

## *Sensation/Perception*

A central function of the mind is integrating the extensive information collected through the body's many sources of sensory reception. Sensory input includes information about touch, pressure, pain, and temperature collected from nerve endings throughout the body. Areas of the cerebral cortex have been found to correspond to specific parts of the body. When these areas are activated by electrical stimulation, the result is a sensation in the corresponding body part. Figure 2.5 shows a strip of the cerebral cortex, located on the postcentral gyri, which contains areas that correspond to different parts of the body. These are illustrated in a drawing of a "homunculus" (i.e., "little person") in which the size of various body parts on the drawing are representative of the area of cerebral cortex devoted to them. For example, the face and lips of the somatosensory homunculus are large because a relatively large area of cortex is connected to them and, correspondingly, they have more sensory receptivity than many other parts of the body. That is why being kissed on the face or lips can be so pleasurable.

Another type of sensory input is proprioceptive, coming from movement receptors in joints and muscles throughout the body. The mind also integrates sensory input from special visual, auditory (hearing), olfactory (smell), and gustatory (taste) receptors.

Many parts of the brain are involved with the processing of sensory input, and specific areas of the cerebral cortex have a role in processing special sensory information, such as visual and auditory input. The mind appears to make sense of the large amount of incoming information through the web of interconnections that are established in the brain. Instantaneously, meaning is assigned on the basis of

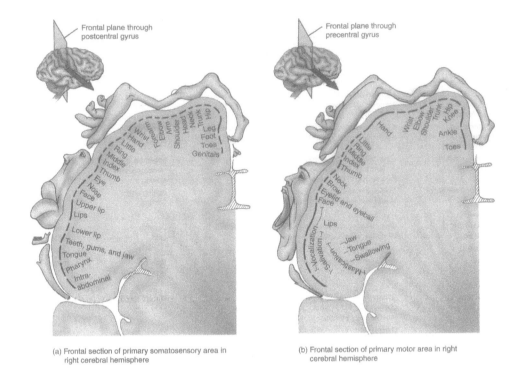

(a) Frontal section of primary somatosensory area in right cerebral hemisphere

(b) Frontal section of primary motor area in right cerebral hemisphere

**Figure 2.5:** Somatosensory homunculus

*Source*: Tortora, G., & Grabowski, S.R. (2002). *Principles of anatomy and physiology* (10th ed., p. 508). Hoboken, NJ: John Wiley & Sons.

recognized patterns and combinations. In this way, the mind accomplishes a complex perception of events through signals received from multiple sources. For example, a bright flash of light across the sky followed by a thunderous boom will immediately be identified as an electrical storm. The perception may also invoke a flood of emotions and memories.

When the mind is healthy, the analysis and perception of sensory input will be relatively accurate. Under the influence of various psychoactive substances, or when mental health is impaired, the mind may create distorted perception. Thus, the rustling of wind might be misperceived to be a human voice, or the touch of bed sheets on one's skin to be crawling insects.

## *Movement*

Both simple and complex movements of the body are generated through mental activity involving multiple areas of the brain working together in synchrony. Areas of the **cerebral hemispheres**, called the "motor cortex," play a key role in sending signals to the many muscles of the body. Movement is often modulated through the integration of sensory information received in rapid sequence and appears to be adjusted by information about balance and coordination through activity in the cerebellum, the lobe of the brain located at the back and bottom of the skull. Complex physical actions, such as running on uneven ground, require rapid coordination of muscle groups and immediate integration of proprioceptive and visual sensory information.

An individual's motor activity may reflect his or her mental state. Good mental health is generally associated with a good balance of motor activity, characterized by the ability to assume a comfortable resting state as well as the capacity to shift into motion easily. Someone who is in a state of hyperarousal and agitation may demonstrate hyperactive movements, with an inability to assume a resting state. This may result from the use of stimulant drugs such as cocaine, methamphetamine, or high doses of caffeine and may occur as a feature of certain mental disorders. Conversely, some mental states will result in the profound slowing of psychomotor activity. This may occur in individuals with severe forms of depressive illness or accompany the use of drugs with sedative properties, for example, opiates and alcohol.

## *Thought, Emotion, and Memory*

These complex mental functions form the foundation of mankind's accomplishments in science, art, literature, architecture, philosophy, and other endeavours. The capacity of the human mind to generate ideas, apply reasoning, attach emotional significance, and build banks of knowledge has distinguished humans from other animals and has permitted the creation of human civilizations.

We have barely scratched the surface in our attempts to understand the brain mechanisms that are involved with thought, emotion, and memory. These functions are inter-related and they involve simultaneous activity in many areas of the brain.

Thought and reasoning appear to draw on the immense interconnectivity of neurons in the cerebral hemispheres as well as those in other regions of the brain. The relative size and architectural complexity of the human cerebral hemispheres supersede parallel structures in other animals and facilitate the advanced capacity of the human mind for thinking and reasoning. With good mental health, an individual is able to think and reason clearly, make use of stored knowledge, and draw logical inferences. Once again, under the influence of certain psychoactive substances or with the appearance of some mental disorders, thinking and reasoning can become markedly distorted. In these circumstances, illogical or unlikely inferences can be drawn, resulting in delusions, that is, fixed false beliefs.

Emotions often occur in connection with thoughts or ideas and are often initiated by sensory input and memories. The **limbic system** refers to a series of interconnected structures in different regions of the brain that have been found to be important in producing mood and emotions. Areas of the brain that are part of the limbic system include the cingulate gyrus, thalamus, hypothalamus, amygdala, and hippocampus. Some of these structures also appear to play an important role in long-term memory. Another structure that plays an important role in emotion is the nucleus accumbens, an area which becomes active with pleasurable behaviours, such as eating food or having sex. This area is also thought to be involved in the pleasurable feelings induced by various psychoactive drugs.

**Mood** refers to the predominant background emotional state that persists in an individual over an extended period of time. A common mental health problem is depressed mood, in which feelings of sadness, lack of pleasure, and decreased interest persist. Mood can also be elevated excessively as in manic or hypomanic states. Good mental health involves the capacity to be emotionally responsive without experiencing extreme or labile (i.e., rapidly shifting and unstable) mood swings.

Memory involves the ability to store, retain, and retrieve information and is necessary for reasoning and learning. Some of the brain areas in the limbic system, such as the amygdala and hippocampus, appear to play an important role, and it is thought that memory involves the enhancement of interconnections among neurons through repeated stimulation, known as long-term potentiation (Bliss & Collingridge, 1993). This process is thought to occur through changes in neurotransmitter function at the synapses, resulting in the potentiated neurotransmission. Good mental health includes the capacity for both short-term and long-term memory. Memory can be impaired as a result of various mental disorders, injuries, nutritional deficits, or damage incurred through use of some psychoactive substances.

---

### Box 2.3: Anosognosia

Anosognosia is a symptom in which an individual does not have the ability to recognize that he or she has a specific disability. It has been found to be the result of damage to areas in the cerebral hemispheres, i.e., within the parietal and frontal lobes, and often occurs following a stroke (sudden damage to brain cells caused either by the rupture of blood vessels supplying the brain or by a blockage of blood vessels to the brain). An example of anosognosia would be a person with a paralyzed arm, who is completely unable to recognize that fact. Even if a physician tries to bring the paralyzed arm to the person's attention, he/she does not appear to recognize or acknowledge the paralysis whatsoever. More recently, the symptom of anosognosia has been considered to be operating among individuals with certain mental disorders. For example, it is thought that individuals with schizophrenic disorders may have anosognosia and are thus unable to recognize that they are experiencing hallucinations and delusions. Whether this inability may be the result of some neurological impairment is not yet known and requires further research.

---

## Personality and Patterns of Behaviour

**Personality** refers to the enduring behavioural traits and characteristics of an individual. We generally make inferences about an individual's personality on the basis of the characteristic behaviour patterns that are observed. For example, one personality dimension is introversion-extraversion, and refers to the degree to which individuals tend to be shy, reserved, and inward-oriented (i.e., introverted) or outgoing and oriented toward interaction with others (i.e., extraverted). An individual's personality features are considered to exist along a continuum and, although some people will fall at extreme ends of the spectrum, the majority will be found closer to the middle. Research indicates that personality is both genetically determined and influenced by environmental factors (Plomin et al., 2013). Although we each inherit a proclivity toward particular personality features, these features can be shaped by interpersonal experiences and by repeated exposure to circumstances that either reinforce or inhibit particular personality traits.

Good mental health does not imply a particular set of personality characteristics; a wide variety of personality configurations and behaviour patterns will be found in people with good mental health. Moreover, norms for personality and behaviour often vary across cultures and subcultures (Smith et al., 2013). For instance, some cultures tend to consider extraverted, emotionally expressive behaviour to be normal, whereas other cultures favour more reserve and restriction of emotional expression. We discuss this in more depth in Chapter 9.

If an individual's personality or pattern of behaviour deviates markedly from cultural expectations, and is inflexible and pervasive across many circumstances, then

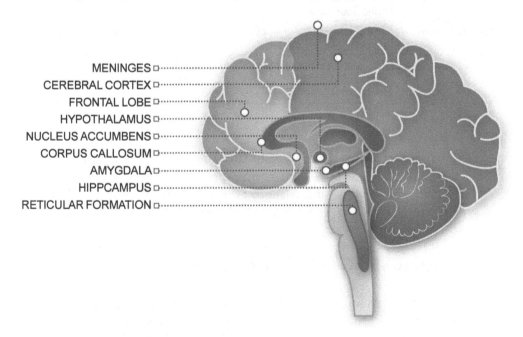

MENINGES
CEREBRAL CORTEX
FRONTAL LOBE
HYPOTHALAMUS
NUCLEUS ACCUMBENS
CORPUS CALLOSUM
AMYGDALA
HIPPOCAMPUS
RETICULAR FORMATION

**Figure 2.6:** Brain structures. See Table 2.1 for description of the functions associated with each of these brain structures.

*Source*: Daniel Wierzbicki, Designer

**Table 2.1: Brain structures and associated functions**

| Brain Structure | Function |
| --- | --- |
| Cerebral cortex | This outer layer of the cerebral hemispheres consists of grey matter (composed primarily of neuronal cell bodies and unmyelinated axons) and has sensory, motor, and association areas. The association areas enable perception of the world and produce thought and language. |
| Frontal lobe | This area at the front of the brain plays a large role in emotional expression, reasoning, judgment, memory, problem solving, planning, decision-making, and language. |
| Hypothalamus | Located at the base of the brain, the hypothalamus controls appetite, sleep, aggression, and sex drive. It is also responsible for regulating body temperature, blood pressure, emotions, and hormone secretion. |
| Nucleus accumbens | The nucleus accumbens is the pleasure centre of the brain. When we do something rewarding (e.g., eat, have sex) there is an increased level of dopamine in the nucleus accumbens. |
| Amygdala | The size and shape of an almond, the amygdala is alert to the needs of basic survival and emotional reactions (e.g., anger, fear). |
| Hippocampus | This area of the brain is responsible for processing new memories for long-term storage. |
| Reticular formation | The reticular formation is responsible for maintaining a state of alert consciousness. |
| Corpus callosum | The corpus callosum delivers messages between the two brain hemispheres. |
| Meninges | The meninges wrap the brain in protective layers filled with cerebrospinal fluid and thus act as a "shock absorber" to help protect the brain from injury. |

the person may be considered to have a personality disorder. Generally, an individual considered to have a personality disorder will experience distress or impairment in his or her capacity to function and relate to others. Individuals with certain forms of personality disorder may be likely to invoke distress in the people around them.

# Brain Function and Good Mental Health

In the above section, we listed many different mental functions. It is important to note that good mental health does not require perfect function in every sphere of mental life. The definition of mental health provided in Chapter 1 describes a state of emotional and psychological well-being in which an individual is able to use his or her cognitive and emotional capabilities, function in society, and meet the ordinary demands of everyday life. Thus, just as we might have a problem with high blood pressure yet be able to control this and enjoy good overall physical health, we may also have a particular challenge with one or more mental functions yet still achieve overall good mental health.

## Genetics and Epigenetics of Mental Health and Illness

Just as we inherit physical characteristics from our biological parents, we also appear to inherit mental characteristics. If both of your biological parents are tall and have green eyes, then you are much more likely than average to be tall and have green eyes. However, despite your tall, green-eyed parents, you could be short and have brown eyes. Similarly, if both of your biological parents are very shy and introverted, you are more likely to be shy and introverted, but you might be socially confident and outgoing instead. Although the likelihood of sharing traits with your ancestors is heightened as a result of genetic transmission, it remains very possible that you will demonstrate a different combination of traits.

Genes are segments of DNA that are contained in the nuclei of all cells in our bodies. The coding of the segments provides "instructions" that guide the development and function of our bodies. Thus, just as there are certain genes (DNA sequence segments) that determine the colour of our eyes, there are genes that determine our mental characteristics, such as whether we are likely to be shy and introverted or confident and extraverted. However, genetic transmission of mental characteristics appears to be highly complex, involving multiple gene loci (Rosoff, 2010).

Even if we inherit the genes for a certain trait or illness, we may not develop the condition. This is partly due to **epigenetics**, which can be defined as functions at the molecular level affecting gene expression that operate in addition to DNA sequencing transmission. Thus, the "epi" in epigenetics can be thought of as meaning "in addition to" genetics. This explains why "identical" (monozygotic) twins are not really identical, physically or mentally. Although they have nearly identical DNA, monozygotic twins are exposed to different environmental influences both in the womb and throughout the rest of their lives, during which genes are switched on or off. These epigenetic variations and other environmental influences alter the phenotype, that is, the observable characteristics that result from the interaction of the genotype and environmental factors. For example, monozygotic twins do not have the same fingerprints because environmental factors in the womb result in different whorls and patterns developing at the fingertips. If one monozygotic twin has a schizophrenic illness, the chance that the other twin will have schizophrenia is only about 40 percent (Kendler, 1983). Although a 40 percent chance is much higher than the risk among the general population of having schizophrenia (less than 1 percent), a monozygotic twin of someone with schizophrenia does not have a 100 percent chance of having the illness, which would be the case if genetic transmission were completely deterministic.

**Figure 2.7:** Pictured here is a strand of DNA, which is contained within the nuclei of all cells in our bodies. The coding of the segments provides "instructions" that guide the development and function of our bodies.

*Source*: luismmolina/iStockphoto

Once again, this shows that genetic factors have significant influence but play only a partial role in determining mental health and illness. Some of the environmental factors thought to be important in influencing mental health or mental illness include exposure to extreme stress or deprivation in early life; exposure to environmental toxins (such as lead or mercury); and diet. There is growing evidence that exposures such as these in utero or early in life may lead to longstanding mental health problems throughout the life course (Lester, Marsit, Conradt, Bromer, & Padbury, 2012; Stuffrein-Roberts, Joyce, & Kennedy, 2008).

## Cellular Activity in the Brain

As discussed earlier in this chapter, the brain contains approximately 100 billion brain cells or neurons that comprise an intricate web of electrochemical connections sending multiple electrical signals shooting at a rapid pace throughout the brain and along nerves leading to all other parts of the body. How is the electrical energy supplied to fuel the brain cells? What serves as the "battery" to keep the brain going strong? The answer is adenosine triphosphate (ATP), a macromolecule that, along with DNA (another macromolecule), constitutes the most important building block of all living organisms. ATP powers virtually every activity of the cell and organism, including generating electrical energy in neurons. ATP is a complex molecule that contains the nucleoside adenosine and a tail consisting of three phosphates, which have high-energy bonds. Energy is released from the ATP molecule by a reaction that breaks off one of the phosphates, leaving ADP, or adenosine diphosphate. Immediately, the cell mitochondria reattach a phosphate group, thus producing ATP and "recharging" the battery: "[H]ooking and unhooking that last phosphate [on ATP] is what keeps the whole world operating" (Trefil, 1992, p. 93).

At any one instant, there are about a billion ATP molecules in each cell of the human body. As they release energy (by the breaking of the high-energy phosphate bonds), they are being replenished continually. Food and oxygen are required to provide the necessary molecular ingredients to rebuild the ATP molecules. In neurons, ATP supplies the energy needed for electrical activity, for transport of chemical messengers across synapses, and for other cellular functions. Neurons require approximately twice the energy supply of other cells, and the brain uses about 10 percent of the entire supply of energy in the human body due to the high demands of neural electrical transmission.

## Brain Nutrients and the Blood-Brain Barrier

Unlike other cells in the human body, which use various nutrients derived from food as fuel, brain cells or neurons use only glucose. Other nutrients do not fuel the brain because of the **blood-brain barrier**. This structure surrounds the blood capillaries that supply the brain and spinal cord and allows only small molecules to pass through its membranes. The blood-brain barrier allows essential metabolites, such as oxygen and glucose, to pass from the blood to the brain but blocks most larger molecules, including most drugs, hormones, viruses, and bacteria. Despite the protection of the blood-brain barrier, it is possible for some harmful toxins to reach the brain. Molecules that are small and those that are lipid-soluble can pass through the barrier. Some viruses and certain toxins, such as lead and mercury, can enter and have damaging effects on brain function; children, whose brains are developing, are particularly susceptible.

Neurons cannot store glucose and, consequently, a constant supply must be delivered for the brain to be adequately fuelled. Glucose is supplied from carbohydrates, found primarily in grains (such as rice, pasta, bread), legumes, fruits and vegetables, and refined sugar, that we eat. Glucose levels are usually maintained at adequate levels by various homeostatic mechanisms. However, in unusual circumstances that cause blood glucose levels to drop to low levels, such as prolonged starvation (including starvation that occurs in people with anorexia nervosa), or when someone with diabetes receives too high a dose of insulin (a hormone that facilitates the uptake of glucose by cells), brain function is adversely affected. Without adequate levels of glucose, brain cells cannot function properly

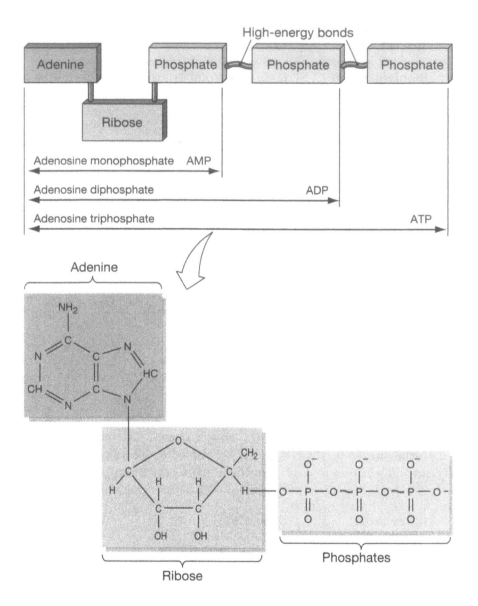

**Figure 2.8:** ATP is the macromolecule that allows us to make energy for all of our cells, including our neurons. Often referred to as the "powerhouse" of the cell, ATP is the most important building block in living organisms.

*Source*: Martini, F.H. (2004). *Fundamentals of anatomy and physiology* (6th ed., p. 59). San Francisco, CA: Pearson Education.

and one quickly becomes unable to think clearly. Very low blood glucose will disable brain function, cause loss of consciousness, and possibly lead to death.

The brain also requires a constant supply of oxygen to be delivered via the bloodstream and utilizes much more oxygen than other parts of the body. The brain uses about 20 percent of the body's oxygen yet only constitutes about 2 percent of the body's weight. Consequently, the brain is particularly sensitive to a lack of oxygen (hypoxia) and large numbers of brain cells will begin to die after about five minutes without oxygen.

In addition to glucose and oxygen, the brain requires an adequate supply of certain vitamins for healthy function. A number of the B vitamins, particularly B1 (thiamine), B3 (niacin), and B12 (cyanocobalanin), are necessary for healthy neuronal activity. The body generally maintains adequate stores of these vitamins, but in unusual circumstances these vitamins can become depleted. Prolonged starvation or malnutrition can lead to deficiencies in B vitamins, as can chronic use of alcohol and certain forms of cancer and other diseases. Deficiencies of these B vitamins can cause serious brain deficits, including disturbances of memory and thinking.

## The Brain's Shock Absorbers: The Meninges and Cerebrospinal Fluid

Since the precious supercomputer that we carry around on top of our necks is so essential to human life, it is not surprising that the body has a series of protective envelopes and shock absorbers to diminish the likelihood of damage or trauma to the brain. Inside the hard casing of the skull, there are three separate protective membranes surrounding the brain, called the **meninges**. Furthermore, the brain is bathed in cerebrospinal fluid, a fluid shock absorber held tightly in place by the meninges.

When we sustain a blow to the head, the brain is protected by the meninges and cerebrospinal fluid. However, if the trauma is too great for the protective shock absorption they provide, bleeding or damage to brain tissue may occur. Repeated studies now confirm that even minor repeated trauma to the head (without loss of consciousness), such as commonly occur in many sports activities, causes substantial damage to the human brain (Baugh et al., 2012; Gavett, Stern, & McKee, 2011). Recent findings about the susceptibility of the brain to even minor head trauma has led to increased public health efforts to increase the use of helmets and protective headgear in various sports activities and to enhance safety features (such as seat belts and airbags) in motor vehicles.

# Hormones and Mental Health

In addition to the complex and sophisticated electrochemical network of neurons, the human body produces various **hormones**, that is, chemical messengers released by cells that affect cells elsewhere in the body. Hormones provide an additional mechanism for regulating and changing mental function and behaviour. They are located in many different sites in the body, usually stored in glands that secrete them into the bloodstream under certain conditions. For example, hormones are stored in the pituitary gland (a small structure located at the base of the brain), the thyroid gland (a gland wrapped around the trachea in the front of the neck), the adrenal glands (triangular glands that sit on top of each kidney), the pancreas (located in the abdomen), and in the ovaries and testes (in women and men, respectively).

The different hormones secreted by these and other glands each have specific effects on the body's function, and many of these hormones can affect the brain and nervous system. For example, adrenaline, the hormone secreted by the adrenal glands, stimulates the brain and snaps it into an emergency high-alert mode. Adrenaline is secreted when we are under threat or experience fear, pain, and other danger signals. It can also be secreted when we are in a competitive situation and need to push our bodies to operate at peak physical performance.

Hormones can be thought of as controls on a music sound system, like those controlling volume or tone. Although changing these parameters will not change the piece of music that is being played, shifts in volume or tone will create profound changes in the character of the sound. Similarly, the release of hormones can create changes in general characteristics of mental activity, such as speeding up or slowing down thought and intensifying or diminishing memory and emotional responsiveness.

Women may experience changes in mood in association with hormonal changes that occur during menstrual cycles, during and following pregnancy, and through menopause. Estrogen and progesterone, the ovarian hormones that regulate menstruation, appear to have significant impact on mood and other mental functions. However, the mechanism of action is not yet understood. Testosterone, a hormone released by the testes in males (and released in smaller amounts by the ovaries in females), also appears to have a significant effect on mental function and behaviour, including regulation of one's libido (i.e., sexual drive) and levels of mental energy. Testosterone levels drop with aging, and some men and women may experience an associated loss of libido and a decrease in mental energy associated with lowered testosterone levels. We will discuss some of the unique features of women's and men's mental health in Chapter 8.

The "master control" for the release of the many hormones is the hypothalamus, a complex region of the brain containing a number of nuclei involved in the regulation of emotion, appetite, body temperature, and other functions. The hypothalamus is directly connected to the pituitary gland, which is located directly below the area of the brain where the hypothalamus is situated. The hypothalamus signals the pituitary gland to release particular hormones (i.e., releasing factors) into the bloodstream, which in turn signal glands in other parts of the body, such as the thyroid gland, adrenal glands, and ovaries, to release their hormones.

Usually, levels of hormones are well regulated by the body. However, certain illnesses can cause hormone levels to be too high or low; this can lead to mental changes, such as increased anxiety or decreased mental energy. Research studies indicate that children who are exposed to repeated stress may develop changes in their hormonal regulatory systems that are associated with chronic anxiety. This appears to occur as a result of changes that cause the adrenal glands to attenuate the release of cortisol (Hertzman & Frank, 2006).

## Light, Darkness, and Mental Health

Similar to other mammals, human biology appears to be affected by changes in the seasons and cycles of light and darkness. Changes in exposure to daylight that occur throughout the seasons, and which may occur more abruptly when we travel to very different time zones or different latitudes, alter the synchronization of our internal biological rhythms. We each have a type of internal biological clock that can be reset by changes in exposure to bright light. If we travel to a very different time zone, we are likely to experience jet lag in which our internal biological clock becomes confused and our internal biological rhythms go out of sync. That is why we can feel so crummy and can have difficulty sleeping when we have jet lag. People who travel frequently across time zones, such as pilots and other airline crew, are trained to maintain their patterns according to a fixed time zone in order to minimize the de-synchronization of their biological clocks.

During the winter months in Canada, daylight hours shorten and many people experience an unpleasant response known as Seasonal Affective Disorder (SAD), in which they have difficulty sleeping and exhibit other symptoms of depression. People who live at high latitudes, that is, either in the far northern or southern hemisphere, will go through long periods in the winter during which there is very little daylight. Research studies have shown that people who live in areas with long periods of darkness are more prone to developing SAD (Kegel et al., 2009). There may be biological reasons why people tend to feel happy and energetic in sunny climates and moody when there is little light.

Researchers have found that people who suffer from SAD often experience relief from depression by being exposed to bright light each morning (Westrin & Lam, 2007). Special light boxes that generate enough bright light (10,000 LUX for 30 minutes) have been created and are sometimes prescribed for use by people with SAD.

**Figure 2.9:** Some individuals will experience Seasonal Affective Disorder (SAD) in response to the longer dark hours during winter months. This photo was taken in the small northern community of Carmacks in Yukon Territory, Canada.

*Source:* Brenden Westman, Photographer

## Plasticity and Regenerativity of the Brain

As described earlier in this chapter, the brain is more than a collection of independent centres, each responsible for particular functions; these centres work together in a coordinated, integrated manner. Furthermore, the brain has a high degree of plasticity so that functions of the brain may be taken over by different areas if there is damage or loss of brain tissue. For example, such plasticity can occur between the two sides of the brain.

If a line is drawn, dividing the brain equally into left and right halves, it can then be seen that the brain is similar to many other parts of the body, with symmetry in structure between its left and right sides. A large band of fibres called the "corpus callosum" connects the right and left sides of the brain.

Scientists have found differentiation of function between the right and left sides of the brain. You may have heard that the left side of the brain is more focused on functions such as mathematics and logic whereas the right side of the brain is more involved in artistic and intuitive functions and abilities, but the reality is more complex. The plasticity of the brain allows different regions, including the right and left hemispheres, to shift functions.

Recently, it was discovered that brain cells are generated throughout life. This discovery of adult neurogenesis overturned the previous view that new brain cells were not generated after fetal development and that we gradually lose brain cells throughout our lifetimes, never to be regained (Gage, 2002; Reynolds & Weiss, 1992). Many neuroscientists now consider generation of neurons in the hippocampus to be important for learning and memory. As disturbances of hippocampal function are thought to be present in various mental disorders, including mood and anxiety disorders and schizophrenia, scientists hope that discoveries regarding adult hippocampal neurogenesis may help to develop new treatments and interventions (Schoenfeld & Cameron, 2015). The important discovery of adult neurogenesis reversed a long-standing scientific belief and is a good reminder to us that some of our current scientific ideas will be revised in the future as we acquire new information.

## Conclusion

In this chapter, we have described various structures and functions of the brain in both mental health and illness. We emphasized that brain regions do not operate independently, but rather in an integrated and coordinated manner. We identified a number of biological influences on brain function, including genetics, epigenetics, nutrition, hormones, and exposure to cycles of light and darkness. We also discussed the capacity of the brain to shift functions from one region to another (i.e., plasticity), and its ability to regenerate its own cells.

Brain function is fascinating and complex; it is no wonder that so many students and scientists are captivated by the study of the brain. However, do not fall into the trap of reductionism and convince yourself that all mental processes and human behaviour can be explained by brain function. In the next chapter, we hope to convince you that a full understanding of mental health and mental illness also requires knowledge provided by the social sciences.

## Glossary

**blood-brain barrier:** The structure that surrounds the blood capillaries that supply the brain and spinal cord and allows only small molecules to pass through its membranes.

**cerebral hemisphere:** One of two regions of the brain; the left and right cerebral hemispheres.

**epigenetics:** Functions at the molecular level affecting gene expression that operate in addition to DNA sequencing transmission.

**hormones:** Chemical messengers released by cells that affect cells elsewhere in the body.

**limbic system:** A series of interconnected structures in different regions of the brain that are important in producing mood and emotions.

**meninges:** Three separate protective envelopes surrounding the brain.

**mood:** The predominant background emotional state that persists in an individual over an extended period of time.

**neurons:** Cells of the brain.

**neurotransmitters:** Chemicals that allow the transmission of signals from one neuron to another.

**personality:** The enduring behavioural traits and characteristics of an individual.

## Critical Thinking Questions

1. How do neurons transmit messages?
2. Select a region of the brain and describe how it can affect a person's mental health.
3. What role do genetics play in determining mental health and illness?
4. Name two hormones that can affect a person's mental health.
5. What role does biology play in understanding human behaviour and mental health?

## Recommended Readings

Carter, R. (2009). *Human Brain Book*. London: Dorling Kindersley.

Frith, C. (2007). *Making up the Mind: How the Brain Creates Our Mental World*. Oxford: Wiley-Blackwell.

Kendler, K.S., & Prescott, C.A. (2006). *Genes, Environment, and Psychopathology: Understanding the Causes of Psychiatric and Substance Use Disorders*. New York: Guildford Press.

LeDoux, J. (2002). *Synaptic Self: How Our Brains Become Who We Are*. New York: Viking Press.

Schwartz, J.M., & Begley, S. (2002). *The Mind and the Brain: Neuroplasticity and the Power of Mental Force*. New York: HarperCollins.

## Recommended Websites

Blue Brain Project. http://bluebrain.epfl.ch/

The Brain from Top to Bottom. http://thebrain.mcgill.ca/

The Hormones of the Human. Kimball's Biology Pages. http://users.rcn.com/jkimball.ma.ultranet/BiologyPages/H/Hormones.html

The Human Brain. The Franklin Institute. http://learn.fi.edu/learn/brain/

The Medical Biochemistry Page. Michael W. King. Biochemistry of Nerve Transmission. http://themedicalbiochemistrypage.org/nerves.html

# References

Baugh, C.M., Stamm, J.M., Riley, D.O., Gavett, B.E., Shenton, M.E., Lin, A., Nowinski, C.J., Cantu, R.C., McKee, A.C., & Stern, R.A. (2012). Chronic traumatic encephalopathy: Neurodegeneration following repetitive concussive and subconcussive brain trauma. *Brain Imaging and Behavior*, 6(2), 244–254.

Bliss, T.V.P., & Collingridge, G.L. (1993). A synaptic model of memory: Long-term potentiation in the hippocampus. *Nature*, 361(6407), 31–39.

Boutrel, B., & Koob, G.F. (2004). What keeps us awake: The neuropharmacology of stimulants and wakefulness-promoting medications. *Sleep*, 27(6), 1181–1194.

Delmonte, M.M. (1984). Physiological responses during meditation and rest. *Biofeedback and Self-Regulation*, 9(2), 181–200.

Eysenck, M.W., & Keane, M.T. (2015). *Cognitive psychology: A student's handbook* (7th ed.). New York: Psychology Press.

Gage, F.H. (2002). Neurogenesis in the adult brain. *Journal of Neuroscience*, 22(3), 212–213.

Gavett, B.E., Stern, R.A., & McKee, A.C. (2011). Chronic traumatic encephalopathy: A potential late effect of sport-related concussive and subconcussive head trauma. *Clinics in Sports Medicine*, 30(1), 179–188.

Hertzman, C., & Frank, J. (2006). Biological pathways linking the social environment, development, and health. In J. Heymann, C. Hertzman, M.L. Barer, & R.G. Evans (Eds.), *Healthier societies: From analysis to action* (pp. 35–57). New York: Oxford University Press.

Kegel, M., Dam, H., Ali, F., & Bjerregaard, P. (2009). The prevalence of seasonal affective disorder (SAD) in Greenland is related to latitude. *Nordic Journal of Psychiatry*, 63(4), 331–335.

Kendler, K.S. (1983). Overview: A current perspective on twin studies of schizophrenia. *American Journal of Psychiatry*, 140(11), 1413–1425.

Kothari, L.K., Bordia, A., & Gupta, O.P. (1973). The yogic claim of voluntary control over the heart beat: An unusual demonstration. *American Heart Journal*, 86, 282–284.

Lee, F.S., Heimer, H., Giedd, J.N., Lein, E.S., Šestan, N., Weinberger, D.R., & Casey, B.J. (2014). Adolescent mental health: Opportunity and obligation. *Science*, 346(6209), 547–549. doi: 10.1126/science.1260497

Lester, B.M., Marsit, C.J., Conradt, E., Bromer, C., & Padbury, J.F. (2012). Behavioral epigenetics and the developmental origins of child mental health disorders. *Journal of Developmental Origins of Health and Disease*, 3(6), 395–408. doi:10.1017/S2040174412000426

Markram, H. (2006). The blue brain project. *Nature Reviews Neuroscience*, 7, 153–160.

McCormick, R.M. (2009). First Nations counsellor training in British Columbia: Strengthening the circle. *Canadian Journal of Community Mental Health*, 16(2), 91–99.

Perez Velazquez, J.L., & Wennberg, R. (2009). *Coordinated activity in the brain: Measurements and relevance to brain function and behavior.* New York: Springer Science & Business Media.

Plomin, R., DeFries, J.C., Knopik, V.S., & Neiderheiser, J. (2013). *Behavioral genetics* (6th ed.). New York: Worth Publishers.

Reynolds, B.A., & Weiss, S. (1992). Generation of neurons and astrocytes from isolated cells of the adult mammalian central nervous system. *Science*, 255(5052), 1707–1710.

Rosoff, P.M. (2010). In search of the mommy gene: Truth and consequences in behavioral genetics. *Science, Technology & Human Values*, 35(2), 200–243.

Schoenfeld, T.J., & Cameron, H.A. (2015). Adult neurogenesis and mental illness. *Neuropsychopharmacology*, 40(1), 113–128. doi: 10.1038/npp.2014.230

Smith, P.B., Fischer, R., Vignoles, V.L., & Bond, M. (2013). *Understanding social psychology across cultures: Engaging with others in a changing world.* London: SAGE.

Statistics Canada. (2008). Beverage consumption of Canadian adults. *Health Reports*, 19(4). Catalogue no. 82-003-X. Retrieved from www.statcan.gc.ca/pub/82-003-x/2008004/article/6500240-eng.htm

Stuffrein-Roberts, S., Joyce, P.R., & Kennedy, M.A. (2008). Role of epigenetics in mental disorders. *Australian & New Zealand Journal of Psychiatry*, 42(2), 97–107.

Trefil, J. (1992). *1001 things everyone should know about science.* New York: Doubleday.

von der Malsburg, C., Phillips, W.A., & Singer, W. (2010). *Dynamic coordination in the brain: From neurons to mind.* Cambridge, MA & London: MIT Press.

Wallace, R.K. (1970). Physiological effects of transcendental meditation. *Science*, 167(926), 1751–1754.

Westrin, A., & Lam, R.W. (2007). Seasonal affective disorder: A clinical update. *Annals of Clinical Psychiatry*, 19(4), 239–246.

Williams, R.W., & Herrup, K. (1988). The control of neuron number. *Annual Review of Neuroscience*, 11, 423–453.

# Chapter 3

# MENTAL HEALTH EXAMINED THROUGH THE SOCIAL SCIENCES

Man, the molecule of society, is the subject of social science.
—Henry Charles Carey (economist and chief economic advisor to 16th US President Abraham Lincoln)

## Introduction

In this chapter, we draw on knowledge about mental health and illness accumulated by the social sciences. The social sciences use the methods of scientific inquiry: careful and systematic data collection, analysis, and interpretation. Examples of social sciences include the disciplines of anthropology, criminology, economics, geography, history, political science, psychology, and sociology. A contrast is often drawn between these sciences and physical sciences such as biology, chemistry, and neuroscience. We examine some of the more important factors identified within the realm of social sciences, both at the level of the individual and the level of populations. Since a vast body of knowledge relevant to mental health and mental illness has been explored by social scientists, we will only be able to touch on a small sample of important ideas and discoveries. This chapter will highlight some topics we find intriguing and we recommend further reading at the end of the chapter for those who would like to explore social sciences in more depth.

## Theories of Individual and Group Behaviour

As we mentioned in the first chapter, psychoanalysis has had a substantial influence on ideas about mental health and illness. Developed in the beginning of the 20th century by Sigmund Freud, a Viennese psychiatrist, psychoanalysis included many ideas; some of these continue to receive attention whereas others have been dismissed.

Freud believed that the human behaviour we observe may be understood only by looking into deeper forces and conflicts operating below the level of awareness, that is, in the **unconscious mind** (Freud, 1901).

Freud asserted that humans are embroiled in a constant conflict between two aspects of the mind: the id, which is the source of instinctual drives (aggression and sexual desire), and the superego, an inner representation of societal norms and cultural conventions (Freud, 1901). Instinctual drives are passed on as part of our evolutionary heritage, whereas societal norms are shaped by our social and family environment. For example, an ordinary college student experiences the sudden wish to embrace an attractive fellow student passionately while in the middle of a class; this represents a conflict between an instinctual drive and a societal norm and would cause stress for this student. Freud theorized that such conflicts are typically resolved by repressing the unacceptable drive, that is, by pushing it below awareness. When this mechanism of repression is unsuccessful, a person may develop mental health problems such as depression or anxiety. Freud daringly proposed that, during childhood, we all have sexual desires toward our parents that are in direct conflict with our societal norms, and, as a result, we end up with emotional conflicts and problems (Freud, 1910). According to psychoanalytic theory, we are unaware of this conflict and repression, because it occurs in the unconscious mind. Psychoanalytic ideas are considered a part of "depth psychology," which plumbs the depths of the human psyche (Gay, 1995). In recent decades, the fields of psychiatry, psychology, nursing, and social work have mostly distanced themselves from psychoanalytic ideas (Bornstein, 2001). However, the appeal of these ideas remains strong in various creative disciplines such as literature, dance, and the visual arts.

Whether we embrace or dismiss his ideas and theories, Freud is considered to have had a great impact on Western thought—in part, because he initiated an awakening of interest in the human psyche and sparked exploration and analysis of human behaviour. In the first half of the 20th century, psychoanalytic theories were the subject of intense intellectual debate in Europe, soon spreading to other continents. Many creative thinkers devoted themselves to extending psychoanalytic theory and practice. Two of the most famous individuals who emerged from Freud's immediate circle were Alfred Adler and Carl Jung. Adler was concerned with the ways in which social structures may cause humans to feel helpless or powerless—he labelled this the **inferiority complex** (Adler, 1956). Adler asserted that much of human striving can be understood as an attempt to overcome the inferiority complex and increase one's sense of personal power and self-esteem. Meanwhile, Carl Jung took a radically different approach and asserted that we all share a very deep level of our mind in the form of the **collective unconscious** (Jung, 1981). Jung understood human personality in terms of archetypes, mythic figures contained in the collective unconscious that show us different ways we might be in the world. For example, the archetype of the *puer aeternus* is like a perpetual child who never settles down or accepts commitment. Jung's ideas appeal to those who favour a more spiritual and non-materialistic approach to understanding mental health.

However, many theorists and practitioners became skeptical of these "depth psychology" approaches and sought theoretical frameworks that would be less complicated and esoteric. The field of psychology developed a straightforward theoretical framework called **behaviourism** that aimed to understand how behaviour is shaped by the application of various stimuli, that of rewards and punishments (Skinner, 1938; Watson, 1924). In its early phases, behaviourism used animal research (often studying laboratory mice and rats) to examine the effects of various patterns of reward and punishment on behaviour. The Russian physiologist Ivan Pavlov was one of the first to examine behaviour in relation to environmental stimuli through his research on dogs (Pavlov, 1927). Such research on behaviour proved to be accurate in describing how humans learn behaviour, too. For example, if you reward a behaviour intermittently and unpredictably, the resulting behaviour change will last longer than if the reward is given every time the behaviour is carried out. (Think about how stubbornly people will continue gambling, where the rewards are intermittent and unpredictable.)

Behaviour therapy applies behaviourist principles to help individuals with mental health problems. It aims to identify the ways in which people with mental health problems have learned maladaptive responses to their environments. One type of behavioural learning involves **classical conditioning**. An example of this would be

Figure 3.1: Lab rat

*Source:* Joe Cicak/iStockphoto

to pair a stimulus that elicits a strong negative response (an electric shock) with a neutral stimulus (a soft light)—as these two stimuli are repeatedly paired, the light begins to elicit a strong negative response as well. At a more complex level, someone who had been harshly disciplined by several teachers might develop a conditioned fear response to all authority figures. This kind of fear response might result in a marked tendency to avoid contact with such figures. This would amount to a phobia that could severely limit someone's ability to complete education or function successfully in a job. Another way in which a maladaptive response might be learned is through **instrumental conditioning**, in which one has been rewarded or punished for a particular kind of behaviour, increasing or decreasing the frequency of the behaviour (Skinner, 1953). Most of our learning occurs through instrumental conditioning. For example, when you receive a high mark for demonstrating your knowledge of course material, you have been rewarded for working hard to reach that level of achievement, and this is likely to increase your tendency to work hard in other courses and jobs. When you receive a very low mark for a course to which you have not been giving much attention, this is a punishment that will likely discourage future inattentive behaviour. This can be considered to be a form of adaptive learning. In contrast, a child who cannot obtain the interest or attention of his parents or siblings other than when he exhibits disruptive, bothersome behaviour may experience maladaptive learning. By conceptualizing mental health problems as expressions of maladaptive learning, whether through classical or instrumental conditioning, we gain a powerful tool to understand behaviours shown by individuals with mental disorders that would otherwise be difficult to understand.

Over recent decades, behaviour therapy has largely been supplanted by a more wide-ranging approach called Cognitive Behavioural Therapy (CBT) (Rachman, 1997). This approach adds a focus on our thoughts or cognitions and how they relate to our behaviours. We'll learn more about CBT when we review treatments for mental health problems in Chapter 12.

Social scientists have also been intrigued by the way behaviour changes when people are in large groups or crowds. Sociologists have noted many examples of people acting differently when in large groups than they would normally as individuals, and this is sometimes referred to as **herd behaviour** (Raafat, Chater, & Frith, 2009). For example, people in a large group are more likely to help an individual in distress when they see others extending help but more likely to do nothing if others are ignoring the individual's distress.

## Development, Families, and Mental Health

Social scientists have focused attention on childhood development because it is a time when individuals learn so much at a very rapid pace. Childhood is a critical period that establishes lifelong patterns of personality and behaviour, echoing the famous

## Box 3.1: The Mental Health of Social Groups

In sociology, it has been questioned whether social groups themselves can be viewed as having good or poor mental health. Consider the surprising behaviour of crowds: excited mobs have been known to act more violently and irrationally than any one individual member would. This phenomenon is referred to as "the madness of crowds" (Mackay, [1841] 1980). Crowd members may lose their individuality and be subsumed by the group's emotions. Each person is subject to contagion and suggestion, virtually hypnotized into doing things that might otherwise be repugnant. When viewed in this way, one can think of the crowd as exhibiting poor mental health when it engages in actions that are irrational, impulsive, and destructive.

**Figure 3.2:** Riots provide an example of how crowd behaviour can quickly become out of control. This picture shows a young man being arrested by police during a riot.

*Source:* Nicole S. Young/iStockphoto

dictum of the Jesuit priesthood: "Give me a child up until he is seven and I will give you the man." Although it is true that childhood is a particularly important period for mental development, our minds continue to develop and change throughout our lives (Rutter & Taylor, 1989).

**Table 3.1: Summary of Erik Erikson's developmental stages**

| Stage | Ages | Basic conflict | Summary |
|---|---|---|---|
| **1. Oral-sensory** | Birth to 18 months | Trust vs. mistrust | The infant must form a first loving, trusting relationship with the caregiver, or develop a sense of mistrust. |
| **2. Muscular-anal** | 18 months to 3 years | Autonomy vs. shame/doubt | The child's energies are directed toward the development of physical skills, including walking, grasping, and rectal sphincter control. The child learns control but may develop shame and doubt if not handled well. |
| **3. Locomotor** | 3 to 6 years | Initiative vs. guilt | The child continues to become more assertive and to take more initiative, but may be too forceful, leading to guilt feelings. |
| **4. Latency** | 6 to 12 years | Industry vs. inferiority | The child must deal with demands to learn new skills or risk a sense of inferiority, failure, and incompetence. |
| **5. Adolescence** | 12 to 19 years | Identity vs. role confusion | The teenager must achieve a sense of identity in occupation, sex roles, politics, and religion. |
| **6. Young adulthood** | 19 to 40 years | Intimacy vs. isolation | The young adult must develop intimate relationships or suffer feelings of isolation. |
| **7. Middle adulthood** | 40 to 65 years | Generativity vs. stagnation | Each adult must find some way to satisfy and support the next generation. |
| **8. Maturity** | 65 to death | Ego integrity vs. despair | The culmination is a sense of oneself as one is and of feeling fulfilled. |

*Source:* Cramer, C., Flynn, B., & LaFave, A. (1997). Erik Erikson's 8 stages of psychosocial development: Summary chart. Retrieved from web.cortland.edu/andersmd/ERIK/sum.HTML

Among the best-known theories of development are those of Erik Erikson, who presented a view of identity development as proceeding through a series of stages across the lifespan (Erikson, [1950] 1993; Erikson & Erikson, 1987). Through infancy and childhood, our identities are defined by our parents and immediate social environment. In adolescence, we begin to question the identity we have been "given" and think about our *own* values and goals. By adulthood, we have preferably worked out our own identity and are striving to reach goals that have personal meaning (see Table 3.1). According to Erikson's theory, failure to navigate each of the stages of identity development can result in mental health problems, whose form will reflect the particular transition that was unsuccessfully completed. For example, the late adolescence/early adult stage of identity formation involves the establishment of occupational and relationship choices—individuals who have difficulty completing this stage may remain in a state of identity diffusion, in which they feel lost, directionless, and anxious (Kroger, Martinussen, & Marcia, 2010). Another stage, associated with the elderly, is that of Integrity, in which individuals must find meaningful ways to look back at their lives; individuals who have difficulty with this stage may experience despair, and feel that their lives have been empty or meaningless.

**Table 3.2: Kohlberg's stages of moral development**

| Level | Stage | Summary |
|---|---|---|
| Level One: **Pre-conventional morality** | Stage 1: Punishment-obedience orientation | An action is perceived to be morally wrong if punishment is received. Young children use this form of reasoning. |
| | Stage 2: Instrumental relativist orientation | Actions are determined by "what's in it for me?" Others' needs are considered only on the basis of self-interest. |
| Level Two: **Conventional morality** | Stage 3: Good boy-nice girl orientation | Individuals are receptive to approval or disapproval by others and moral decisions are influenced by a desire to be liked and accepted. |
| | Stage 4: Law and order orientation | Actions are based on social conventions and what is right and wrong, and obligations to uphold laws and societal rules. |
| Level Three: **Post-conventional morality** | Stage 5: Social contract orientation | Individuals are understood to hold different positions and decisions are made based on wishes of the majority and through compromise. |
| | Stage 6: Universal ethical principle orientation | Decisions are made through abstract reasoning about what is right according to universal ethical principles. |

Erikson's theory is only one of a number of sophisticated theories of psychological development. We won't be able to discuss most of these, but it is worth noting Kohlberg's theory of moral development. This theory explains the stages by which individuals develop the ability to reason out the moral aspects of situations in order to make appropriate ethical decisions (see Table 3.2). Although Kohlberg described six stages of moral development, he proposed that most adults do not progress beyond the third or fourth stage and many operate at more primitive levels throughout their lives (Kohlberg, 1976). At the most advanced stage, individuals choose their actions by viewing situations from various perspectives and trying to achieve the best balance of benefits among the different participants according to universal principles of justice.

How does Kohlberg's theory help us to understand mental health? It can help to explain how certain people become anti-social, that is, willing to ignore others' rights and act in violent or destructive ways. Even violent criminals will typically express some kind of moral justification for their actions, though their moral reasoning is crude and maladaptive (e.g., built on a primitive notion of personal vengeance) and corresponds to the lower stages of Kohlberg's developmental framework.

Since our behaviour and development is strongly influenced by our families, various theories have been advanced to explain family interactions and create family therapy approaches. For example, a systems theory model, developed by Olson, Russell, and Sprenkle (1989), describes families in terms of three dimensions: family cohesion, flexibility, and communication. "Family cohesion" is defined by the degree of emotional bonding among family members and is viewed as connected, separated, disengaged, or enmeshed. "Family flexibility" refers to the amount of change that is tolerated in the family's leadership and relationship rules and is flexible, structured, rigid, or chaotic. "Family communication" describes the listening skills, self-disclosure, clarity, and respect in communications among family members.

In recent years, family theorists have questioned traditional theories and have criticized the contention that there is a "normal" set of behaviours that characterizes families. It has been pointed out that certain kinds of families and family members have been dominated and oppressed by those in more powerful positions in society (including scientists and therapists), and therefore we should be wary of theories that proscribe what is "normal." Some family theorists have embraced **social constructionism**, which posits that there is no objective truth, only a variety of subjective views developed through dialogue with others (Burr, 1995; Loseke, 2011). We discuss this perspective in the following section.

## Society and Mental Health

It has long been recognized that there is a relationship between an individual's mental health and the sense of connection to the society in which he or she lives. This relationship was articulated by Emile Durkheim, a sociologist who argued that people living in societies undergoing a high degree of turbulence or fragmentation would experience a state of **anomie**, that is, a condition where social and/or moral norms are confused, unclear, or simply absent. Durkheim felt that this lack of connectedness would result in feelings of alienation and isolation (Durkheim, [1897] 1997). Durkheim believed that individuals experiencing anomie would be at an increased risk of suicide. Recent sociological research has built upon Durkheim's foundation to show that individuals with low levels of connections to social networks, that is, lacking family connections, friendships, or membership in religious or voluntary groups, have relatively poor mental health and higher rates of mortality (Smith & Christakis, 2008). Conversely, connectedness to social networks is positively correlated with mental health.

**Figure 3.3:** This photo taken at a young woman's graduation demonstrates the emotional bonding and connectedness between father and daughter.

*Source:* skynesher/iStockphoto

Social scientists have concluded that each of us must feel that we are meeting the expectations of our social group, yet some experience this as a painful struggle. Those who perceive large discrepancies between their self-images and who they feel they ought to be may feel considerable anxiety and distress. To escape these painful feelings, these individuals may use escape strategies (Wild et al., 2008), such as alcohol and drug use, overeating, and even suicide.

---

**Box 3.2: Generations and Birth Cohorts**

You have likely heard of generational groups such as the "Baby Boomers" (born approximately 1946–1960), "Generation X" (born approximately 1960–1980), and "Millennials" (born 1980–1995). Epidemiologists and social scientists often refer to such generational groupings as **birth cohorts** (i.e., groups of people born at the same time who then grow up together) and have found that various facets of our behaviour seems to be strongly predicted by membership in a specific birth cohort. People in the same birth cohort are generally exposed to the same social events and these often have powerful impacts on key beliefs, values, anxieties, and behaviour patterns. Baby Boomers came of age during a time of rapid social change, increased freedom, and relative affluence. Experimentation with psychoactive substances was common and socially accepted during their teenage and young adult years. Even as they age, they continue to have high rates of substance use and misuse. Members of the Generation X birth cohort, when compared to previous generations, have been found to be more heterogeneous and socially diverse in regard to characteristics such as ethnicity, culture, sexual orientation, gender identity, and religious identity. Millennials are unique in their facility and comfort with technology in everyday life since they grew up at a time when computer, Internet, and mobile device technology advanced at a rapid pace. They also came of age at a time when economic pressures increased and housing and job markets became more difficult to crack. Rates of depression, anxiety, substance use, and other mental health characteristics have been shown to be strongly associated with birth cohorts.

---

A provocative theory that emerged in the social sciences is social constructionism, which argues that "scientific concepts" and "facts" are based upon social norms, rather than a bedrock of absolute reality (Burr, 1995). In this view, scientific concepts or laws are constructed within the context of science itself as a type of social organization. The social constructionist view holds that conceptions of mental health are socially constructed, they vary across societies, and all of them are "correct." From this perspective, there are many equally valid ways to define mental health and construe mental illness.

## *Politics, Economics, and Mental Health*

Stable political and economic conditions foster good mental health, whereas periods of political or economic instability have detrimental impacts on populations. For example, suicide rates increased dramatically in Asia during the economic crisis of 1997/98 in which many people lost their jobs (Chang et al., 2009) and rates of suicide in Greece similarly increased during the economic crisis there in 2011/12 (Rachiotis et al., 2015). The atrocities of war, which may include substantial loss of life and property, displacement from communities, and even extrajudicial execution

---

**Box 3.3: Social Constructionism**

Imagine a man who states that he is inhabited by a god and has been chosen as a sacred spokesman. This man would be viewed by conventional mental health practitioners in Western society as suffering from a delusional belief, a symptom of psychosis; but in another society that same person might be accepted as a shaman truly possessed by a deity. The social constructionist would not be surprised to find such different views of this man's mental health and, further, would insist that each is correct for its respective society. Needless to say, social constructionism has engendered a great deal of controversy within the social sciences. You might want to explore this fascinating controversy, but don't assume that social constructionism is easily disproven. Consider the individual we've described above. Some would argue that he must be schizophrenic, and schizophrenia is caused by a dysfunctional brain, but there really isn't much hard scientific evidence that proves the theory that schizophrenia involves brain pathology. And if we can't prove that this person has a mental disease, would we have to acknowledge that he just *might* be a shaman?

---

and torture, can have far-reaching effects on the mental health of a population (Dimitry, 2012; Silove, 1999).

Canadians have enjoyed relative political and economic stability and peace for many decades. However, there are groups within Canadian society who have experienced political and economic hardships similar to many residents of poor and war-ravaged countries. For example, refugees who have fled or been forced out of countries in which they were subjected to human rights abuses frequently experience substantial mental health problems. Members of Canada's armed forces who have served in combat zones or have witnessed traumatic events are also at high risk of mental health problems. Studies of Canadian military personnel returning from Afghanistan have found that 28 percent suffered from at least one mental health problem (Fikretoglu et al., 2007; Paré & Radford, 2013).

Many members of Canada's Aboriginal communities experienced terrible losses in previous generations. For a period of more than 100 years, Aboriginal children were forcibly placed in residential schools where they were separated from their families and required to abandon their cultural and linguistic heritages. Many people who went through the residential school system describe psychological, physical, and sexual abuse while they were residents in the schools. The detrimental effects of residential schools on Aboriginal people are considered to result in a form of post-traumatic stress disorder (PTSD) termed **residential school syndrome**. Its symptoms are described by Canadian psychiatrist Charles Brasfield:

> recurrent intrusive memories, nightmares, occasional flashbacks, and quite striking avoidance of anything that might be reminiscent of the Indian residential school experience.

**Figure 3.4:** People living in war-torn countries experience turbulence and uncertainty, which can lead to poor mental health outcomes.

*Source:* iStockphoto

At the same time, there is often a significant detachment from others, and relationship difficulties are common. There is often diminished interest and participation in aboriginal cultural activities and markedly deficient knowledge of traditional culture and skills. Often there is markedly increased arousal including sleep difficulties, anger management difficulties, and impaired concentration. As might be the case for anyone attending a boarding school with inadequate parenting, parenting skills are often deficient. Strikingly, there is a persistent tendency to abuse alcohol or sedative medication drugs, often starting at a very young age. (Brasfield, 2001, p. 79)

## *Social Determinants of Health*

**Social determinants of health** are defined as the socio-political and economic factors that influence the health of individuals and broad populations. There is no universally accepted list of social determinants of health; however, Canadian health policy professor Dennis Raphael and a group of co-authors have undertaken a detailed exploration of the following list of 12 key social determinants of health especially relevant to Canadians (Raphael, 2008):

- Income and its distribution
- Housing
- Education
- Early life
- Gender
- Employment and working conditions
- Unemployment and employment security
- Aboriginal status
- Social exclusion
- Social safety net
- Food security
- Health care services

Of course, many of these factors are correlated, for example, people who have higher incomes will usually have better housing, more stable employment, and greater education than those with lower incomes. Social determinants have a profound influence on health; in fact, they have a greater impact on health than behavioural risk factors such as diet, physical activity, smoking, and use of alcohol (Benzeval et al., 2001). Researchers continue to explore which social determinants have the strongest influence on the health of individuals and populations. It is important to recognize that social determinants of health, such as gender, ethnicity, and education, do not impact or influence a person in isolation. Instead, they are experienced alongside each other and interact on multiple levels—a concept known as "intersectionality" (Hankivsky & Cormier, 2009). Emerging from feminist theory, sociologists such as Patricia Hill Collins argue that patterns of oppression are often tied together and influenced by the intersectional systems of society (Collins, 2000). As an example, it was recognized that the experiences of white, middle-class women were often very different from those of immigrant, poor, or disabled women. When considering how female gender affects health, it became evident that women are not a homogeneous group, and an intersectional analysis is required to understand the relationships among various social determinants and health outcomes.

The WHO has described poverty as the greatest cause of suffering on earth (WHO, 1995). It will not surprise you that poverty is strongly correlated with poor health; the relationship between individual income and health is well established. This holds true for mental health conditions such as mood disorders, anxiety disorders, developmental problems, hyperactivity, and suicidal behaviour, each of which has been found to be much more prevalent among people living in poverty (Farr, 2000; Sareen et al., 2011). Table 3.3. shows a few of the findings of a study by Sareen and colleagues

(2011) that examined the relationship between income and mental disorder in a large population-based study. Individuals in the lowest income bracket (i.e., income less than $20,000 per year) were far more likely to have had mood disorders or have made suicide attempts than those in higher income groups.

**Table 3.3: Rates of mood disorders, suicide attempts, and other mental health conditions by income**

| Annual household income | ≤ $19,999 | $20,000–$39,999 | $40,000–$69,999 | ≥ $70,000 |
|---|---|---|---|---|
| Any Lifetime Mood Disorder | 1.80 (1.50–2.16) | 1.36 (1.18–1.37) | 1.05 (0.95–1.24) | 1.00 (Reference) |
| Lifetime Suicide Attempt | 3.66 (2.56–5.24) | 2.33 (1.44–2.87) | 1.52 (1.09–2.13) | 1.00 (Reference) |

*Source:* Sareen, J., Afifi, T.O., McMillan, K.A., & Asmundson, G.J.G. (2011). Relationship between household income and mental disorders: Findings from a population-based longitudinal study. *Archives of General Psychiatry*, 68(4), 419–426. doi: 10.1001/archgenpsychiatry.2011.15

Poverty is thought to have an impact on mental health through various mechanisms. These mechanisms include the stress of obtaining material necessities and sustaining oneself or one's family. Poverty also increases the likelihood that one will live in an unsafe environment and be exposed to criminal activity, violence, and illicit drug use. Exposure to each of these will, in turn, increase the likelihood of developing significant mental health problems. People who are living in poverty will also have greater limitations in their abilities to access treatment or get time away from work. These proposed links between low income and poor health have been described as "absolute deprivation theory" (Lynch et al., 2004; Phipps, 2003).

Although self-reported emotional well-being and mental health increases with higher income levels, the relationship between individual income and emotional well-being is not linear. As income levels increase, there is a diminishing increase in emotional well-being and this has been described as the "law of marginal utility of income." Lower incomes are correlated with poorer emotional well-being; however, there is a point above which there is little added benefit to one's emotional well-being of having a greater income (Kahneman & Deaton 2010). This relationship is depicted in Figure 3.5.

The relationship of mental health and emotional well-being to income levels has been found to be complex. In countries such as Canada and the US that have experienced increasing affluence over recent decades, people are less happy and experience poorer emotional well-being than during preceding decades when people had less material wealth (Layard, 2005). This has been explained by relative deprivation

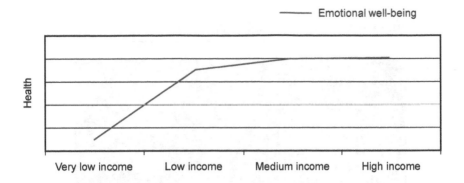

**Figure 3.5:** Relationship of individual income and emotional well-being. Kahneman and Deaton (2010) found that, although emotional well-being rises with income, there is a marginal increase, and an increase in income above medium income levels does not lead to further increases in emotional well-being.

*Source:* Kahneman, D., & Deaton, A. (2010). High income improves evaluation of life but not emotional well-being. *Proceedings of the National Academy of Sciences of the United States of America*, 107(38), 16489–16493. doi: 10.1073/pnas.1011492107

theory, which posits that individuals assess their satisfaction with their material wealth by comparing themselves with others and often perceive themselves to be deprived, leading to considerable psychosocial stress (Marmot, 2006). Citizens of countries with large gaps between rich and poor (i.e., income inequality) tend to have poorer health overall than citizens of countries in which there is a smaller disparity between the wealthiest and poorest (Wilkinson & Pickett, 2006). However, research to date has not been able to show definitively that income inequality is correlated with poorer mental health (Lordan, Rao, & Bechtel, 2012).

*Housing and Mental Health*
Housing is one of the social determinants of health and certainly the absence of adequate housing has a huge impact on mental health. Stable and secure housing provides the safety that people need to be able to function in their day-to-day lives. Those without such security are subject to fear and stress.

Homelessness refers to the lack of a regular, fixed, or adequate night-time address, and includes those who live in temporary shelters or in public or private spaces that are not intended for human habitation, such as streets, parks, cars, bus stations, or abandoned buildings. In Canada, it is estimated that between 150,000 and 300,000 people are homeless in a given year, counting not only those who live on the street or in shelters but also those living in housing that does not meet even the most basic standards (Laird, 2007). The homeless population includes not only single men, but also single women, youth who have run away from home, and families with young children. Figure 3.7 shows recent information about the homeless population in

## Box 3.4: Bhutan and Gross National Happiness

Figure 3.6: A cliffside monastery in Bhutan, where former King Jigme Singye Wangchuck began measuring Gross National Happiness as opposed to Gross Domestic Product.

*Source:* Steve Geer/iStockphoto

At the population level, good mental health is closely related to both life satisfaction and subjective happiness, each of which can be measured by polls and questionnaires. The Kingdom of Bhutan is a nation in Asia that has maintained a focus on spiritual values and has resisted the lure of modern materialism. Despite being a relatively poor country, Bhutan's population has been found to have high levels of subjective happiness (ranking 8th of 178 countries). Former King Jigme Singye Wangchuck coined the term "Gross National Happiness" to emphasize its importance in distinction from the common drive for increasing the Gross Domestic Product, which is a measure of material wealth. But note that there has been controversy about the Gross National Happiness index. A prominent critic is Dr. David Luechauer at Purdue University, who suggests that a focus on Gross National Happiness may serve as a distraction from tackling real social and economic problems: "I questioned why Bhutanese leaders were out promoting Bhutan's Gross National Happiness as an economic development model to follow when conditions in the country were so deplorable—dilapidated housing, unsanitary medical facilities, inability to procure healthcare" (Luechauer, July 21, 2013).

Vancouver as an example. Many people may be homeless for a brief period, but there is a group of people who are chronically homeless. A large proportion of homeless individuals have mental health problems, including difficulties with substance use that predated their homelessness (Krausz et al., 2013). Moreover, if one's mental health was okay before becoming homeless, living without stable shelter would certainly create mental health problems.

For those of us who have never had to contemplate surviving without stable housing, it may be difficult to imagine why someone would consider living on the street, or sleeping in a doorway or under a bridge, possibly using only cardboard boxes as shelter. In particular, it might be hard to understand why someone would choose to sleep on the street even when a temporary shelter is offered as an alternative. Yet, many who are homeless prefer life on the street because they consider shelters or low-quality housing to hold greater dangers, including bedbugs, rodents, fires, or encounters with people who are threatening or aggressive. You might ask why safe and secure housing is not provided to all citizens in Canada. To answer this question, you might consider that people who are poor, mentally ill, or stigmatized are often without much political influence. A prominent research study undertaken by the Mental Health Commission of Canada has raised awareness about the relationship of mental illness and homelessness. Known as the "At Home/Chez Soi" trial, the study examined the outcomes of providing a "housing first" approach. Unlike traditional approaches, which require that people accept treatment for mental illnesses or stop using drugs or alcohol before they are provided with housing, the housing first model does not have these requirements and, instead, homeless individuals are moved immediately into their own apartments. The At Home/Chez Soi study was undertaken in five Canadian cities (Vancouver, Winnipeg, Toronto, Montreal, and Moncton) and examined the impact and outcomes of particular treatment services (Goering & Streiner, 2015). The At Home/Chez Soi study found the housing first model to be effective in enabling people with mental illness who are homeless to find and maintain stable housing for extended periods of time.

# Who are "the homeless"?
### 1,803 living in shelters or on the street

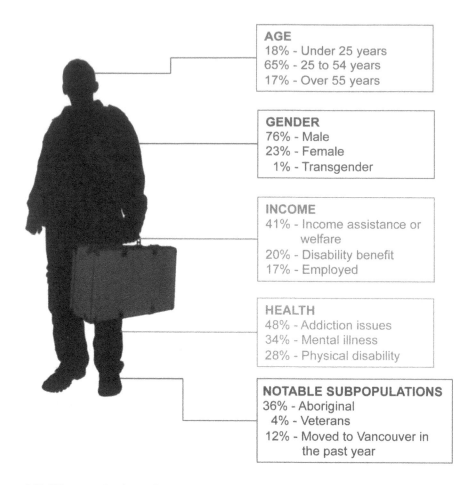

**AGE**
18% - Under 25 years
65% - 25 to 54 years
17% - Over 55 years

**GENDER**
76% - Male
23% - Female
 1% - Transgender

**INCOME**
41% - Income assistance or
       welfare
20% - Disability benefit
17% - Employed

**HEALTH**
48% - Addiction issues
34% - Mental illness
28% - Physical disability

**NOTABLE SUBPOPULATIONS**
36% - Aboriginal
 4% - Veterans
12% - Moved to Vancouver in
       the past year

**Figure 3.7:** Who are the homeless in Vancouver?

*Source:* Adapted from Street to Home Foundation. (2014). *Street to Home 2014 Annual Report.*
Vancouver: Street to Home Foundation, p. 4. Data from 2014 City of Vancouver Homeless Count.
Retrieved March 31, 2016 from http://streetohome.org/about-streetohome/annual-report.

Individuals who received housing first spent 73 percent of their time in stable
housing, whereas a comparison group who did not receive housing first spent
32 percent of their time in stable housing (Aubry, Nelson, & Tsemberis, 2015).
Housing first also led to improvements in community function and quality of
life; however, the receipt of housing first does not adequately address the high
rate of mental health and physical health problems or substance use disorders
among this population.

**Figure 3.8:** Many people who are homeless and unemployed survive by collecting various second-hand items and selling them on the street.

*Source*: Soroush Moallef, Photographer

> **Box 3.5: Street to Home Foundation**
>
> In response to the complex issue of homelessness in Vancouver, the Street to Home Foundation was established in 2008, bringing together individuals from the private, public, and non-profit sectors. Although they themselves do not provide housing, they work to increase access to permanent housing for homeless individuals in Vancouver. In addition to providing support for housing, the Street to Home Foundation is also working on numerous strategies to prevent homelessness. One such strategy is providing support and funding for the Vancouver Rent Bank, a program that provides interest-free loans to individuals who are at risk for eviction or having their utilities cut off. Drawing on success from other cities and like organizations, a large focus for the Street to Home Foundation is strategic homeless prevention programs that focus on employment and job placement. This is particularly beneficial for those who are considered to be transitionally homeless, and may only require emergency shelter or supportive housing for a brief period of time, or may not qualify for long-term services.

# Conclusion

In this chapter, we have examined concepts of mental health through the social sciences. Some prominent theories developed to explain individual and group behaviour are psychoanalysis, behaviourism, systems theory, and social constructionism. Theories have also been formulated to explain the development of identity and moral reasoning throughout the lifecourse. Socio-political and economic factors also play important roles in determining mental health; social determinants of health include income, Aboriginal status, education, housing, and other factors.

# Glossary

**anomie:** A condition where social and/or moral norms are confused, unclear, or simply absent.

**behaviourism:** Understanding how behaviour is shaped by the application of various stimuli, such as rewards and punishments.

**birth cohorts:** Groups of people who were born at the same time and therefore often have had the same exposure to various social and temporal events that may shape their behaviour.

**classical conditioning:** A learning response that involves associations between environmental stimulus and a naturally occurring stimulus.

**collective unconscious:** The very deep level of our minds, shared by all humans.

**herd behaviour:** Describes how people act differently when in large groups than they would normally as individuals.

**inferiority complex:** The ways in which social structures may cause humans to feel helpless or powerless.

**instrumental conditioning:** A learning response in which reward or punishment for a particular behaviour increases or decreases the frequency of the behaviour.

**residential school syndrome:** A form of post-traumatic stress disorder resulting from the detrimental effects of residential schools on Aboriginal people.

**social constructionism:** A theory that states that there is no objective truth, only a variety of subjective views developed through dialogue with others.

**social determinants of health:** The socio-political and economic factors that influence the health of individuals and broad populations.

**unconscious mind:** The part of the mind that holds feelings, thoughts, desires, and conflict of which is the person is unaware.

## Critical Thinking Questions

1. Select and describe one social scientist's theory of interest to you.
2. Compare and contrast classical conditioning and instrumental conditioning.
3. How does Erikson's theory help us to understand mental health?
4. Explain how an individual's mental health is related to his or her sense of connection to the society in which they live.
5. Choose one of the social determinants of health and explain how that determinant can affect the mental health of a population.

## Recommended Readings

Aneshensel, C.S., Phelan, J.C., & Bierman, A. (Eds.). (2012). *Handbook of the Sociology of Mental Health*. New York: Springer Science & Business Media.

Freud, S. (1989). *Civilization and Its Discontents*. New York: W.W. Norton and Company.

Marmot, M. (2012). *Status Syndrome: How Your Social Standing Directly Affects Your Health*. New York: Bloomsbury Publishing.

Raphael, D. (Ed.). (2009). *Social Determinants of Health: Canadian Perspectives* (2nd ed.). Toronto: Canadian Scholars' Press.

Rholes, W.S., & Simpson, J.A. (Eds.). (2006). *Adult Attachment: Theory, Research, and Clinical Implications*. New York: Guildford Press.

## Recommended Websites

Athabasca University. Centre for Psychology Resources. http://psych.athabascau.ca/html/aupr/psycres.shtml

Introduction to Psychology—1st Canadian Edition. http://opentextbc.ca/introduction
    topsychology/
The Socio Web. www.socioweb.com
Tools of Change—Social Marketers. www.toolsofchange.com/en/programs/social-
    marketers/
University of Michigan. Institute for Social Research. www.isr.umich.edu/home/
Wikipedia. Social Sciences. http://en.wikipedia.org/wiki/Social_sciences

---

# References

Adler, A. (1956). *The individual psychology of Alfred Adler*, eds. H.L. Ansbacher &
    R.R. Ansbacher. New York: Harper Torchbooks.
Aubry, T., Nelson, G., & Tsemberis, S. (2015). Housing first for people with severe
    mental illness who are homeless: A review of the research and findings from
    the At Home-Chez Soi demonstration project. *Canadian Journal of Psychiatry*,
    60(11), 467–474.
Benzeval, M., Dilnot, A., Judge, K., & Taylor, J. (2001). Income and health over the
    lifecourse: Evidence and policy implications. In H. Graham (Ed.), *Understanding
    health inequalities* (pp. 96–112). Buckingham: Open University Press.
Bornstein, R.F. (2001). The impending death of psychoanalysis. *Psychoanalytical
    Psychology*, 18, 3–20.
Brasfield, C.R. (2001). Residential school syndrome. *British Columbia Medical Journal*,
    43(2), 78–81.
Burr, V. (1995). *An introduction to social constructionism*. London: Routledge.
Chang, S.S., Gunnell, D., Sterne, J.A.C., Lu, T.H., & Cheng, A.T.A. (2009). Was
    the economic crisis 1997–1998 responsible for rising suicide rates in East/
    Southeast Asia? A time-trend analysis for Japan, Hong Kong, South Korea,
    Taiwan, Singapore and Thailand. *Social Science and Medicine*, 68(7), 1322–1331.
Collins, P.H. (2000). Gender, black feminism, and black political economy. *Annals
    of the American Academy of Political and Social Science*, 568, 41–53.
Dimitry, L. (2012). A systematic review on the mental health of children and
    adolescents in areas of armed conflict in the Middle East. *Child: Care, Health &
    Development*, 38(2), 153–161. doi: 10.1111/j.1365-2214.2011.01246.x
Durkheim, E. ([1897] 1997). *Suicide*. New York: The Free Press.
Erikson, E. ([1950] 1993). *Childhood and society*. New York: W.W. Norton &
    Company.
Erikson, E., & Erikson, J.M. (1987). *The life cycle completed*. New York: W.W. Norton
    & Company.
Farr, W. (2000). Vital statistics: Memorial volume of selections from the reports and
    writings. 1885. *Bulletin of the World Health Organization*, 78(1), 88–95.
Fikretoglu, D., Brunet, A., Guay, S., & Pedlar, D. (2007). Mental health treatment
    seeking by military members with posttraumatic stress disorder: Findings on rates,

characteristics, and predictors from a nationally representative sample of Canadian military sample. *Canadian Journal of Psychiatry*, 52(2), 103–110.

Freud, S. (1901). *The psychopathology of everyday life*. London: T. Fisher Unwin.

Freud, S. (1910). The origin and development of psychoanalysis. *American Journal of Psychology*, 21(2), 181–218.

Gay, P. (1995). *The Freud reader*. New York: Norton.

Goering, P.N., Streiner, D.L., Adair, C., Aubry, T., Barker, J., Distasio, J., Hwang, S.W.,

Goering, P., & Streiner D.L. (2015). Putting housing first: The evidence and impact. *Canadian Journal of Psychiatry*, 60(11), 465–466.

Hankivsky, O., & Cormier, R. (2009). *Intersectionality: Moving women's health research and policy forward*. Vancouver: Women's Health Research Network.

Jung, C. (1981). *The archetypes and the collective unconscious*. Princeton, NJ: Princeton University Press.

Kahneman, D., & Deaton, A. (2010). High income improves evaluation of life but not emotional well-being. *Proceedings of the National Academy of Sciences of the United States of America*, 107(38), 16489–16493. doi: 10.1073/pnas.1011492107

Kohlberg, L. (1976). Moral stages and moralization: The cognitive-developmental approach. In T. Lickona (Ed.), *Moral development and behavior: Theory, research, and social issues* (pp. 31–53). New York: Holt, Rinehard, and Winston.

Krausz, R.M., Clarkson, A.F., Strehlau, V., Torchalla, I., Li, K., & Schuetz, C.G. (2013). Mental disorder, service use, and barriers to care among 500 homeless people in 3 different urban settings. *Social Psychiatry and Psychiatric Epidemiology*, 48(8), 1235–1243. doi: 10.1007/s00127-012-0649-8

Kroger, J., Martinussen, M., & Marcia, J.E. (2010). Identity status change during adolescence and young adult: A meta-analysis. *Journal of Adolescence*, 33(5), 683–698.

Laird, G. (2007). *Homelessness in a growth economy: Canada's 21st century paradox*. Sheldon Chumir Foundation for Ethics in Leadership. Retrieved from http://www.chumirethicsfoundation.ca/files/pdf/SHELTER.pdf

Layard, R. (2005). *Happiness: Lessons from a new science*. London: Penguin.

Lordan, G., Rao, P., & Bechtel, L. (2012). Inequality and Mental Health. School of Economics, University of Queensland, Australia. Retrieved from ideas.repec.org/p/qld/uq2004/456.html

Loseke, D.R. (2011). *Thinking about social problems: An introduction to constructionist perspectives*. New Jersey: Transaction Books.

Luechauer, D.L. (2013). The false promises of Bhutan's Gross National Happiness. *Global South Development Magazine*. Retrieved from www.gsdmagazine.org/the-false-promises-of-bhutans-gross-national-happiness/

Lynch, J., Smith, G.D., Harper, S., Hillemeier, M., Ross, N., Kaplan, G.A., & Wolfson, M. (2004). Is income inequality a determinant of population health? Part 1. A systematic review. *The Milbank Quarterly*, 82(1), 5–99.

Mackay, C. ([1841] 1980). *Extraordinary popular delusions and the madness of crowds*. New York: Harmony Books.

Marmot, M.G. (2006). Status syndrome: A challenge to medicine. *Journal of the American Medical Association*, 295(11), 1304–1307.

Olson, D.H., Russell, C.S., & Sprenkle, D.H. (1989). *Circumplex model: Systemic assessment and treatment of families*. London: Haworth Press.

Paré, J.R., & Radford, M. (2013). *Current issues in mental health in Canada: Mental health in the Canadian Forces and among veterans*. Publication no. 2013-91-E. Ottawa: Library of Parliament. Retrieved from http://www.lop.parl.gc.ca/content/lop/ResearchPublications/2013-91-e.pdf

Pavlov, I.P. (1927). *Conditioned reflexes: An investigation of the physiological activity of the cerebral cortex* (G.V. Anrep, Ed. and Trans.). London: Oxford University Press.

Phipps, S. (2003). *The impact of poverty on health: A scan of research literature*. Ottawa: Canadian Institute for Health Information.

Raafat, R.M., Chater, N., & Frith, C. (2009). Herding in humans. *Trends in Cognitive Sciences*, 13(10), 420–428.

Rachiotis, G., Stuckler, D., McKee, M., & Hadjichristodoulou, C. (2015). What has happened to suicides during the Greek economic crisis? Findings from an ecological study of suicides and their determinants (2003–2012). *British Medical Journal Open*, 5(3), e007295-e007295. doi: 10.1136/bmjopen-2014-007295

Rachman, S. (1997). The evolution of cognitive behaviour therapy. In D. Clark, C.G. Fairburn, & M.G. Gelder (Eds.), *Science and practice of cognitive behaviour therapy* (pp. 1–26). Oxford: Oxford University Press.

Raphael, D. (2008). Social determinants of health: An overview of key issues and themes. In D. Raphael (Ed.), *Social determinants of health* (2nd ed.). Toronto: Canadian Scholars' Press.

Rutter, M., & Taylor, E.A. (1989). Developmental psychology. In E. Taylor & J. Green (Eds.), *Research and innovation on the road to modern child psychiatry*, Vol. 2 (pp. 3–32). Glasgow: Bell & Bain Limited.

Sareen, J., Afifi, T.O., McMillan, K.A., & Asmundson, G.J.G. (2011). Relationship between household income and mental disorders: Findings from a population-based longitudinal study. *Archives of General Psychiatry*, 68(4), 419–426. doi: 10.1001/archgenpsychiatry.2011.15

Silove, D. (1999). The psychosocial effects of torture, mass human rights violations, and refugee trauma: Toward an integrated conceptual framework. *Journal of Nervous and Mental Disease*, 187(4), 200–207. doi: 10.1097/00005053-199904000-00002

Skinner, B.F. (1938). *The behavior of organisms*. New York: Appleton-Century-Crofts.

Skinner, B.F. (1953). *Science and human behavior*. Oxford: Macmillan.

Smith, K.P., & Christakis, N.A. (2008). Social networks and health. *Annual Review of Sociology*, 34(1), 405–429.

Watson, J.B. (1924). *Behaviorism*. New York: Norton.

Wild, L.G., Flisher, A.J., Bhana, A., & Lombard, C. (2008). Associations among adolescent risk behaviours and self-esteem in six domains. *Journal of Child Psychology and Psychiatry*, 45(8), 1454–1467.

Wilkinson, R.G., & Pickett, K.E. (2006). Income inequality and population health: A review and explanation of the evidence. *Social Science & Medicine*, 62(7), 1768–1784.

World Health Organization. (1995). *The world health report 1995: Bridging the gaps*. Geneva: WHO.

# Chapter 4

# THE SPECTRUM OF
# MENTAL HEALTH PROBLEMS

They called me mad, and I called them mad, and damn them, they outvoted me.
—Nathaniel Porter (playwright)

## Introduction

In its interim report on mental health and illness in Canada, the Standing Senate Committee on Social Affairs, Science and Technology (2004) defined mental health problems and mental disorders as follows:

> **Mental health problems** refer to diminished capacities—whether cognitive, emotional, attentional, interpersonal, motivational or behavioural—that interfere with a person's enjoyment of life or adversely affect interactions with society and the environment. Feelings of low self-esteem, frequent frustration or irritability, burn out, feelings of stress, excessive worrying, are examples of common mental health problems. Over the course of a lifetime, every individual will be likely, at some time, to experience some mental health problems such as these. Usually, they are normal, short-term reactions that occur in response to difficult situations (e.g., school pressures, work-related stress, marital conflict, grief, changes in living arrangements).... Mental health problems that resolve quickly, do not recur and do not result in significant disability do not meet the criteria required for diagnosis of a mental illness. **Mental disorders** or illnesses refer to clinically significant patterns of behavioural or emotional function that are associated with some level of distress, suffering (even to the point of pain and death), or impairment in one or more areas of functioning (e.g., school, work, social and family interactions). (p. 68)

In this chapter, we will discuss some of the limitations and problems with current diagnostic systems and approaches, and provide an overview of the main categories of mental disorders.

## Systems of Diagnostic Classification

There are many different forms of mental disorder, and they vary widely in terms of the course and pattern of illness, the type and severity of symptoms produced, and the degree of disability experienced. An individual may have only one episode of illness, or may have repeated episodes of illness separated by long periods of wellness. Some mental disorders are episodic or cyclical in nature, whereas others are more persistent, with lengthy or frequently recurring episodes.

In Canada, two different classification systems are used for mental disorders: the *International Classification of Diseases* (ICD), Mental Health Section, published by the WHO, and the *Diagnostic and Statistical Manual of Mental Disorders* (DSM) published by the American Psychiatric Association. The DSM classification system addresses psychiatric disorders but no other illnesses and is used exclusively in North America. The ICD system is used internationally and addresses all types of illness. Expert panels refine these classification systems regularly in an effort to enhance diagnostic accuracy and incorporate new research evidence. These two classification systems provide the official definitions of mental disorders that may be diagnosed; each classification system includes more than 300 hundred separate mental disorders. Although Canadian psychiatrists tend to use the DSM system, we have chosen to summarize the ICD system here because it is international in scope and is utilized by the WHO. Further, despite the pervasive influence of the DSM in North America, Canada's official classification system is the ICD-10. Although the 11th version of the ICD is now being developed and tested, the ICD system in current use the 10th version, that is, the ICD-10, and its fifth chapter addresses mental and behavioural disorders. Within each chapter, the ICD-10 identifies blocks or groups of diagnoses that have some similar characteristics. Table 4.1 lists the main ICD-10 Chapter V blocks along with the respective codes for the disorder categories. Later in this chapter, we will provide a brief description of each of these main blocks and summarize prominent diagnostic categories. Individuals who develop mental disorders typically meet criteria for more than one mental disorder at the same time, and many will experience a number of different mental disorders at various points across their lifespans (Kessler et al., 2005).

The introduction of the latest version of the DSM classification system, the DSM-5, has raised considerable controversy and triggered discussion of fundamental issues concerning the act of diagnosing mental disorders. As we indicated in Chapter 1, a basic problem of psychiatric diagnosis is that laboratory tests are not available to establish the presence of mental illnesses. Consequently, there is both a greater reliance upon clinician "experts" for diagnosis and considerable room for disagreement. Notably, the DSM-5 is much less cautious about labelling individuals as "mentally ill" than were previous DSM versions; it loosens the criteria in such a way that many more individuals may now receive psychiatric diagnoses instead of being considered "normal." The developers of the DSM-5 insist that their approach is one that will extend the benefits of psychiatric treatment to a larger proportion of individuals, and that this advantage outweighs the risk of labelling large numbers of people as "mentally ill" who previously would have been described as "normal." As stated eloquently by Allen Frances, a psychiatrist who led the development of the previous DSM version: "DSM-5 pushes psychiatric diagnosis in the wrong direction, will create new false epidemics, and promotes even more medication misuse. The right goal for DSM-5 would have been diagnostic restraint and deflation, not a further unwarranted expansion of diagnosis and treatment" (Frances, 2013).

**Table 4.1: List of blocks of diagnoses in Chapter V of the ICD-10 covering mental and behavioural disorders**

| ICD code | Disorder block |
| --- | --- |
| F00-F09 | Organic, including symptomatic, mental disorders |
| F10-F19 | Mental and behavioural disorders due to psychoactive substance use |
| F20-F29 | Schizophrenia, schizotypal, and delusional disorders |
| F30-F39 | Mood (affective) disorders |
| F40-F49 | Neurotic, stress-related, and somatoform disorders |
| F50-F59 | Behavioural syndromes associated with physiological disturbances and physical factors |
| F60-F69 | Disorders of adult personality and behaviour |
| F70-F79 | Mental retardation |
| F80-F89 | Disorders of psychological development |
| F90-F98 | Behavioural and emotional disorders with onset usually occurring in childhood and adolescence |
| F99 | Unclassified mental disorders |

*Source:* Adapted from World Health Organization. (1992). *The ICD-10 classification of mental and behavioural disorders*. Retrieved from www.who.int/classifications/icd/en/GRNBOOK.pdf

## Concerns about Diagnostic Classification

Unfortunately, receipt of a psychiatric diagnosis can cause an individual various problems. As we will discuss in Chapter 6, people who are designated as "mentally ill" are often subject to serious discrimination within Canadian society because of widespread fear and misunderstanding. A person who carries a diagnosis of mental illness may suffer loss of relationships, ostracism at work, or exclusion from employment and housing opportunities (Bawaskar, 2006). Some people who have been given diagnoses of mental illness by psychiatrists feel that their lives have been damaged as a result (Caplan & Cosgrove, 2004) and it is not uncommon to find anti-psychiatry protests organized to bring attention to such concerns (see Figure 4.1).

**Figure 4.1:** Display panel from the Psychiatry: An Industry of Death museum at Worldcon 2006, Anaheim, California

*Source:* Wikimedia Commons/gruntzooki

Criticisms regarding the diagnosis of mental disorders include problems with reliability and validity, effects of labelling, cultural relativity, and political and economic misuses of diagnoses. We will discuss each of these in turn.

## Problems with Reliability and Validity

**Reliability** refers to the *consistency* of results when a measurement (including a diagnostic test) is repeated. For example, if someone is examined and diagnosed with a schizophrenic disorder at one point in time, will that person receive the same diagnosis if examined at a different point in time? Will different examiners produce the same diagnosis? As is the case with other medical diagnoses, the reliability of mental disorder diagnoses is far below 100 percent. **Validity** refers to whether a measurement (including a diagnostic test) really captures what it purports to measure. Thus, when a diagnostician describes someone as having schizophrenia, does this truly indicate that the person has schizophrenia? Perhaps this person presents with similar symptoms as a result of drug use or some other mental health problem. Even if a diagnosis has high reliability (consistency), its validity may be poor. Thus, in our example, a diagnostician might consistently give a diagnosis of schizophrenia (i.e., high reliability) to a person who has similar symptoms but doesn't really have a schizophrenic disorder (i.e., poor validity).

Diagnoses of mental disorders are criticized as being vague, arbitrary, and unscientific (Grob & Horwitz, 2009). These criticisms reflect the fact that most mental disorder diagnoses are simply descriptive of patterns of observed symptoms. Very few are clearly linked to specific causes or mechanisms of action, that is, specific biochemical or psychological steps that explain how the disorder occurs. For example, the diagnosis of depressive disorder describes a core set of symptoms often found together (e.g., sadness, loss of interest, lack of energy), but there may be many mechanisms that lead to the same symptom complex; there may be many different underlying problems. Imagine that we have used the term "abdominal pain disorder" to describe a group of different conditions (e.g., peptic ulcer disease, stomach cancer, and appendicitis) without knowing the cause of these conditions. If we did this, each of these conditions would be considered an instance of abdominal pain disorder, and we would not understand the actual problem. Such a vague diagnosis would contribute little to our understanding of the problem, its appropriate treatment, and its likely outcome. Analogously, the diagnosis of depressive disorder may be far too broad to be of much benefit. Without understanding underlying causes and mechanisms, the current diagnostic classification of mental disorders may not provide a valid or meaningful reflection of the actual conditions.

## *Effects of Labelling*

**Labelling theory** emerged from the disciplines of sociology and criminology and describes the tendency of dominant groups to negatively label minority groups (Murphy,

---

### Box 4.1: Validity of Psychiatric Diagnoses

A famous experiment conducted by David Rosenhan in the 1970s highlighted the questionable validity of psychiatric diagnoses. Rosenhan assembled a group of students and others who pretended to have mental illnesses and sought admission to 12 different psychiatric hospitals. When they were assessed, the "fake patients" (who gave false names and employment information but provided other biographical information accurately) pretended to be hearing voices but claimed no other symptoms or problems. All were admitted and received diagnoses of schizophrenia or bipolar disorder. Once they were admitted, they acted normally and no longer reported any symptoms. None were identified as imposters by the hospital staff. Only when they agreed to accept the diagnosis they were given and take antipsychotic medications were they allowed to leave; their hospital stays ranged from 7 to 52 days. In a second part of the study, staff members at one psychiatric hospital were asked to detect fake patients over a three-month period, yet in actuality none had been admitted to that hospital. Nevertheless, the hospital staff members identified large numbers of patients they considered to be impostors. In his publication in the journal *Science*, Rosenhan (1973) concluded: "It is clear that we cannot distinguish the sane from the insane in psychiatric hospitals" (p. 254).

1976; Scheff, 1966). The theory states that deviance is caused when individuals who are labelled internalize the label, eventually leading them to take on the traits and behaviours that conform to the label (Roman & Trice, 1968). Psychiatric diagnoses are considered by some to constitute an example of labelling that carries negative consequences (Link & Phelan, 2012). In Chapter 6, we will discuss the profound discrimination that people experience as a result of being identified as "mentally ill."

### *Cultural Relativity*

The extent to which diagnoses of mental disorders are valid across different cultures has been questioned (Murphy, 1976). A classification of mental disorder developed in one culture may not be applicable to other cultural groups (Lefley, 2006). For example, people in Canada's First Nations, Inuit, and Metis communities have declared that the description of mental disorders listed in the DSM or the ICD may not be relevant or meaningful to members of their communities. They feel that the unique historical and cultural events that have shaped the type of mental health problems they encounter are not reflected in the existing diagnostic systems. The psychiatric diagnostic system utilized in Canadian health services may not fit with the spiritual and philosophical framework that is embraced by many Aboriginal people (Smye & Mussell, 2001).

### *Political and Economic Misuses of Diagnoses*

Concerns have been raised about misuses of diagnoses to serve a covert agenda. One concern is that various governments have imprisoned individuals for political purposes by falsely applying diagnoses of mental illness (Bloch & Reddaway, 1984). This can be a nefarious means of circumventing legal and judicial procedures and has been used to detain minority groups and political prisoners for lengthy periods (Vaughan, 1991). Another concern is that diagnoses of mental disorders are promulgated and over-identified for the purpose of selling medications. The pharmaceutical industry and the psychiatric profession have been accused of colluding to manufacture illusory mental illnesses (Atrens, 2011; Cosgrove & Wheeler, 2013). For example, the diagnosis of attention deficit disorder is made when children have difficulty focusing their attention, are easily distracted, and have difficulty sitting or standing still, and standard treatment includes prescription of medications such as methylphenidate (also called Ritalin). Critics contend that psychiatrists and pharmaceutical companies inflate the prevalence of attention deficit disorder for their own economic benefit, while needlessly drugging children who may be simply be bored or overstimulated (Wolinsky, 2005).

## Diagnostic Categories

Given the significant concerns we have identified regarding the diagnosis of mental disorders, you might ask: Why not discard the whole enterprise? What is the purpose

**Figure 4.2:** Mental health and mental illness are construed in different ways by people of various cultural backgrounds. In comparison to the dominant approach in psychiatric diagnostic systems, First Nations, Inuit, and Metis people tend to conceptualize mental health in more holistic and spiritual terms.

*Source:* Chris Sang Yeob Park, Photographer

of diagnosing people with mental illness if it risks causing harm? The usual answer is that diagnosis is meant to provide the means of understanding and addressing mental disorders and to designate the correct treatment to fit the condition. The assumption is made that the benefits of applying a diagnosis outweigh potential risks.

In the following, we provide a short description of the current ICD-10 Chapter V blocks, and we summarize prominent diagnostic categories. The number of mental disorder diagnoses is too large for us to adequately discuss here. We provide recommendations at the end of the chapter for additional reading that can offer more comprehensive listings and descriptions.

## Organic, Including Symptomatic, Mental Disorders

This block is reserved for mental disorders that can be demonstrated to be caused by some disturbance of brain function or damage to brain structures, often as a result of infection, injury, or medical condition (WHO, 2010). That is what the term "**organic mental disorders**" means, and it is used to differentiate this group of disorders from most mental disorders. In most mental disorders, no overt disturbance of brain function or structure can be found; these are described as "**functional mental disorders**." Some organic mental disorders, such as various forms of delirium, are temporary and reversible, whereas other conditions are likely to lead to progressive or irreversible deficits.

Delirium refers to a syndrome in which there is a disturbance of brain function with confusion, memory loss, disturbed levels of consciousness, and distorted perception. It can be caused by an infection or other medical illness and often occurs following surgery, particularly in the elderly and in people with medical conditions. Delirium ranges in severity from mild to very severe, but it generally resolves in a relatively short period of time.

In contrast, dementia is a progressive degenerative disease that involves loss of neurons from the cerebral cortex and other areas of the brain. Alzheimer's disease is the most common cause of dementia and occurs predominately in older adults. However, Alzheimer's disease and other forms of dementia can occur earlier in adulthood, albeit less commonly. The brain of an individual with Alzheimer's disease will have plaques, which are clumps of protein, and these may contribute to the destruction and loss of neurons. Tangles, which are twisted threads of protein, are also found to be present and are thought to interfere with the transport of nutrients to brain cells. Memory loss is the most prominent early symptom of Alzheimer's disease, often followed by a slow deterioration of cognitive functions, personality features, and physical capacity. Some individuals experience hallucinations, delusions, seizures, and aggressive behaviour as a function of the disease.

Other organic mental disorders can occur in which the prominent symptoms may be any of the following: mood problems (such as depression or mania), anxiety, psychotic symptoms similar to schizophrenia, and personality changes.

## *Mental and Behavioural Disorders Due to Psychoactive Substance Use*

A diagnosis of any of this group of mental disorders indicates that the cause is the use of a psychoactive substance, which may or may not have been medically prescribed (WHO, 2010). The individual diagnosis is based on the type of substance that is implicated (i.e., alcohol, opioids, cannabinoids, sedatives, cocaine or other stimulants, hallucinogens, tobacco, solvents, and others) and it designates various clinical conditions that can occur.

Acute intoxication denotes acute disruptions in cognition, emotion, level of consciousness, and other mental function subsequent to substance use. The ICD-10 describes harmful use as

> a pattern of psychoactive substance use that is causing damage to health. The damage may be physical (as in cases of hepatitis from the self-administration of injected psychoactive substances) or mental (e.g., episodes of depressive disorder secondary to heavy consumption of alcohol). (WHO, 2010)

Other clinical conditions that may be designated include syndromes involving dependence, withdrawal, and psychosis. We consider the topic of substance use to be so important that we have devoted an entire chapter to its discussion (Chapter 5) and we define these syndromes there.

**Figure 4.3:** Marijuana is the most commonly used illicit substance in Canada. Persistent, high-frequency use is associated with a number of poor mental health outcomes.

*Source:* BraunS/iStockPhoto

Concurrent disorders refer to the combination of a substance use disorder and another mental disorder. For example, someone who meets diagnostic criteria for both alcohol dependence disorder and major depressive disorder would be considered to have a concurrent disorder. Epidemiological studies have found that concurrent disorders are very common (Canadian Centre on Substance Abuse, 2009) and, in our chapter on treatment (Chapter 12), we will discuss specialized treatment approaches for concurrent disorders that have been developed in recent decades.

## *Schizophrenia, Schizotypal, and Delusional Disorders*

Schizophrenic disorders usually emerge in adolescence or early adulthood but occasionally develop during childhood or later in adulthood (Eaton, Chen, & Bromet, 2011). Schizophrenia is a relatively infrequent disorder, with a lifetime prevalence of approximately 0.55 percent (although there is considerable variation between geographic regions) (Goldner et al., 2002). Schizophrenia affects a person's thinking, with the presence of delusions, that is, intensely held irrational beliefs. For example, delusional beliefs might include the conviction that alien beings are monitoring one's thoughts and causing major world events to occur. Delusions may be paranoid, involving beliefs that there is some imminent danger, or that someone is being followed or persecuted. Paranoid delusions can be extremely frightening and often create terrible distress and suffering. Grandiose delusions are also common, and they involve false beliefs about possessing superior abilities, powers, or influence over others or world events. Religious delusions may also occur, for example, believing oneself to be a spiritual saviour. Hallucinations, false sensory experiences generated by an individual's mind, are also typical features of schizophrenic disorders. Most often, people with schizophrenic disorders experience auditory hallucinations in which they are convinced that they are hearing voices or sounds; hallucinations involving other senses can also occur. Delusions and hallucinations are categorized as positive symptoms of schizophrenia. This does not mean that these are positive in the sense that they are beneficial or desirable, only that they are symptoms that occur in addition to usual cognitive and sensory experience. Schizophrenic disorders are also characterized by negative symptoms in which the person has reduced motivational drive and activity level. Schizophrenic disorders usually begin slowly with prodromal symptoms, that is, early symptoms that indicate the start of illness, and often manifest in cycles of alternating remission and relapse.

---

### Box 4.2: "The Son Who Vanished ..." by Erin Anderssen

On a September evening almost nine years ago, Susan and Jay Bigelow called 911, then sat down to dinner in their Toronto home, waiting for the police to come and take away the stranger at the dining-room table who was once their son.

For 19 years, they had raised a cheerful, outgoing boy named Jesse Bigelow, who had lots of friends, was chased by girls and sang in a rock band called, in an odd foreshadowing, Mental Distortion.

Then, slowly, helplessly, they watched Jesse Bigelow vanish, as surely as if he had been kidnapped. They didn't recognize the shaggy, bearded intruder who now lay like a zombie in the bedroom upstairs and ranted at them about God.

**Jay:** The first thing you notice is that, all of a sudden, he is not associating with his friends as regularly as he had been. He became very withdrawn. And he was not having as much social contact.

**Jesse:** I went from being very sociable to being weird and more reserved and very moody. I became paranoid. If there was a group of people in the schoolyard talking and laughing, I started to believe they were laughing at me.

**Susan:** Then one day, he came home and told me that he thought people on the subway had been talking about him.

For several months, Jesse's parents hoped that it really was just "a bad patch." But by the late spring of 1999, Jesse was clearly psychotic.

It was devastating: Jay had always been close to Jesse, but now his son refused to speak to him and began to refer to his father as the Devil. The family, who'd never attended church, couldn't make sense of this newly found religious fervour. "It was very scary," his mother says, as Jesse's delusions intensified.

**Jesse:** I started hearing voices. I would hear my own voice in my head as my regular thoughts, but then I had additional voices. On my left side, I heard a very disruptive commanding male voice that I thought was the Devil. On the right side, I would hear a very soothing, calming female voice that I thought was the Virgin Mary.

**Jay:** There'd be times when he'd go to his room and spend hours and hours on end lying in bed, doing nothing but basically staring at the ceiling. And every hour or so, you might hear maniacal laughter, or sometimes you'd hear talking. Of course, what he was really doing was interacting with the voices.

**Jesse:** ... But I really, really believed I was Jesus Christ at that time. Now I look back, no human being can be Jesus Christ. That's impossible....

In the elevator after the first meeting with Jesse's doctor at the Centre for Addiction and Mental Health in Toronto, his parents were reeling from the diagnosis. Susan looked at Jay: "This is a death sentence," she said. Only about one-third of people diagnosed with schizophrenia make a full recovery and, even then, the disease is a chronic condition....

For four months, his doctors experimented with medications.... At last he showed progress on a new antipsychotic called Clozapine.

Even so, it was a year before they began to see signs of the old Jesse. He could follow a conversation. He showered. He spoke less often about the voices. He began to talk about getting a job....

If you met Jesse Bigelow today, more than eight years since his release from the hospital, it would never cross your mind that he had a mental illness....

Over the years, he has reclaimed his life, piece by piece, and in many ways started fresh. He falls within the lucky percentage of people with schizophrenia who are able, through medication, to control the disease.

Now 29, he attends a United Church faithfully (something he never would have done before his diagnosis) and sings with a band in a local pub on Sunday nights.... Healthy as he is, Jesse is not cured. At times, he has experienced "breakthrough symptoms," times when his medication, which comes with a risk of serious side effects, must be increased....

**Susan:** The thing that bothers me is that there were so many times we could have said, "Just get out." And he would have been living on the street—or dying on the street. I think that's the most frightening. There are so many people on the street with mental illness, and that's what happened. I understand. You just can't put up with them anymore. But you have to.

**Jay:** Don't give up hope. When it looks really bleak, there is room to get better.

*Source:* E. Anderssen. (June 20, 2008). The son who vanished.... *The Globe and Mail.* Retrieved from http://www.theglobeandmail.com/life/health-and-fitness/the-son-who-vanished/article560793/

Schizotypal disorders refer to conditions in which disturbances in thinking and eccentric behaviour occur that are similar to symptoms seen in schizophrenic disorders but generally milder in nature. A variety of other diagnoses are included in this block, and they are characterized by the existence of delusional symptoms that may be transient or persistent (WHO, 2010).

## Mood (Affective) Disorders

Mood disorders include major depressive disorder, bipolar disorder, and a number of related diagnostic categories (WHO, 2010). Mood disorders are relatively common. Major depressive disorder has a lifetime prevalence of 6.7 percent, Dysthymia has a lifetime prevalence of 3.6 percent, and Bipolar I has a lifetime prevalence of 0.8 percent) (Waraich et al., 2004). As is the case for almost all mental disorder diagnoses, mood disorders cover a very wide spectrum of severity and disability. In some situations, a mood disorder can be a mild, brief episode that resolves spontaneously. At the other extreme, mood disorders can be extremely debilitating, persistent, recurrent, and resistant to treatment. Major depressive disorder (previously referred to as unipolar depression) is characterized by one or more depressive episode lasting at least two weeks that is accompanied by at least four additional symptoms of depression (e.g., fatigue or loss of energy, insomnia or sleeping too much, feelings of worthlessness, significant weight loss or weight gain) (WHO, 2010). Bipolar disorder, which is also known as "manic depressive illness," is a condition that involves both substantial elevations of mood (i.e., episodes of mania or hypomania) and depressed mood (WHO, 2010). Bipolar disorder most often begins in late adolescence or early adulthood, but can also develop during childhood or later in adulthood.

## *Neurotic, Stress-Related, and Somatoform Disorders*

The acceptability of the term "neurotic disorders" is somewhat controversial and has been discarded by many health care professionals. Originally, it referred to mental conditions that were not psychotic in nature, that is to say, individuals retained their capacity to think clearly and did not experience delusions or hallucinations. However, the term has now taken on other connotations in everyday language and is sometimes used in a disparaging manner to refer to people who are emotionally unstable. This block includes various anxiety disorders such as generalized anxiety disorder, phobic anxiety disorder, panic disorder, agoraphobia, and obsessive-compulsive disorder (WHO, 2010).

Anxiety disorders are relatively common, with a lifetime prevalence (averaging across anxiety disorder categories) of 16.6 percent (Somers et al., 2006). Generalized anxiety disorder is defined by a protracted period of anxiety and worry accompanied by multiple symptoms such as muscle tension, easy fatigability, poor concentration, insomnia, and irritability. Phobic anxiety disorders involve excessive fears in relation to certain objects or situations (e.g., animals, insects, heights, bridges, elevators). Panic disorder is diagnosed when an individual has experienced multiple panic attacks, that is, episodes of intense and acute distress with a sense of impending doom, accompanied by characteristic physical symptoms (e.g., sweating, palpitations, difficulty breathing, dizziness) and persistent concern about the likelihood of having more attacks. Obsessive-compulsive disorder is characterized by obsessions, consisting of intrusive and persistent thoughts, ideas, impulses, or images that are inappropriate or irrational and cause marked anxiety or distress, and compulsions, which are repetitive or ritualistic behaviours (such as handwashing) or mental acts (such as counting) that sometimes occur in response to an obsession. Anxiety disorders tend to start early in life (during childhood or adolescence) and often persist for many years.

This block also includes stress reactions and adjustment disorders, which are conditions that are considered to be a response to some particular stressor, such as the loss of a job or a death in the family. The diagnosis of adjustment disorder indicates that the individual has developed symptoms that are more intense or prolonged than expected. PTSD involves flashbacks, disturbing dreams, persistent frightening thoughts and memories, anger, or irritability in response to a terrifying experience in which physical harm occurred or was threatened (such as violence or a natural disaster). Another group of disorders in this block is known as "somatoform disorders," described in the ICD-10 as follows: "The main feature is repeated presentation of physical symptoms together with persistent requests for medical investigations, in spite of repeated negative findings and reassurances by doctors that the symptoms have no physical basis. If any physical disorders are present, they do not explain the nature and extent of the symptoms or the distress and preoccupation of the patient" (WHO, 2010).

## *Behavioural Syndromes Associated with Physiological Disturbances and Physical Factors*

This block includes eating disorders, sleep disorders, sexual dysfunction not caused by organic illness, and mental disorders associated with the puerperium (i.e., experienced by a woman following the delivery of a baby) (WHO, 2010).

Eating disorders involve a serious disturbance in eating behaviour—either eating too much or too little—in addition to extreme concern or preoccupation with body weight or shape (WHO, 2010). As a result of the nutritional and metabolic consequences of severe eating disorders, they can cause serious medical problems that may be life-threatening (Johnson et al., 2002). The most common eating disorders are binge-eating disorder and bulimia nervosa. Binge-eating disorder is a condition characterized by episodes in which an individual feels compelled to eat large amounts of food in an uncontrolled manner, experiencing profound distress and self-denigration. The episodes of binge eating are not followed by any compensatory activities, (i.e., self-induced vomiting, intense exercise, or laxative use to avert weight gain). Bulimia nervosa, in contrast, is marked by both binge-eating episodes and regular compensatory activities. Anorexia nervosa is characterized by low body weight, intense fear of weight gain, disturbed eating behaviour, and an inaccurate perception of one's own body weight or shape. Eating disorders often arise in adolescence and affect females disproportionately (National Eating Disorder Information Centre, 2008).

**Figure 4.4:** People suffering from eating disorders such as anorexia are excessively fearful of weight gain.

*Source:* Ximagination/iStockphoto

Disturbances of sleep are common features of various mental disorders such as major depressive disorder, bipolar disorder, anorexia nervosa, and many others.

A sleep disorder is diagnosed when sleep disturbance is a prominent feature and when emotional causes are considered to be a primary factor in causing the sleep disturbance. Diagnoses include insomnia (i.e., unsatisfactory quantity or quality of sleep), hypersomnia (excessive sleepiness), disorder of the sleep-wake cycle, sleepwalking, night terrors, and nightmares (WHO, 2010).

"Sexual dysfunction not caused by organic illness" refers to a group of disorders in which individuals experience difficulties in sexual function or response. Disorders include lack or loss of sexual desire, sexual aversion, and lack of sexual enjoyment, excessive sexual desire, premature ejaculation, and non-organic dyspareunia (i.e., pain during sexual intercourse when there is no physical cause) (WHO, 2010).

After giving birth, some women develop significant symptoms of mental disorder. Mental disorders associated with the puerperium are diagnosed when these occur within six weeks of the delivery. Diagnoses are classified according to their severity and include postpartum depression and puerperal psychosis (WHO, 2010).

## Disorders of Adult Personality and Behaviour

Personality disorders include a number of disorders that vary considerably in their characteristics and patterns of behaviour. However, they all share the following characteristics: an enduring pattern of inner experience and behaviour that deviates from the expectations of society; and behavioural patterns that are pervasive, inflexible, and stable over time, creating distress and/or impairment. The onset of personality disorders usually occurs in adolescence or early adulthood; they can also become apparent in mid-adulthood.

Some forms of personality disorder result in suffering that primarily affects the individual, for example, avoidant personality disorder, which is characterized by feelings of extreme discomfort and intense self-criticism in social circumstances, leading to marked loneliness and isolation despite intense longings for social contact. Other forms of personality disorder tend to cause distress to those who are in proximity to the individual. For example, anti-social personality disorder involves a pervasive pattern of disregard for and violation of the rights of others and often includes repeated criminal activity, impulsive violent behaviour, deceitfulness, and lack of remorse.

This block also includes habit and impulse disorders, described in the ICD-10 as follows: "They are characterized by repeated acts that have no clear rational motivation, cannot be controlled, and generally harm the patient's own interests and those of other people. The patient reports that the behaviour is associated with impulses to action. The cause of these disorders is not understood and they are grouped together because of broad descriptive similarities, not because they are known to share any other important features" (WHO, 2010). Diagnoses in this group include pathological gambling, pathological fire-setting (pyromania), and pathological stealing (kleptomania).

This block of disorders also includes a group of gender identity disorders. Now commonly known by the umbrella term "transgender" this group includes the diagnosis of **transsexualism**, that is, a desire to live and be accepted as a member of the opposite sex, usually accompanied by a sense of discomfort with one's anatomic sex and a wish to have surgery and hormonal treatment to make one's body as congruent as possible with one's preferred sex. Another diagnosis within this group is dual-role transvestitism, in which the individual wears the clothing of the opposite sex to enjoy the temporary experience but without any desire for a more permanent sex change or associated surgical reassignment. We will return to a discussion of gender identity disorders in Chapter 8, where we address gender and mental health.

Another group of disorders included in this block is designated as disorders of sexual preference (WHO, 2010). One diagnosis in this group is fetishism, which is the reliance on some non-living object, such as articles of clothing or footwear, as a stimulus for sexual arousal and sexual gratification. Exhibitionism involves recurrent exposure of the genitalia to strangers or to people in public places without inviting or intending closer contact, and, typically, there is sexual excitement at the time of the exposure. Voyeurism refers to a recurrent or persistent tendency to look at people engaging in sexual or intimate behaviour, such as undressing. This is carried out without the observed people being aware and usually leads to sexual excitement and masturbation. The diagnosis of pedophilia denotes a sexual preference for children usually of prepubertal or early pubertal age. Sadomasochism is defined as a preference

**Figure 4.5:** In dual-role transvestitism, the individual wears the clothing of the opposite sex to enjoy the temporary experience but has no desire for a more permanent sex change.

*Source*: iulianvalentin/iStockphoto

**Figure 4.6:** Individuals who experience sadomasochism have a preference for sexual activity that involves the infliction of pain, humiliation, or bondage.

*Source*: Maks08/iStockphoto

for sexual activity that involves the infliction of pain, humiliation, or bondage. If the subject prefers to be the recipient of such stimulation, this is called "masochism"; if the provider, "sadism." Often such an individual obtains sexual excitement from both sadistic and masochistic activities.

## *Mental Retardation*

In the ICD-10, mental retardation is defined as: "A condition of arrested or incomplete development of the mind, which is especially characterized by impairment of skills manifested during the developmental period, skills which contribute to the overall level of intelligence, i.e. cognitive, language, motor, and social abilities" (WHO, 2010). In Canada, the terms "developmental disability" or "intellectual disability" are commonly used instead of mental retardation, in part to prevent the misconception that the condition is characterized by a retardation (i.e., slowing) of normal mental development. The move away from use of the term "mental retardation" is also a response to the pejorative use of the term sometimes encountered in everyday language. In Chapter 6, we discuss the profound negative impact that occurs as a result of the discriminatory and cruel behaviour that individuals with mental disorders often experience.

The degree of impairment of cognition, language, and intellect varies across a wide spectrum in people affected by mental retardation. Distinctions are made on the basis of standard intelligence testing, with average Intelligence Quotient (IQ) being 100. Diagnosis specifies mild mental retardation (IQ 50 to 69), moderate mental retardation (IQ 35 to 49), severe mental retardation (IQ 20 to 34) and profound mental retardation (IQ below 20). The latter group corresponds to a mental age of less than three years old.

## Disorders of Psychological Development

This block of disorders involves the impairment or delay of functions such as language, visuo-spatial skills, and arithmetic abilities, but disorders in this category do not entail global impairments as seen in mental retardation. Usually, the delay or impairment is present at an early age and diminishes as the individual ages. However, milder deficits often remain in adult life (WHO, 2010).

Many of the diagnoses included in this block describe conditions in which the deficits are circumscribed to a specific function, such as reading or expressing speech. Other diagnoses, such as autism, are more pervasive in nature and cause significant impairments in social interaction and communication. Autism, which involves impairment that is manifested before the age of three years, is also characterized by stereotyped, repetitive behaviour. A more complete discussion of autism is provided in Chapter 7.

## Behavioural and Emotional Disorders with Onset Usually Occurring in Childhood and Adolescence

The ICD-10 also includes a block of disorders that affect children and adolescents. These include attention deficit disorder, conduct disorder, separation anxiety, tic disorders, and many other conditions (WHO, 2010). We will discuss these disorders in Chapter 7, which is devoted to a discussion of mental health and illness in children and adolescents.

## Unspecified Mental Disorder

This is a category for conditions that do not fit into any of the existing diagnostic groups. The ICD-10 urges the diagnostician to avoid use of this category unless absolutely necessary (WHO, 2010).

# Conclusion

A great deal of effort has gone into the diagnostic classification of mental disorders. Although these efforts are limited by problems of reliability and validity, they remain a central means of organizing our understanding of behavioural conditions and help to delineate treatment approaches. Care must be taken to avoid harms that may occur as a result of diagnostic labelling in view of the widespread stigma and discrimination toward people with mental illness that persists in our societies.

## Glossary

**functional mental disorders:** Mental disorders in which no overt disturbance of brain function or structure can be found.

**labelling theory:** The theory that deviance is caused when individuals who are labelled internalize the label, eventually leading them to take on the traits and behaviours that conform to the label.

**mental disorders:** Clinically significant patterns of behavioural or emotional functioning that are associated with some level of distress, suffering, or impairment in one or more areas of functioning (e.g., school, work, social and family interactions).

**mental health problems:** Diminished capacities, whether cognitive, emotional, attentional, interpersonal, motivational, or behavioural, that interfere with a person's enjoyment of life or adversely affect interactions with society and the environment.

**organic mental disorders:** Mental disorders caused by some disturbance of brain function or damage to brain structures, often as a result of infection, injury, or medical condition.

**reliability:** The *consistency* of results when a measurement (including a diagnostic test) is repeated.

**transsexualism:** The desire for and pursuit of change to one's sexual identity.

**validity:** Whether a measure (including a diagnostic test) really captures what it purports to measure.

## Critical Thinking Questions

1. What is the difference between mental health problems and mental disorders?
2. What are some of the challenges with current diagnostic classification?
3. Provide examples of political and economic misuses of diagnosis.
4. What role does culture play in understanding mental health and illness?
5. Briefly describe the ICD-10 Chapter V blocks.

## Recommended Readings

Brown, T., & Scheid, T.L. (Eds.). (2010). *A Handbook for the Study of Mental Health: Social Contexts, Theories, and Systems.* New York: Cambridge University Press.

Conrad, P. (2007). *The Medicalization of Society: On the Transformation of Human Conditions into Treatable Disorders.* Baltimore: Hopkins Fulfillment Service.

Horwitz, A.V. (2003). *Creating Mental Illness.* Chicago: University of Chicago Press.

Kutchins, H., & Kirk, S.A. (2003). *Making Us Crazy: DSM: The Psychiatric Bible and the Creation of Mental Disorders.* New York: Free Press.

Morrison, J. (2010). *Diagnosis Made Easier: Principles and Techniques for Mental Health Clinicians.* New York: Guilford Press.

World Health Organization. (2010). *ICD-10: Version 2010.* Retrieved from http://www.who.int/classifications/icd/en/

## Recommended Websites

Internet Mental Health. www.mentalhealth.com/

Public Health Agency of Canada. Mental Health. www.phac-aspc.gc.ca/mh-sm/index-eng.php

World Health Organization. Mental Health. www.who.int/topics/mental_health/en/

## References

Atrens, D.M. (2011). Big pharma and the manufacture of madness. *Quadrant,* 55(1–2).

Bawaskar, H.S. (2006). The many stigmas of mental illness. *The Lancet,* 367(9520), 1396–1397.

Bloch, S., & Reddaway, P. (1984). *Soviet psychiatric abuse: The shadow over world psychiatry.* New York: Westview Press.

Canadian Centre on Substance Abuse. (2009). *Concurrent disorders: Substance abuse in Canada.* Ottawa: Canadian Centre on Substance Abuse.

Caplan, P.C., & Cosgrove, L. (Eds.). (2004). *Bias in psychiatric diagnosis.* Toronto: Jason Aronson.

Cosgrove, L., & Wheeler, E.E. (2013). Industry's colonization of psychiatry: Ethical and practical implications of financial conflicts of interest in the DSM-5. *Feminism & Psychology,* 23(1), 93–106. doi: 10.1177/0959353512467972

Eaton, W. W., Chen, C.Y., & Bromet, E.J. (2011). Epidemiology of schizophrenia. In M.T. Tsuang, M. Tohen, & P.B. Jones (Eds.), Textbook of psychiatric epidemiology (3rd ed.). Chichester, UK: John Wiley & Sons. doi: 10.1002/9780470976739.ch16

Frances, A. (2013). *Saving normal: An insider's revolt against out-of-control psychiatric diagnosis, DSM-5, Big Pharma, and the medicalization of ordinary life.* New York: HarperCollins.

Goldner, E.M., Hsu, L., Waraich, P., & Somers, J.M. (2002). Prevalence and incidence studies of schizophrenic disorders: A systematic review of the literature. *The Canadian Journal of Psychiatry,* 47(9), 833–843.

Grob, G.N., & Horwitz, A.V. (2009). *Diagnosis, therapy, and evidence: Conundrums in modern American medicine*. New Brunswick, NJ: Rutgers University Press.

Johnson, J.G., Cohen, P., Kasen, S., & Brook, J.S. (2002). Eating disorders during adolescence and the risk for physical and mental disorders during early adulthood. *Archives of General Psychiatry*, 59(6), 545–552.

Kessler, R.C., Chiu, W.T., Demler, O., & Walters, E.E. (2005). Prevalence, severity, and comorbidity of 12-month DSM-IV disorders in the National Comorbidity Survey Replication. *Archives of General Psychiatry*, 62, 617–627.

Lefley, H.P. (2006). Mental health systems in a cross-cultural context. In A.V. Horwitz & T.L. Scheid (Eds.), *A handbook for the study of mental health: Social contexts, theories, and systems* (pp. 295–314). New York: Cambridge University Press.

Link, B.G., & Phelan, J.C. (2012). Labelling and stigma. In C.S. Aneshensel, J.C. Phelan, & A. Bierman (Eds.), *Handbook of the sociology of mental health* (p. 525–543. New York: Springer. doi: 10.1007/978-94-007-4276-5_25

Murphy, J. (1976). Psychiatric labeling in cross-cultural perspective: Similar kinds of disturbed behavior appear to be labeled abnormal in diverse cultures. *Science*, 191, 1019–1028.

National Eating Disorder Information Centre. (2008). *Know the facts*. Retrieved from www.nedic.ca/knowthefacts/statistics.shtml

Roman, P.M., & Trice, H.M. (1968). The sick role, labeling theory, and the deviant drinker. *International Journal of Social Psychiatry*, 14, 245–251.

Rosenhan, D.L. (1973). On being sane in insane places. *Science*, 179(70), 250–258.

Scheff, T.J. (1966). *Being mentally ill: A sociological theory*. Chicago: Aldine.

Smye, V., & Mussell, B. (2001). *Aboriginal mental health: 'What works best?'*, a discussion paper. Retrieved from www.london.cmha.ca/data/1/rec_docs/1598_Aboriginal%20Mental%20Health%20What%20Works%20Best.pdf

Somers, J.M., Goldner, E.M., Waraich, P., & Hsu, L. (2006). Prevalence and incidence studies of anxiety disorders: A systematic review of the literature. *Canadian Journal of Psychiatry*, 51(2), 100–113.

Standing Senate Committee on Social Affairs, Science and Technology. (2004). *Mental health, mental illness and addiction: Overview of policies and programs in Canada*. Ottawa: Parliament of Canada. Retrieved from http://www.parl.gc.ca/Content/SEN/Committee/381/soci/rep/report1/repintnov04vol1-e.pdf

Vaughan, M. (1991). *Curing their ills: Colonial power and African illness*. Stanford, CA: Stanford University Press.

Waraich, P., Goldner, E.M., Somers, J.M., & Hsu, L. (2004). Prevalence and incidence studies of mood disorders: A systematic review of the literature. *Canadian Journal of Psychiatry*, 49(2), 124–138.

Wolinsky, H. (2005). Disease mongering and drug marketing. *Science and Society*, 6(7), 612–614.

World Health Organization. (2010). ICD-10: Version 2010. Retrieved from www.who.int/classifications/icd/en/

# Chapter 5

# SUBSTANCE USE, DEPENDENCE, AND ADDICTIVE BEHAVIOUR

I can honestly say all the bad things that ever happened to me were directly attributed to drugs and alcohol. I mean, I would never urinate at the Alamo at nine o'clock in the morning dressed in a woman's evening dress sober.
—Ozzy Osborne (former lead vocalist of heavy metal band Black Sabbath)

## Introduction

Substance use refers to the use of psychoactive substances, such as drugs, alcohol, plant materials, and chemicals, which cause noticeable changes in mental function. Substances may be eaten or drunk in pure form or brewed in some type of beverage. They may be snorted, inhaled as smoke or vapour, dissolved under the tongue, absorbed through the skin from a patch or poultice, injected intramuscularly or intravenously, or inserted into the anus or urethra. The use of psychoactive substances is very common, both **licit substance use** (use of substances that are not regulated by prevailing laws and use of regulated substances in compliance with laws and regulations) and **illicit substance use** (use that is in contravention of existing laws and regulations).

In this chapter, we will discuss each of the main classes of psychoactive substances that have a prominent presence and impact in Canada, including alcohol, tobacco, cannabinoids, stimulants, opioids, sedatives, hallucinogens, inhalants, and dissociatives. We will examine substance use from individual- and population-based perspectives, revealing the effects that substance use has on individuals and reviewing the extent of substance use among the Canadian population. In Chapter 15, we will return to the issue of substance use by reviewing important public policy and ethical considerations and discussing how these issues are being grappled with by members of Canadian society.

Although substance use disorders are considered to be one group of mental disorders described in diagnostic classification systems (such as the DSM and the

ICD), we consider this topic to be so important that it requires a dedicated chapter. It has been found that substance use disorders often co-occur with other mental health problems. Nevertheless, substance use warrants careful study and attention in its own right. The fields of research and practice that address substance use have a long history separate from parallel fields that focus on other mental health conditions. Many researchers and practitioners have specialized in addressing substance use and addictions, and there is a large body of knowledge in the field that requires attention. In the past, this has often been neglected by students and teachers when addressing mental health.

## Substance Use, Dependence, and Addiction

Substance use exists across a wide spectrum. Not all substance use is harmful or problematic and, under certain circumstances, substance use can be considered to be beneficial to many individuals. For example, the modest use of alcohol is experienced as a pleasure and benefit to many individuals who enjoy an occasional cocktail, glass of wine, or cold beer (possibly a warm beer if you are from the British Isles). For many people, the modest use of alcohol enhances the enjoyment of social events, adds to the taste of food, and helps one to relax and unwind. Of course, there are some individuals who have great difficulty limiting themselves to a modest use of alcohol and end up suffering from the harmful effects associated with higher levels of alcohol use. There are also some people who respond negatively to even the smallest amounts of alcohol. These are examples of the wide range of responses that people may have to the use of alcohol; this also holds true in relation to other psychoactive substances.

How do psychoactive substances exert their effects? Brain cell receptors are stimulated or inhibited by molecules contained in the substance, causing changes in various mental activities. For example, alcohol is quickly transferred from the stomach and small intestine to the bloodstream, where it circulates to the brain. Alcohol (known scientifically as ethanol) is a relatively small molecule (see Figure 5.1) and, consequently, it passes through the blood-brain barrier easily.

Once ethanol molecules reach brain cells, they have a biochemical effect on neurotransmitter function, suppressing the activity of excitatory nerve pathways and increasing the activity of inhibitory nerve pathways. In low doses, the effects of ethanol will often result in feelings of general relaxation and euphoria, but, in higher doses, the effects will cause loss of coordination in body movements, lapses in judgment, and a diminished attention span. In very high doses, alcohol can cause stupor, coma, and even death.

Let us look at the effect of opium, another psychoactive substance, on the brain. Opium is derived from the sticky resin of the opium poppy, and, once dried, it looks like tar. Opium contains a number of alkaloids (i.e., chemical compounds found in various plants and fungi) that have psychoactive properties, with the most active alkaloid being morphine, which is a much larger molecule than ethanol.

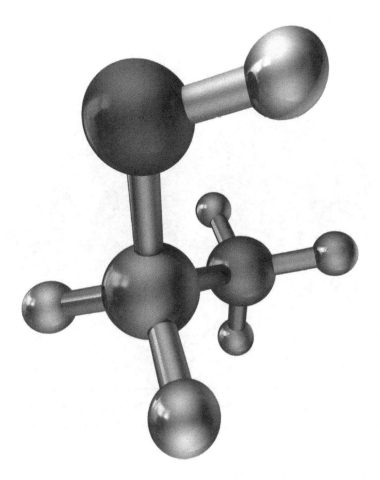

**Figure 5.1:** Ethanol (alcohol) is a relatively small molecule that passes easily through the blood-brain barrier and affects the actions of various neurotransmitters on brain function.

*Source*: Martin McCarthy/iStockphoto

The effect of morphine and other psychoactive alkaloids found in opium is mediated by their effect on particular receptors, called mu receptors, located on neurons and other cells in the body. Like ethanol, morphine and other opioid alkaloids affect neurotransmitter activity and alter function in many areas of the brain.

It has been found that psychological and environmental factors have a large mediating effect on the degree of intoxication and the particular behavioural effects experienced by individuals when they use psychoactive substances (Birak, Higgs, & Terry, 2011). For example, research studies have shown that the effects of alcohol on an individual are strongly related to the expectations that exist within a particular society or cultural group. In societies in which drunkenness is considered to be a "time out" from usual social sanctions and behaviours, it is common for a person who imbibes

**Figure 5.2:** Two opium poppies at different stages. The poppy on the left has dumped tasty seeds, used for pastries and sauces. The poppy on the right is at an earlier stage, used to harvest juice for heroin.

*Source:* Stephanie Horrocks/iStockphoto

to act in a disinhibited manner. Nevertheless, even in these societies, behaviour will usually be kept within certain social norms.

As we have mentioned, substance use can be understood to occur across a wide spectrum, from beneficial use at one extreme, to profoundly harmful use at the other, as shown in Figure 5.3.

We have already discussed the notion of beneficial use of substances, which is the case for many people when they enjoy alcoholic beverages in moderation or enjoy a morning coffee that helps stimulate them at the beginning of the day. In addition, psychoactive substances are prescribed by physicians for therapeutic purposes, such as the use of a sedative drug during surgery or the use of an anti-anxiety medication to treat uncomfortable anxiety symptoms.

However, psychoactive substances can also create much harm as a result of their direct effects on the brain or other organs or because of indirect effects caused by a variety of physical, social, and psychological factors that accompany substance use. For example, we are all familiar with the harms caused by smoking tobacco. Inhaling

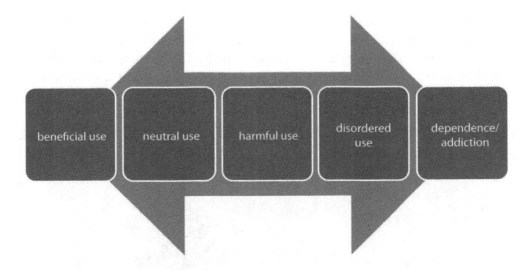

**Figure 5.3:** The spectrum of substance abuse

smoke containing tars and other carcinogens involves serious damage to the lungs, heart, and other organs. Yet, for many smokers, the brain's craving for the continued delivery of nicotine, the psychoactive substance contained in tobacco, is strong enough to overwhelm their good sense that tobacco smoking comes with too high a risk of disease and early death. Note that the main negative effects of tobacco are unrelated to its psychoactive properties; instead they consist of physical harms that result from smoking it. This is also the case with some other psychoactive substances, in which the mode of delivery results in substantial physical harms. Other examples of such indirect harms include severe infections frequently contracted by intravenous drug users, and neurological damage or blindness experienced by some people who drink high doses of alcohol.

Diagnostic conventions identify individuals as having a **substance use disorder** when they are engaged in a pattern of behaviour that involves ongoing use of substances causing harm, either through detrimental physical or mental effects, or negative impact on the welfare of others. In addition to health problems, common adverse consequences of substance use include failure to meet work, family, or school obligations; interpersonal conflicts; and legal problems. Substance use disorders are implicated in a sizable proportion of injuries, motor vehicle accidents, and instances of interpersonal violence.

An important concept is **dependence**. This refers to a state that develops once someone uses a substance for some period of time, in which it becomes very difficult to stop use of the substance as a result of the physiological changes that have occurred. As a result of regular substance use, certain cell functions accommodate to the presence of the substance in the body. This accommodation is called **tolerance**, and it means that the body will need a higher dose of the substance to create the effects that a smaller dose would have achieved previously. This accommodation also means that, if the substance is no longer used, the body experiences **withdrawal**, that is, physical and mental symptoms that are often very uncomfortable. The symptoms of withdrawal that develop are related to the effect of the particular substance, and some substances cause particularly strong withdrawal symptoms.

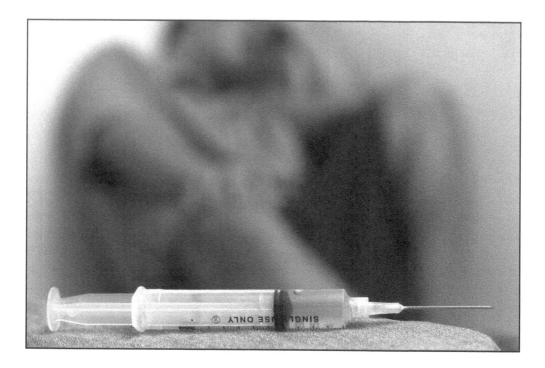

**Figure 5.4:** Stopping the use of heroin causes a severe withdrawal syndrome within 24 hours.

*Source:* GetStock/Palangsi

For example, heroin (or diacetylmorphine hydrochloride, as it is known by scientists), a synthetic substance that has similar but stronger effects to naturally occurring opiates, is associated with a very severe withdrawal syndrome. If heroin is used continuously for as little as three days, then substantial withdrawal symptoms appear within 24 hours after it is stopped. Withdrawal from heroin is usually followed by intense physical symptoms, including cold sweats, chills, insomnia, malaise, cramp-like pains, nausea, vomiting, diarrhea, and fever. For many heroin users, withdrawal is so terrible that they are driven to get a "fix" (i.e., a dose) of heroin even when they wish deeply that they could break the cycle of dependence.

The phenomena of tolerance and withdrawal appear to be caused by sustained changes in the release and uptake of neurotransmitters at the synaptic junctions of various cells in the body. For example, repeated use of heroin and other opioids are associated with marked changes in a variety of neurotransmitters that coincide with the emergence of tolerance and withdrawal.

In addition to physiological dependence on psychoactive substances (with the development of tolerance and withdrawal, as described above), **psychological dependence** may occur in which an individual experiences intense cravings, anxiety, irritability, or other feelings of distress when substance use is stopped. Although described as a "psychological" dependence, the cravings, anxiety, irritability, and other symptoms may have a physiological basis, caused by the same type of alterations in neurotransmitter function as described above. Yet, as we discussed in Chapter 1, it is unlikely that a purely physiological explanation fully explains such phenomena. Undoubtedly, there are many other factors that influence the presence of cravings and other features of psychological dependence. For example, cravings have been found to be much more intense when an individual is exposed to stress or when one is in an environment that is associated with use of the drug (Preston & Epstein, 2011).

**Addiction** to a substance is defined as the compulsive use of it despite its adverse consequences. The meaning and usage of the term "addiction" has changed over time. Originally, the term was synonymous with physiological dependence and, over time, was also used to denote psychological dependence. More recently, the term has been extended beyond its original connection to substance use. Addiction is now used to denote other compulsive behaviours, such as gambling and sexual behaviour, which persist despite causing significant adverse consequences. In its popular use, addiction also refers to harms that result, for example, to others, and often carries the negative connotation of a criminal/moral model of thought about substance use as deviant behaviour.

In its more severe manifestations, addiction is responsible for horrific levels of human suffering and misery. Individuals who are in the throes of a severe addiction are often so overtaken by their compulsive behaviour that everything else in their lives may be sacrificed. The devastating effects on people with severe addictions are heartbreaking. Commonly, people with addictions will immediately and repeatedly spend their last dollar to get another fix, using up any resources they could have had for basic sustenance, such as shelter or housing. This contributes to homelessness and nutritional deprivation among people with addictions. Very serious health problems develop, both because of the direct harmful effects of substance use on the body and because of indirect harms, such as infections caused by intravenous injection, malnutrition, and inadequate sanitation and living conditions. Involvement in sex work and property crime is often resorted to in order to obtain money for the next fix, resulting in exposure to violence and criminalization. People with severe addictions constitute one of the most ill and most impoverished populations in Canada (Keller et al., 2013).

We have seen that the negative health consequences for individuals with substance use disorders and addictions can be devastating. However, substance use can lead to profound risks and harms even when someone does not have an addiction or substance

**Figure 5.5:** This photo was taken in a bar in the Downtown Eastside of Vancouver.

*Source:* Chris Sang Yeob Park, Photographer

use disorder. For example, many teenagers and young people who experiment with substance use end up in dire circumstances. Serious accidents caused by intoxication rob many young people of their lives or cause lifelong disability or suffering. It has been estimated that hazardous alcohol use is the leading cause of morbidity among young people aged 10 to 24 years worldwide (Gore et al., 2011) and alone causes approximately one-third of all deaths in males aged 15 to 29 years in economically developed countries such as Canada (Toumbourou et al., 2007). In fact, the WHO has identified alcohol as the second leading risk factor (out of 26 risk factors) for morbidity, mortality, and disability, surpassed only by tobacco (WHO, 2011). Rape, sexual abuse, physical violence, and other criminal acts often occur in conjunction with substance use and can result in profound sequelae and long-lasting harm.

## Substances Commonly Used in Canada

As there are many hundreds of substances used for known psychoactive effects, we will not attempt to catalogue all of these. Instead, we will discuss substances that are in relatively widespread use in Canada, emphasizing those that are used by a large proportion of the population.

### *Alcohol*

For most Canadians, the use of alcohol is accepted as a normal part of our lives. According to a recent national survey, almost 80 percent of Canadians 15 years of age and older reported consuming alcohol in the previous year, and around 20 percent of Canadians who consume alcohol do so at levels above the low-risk drinking guidelines (Health Canada, 2012a). It is easy for us to forget that, in other parts of the world, alcohol is considered dangerous and deemed illegal, and its use can warrant serious punishment.

However, even in Canada, alcohol was once widely prohibited. From the early 1900s to the 1920s, the use or sale of alcohol was illegal in most parts of the country. In a federal referendum held in 1898, 51 percent voted for prohibition, whereas 49 percent voted against it. Prohibition had a majority in all provinces except Quebec, where 81 percent voted against it (likely because of the French cultural tradition of valuing wine as one as life's great pleasures).

How can we explain the divergent opinions about alcohol? Why do some people and some societies consider alcohol in a positive light while others feel strongly that alcohol should be avoided or even outlawed? In part, this is because of the wide spectrum of human behaviour and the consequences associated with alcohol use. For most Canadians, alcohol has a neutral or positive impact on their lives. However, for a smaller proportion of Canadian society, alcohol is associated with profound harms and sorrow (Health Canada, 2012a). How do we best balance the value to Canadians of being able to enjoy drinking alcohol against the risks and harms that exist for some in the population? Certainly, the extent of risk and harm to Canadians associated with alcohol use is very real and cannot be ignored. For example, using 2002 data, Rehm and colleagues found that alcohol resulted in 195,970 hospital visits, costing Canadians almost $1.5 billion in direct health care costs alone (Rehm et al., 2006), and according to a recent report from the Canadian Public Health Association, "Globally and in Canada, alcohol's net effect is negative" (Canadian Public Health Association, 2011, p. 1). Each year, alcohol is identified as being responsible for a large number of deaths caused by trauma (e.g., motor vehicle accidents, fires, falls, and other accidents), acute alcohol poisoning, and cirrhosis of the liver. We have already mentioned that alcohol is often implicated in many other tragedies, such as violent and criminal behaviour, suicide, unsafe sex and unwanted pregnancies, and serious problems in the workplace.

Some sectors of Canadian society have suffered disproportionately with the negative consequences of alcohol use. Many Aboriginal people have experienced devastating harm as a result of alcohol use in their communities. Scientists have examined whether First Nations, Inuit, and Metis people may be more prone to the effects of alcohol than people of European descent. Some of the differences in vulnerability to the effects of alcohol may result from genetically determined variations in the body's ability to metabolize (break down) and eliminate alcohol from the body through the activity of enzymes such as aldehyde dehydrogenase. For example, it has been confirmed that many people of Asian heritage inherit genes that produce enzymes that are relatively inactive in breaking down alcohol. Such individuals appear to be more prone to a flushing of the skin when they drink alcohol, often experience noxious effects when they drink, and have been found to be less prone to becoming alcohol dependent (ostensibly because drinking more than very small amounts of alcohol is immediately unpleasant) (Li, Zhao, & Gelernter, 2012). Although research about the influence of genetic factors on alcohol use among First Nations, Inuit, and Metis populations is not definitive, it is possible that such genetic factors may help explain the high prevalence of alcohol problems. However, it appears likely that historical, social, political, economic, and psychological factors, such as those discussed in Chapter 9, have been the greatest contributors to the higher prevalence of problems with alcohol experienced by Canadian Aboriginal peoples.

## *Tobacco*

The smoking of tobacco in pipes, cigars, and cigarettes has been popular in Canada since the earliest years of Confederation. Although Aboriginal people used tobacco, it is thought they did so primarily as a component of ceremonial rituals. However, on the arrival of Europeans, tobacco quickly became popularized as a trade item and recreational drug. The habit of smoking tobacco frequently throughout the day appears to have been initiated in the Americas by European settlers, and the large tobacco-growing industry in the southern United States promoted the widespread use of tobacco.

The psychoactive substance in tobacco smoke is nicotine. When tobacco smoke is inhaled, nicotine travels quickly to the brain and acts on receptors there and elsewhere in the body, altering neurotransmitters such as dopamine and leading to feelings of relaxation, alertness, and euphoria, and appetite suppression. Due to nicotine's properties, physical dependence develops quickly with the repeated smoking of tobacco, and psychological dependence appears to be a significant factor in its addictive potential. Tobacco use has become widespread; it is estimated that approximately 1.1 billion people smoke tobacco, approximately one-third of the world's adult population. It has now become well known that tobacco causes substantial harm through damage to organs and the precipitation of various forms of cancer and other diseases. Lung diseases, such as lung cancer and chronic obstructive pulmonary disease, are particularly common, but tobacco also causes heart disease, diseases of the digestive tract, and many other serious detrimental effects on health. The WHO estimates that tobacco use currently causes 6 million deaths per year and considers it to be the leading preventable cause of death worldwide (WHO, 2015). Canada has made more progress in tobacco control in recent years than most other countries in the world and has seen a dramatic decline in tobacco consumption from previous decades. Various countries are modelling their efforts on Canada's Federal Tobacco Control Strategy (Health Canada, 2012b).

## *Cannabinoids*

Cannabis (marijuana) has been used as an intoxicant for many centuries. Tetrahydrocannabinol (THC) is the main psychoactive ingredient contained in the cannabis plant, but there are many others. Most commonly, the dried buds and leaves of the plant (marijuana or ganja) or hashish, a resin, which is extracted from the plant containing the trichomes in which the THC is most highly concentrated, is smoked.

THC binds to cannabinoid receptors on cells throughout the brain and influences neurotransmission that causes activation of various brain centres. Common effects include feelings of euphoria, relaxation, altered perception of time and sensory stimulation, and an increased appetite ("the munchies"). However, as is true with most psychoactive substances, individuals will respond quite differently to cannabis; some people find that cannabis causes them to feel highly anxious or paranoid. In the early 1990s, scientists conducting research on cannabis identified that the human body creates its own (i.e., endogenous) neurotransmitters that also bind to the cannabinoid receptors. Anandamide was the first isolated endogenous neurotransmitter; it binds to the cannabinoid receptor and has effects similar to THC. A number of other endogenous cannabinoid neurotransmitters have since been isolated and researchers continue to explore their actions and potential therapeutic uses.

Given that use of cannabis is currently illegal in Canada, it is surprisingly common. In a recent epidemiological survey, approximately 10 percent of Canadians 15 years of age and older had used cannabis in the previous year, while about 40 percent reported having used cannabis in their lifetimes, making it the most commonly used illicit drug in Canada (Health Canada, 2012a). Rates of cannabis use in Canada have oscillated substantially in recent decades. Among some sub-populations of adolescents in Canada, cannabis use is more common than tobacco use.

Reliable information about the health risks and benefits of cannabis is limited and inconclusive (Moffat, Jenkins, & Johnson, 2013). Although levels of tars and other toxic substances have been found to be even higher in cannabis smoke than in cigarette smoke, it has not been shown that cannabis use by itself is linked to lung cancer or respiratory damage (Pletcher et al., 2012). Use of a vaporizer (which heats the cannabis to a high enough temperature to release vapour without creating smoke) results in a significantly lower concentration of noxious substances being inhaled in comparison with conventional methods of smoking with pipes or in "joints" (i.e., rolled up in cigarette papers). Cannabis intoxication does seem to play a role in many injuries, including motor vehicle accidents (Asbridge, Hayden, & Cartwright, 2012). Some heavy users develop dependence and may experience cognitive impairment that may not be fully reversed even after discontinuation of cannabis use (Solowij et al., 2002). There is evidence that cannabis use is associated with the development of psychosis in young people but the directionality of the link is unclear; cannabis may play a role in inducing psychosis or, alternatively, people who are developing psychosis may be more likely to use cannabis (Kuepper et al., 2011; McGrath et al., 2010). While some people with schizophrenia and other psychotic illnesses appear to have an exacerbation of psychotic symptoms with the use of cannabis (Hall, Degenhardt, & Teesson, 2004), some research suggests no association between cannabis use and psychotic symptomology (Barrowclough et al., 2013).

A review of evidence has indicated that the health harms associated with cannabis use increase with the frequency of use (Fischer et al., 2011); the authors have provided guidelines for reducing risk associated with cannabis use. In recent years, there has been evidence for potentially beneficial effects of cannabinoids in the treatment of chronic pain and other medical conditions for some patients.

## Stimulants

The most commonly used psychoactive substance in Canada is caffeine, a stimulant that has the effect of increasing alertness and temporarily warding off drowsiness. We have already mentioned that coffee and other caffeine-containing drinks are drunk daily by more than 75 percent of adult Canadians. Intake of large amounts of caffeine-containing substances can cause caffeinism, in which the following symptoms are common: nervousness, irritability, insomnia, muscle twitches, and palpitations. High use also increases stomach acid and can cause various esophageal and gastrointestinal problems, including peptic ulcers. Most coffee drinkers would find it very difficult to eliminate coffee from their daily routines, and cessation or reduction of coffee intake is likely to result in a withdrawal syndrome characterized by headache, fatigue, nausea, and depressed mood.

**Figure 5.6:** Coca leaves for sale in a Peruvian street market

*Source:* Brasil2/iStockphoto

For at least a thousand years, indigenous people in South America have been chewing the leaves of the coca plant for its stimulant properties. By the 19th century, European physicians and chemists began to experiment with extracts of coca leaves for medicinal and stimulant properties. Various tinctures and mixtures included extracts from the coca plant, and the original recipe for Coca-Cola included a "pinch" of coca leaves. Coca extracts were given to soldiers and pilots to help them resist sleep. Chemists isolated cocaine, the psychoactive substance contained in the coca leaves, and, in recent decades, cocaine has been found to cause alterations in levels of neurotransmitters such as dopamine and serotonin in various brain centres.

Cocaine is the second most commonly used illicit drug in Canada (after cannabis), and a recent epidemiological survey indicated that approximately 1 percent of Canadians had used cocaine during the previous year (Health Canada, 2012a). As we have discussed, individuals vary in their responses to psychoactive substances, and this certainly holds true in regard to cocaine use. Often, cocaine induces euphoria and a sense of increased energy, physical prowess, and ability. However, it is also common for people to become angry, mean-spirited, and argumentative, and violent behaviour often accompanies cocaine use. In high doses, cocaine often causes paranoia and psychosis.

Cocaine is taken in various forms using different routes of administration. Snorting (i.e., insufflation) of cocaine powder is likely the most common way cocaine is used in

**Figure 5.7:** Cocaine is ingested by snorting, smoking, and injecting. Here, a woman is pictured snorting cocaine.

*Source:* Mlenny/iStockphoto

Canada, often as part of the "club scene." Smoking of either freebase or crack cocaine (chemical preparations of cocaine that vaporize at low temperatures) emerged a few decades ago and quickly spread to communities throughout the world, particularly to poor neighbourhoods in which drug use and crime rates were high. Freebase and crack cocaine deliver a much more immediate and powerful intoxication and induce strong cravings and psychological dependence that are difficult to overcome. Cocaine can also be injected intravenously, leading to high rates of serious complications, including infections and heart disease. Taken in any form—whether snorted, smoked, or injected—cocaine causes profound health problems and has become closely associated with such social problems as prostitution, theft, and violent criminal behaviour.

Another stimulant that has been in prominent use in Canada is methamphetamine, also known in street terms as "crystal," "meth," and "crank," among others. This substance can be made in illicit laboratories with ingredients that are readily available in household products or over-the-counter medications. Consequently, methamphetamine can be produced and sold cheaply. It is a potent stimulant of the central nervous system and affects neurotransmitters, resulting in feelings of euphoria, insomnia, increased sexual interest, increased heart rate, increased body temperature, and loss of appetite. Methamphetamine can have a high addictive potential, particularly when smoked or injected. It has been used often among street youth and has sometimes been popular in gay society as a drug to enhance sexual interest and experience. It is of particular concern that methamphetamine has been found to result in structural and functional damage to the brain that appears irreversible (National Institute on Drug Abuse, 2008). Methamphetamine production and distribution was the focus of the popular television series *Breaking Bad*, in which the main character, Walter White, a science teacher diagnosed with cancer, decided to "cook" meth in order to make money to support his medical treatment. The show demonstrated how the substance is often created in makeshift laboratories, with one of the initial meth productions taking place in an RV. *Breaking Bad* also portrayed the dangers of production (e.g., the release of toxic chemicals), as well as the violence and crime associated with the drug trade.

**Figure 5.8:** Methamphetamine is smoked using a pipe.

*Source:* KarenMower/iStockphoto

Ecstasy or methylenedioxymethamphetamine (MDMA) is similar in chemical structure to amphetamines. However, its psychoactive effects appear unique, and it is known to have hallucinogenic qualities. In addition to feelings of euphoria, MDMA is often described as increasing feelings of intimacy and empathy (and is sometimes called "the love drug"). Common street names for MDMA include "molly," and "X." Like other stimulants, MDMA gives the perception of increased energy and loss of appetite. In recent decades, MDMA became popular in raves and other dance club scenes. Intense hyperthermia (increased body temperature) is a significant risk associated with MDMA. Long-term health risks are unclear, and the overall risk or safety of MDMA is still in debate.

## Opiates and Opioids

Opiates are drugs derived from the opium poppy and include opium, morphine, codeine, and heroin. Opioids are psychoactive substances that are synthesized to have chemical structures and properties similar to opiates. Opioids include heroin, morphine, codeine, methadone, oxycodone, hydrocodone, fentanyl, and hydromorphone. Some opioids (e.g., heroin) are often injected intravenously or smoked (smoking heroin is known as "chasing the dragon") while other opioids (e.g., oxycodone) are usually ingested as pills. Their potent analgesic (pain-killing) properties have made opioids highly valuable as medicines for many centuries. They also induce intense feelings of euphoria and have high addictive potential, inducing strong physical and psychological dependence. During one period in China's history (the early 20th century), more than 25 percent of adults were addicted to opium (McCoy, 2004), and during the 1960s, a similar proportion of American soldiers became addicted to heroin and other opioids when serving in the Vietnam War (Robins, Helzer, & Davis, 1975). A growing problem in recent years has been the rise of non-medicinal use of opioids. Fentanyl, a synthetic opioid that is up to 100 percent more potent than morphine, has gained much attention due to a significant spike in deaths attributed to the substance. For example, between 2009 and 2014, it is estimated that there has been one fentanyl-related death every three days (Canadian Community Epidemiology Network on Drug Use, 2015). The majority of fentanyl victims are believed to be unaware that they are ingesting the drug, which is added to other commonly used substances (e.g., oxycodone, cocaine). The rise in fentanyl-related deaths has sparked campaigns across the country to encourage people to know the source of their drugs and to be in the presence of others when using substances (Canadian Community Epidemiology Network on Drug Use, 2015).

**Figure 5.9:** Preparing heroin for injection

*Source:* ermingut/iStockphoto

---

**Box 5.1: Heroin Use among Musicians and Actors**

Many talented musicians and actors have had their lives diminished or ended by addiction to heroin—a powerful opiate that is commonly injected intravenously. Ray Charles, Philip Seymour Hoffman, John Lennon, Jimi Hendrix, Jim Morrison, Janis Joplin, Cory Monteith, and Kurt Cobain are but a few of the many whose lives have taken this turn. Some musicians and actors seem to be at particular risk for drug use and addiction.

---

## *Sedatives*

A wide variety of substances with different chemical structures have psychoactive effects in which sedation is a prominent feature. In general, sedatives depress function in brain centres that govern wakefulness and alertness. Barbiturates (such as amobarbital and secobarbital) are potent sedatives that are used widely to induce anesthesia during surgery. Because they are associated with a strong physical dependence, they are tightly controlled and rarely prescribed for other purposes. Benzodiazepines (such as diazepam and lorazepam) also have strong sedative effects, and are commonly used to induce anesthesia for medical procedures. In lower doses, benzodiazepines can be used as anxiolytics (i.e., to reduce anxiety) and as soporifics (sleeping pills). Two commonly used club drugs are flunitrazepam and gamma hydroxybutyrate (GHB). Flunitrazepam, (more commonly known by its trade name "Rohypnol"), is a benzodiazepine tranquilizer that induces sedation, muscle relaxation, confusion, memory loss, dizziness, and impaired coordination. Flunitrazepam has legitimate medical purposes and has been used for sedation before medical procedures in some countries. However, it is also frequently used as a "club drug" and has become infamous as a drug used in committing sexual assaults. That is why one of its street names is "the date rape drug." Also known as "roofies," flunitrazepam is produced as a small white tablet and is colourless, tasteless, and odourless. The effects are almost immediate, and can last anywhere from 8 to 24 hours, depending on the dose. Repeated use of flunitrazepam over a period of time can result in physical and psychological dependence, and can cause withdrawal symptoms if regular use is abruptly stopped.

GHB is a central nervous system depressant that is known on the street as "G," "Georgia home boy," and "liquid ecstasy." Due to its properties and its effects at higher doses, GHB is also used by perpetrators of sexual assault. At lower doses, GHB produces euphoric and sedative effects, similar to alcohol. Individuals have reported feeling relaxed, happy, and sociable, and having an increased libido. With frequent use, GHB can cause severe physical addiction, and can result in extreme withdrawal symptoms. The use of GHB has been associated with adverse acute health effects such as coma and seizures and has been linked to overdoses and deaths.

## Hallucinogens

Hallucinogens are substances that cause significant alterations in sensory perception, emotion, and thought, inducing experiences that are unusual and outside the bounds of normal consciousness. Hallucinogens have been used in the shamanic and spiritual practices of various cultures for centuries and became popularized in the Western world during the 1960s as part of the counterculture movement.

A wide variety of naturally occurring and synthesized substances are classified as hallucinogens. The peyote cactus, which contains the hallucinogen mescaline, and the psilocybin mushroom ("magic mushroom"), have been used by indigenous people in Central and South America for centuries as entheogens, that is, drugs used to bring on spiritual experiences. Lysergic acid diethylamide (LSD) was synthesized from ergot, a fungus that grows on grains, by Swiss chemist Albert Hoffman. After absorbing a small amount through his skin, Hoffman described seeing through his closed eyes "fantastic pictures, extraordinary shapes with intense, kaleidoscopic play of colors." (Hoffman, 1980, p. 15).

---

**Box 5.2: Medical Use of Hallucinogenic Drugs**

A curious and unethical chapter in the history of psychiatric treatment in Canada occurred during the 1950s in a Montreal hospital, when psychiatrist Dr. Ewen Cameron conducted experiments on patients in which they were given LSD and other hallucinogenic drugs without obtaining informed consent. These experiments were funded by the US Central Intelligence Agency because it was interested in Dr. Cameron's theories, in which he aimed to erase existing memories and "rebuild" the psyche (Collins, 1998). In more recent years, there has been resurgence in the medical use of hallucinogenic drugs. The psychoactive substances found in magic mushrooms, LSD, ketamine, and MDMA have all been used in the recent treatment of patients experiencing mental disorders such as PTSD, depression, and anxiety (Grescoe, 2013). In 2013, a study exploring the use of MDMA for the treatment of PTSD was approved by Health Canada.

---

## Inhalants

Inhalants are particularly dangerous substances when used for their psychoactive effects. Glue, gasoline, paint, butane, and other solvents can cause intoxication when inhaled and often cause damage to the central nervous system; hearing loss; lung, heart, and brain damage; and can sometimes cause sudden death. Inhalant use is particularly prevalent among young people who are living in especially marginalized circumstances, such as homeless youth and some Aboriginal youth in rural and remote communities. Studies have indicated that the majority of first-time inhalant use occurs between the ages of 12 and 16 years (Dell et al., 2011), and that, on some Aboriginal reserves, more than 50 percent of youth under 18 years of age have inhaled solvents (Collin, 2006).

## Dissociatives

Dissociative drugs distort perceptions of sight and sound, and cause users to feel a disconnection from reality. Two such drugs are ketamine and phencyclidine (PCP), each dissociative anesthetics that were originally produced for medical purposes, but are now used predominantly in veterinary practice due to their adverse effects. Ketamine, popularly known as "K," "special K," or "vitamin K," can be snorted or injected but is often smoked together with tobacco or cannabis. Ketamine causes a dream-like state that users describe as an "out of body experience." When in this state, users experience a disconnection from bodily sensations, which is be potentially dangerous as it can lead the individual to disregard pain or hazards. When taken in high doses, ketamine can cause vomiting, anxiety, hallucinations, temporary paralysis, and blackouts, and as such has been associated with sexual assault. PCP causes individuals to feel a sense of numbness and invulnerability. The use of PCP was discontinued in medical practice as it was found to cause individuals to become agitated, delusional, and irrational. It continues to be produced, albeit illicitly, and is sold on the street despite having a reputation for causing unfavourable reactions. Some users experience psychotic symptoms, such as hallucinations and paranoia.

In addition to synthetic dissociative drugs, there are also naturally occurring substances, such as the salvia divinorum herb, that cause dissociative effects. Growing natively in Mexico, salvia leaves are chewed or smoked and cause short and intense psychedelic changes in visual and body perceptions, mood, emotions, and a feeling of detachment from reality. Salvia is not currently a controlled substance and is regulated by Health Canada as a "natural health product," although there are no licences to sell it. Recently, governments across North America have been working to add it to the list of controlled substances.

## Club Drugs

The term "club drugs" is used to describe drugs that are commonly used at night clubs, all-night parties, and raves, particularly by youth and young adults. Users of these drugs believe they enhance their party experience and often prefer these substances to those that they perceive to be "harder" drugs, such as cocaine or methamphetamine. The drugs that are included in this group may not be similar in chemical composition or effect (e.g., some are stimulants and others are sedatives), however, the relative low cost and easy accessibility of these drugs has increased their popularity in recent years. Several of the drugs described above are commonly used as club drugs (e.g., MDMA, ketamine, flunitraepam, and GHB).

**Box 5.3: ANKORS Harm-Reduction Services**

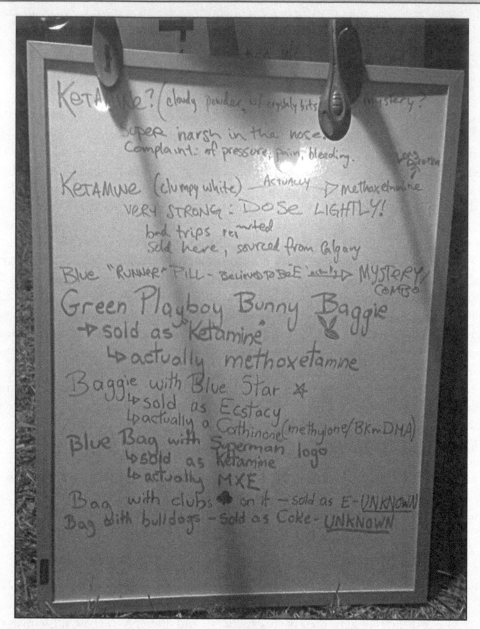

**Figure 5.10:** A whiteboard outside the ANKORS harm-reduction tent at Shambhala Music Festival warns partiers of misrepresented drugs they have found from drug presence testing.

*Source:* www.ankorsvolunteer.com

In recent years, electronic dance music festivals have become widely popular across North America. One of largest festivals, Shambhala Music Festival, takes place for one week every summer on the Salmo River Ranch, located in the West Kootenay region of British Columbia. Shambhala brings together around 15,000 music enthusiasts each year, many of whom are young and experienced drug users. The large crowds of partiers combined with the use of drugs and alcohol increases the issues of bingeing, overdose, and sexual assault. In order to reduce such negative occurrences, ANKORS, a non-profit organization funded by Interior Health and the Public Health Agency of Canada, offers an array of harm-reduction services. One of the main services offered is pill and powder drug-presence testing. Often, the true nature of a drug that people have purchased is not actually what was represented when sold to them. For instance, individuals who thought they purchased ketamine have actually been sold PMMA, MXE, 2-CI, and other substances, many of which can be extremely dangerous. Drug tests are offered free of charge and without any repercussion from law enforcement for possession of illicit substances. At the 2014 festival, ANKORS performed 2,954 tests with about 30% negative results (i.e., the drug was not what it was sold to be), which prompted 190 people to dispose of their drugs entirely. With the services that ANKORS provides, the Shambhala music festival has seen just one death due to overdose since its establishment 18 years ago. Figure 5.10 depicts the whiteboard outside of the ANKORS tent warning attendees about misrepresented drugs.

## Prescription Drug Use

Historically, the use of street drugs and illicitly distributed substances has garnered the most attention regarding concerns about individual and societal harms. However, there are now indications that difficulties with the use of prescription medications have grown to become a very significant public health problem. Recent reports indicate that prescription drugs are the third most commonly misused substances in Canada after alcohol and marijuana with use rising dramatically from between 2011 and 2012 (the prevalence of prescription drug misuse increased from 3.2 percent to 6.5 percent over that period). Of particular concern is the rising misuse of prescription drugs among youth populations. In a recent Canadian survey, 5 percent of youth indicated having used prescription drugs for recreational purposes (Nasr & Phillips, 2014). There is evidence that prescription drugs have replaced traditional street drugs in major cities in Canada (Fischer et al., 2008). Prescription opioids, such as oxycodone and hydromorphone, are being prescribed more frequently than in the past for severe and chronic pain conditions, which are prevalent among the population. A sharp increase in accidental deaths and hospital admissions related to prescription opioid use has been found. A recent study found that accidental deaths in Ontario related to prescription opioid use doubled from 1991 to 2004, and prescription opioids may now be implicated in up to 50 percent of the total of the estimated 1,000–2,000 annual drug-related accidental deaths in Canada (Dhalla et al., 2009). Efforts are now underway to examine how to best approach control policies that may limit harms that accompany prescription drug use.

## Theoretical Models to Explain Substance Use Disorder

A wide variety of models have been proposed to explain why people become entrenched in patterns of harmful substance use. None have been proven to be correct and, in reality, there may not be a single explanatory model that can adequately explain the full spectrum of substance use disorder that is seen so commonly. (In Chapter 1, we noted that a recent Statistics Canada survey estimated that more than 21 percent of Canadians had substance use disorder in their lifetimes—and that is considered to be a gross underestimate of the true figure!) In his book on substance use and abuse, Csiernik (2016) has classified theories into four categories: the moral model, biological theories, psychological theories, and sociological theories, as shown in Figure 5.6.

Clearly, many diverse perspectives have been taken in efforts to explain addictive behaviour. One perspective that is now generally considered to be a relic of the past is that of the "moral model" and is widely scorned by experts in the field of addiction. The moral model is a belief system based on a dichotomous moral theory in which people are considered fully and individually responsible for their behavioural choices, which may be either good or bad. Those who choose good behaviour should be praised, whereas those who choose bad behaviour should be punished. Since addiction is a "bad habit," it follows that addicts should be punished. Much of the stigma faced by individuals with addiction problems is based on this underlying moral model that labels anyone with a "bad habit" as a "bad person." The downside of the moral model has become increasingly clear over the years. Alcohol prohibition (in the United States and Canada) failed to eliminate drinking behaviour but increased criminal activity through black market sales of alcohol. Programs that were once attempted in Canada requiring people addicted to heroin to undergo compulsory treatment were considered unsuccessful and were discontinued in the 1970s. The "War on Drugs" which was waged by the US has led to the highest incarceration rate in American history with little evidence of reduced illegal drug use as a result. People with addiction problems are stigmatized and are often demoralized by feelings of self-blame, shame, and guilt to the extent that they are unwilling or unable to seek help or treatment.

## The Impact of Substance Use in Canada

As we have described, substance use ranges widely from beneficial use, at one extreme, to profoundly harmful use, at the other. A scholarly effort to estimate the overall costs and harms to Canadian society of substance use has been undertaken by Rehm

**Table 5.1: Theories of addiction**

| The moral model | The moral model upholds that any drug use is inherently wrong and sinful, and addiction is a result of poor personal choices. There is no research evidence in support of this theory. |
|---|---|
| Biological theories | Biological theories attempt to find a chemical or physiological cause for addiction. These include:<br>• Disease (medical) model<br>• Neurobiology<br>• Genetic theory<br>• Brain dysfunction theory<br>• Biochemical theories<br>• Allergy theory |
| Psychological theories | Psychological theories focus on individuals' behaviour, and study how they are learned, modified, and reinforced. These theories include:<br>• Learning theory<br>• Personality theory<br>• Psychodynamic theory<br>• Humanistic theory<br>• Attachment theory<br>• Rational theory |
| Sociological theories | Sociological theories propose that addiction is influenced by socio-cultural events, and that politics, cultural norms, media, and how drugs are regulated in society should be considered. These include:<br>• Cultural theories<br>• Sub-cultural theories<br>• Deviant behaviour theory<br>• Marxist theory<br>• Availability-control theory<br>• Environmental stress theory |

*Source:* Adapted from Csiernik, R. (2016). *Substance use and abuse: Everything matters* (2nd ed.). Toronto: Canadian Scholars' Press.

and colleagues. They report that the burden to Canadian society is extremely high, with both direct impact on health care and criminal justice costs, and indirect losses of productivity resulting from disability and premature death. Based on 2002 data, the total annual cost of substance abuse in Canada was estimated to be $39.8 billion (Rehm et al., 2006).

The extraordinary harm, suffering, and loss that is associated with substance use has led to a variety of efforts and approaches to prevent such negative consequences and to reduce harms to individuals, families, and society. This text offers further discussion of the efforts that are in place in Canada to respond to substance use problems. In Chapter 12, we will discuss the treatments that have been developed for individuals having difficulties with substance use. In Chapter 15, we will address the approaches that are taken at populations and public-health levels by governments in Canada to minimize substance use and its associated harms.

## Your Own Substance Use

Since problematic substance use is so common, we encourage you to consider whether your own use of substances is generally healthy or whether there are times when you are using substances in less healthy ways. Whether it be caffeine, alcohol, cannabinoids, or one of the less commonly used (but often riskier and more dangerous) drugs, there is always a chance that you could end up experiencing problems if your pattern of use is less than healthy. Remember that people respond differently to the use of various substances and, for some people, any substance use can be unhealthy and problematic. If you think there are times when your substance use is potentially unhealthy, then we encourage you to review the section in Chapter 12 titled "Personal Mental Health Tool Kit," where we provide some recommendations about maintaining good mental health.

## Conclusion

It is clear that psychoactive substance use is very common and widespread throughout the Canadian population. Many psychoactive substances are derived from plant materials or are synthesized by chemical procedures. They exert their effects by binding to various receptors that modulate neuronal transmission in the brain and may result in mental stimulation, sedation, or cause changes in perception, cognition, mood, and behaviour. For the most part, judicious use of certain substances (e.g., having coffee or tea in the morning, or drinking small amounts of alcohol in social circumstances) can be innocuous or even beneficial. However, many people experience substantial harm as a result of substance use due to intoxication or physical or psychological dependence, or as victims of accidents or crimes that involve substance use.

We have provided brief descriptions of the substances that are most commonly used in Canada. Although specific substances exert characteristic effects on the human body and mind, there is considerable variation in individual responses. Additional recommended readings are listed at the end of this chapter for those who would like more information about the physiological, psychological, and social factors relevant to the substances discussed here, as well as about other substances that have not been mentioned.

## Glossary

**addiction:** The compulsive use of a substance despite its adverse consequences.

**dependence:** A state that develops once someone has used a substance for some time in which it becomes very difficult to stop use because of the physiological changes that have occurred.

**illicit substance use:** Substance use that is in contravention of existing laws and regulations.

**licit substance use:** Use of substances that are not regulated by prevailing laws and use of regulated substances in compliance with laws and regulations.

**psychological dependence:** Occurs when an individual experiences intense cravings, anxiety, irritability, or other feelings of distress when substance use is stopped.

**substance use disorder:** A pattern of behaviour that involves ongoing use of substances causing harm, either through detrimental physical or mental effects, or negative impact on the welfare of others.

**tolerance:** A state in which the body will need a higher dose of the substance to create the effects that a smaller dose would have previously.

**withdrawal:** A state in which the body experiences physical and mental symptoms that are often very uncomfortable when a substance is no longer used.

## Critical Thinking Questions

1. Substance use can be understood to occur across a wide spectrum. Describe each end of the spectrum and provide examples.
2. Discuss the concepts of dependence, tolerance, and withdrawal. How are they related?
3. How do psychological and environmental factors mediate the effect of psychoactive substances?
4. Define addiction and describe the impact it can have on an individual's life and well-being.
5. Select a substance commonly used in Canada and describe its characteristic effects on the human body.

## Recommended Readings

Csiernik, R. (2016). *Substance Use and Abuse: Everything Matters.* (2nd ed.). Toronto: Canadian Scholars' Press.

Gitlow, S. (Ed.). (2007). *Substance Use Disorders: A Practical Guide.* (2nd ed.). Philadelphia: Lippincott Williams & Wilkins.

Miller, W.R., & Carroll, K.M. (Eds.). (2012). *Rethinking Substance Abuse: What the Science Shows, and What We Should Do About It.* New York: Guilford Press.

## Recommended Websites

Canadian Centre on Substance Abuse. www.ccsa.ca/Eng/Pages/default.aspx

Health Canada. Drug Prevention and Treatment. www.hc-sc.gc.ca/hc-ps/drugs-drogues/index-eng.php

Here to Help. Alcohol and Other Drugs. www.heretohelp.bc.ca/self-help-resources

Public Health Agency of Canada. Substance Use/Addictions. www.phac-aspc.gc.ca/chn-rcs/saa-toxicomanie-eng.php?rd=substance_toxico_eng

## References

Asbridge, M., Hayden, J.A., & Cartwright, J.L. (2012). Acute cannabis consumption and motor vehicle collision risk: Systemic review of observational studies and meta-analysis. *British Medical Journal, 344*(2).

Barrowclough, C., Emsley, R., Eisner, E., Beardmore, R., & Wykes, T. (2013). Does change in cannabis use in established psychosis affect clinical outcome? *Schizophrenia Bulletin, 39*(2), 339–348.

Birak, K.S., Higgs, S., & Terry, P. (2011). Conditioned tolerance to the effects of alcohol on inhibitory control in humans. *Alcohol and Alcoholism (Oxford, Oxfordshire), 46*(6), 686–693. doi: 10.1093/alcalc/agr084

Canadian Community Epidemiology Network on Drug Use. (2015). Deaths involving fentanyl in Canada 2009–2014. Retrieved from www.ccsa.ca/Resource%20Library/CCSA-CCENDU-Fentanyl-Deaths-Canada-Bulletin-2015-en.pdf

Canadian Public Health Association. (2011). Too high a cost: A public health approach to alcohol policy in Canada. Retrieved from www.cpha.ca/uploads/positions/position-paper-alcohol_e.pdf

Collin, C. (2006). Substance abuse issues and public policy in Canada: IV. Prevalence of use and its consequences. Retrieved from www2.parl.gc.ca/Content/LOP/ResearchPublications/prb0619-e.htm#csolvent

Collins, A. (1998). *In the sleep room: The story of the CIA brainwashing experiments in Canada.* Toronto: Key Porter Books.

Csiernik, R. (2016). *Substance use and abuse: Everything matters* (2nd ed.). Toronto: Canadian Scholars' Press.

Dell, C.A., Seguin, M., Hopkins, C., Tempier, R., & Lewis, M. (2011). From benzos to berries: Treatment offered at an Aboriginal youth solvent abuse treatment centre relays the importance of culture. *Canadian Journal of Psychiatry, 56*(2), 75–83.

Dhalla, I., Mamdani, M., Sivilotti, M., Kopp, A., Qureshi, O., & Juurlink, D. (2009). Opioid analgesic prescribing and mortality before and after the introduction of long-acting oxycodone in Ontario. *Canadian Medical Association Journal*, 181(12), 891–896.

Fischer, B., Rehm, J., Goldman, B., & Popova, S. (2008). Non-medical use of prescription opioids and public health in Canada: An urgent call for research and interventions development. *Canadian Journal of Public Health/Revue canadienne de Santé publique*, 99(3), 182–184.

Fischer, B., Jeffries, V., Hall, W., Room, R., Goldner, E., & Rehm, J. (2011). Lower risk cannabis use guidelines for Canada (LRCUG): A narrative review of evidence and recommendations. *Canadian Journal of Public Health/Revue canadienne de Santé publique*, 102(5), 324–327. Retrieved from www.jstor.org/stable/41995624

Gore, F.M., Bloem, P., Patton, G.C., Ferguson, J., Joseph, V., Coffey, C., Sawyer, S.M., & Mathers, C.D. (2011). Global burden of disease in young people aged 10-24 years: A systematic analysis. *The Lancet*, 377(9783), 2093–2102.

Grescoe, T. (2013). High hopes: Why science is seeking a pardon for psychedelics. *The Globe and Mail*. Retrieved from www.theglobeandmail.com/technology/science/brain/high-hopes-why-science-is-seeking-a-pardon-for-psychedelics/article7529135/?page=all

Hall, W., Degenhardt, L., & Teesson, M. (2004). Cannabis use and psychotic disorders: An update. *Drug and Alcohol Review*, 23(4), 433–443.

Health Canada. (2012a). Canadian Alcohol and Drug Use Monitoring Survey 2012. Retrieved from www.hc-sc.gc.ca/hc-ps/drugs-drogues/stat/_2012/summary-sommaire-eng.php

Health Canada. (2012b). Federal tobacco control strategy. Retrieved from www.hc-sc.gc.ca/ahc-asc/alt_formats/pdf/performance/eval/ftcs-evaluation-sflt-eng.pdf

Hoffman, A. (1980). *LSD: My problem child*. New York: McGraw-Hill.

Keller, C., Goering, P., Hume, C., Macnaughton, E., O'Campo, P., Sarang, A., Thomson, M., Vallee, C., Watson, A., & Tsemberis, S. (2013). Initial implementation of Housing First in five Canadian cities: How do you make the shoe fit, when one size does not fit all? *American Journal of Psychiatric Rehabilitation*, 16(4), 275–289.

Kuepper, R., van Os, J., Roselind, L., Hans-Ulrich, W., Hofler, M., & Henquet, C. (2011). Continued cannabis use and risk of incidence and persistence of psychotic symptoms: 10-year follow-up cohort study. *British Medical Journal*, 342(7796). doi: http://dx.doi.org/10.1136/bmj.d738

Li, D., Zhao, H., & Gelernter, J. (2012). Strong protective effect of the aldehyde dehydrogenase gene (ALDH2) 504lys (2) allele against alcoholism and alcohol-induced medical diseases in Asians. *Human Genetics*, 131(5), 725–737.

McCoy, A.W. (2004). The stimulus of prohibition: A critical history of the global narcotics trade. In M.K. Steinberg, J.J. Hobbs, & K. Mathewson (Eds.), *Dangerous harvest: Drug plants and the transformation of indigenous landscapes* (pp. 24–111). New York: Oxford University Press.

McGrath, J., Welham, J., Scott, J., Varghese, D., Degenhardt, L., Hayatbakhsh, M.R., Alati, R., Williams, G.M., Bor, W., & Najman, J.M. (2010). Association between cannabis use and psychosis-related outcomes using sibling pair analysis in a cohort of young adults. *Archives of General Psychiatry,* 67(5), 440–447.

Moffat, B.M., Jenkins, E.K., & Johnson, J.L. (2013). Weeding out the information: An ethnographic approach to exploring how young people make sense of the evidence on cannabis. *Harm Reduction Journal,* 10(1), 2–9.

Nasr, W., & Phillips, K. (2014). Current issues in mental health in Canada: Directions in federal substance abuse policy. *Library of Parliament Research Publications.* Retrieved from www.parl.gc.ca/Content/LOP/ResearchPublications/2014-06-e. htm

National Institute on Drug Abuse. (2008). Research report series: Methamphetamine abuse and addiction. Retrieved from www.drugabuse.gov/Researchreports/ Methamph/methamph3.html

Pletcher, M.J., Vittinghoff, E., Kalhan, R., Richman, J., Safford, M., Sidney, S., Lin, F., & Kertesz, S. (2012). Association between marijuana exposure and pulmonary function over 20 years. *Journal of the American Medical Association,* 307(2), 173–181.

Preston, K.L., & Epstein, D.H. (2011). Stress in the daily lives of cocaine and heroin users: Relationship to mood, craving, relapse triggers, and cocaine use. *Psychopharmacology,* 218(1), 29–37.

Rehm, J., Baliunas, D., Brochu, S., Fischer, B., Gnam, W., Patra, J., Popova, S., Sarnocinska-Hart, A., & Taylor, B. (2006). The costs of substance abuse in Canada 2002. Retrieved from www.ccsa.ca/resource%20library/ccsa-011332-2006.pdf

Robins, L.N., Helzer, J.E., & Davis, D.H. (1975). Narcotic use in Southeast Asia and afterward: An interview study of 898 Vietnam returnees. *Archives of General Psychiatry,* 32(8), 955–961.

Solowij, N., Stephens, R.S., Roffman, R.A., Babor, T., Kadden, R., Miller, M., Christiansen, K., McRee, B., & Vendetti, J. (2002). Cognitive functioning of long-term heavy cannabis users seeking treatment. *Journal of the American Medical Association,* 287(9), 1123–1131.

Toumbourou, J.W., Stockwell, T., Neighbors, C., Marlatt, G.A., Sturge, J., & Rehm, J. (2007). Interventions to reduce harm associated with adolescent substance use. *The Lancet,* 369(9570), 1323–1325.

World Health Organization. (2011). Global status report on alcohol and health. Retrieved from www.who.int/substance_abuse/publications/global_alcohol_ report/msbgsruprofiles.pdf

World Health Organization. (2015). Tobacco: Key facts. Retrieved from www.who. int/mediacentre/factsheets/fs339/en/

# Chapter 6

# STIGMA, DISCRIMINATION, AND MENTAL HEALTH IN THE WORKPLACE

Mental illness is nothing to be ashamed of, but stigma and bias shame us all.
—Bill Clinton (42nd US President)

## Introduction

We begin this chapter by examining stigma and discrimination as manifested toward people with mental illness. The Canadian Mental Health Association has long proclaimed that people with mental health problems want the same things in their lives as everyone else, that is, a home, friends, and a job. Stigma and discrimination toward people with mental illness can interfere with all of these basic elements of a person's life. In this chapter, we also deal more broadly with mental health issues in the workplace, addressing the intricate relationship between work and mental health in Canada.

## Stigma and Discrimination

For some people with mental health problems, the stigma and discrimination they experience cause as much, if not more, suffering than the mental health problem itself. **Stigma** can be defined as "a mark of disgrace" or an "attribute that is deeply discrediting" (Link & Phelan, 2001). "Stigma is the situation of the individual who is disqualified from full social acceptance" (Goffman, 1963). The stigmatized individual is "reduced in our minds from a whole and usual person to a tainted, discounted one" (Goffman, 1963). For the most part, stigma results from **prejudicial attitudes**, i.e., unreasonable attitudes that are resistant to rational influence. For example, someone labelled "mentally ill" can be stereotyped as being unpredictable, dangerous, or potentially violent when under stress, and such stereotyping can lead employers to exclude people who have had a mental illness from employment. **Discrimination** has been defined by legal scholars and is generally understood to be "the making of an unjustified distinction [among people] on the basis of a forbidden ground" (Makkonen, 2002), for example, on the basis of gender, ethnicity, age, or disability. However, it is important to note that not all distinctions are considered to be discriminatory. Some distinctions may be deemed to be justifiable as in the following example: "It has been held to be legitimate to impose a minimum age for voting in [national elections]. While this involves differential treatment on the basis of age, it has been held to have an objective and reasonable justification because of the level of maturity that the meaningful exercise of such a political right requires" (Makkonen, 2002).

---

**Box 6.1: The 2006 Canadian Senate Report, *Out of the Shadows at Last***

When Michael Kirby (who was later appointed as the first Chair of the Mental Health Commission of Canada) was a member of the Canadian Senate, he led a committee of senators in a nationwide investigation of mental health in Canada. They were dismayed to hear a large number of personal accounts of profound stigma and discrimination experienced by people with mental health problems. The following excerpts from the Senate Report, *Out of the Shadows at Last* (Kirby & Keon, 2006), recount two of the many heartbreaking stories:

> Broken. Lonely. Hopeless. Ashamed. Rejected. Isolated. Afraid. Unsupported. Lost. Anxious. Disbelieved. Overwhelmed. Embarrassed. Dark. Pained. Desperate. Fading.
>
> I'm a 31-year-old Canadian woman who has been fighting the disease of Depression since my late teenage years. The words above are words that come to my mind when I think of what it's like to live as a Canadian in Canada with Mental Illness. It's pretty sad when you sit around wishing you had any (literally ANY) other disease other than a Mental Illness. There is so much shame, stigma and disbelief that accompany a diagnosis of a mental illness. It's the constant justification that you're actually sick. Why do we who suffer with this debilitating disease have to suffer socially as well?—Kim. (p. 15)

> I was a counsellor, I was a substitute teacher, I was a day-care worker, I worked in a women's shelter, but once they labelled me "mentally ill" I lost all credibility.—Ruth Johnson. (p. 15)

Stigma and discrimination are often prominent in the negative response and resistance that emerge when efforts are made to provide housing for people with mental health problems, as described in the following testimony to the Senate Committee:

> In the process of advocating for more supportive housing, often we must fight NIMBYism, Not In My Backyard; the stigma of mental illness; and zoning bylaws that discriminate against supportive housing. The homeless and mentally ill also have a

right to live wherever they want, like anybody else. Nobody has a right to prevent us from living in their neighbourhood. This is blatant discrimination and a flagrant violation of human rights. How would anybody in this room like it if somebody came up to you and said, "We do not want you living in our neighbourhood"? It does not matter why they say it to you; it is wrong. People are not allowed to prevent Blacks, gays or Jews from living in their neighbourhood because it is considered a hate crime and they should not be allowed to do this to the homeless and mentally ill either. Nobody is criticizing us because of anything we have done wrong. They are criticizing us out of fear and ignorance.—Phillip Dufresne. (p. 12).

*Source*: Kirby, M. J. L. & Keon, W. J. (2006). *Out of the shadows at last: Transforming mental health, mental illness and addiction services in Canada*. Ottawa: The Standing Senate Committee on Social Affairs, Science and Technology.

**Figure 6.1:** Child protesters outside a former extended care facility, joining the protest against turning it into a rehabilitation unit for people with mental illness, 2004.

*Source: The Star* (2004), Sheffield Newspapers

It is easy to notice prominent acts of discrimination, such as racist attacks or protest, but it has been argued that it is the subtle **microaggressions**, that is, everyday minor incidents and slights, and the perception that society is discriminatory, that have a more significant impact on an individual's health (Sue, 2010). Often, these subtle manifestations of stigma and discrimination become incorporated into the "norms" of society and lead to self-stigma and self-discrimination. An individual feels unworthy or guilty, leading to a lack of self-worth and depression as well as abnormal behaviour, such as self-isolation, avoidance behaviour, and introversion (Baral, Kariki, & Newell, 2007).

## *Causes of Stigma and Discrimination*

Negative depictions of people with mental illness in the media are often blamed for perpetuating the harmful stereotypes that underlie stigma and discrimination. Film and television portray the mentally ill as uncontrollable, dangerous misfits. Sensationalist news reports frequently draw attention to rare events that frighten readers and perpetuate the pejorative labelling of "crazies," "psychos," and "lunatics." Although such irresponsible treatment of mental illness in the media contributes to harmful stereotyping, the roots of stigma and discrimination can be found at a deeper level within our psyches and our societies. Negative media images and depictions are often a reflection of insidious fears and prejudices concealed within us.

In trying to understand the roots of prejudice and discrimination, scientists have found that, no matter how open-minded any of us may be, we *all* hold stereotyped beliefs and attitudes about sensitive topics such as race, religion, gender, age, sexuality, skin tone, weight, and disability.

It is likely that, on an evolutionary basis, we are programmed to be wary of people who appear different from ourselves. Humans have a need to feel part of a group, such as a village, clan, team, peer group, or ethnic group; this is described by social psychologists as "in-group/out-group dynamics." Stereotypes about members of an out-group may emerge from an unconscious need for us to differentiate people in other groups to contain potential threats and protect ourselves. If we consider the theories of the psychoanalyst Alfred Adler (whose ideas are mentioned in Chapter 3), then each of us is unconsciously protecting ourselves against feelings of inferiority, frequently searching for ways to feel superior to others in order to maintain our own self-esteem. This is often seen in the amusing interactions of young children when they proclaim: "My toy is better than yours," or "My dad is stronger than yours." As adults, we are more adept at concealing our deep-seated need to feel superior, but it drives our attitudes and behaviours nevertheless.

Clearly, the attitudes and behaviours we hold about an out-group are greatly influenced by social environments. We are likely to be influenced by prejudicial attitudes that are normative in the societies in which we live. White people living in the southeast of the United States in the 1950s were likely to consider it normal to hold attitudes and beliefs about African Americans that would now be considered bigoted, racist, and deplorable. Political and social theorists have noted that economic

**Figure 6.2:** *The Crazies*

*Source:* Overture Films

factors often drive prejudicial attitudes and behaviours. Historians consider one of the factors that contributed to the infamous anti-Semitism (i.e., hatred of Jewish people) in Nazi Germany to have been the economic hardship experienced by Germans before the Second World War. Social scientists have shown that prejudice, bigotry, and discrimination increase when money, jobs, and resources are scarce (Quillian, 1995; Whitley & Kite, 2009). The horrific torture, cruelty, and inhumanity of the Nazi Holocaust serve as a lesson about how powerful and dangerous the forces of prejudice and bigotry become when they are multiplied and spread throughout a society. That such atrocities could occur in a highly developed, educated, and cultured society should give all of us pause and force us to examine the prejudice and discrimination present in our own society.

Despite the deep roots of stigma and discrimination in the human psyche and society, negative attitudes, beliefs, and behaviours can be changed, and most of us work actively to eradicate them when we are aware of their existence. In order to

**Figure 6.3:** A photo still after the execution of Serbs, with Nazi soldiers in the foreground. Other Serbs are seen looking on at the pitiful scene that is to serve as a brutal demonstration of Nazi power.

*Source*: GetStock/topham Picture Point

do so, we must overcome the irrational thinking that underlies stereotypes. Many stereotypes are associated with a fact that is blown out of proportion and taken to irrational conclusions. For example, it is true that some people with mental illnesses can commit violent acts, however, these are rare events. The vast majority of people with mental illnesses will be no more likely to commit violent acts than anyone else. We will find that this type of irrational thinking is a very common human fallibility.

## *Foci of Stigma and Discrimination*

In addition to stigma and discrimination toward people with mental illnesses in general, there are particular groups who are targeted selectively. People with schizophrenia and other psychotic illnesses are often depicted as frightening, dangerous individuals. Yet, most are not dangerous at all and are frightening only for those who do not understand the illness. This is unfortunate because many people with schizophrenia and other psychotic disorders can make impressive recoveries, particularly when they receive good treatment and support early on. But recovery is hindered when they feel shunned and feared by those around them.

People with substance use problems experience particularly vehement stigma and discrimination. There is often little sympathy for those who struggle with substance use problems, and they are commonly blamed for producing their own misery and considered to have "weak morals."

People who belong to more than one stigmatized group are particularly prone to experience prejudice and discrimination. For example, Canadian Aboriginal people who have mental health or substance use problems are likely to be treated badly. People with mental health problems have expressed disappointment about the stigma they experience at the hands of health care providers. Commonly, they feel that physicians, nurses, emergency health care workers, and others disregard their physical health problems, attributing their suffering to mental health conditions. Studies have shown that mental health care providers are not immune to stigma and discrimination toward people with mental illness (Schulze, 2007; Thornicroft, Rose, & Kassam, 2007).

## *Combating Stigma and Discrimination*

While much research is needed to improve our knowledge of stigma reduction, it has been found that stigma is typically reduced when people have increased contact with persons with mental illness, especially hearing about their personal experiences (Corrigan & O'Shaughnessy, 2007; Kolodziej & Johnson, 1996; Pinfold et al., 2005). Studies have also found that large-scale public campaigns to increase awareness and educate people about mental illness can be very effective (Goldney & Fisher, 2008).

Graham Thornicroft and his colleagues have suggested shifting to a focus on policies regarding discrimination against individuals dealing with mental wellness, with the implementation of anti-discrimination laws and policies similar to those that protect people with physical disabilities (Thornicroft et al., 2007). As Timo Makkonen has stated: "Discrimination runs against the most fundamental values of a modern society.... Law is one of the most, if not the most important tool in the fight against discrimination. Hence it is essential that there exists laws against discrimination and that those laws are duly implemented" (Makkonen, 2002).

## *Stigma and Discrimination in the Workplace*

It is especially important to understand the impact of stigma and discrimination in the workplace because individuals with mental health conditions may find themselves unfairly excluded from participating in the work force or subject to unfounded mistrust and rejection by co-workers. Given the central role of occupational function in our society, barriers to occupational participation can have devastating effects on an individual's quality of life and self-esteem.

Although it is certainly true that mental illness may have negative effects on an individual's ability to function in the work setting, it is also true that employers frequently have exaggerated fears about the risks of hiring an individual currently suffering from, or with a history of, mental health conditions. In surveys, employers express unrealistic perceptions that individuals with mental health conditions are simply unable to perform in a work situation and therefore hiring such an individual would represent a threat to the organization, reducing productivity and profitability. The reality of mental illness simply does not support this degree of pessimism, which represents one of the most powerful manifestations of stigma against those with mental health problems. An individual who cannot enter or remain in the work force will be considerably hampered in participating as a full member of society. Furthermore, paid employment enhances mental health by promoting the development of social and occupational skills, as well as raising the individual's financial well-being.

As a result of discrimination against individuals who have had mental health problems, it is common for individuals to conceal such conditions. This can result in a high-frequency of unrecognized and untreated mental health conditions, thereby increasing suffering by employees, negatively affecting productivity, and removing the possibility of early intervention to identify and deal with mental health problems before they cause disability. Given the substantial costs of disability (see below), employers may well be causing themselves more expense and difficulty.

# Mental Health and the Workplace

Over the last decade, there has been a great deal of attention given to ways in which mental health difficulties of employees may affect their work function as well as ways in which characteristics of the workplace may affect the mental health of employees. In the following discussions about how to improve mental health, we will discuss both opportunities to enhance the workplace and approaches geared to helping individuals with their mental health in relation to work.

Mental health problems, whether diagnosable psychiatric disorders or less intense psychological difficulties, may impact an individual's capacity to carry out his or her occupational roles (OECD, 2015). What follows is a description of how these impacts typically manifest.

*Presenteeism.* The employee shows up at work and carries out the basic duties of the job but performs at a much lower level, with poor concentration, forgetfulness, reduced judgment, and less effective problem solving. This results in reduced productivity, increased errors, more workplace accidents, and difficulties with workload management.

*Absenteeism.* The employee takes many sickness days and is repeatedly absent for short periods of time (when suffering from the effects of mood, anxiety, or excessive drinking).

*Poor attitude.* The employee experiences a loss of motivation and feels uncommitted, demoralized, and exhausted—a state referred to as "burnout." Burnout is often associated with presenteeism and may cause a high rate of turnover. When highly skilled and experienced employees leave because of burnout, the cost of recruiting and retraining new employees is substantial.

*Conflict with co-workers or supervisors.* Conflict that is very intense or unresolved over time will have a very negative effect on the workplace—it can create a "toxic" environment where many workers suffer high stress and will be at increased risk for mental health problems.

## Workplace Psychological Risk Factors

A number of **workplace psychological risk factors** have been identified. The presence of these factors increases the likelihood that employees will develop common mental health problems such as depression, anxiety, or excessive substance use. This is not to say that all mental health problems are caused by work stress; clearly, employees bring their own vulnerabilities, mental health difficulties, and personal life problems into the work situation, and it would be unreasonable and unfair to blame workplaces for all psychological problems experienced by employees. But, in many cases, workplace stress contributes significantly to employee mental health problems, whether substantially causing the problem or triggering a pre-existing vulnerability. An example of a workplace psychological risk factor is an extreme lack of control over the flow or sequencing of work tasks. This might increase employees' experienced stress and leave them feeling out of control, which in turn would increase their vulnerability to becoming depressed or anxious.

Each workplace has its own profile of risk factors. Think of jobs you've had: maybe in one job, the boss had a bullying manner that was upsetting for many employees; in another job, it was unclear what exactly you were supposed to be doing; in yet another, a co-worker always passed off work to others, causing intense resentment. And, if several risk factors are highly active at the same time (a bullying boss in a workplace where task requirements are unclear and some workers aren't doing their part), the stress employees experience can be immense! This level of stress raises the likelihood that employees will develop mental health problems.

Figure 6.4: Employees who feel they have little control in the work environment experience greater levels of mental health problems than those who have a sense of autonomy.

*Source*: David H. Lewis/iStockphoto

Within the sociological literature on disability due to health conditions, the concept of a "disabling environment" has been proposed (Siebers, 2008), referring to a physical environment that imposes barriers to access or otherwise impedes an individual's function: "Disability is not a personal defect or deficiency ... it may be primarily the product of a disabling environment" (Hahn, 1991). This may also be applied to mental health problems emerging in a specific workplace environment; if the workplace environment is harsh and unsupportive, it may trigger mental health conditions and resultant disabilities in employees. The usual approach is to label the troubled employees as "ill" or "disabled," in effect stigmatizing them, rather than focusing on disabling or illness-promoting aspects of the workplace environment.

But note that risk factors may also be expressed as *positive* features of the work situation. Instead of speaking of excessive work demand, we could speak of "manageable workload"; instead of bullying management style, we could speak of "supportive leadership." This emphasis on positive factors that are protective of employee mental health is consistent with the broader shift to positive psychology, which insists that it is essential to identify strengths and virtues to be enhanced, rather than only flaws and problems to be overcome (we return to this discussion in Chapter 15).

---

**Box 6.2: Protective Factors for Psychological Health and Safety in the Workplace**

Here are some protective factors for psychological health and safety in the workplace, taken from a workplace survey, Guarding Minds @ Work. These factors are ones that help to protect against mental health problems in workers—when they are insufficiently present in the workplace, psychological risk is increased.

**Organizational Culture:** A work environment characterized by trust, honesty, and fairness.

**Recognition and Reward:** There is appropriate acknowledgment and appreciation of employees' efforts.

**Involvement and Influence:** Employees are included in discussions about how their work is done and how important decisions are made.

**Workload Management:** Tasks and responsibilities can be accomplished successfully within the time available.

**Engagement:** Employees enjoy and feel connected to their work and feel motivated to do their jobs well.

**Balance:** There is recognition of the need for balance between the demands of work, family, and personal life.

*Source:* Guarding Minds @ Work. Gilbert, Bilsker, Shain & Samra, 2012.

---

By maximizing these protective factors, organizations can have a positive effect on their employees' mental health. Organizational policies can focus on recognizing mental health problems at an early stage and ensuring that employees have access to appropriate intervention. An example of this might be a program to train managers to recognize the first signs of depression and arrange access to psychological or medical treatment.

But why would organizations, focused on increasing profitability and productivity, want to invest time and money in reducing psychological risks? There are three motivating reasons for employers to make the commitment to enhancing mental health in their workplaces.

First, most employers feel a sense of responsibility for the physical and psychological safety of their employees. Just as most employers would be alarmed to discover a poorly maintained and physically dangerous piece of machinery in the workplace, they would be alarmed to discover that their employees are subject to psychologically dangerous conditions (e.g., harassment from an intimidating boss, unrealistic work demands leading to neglect of family responsibilities, etc.) likely to trigger mental health problems.

Second, there has been a steady increase in the legal and regulatory requirements on employers to ensure the psychological safety of their workers. Employers have been found legally responsible for maintaining workplaces that contributed to employees' "mental injury"—and therefore liable for large financial penalties. Employers are increasingly seen as having a "duty of care" to keep their workers safe, physically *and* mentally, while on the job.

An alternative to the legal or regulatory approach is that taken by the Mental Health Commission of Canada, which has developed the National Standard on Psychological Health and Safety in the Workplace (Mental Health Commission of Canada, 2015). This is a voluntary standard meant to serve as both:

- a strong statement that organizations should be addressing psychological health and safety, and
- a tool to make it easier for organizations to take action to prevent psychological injury, reduce psychological risk, and promote psychologically healthier workplaces.

The standard was released in 2013. In a bold experiment, the Mental Health Commission of Canada then secured the participation of 40 Canadian organizations, ranging from a small public library to a national telecommunications organization, to implement the standard while being evaluated (Mental Health Commission of Canada, 2015). Evaluation of each organization's journey has been *formative* in nature: that is, focused on the process of change rather than on outcomes, allowing ongoing innovation, feedback to the organizations, and refinement of their implementation plan (Dehar, Casswell, & Duignan, 1993). Findings from this implementation project will be shared across Canada, helping to raise awareness and show organizations how they can take action.

The third motivating reason for employers to make the commitment to enhance mental health in their workplaces is that it is a financially sound decision (Global Business and Economic Roundtable on Addictions and Mental Health, 2000; Mental Health International, 2013). Assuming that employers have decided to address psychological risk factors in their workplaces, how do they go about it? In Canada, the recently developed free on-line tool Guarding Minds @ Work enables employers to measure the protective factors we described above. After employee groups have completed the survey, profiles are provided to employers, giving scores for each factor and indicating which factors are minimal, moderate, or serious concerns. Based on the profiles, action plans are produced, suggesting actions to improve the psychological safety and health of the workplaces and workers.

In the above section, we have discussed ways in which workplaces can promote and support good mental health. In the following, we want to emphasize ways in which the mental health of individuals may relate to their work. Most people will experience mild or moderate mental health problems at some time in their working lives, often temporary, but sometimes recurring. Often these periods co-occur with stressors or life events that can destabilize equilibrium and overcome usual defences. Life events such as deaths, loss, divorce, interpersonal conflicts, and physical health problems are commonly associated with temporary or ongoing problems.

We can view the connection between individual mental health and the workplace as a relationship. On one hand, each person enters the work environment with certain vulnerabilities associated with his or her own biological or psychological makeup, as well as past experiences and stresses in his or her current life situation, and so forth. On the other hand, work settings are associated with fluctuating levels of stress. When workplace stress increases subtly or uncontrollably, the individual worker may develop a mental health problem—for example, someone who tends to use alcohol as a means to manage stress might increase alcohol consumption, which in turn affects his or her job performance and increases workplace stress, and so on. In the early stages of workers developing mental health problems, low-intensity interventions—such as problem solving in conjunction with occupational health professionals or support for mood self-management—can be very helpful. A workbook specifically designed to foster self-management in workers suffering from mood difficulties is Antidepressant Skills @ Work (Centre for Applied Research in Mental Health and Addiction, 2015).

## Short-Term Disability Absence

Individuals who are unable to maintain occupational function as a result of common mental health problems may take a period of short-term disability absence, typically from 1 to 3 months. Deciding whether to take a work absence related to mental health problems, and for how long, is complicated. There are significant advantages and disadvantages to be considered (see Table 6.1). This decision should be made through collaborative problem solving between the individual and his or her health care provider, usually the family physician, by carefully weighing the pros and cons of extended absence from the workplace (Bilsker, Wiseman, & Gilbert, 2006).

**Table 6.1: Benefits and costs of work absence**

| Benefits of work absence | Costs of work absence |
| --- | --- |
| • Removed from occupational stresses<br>• More time to engage in activities conducive to recovery<br>• Less risk of workplace safety incidents | • Inactivity/withdrawal<br>• Social isolation<br>• Secondary anxiety regarding workplace<br>• Prolonged absence is negative prognostic factor regarding whether an individual ever returns to work |

If the short-term disability absence goes well, the individual will receive appropriate support from the health care system, as well as family or friends, and will gradually recover in mood and in the ability to function in the workplace. If it does not go well, the individual will become more discouraged and inactive, retreating from social contact and slipping into more profound depression and anxiety. In addition to medication treatment for psychiatric symptomatology in some cases, cognitive behavioural treatment focused on teaching improved skills for coping with difficult workplace environments, interpersonal conflict, fluctuating work demands, and so forth, can be extremely helpful. Unfortunately, behavioural interventions are infrequently provided.

At some point, a return-to-work will be undertaken. The return-to-work may include some form of accommodation by the employer, that is, an adjustment in the employee's working conditions to allow for particular difficulties related to the return-to-work following a health problem.

> Employers have a duty to accommodate employees with disabilities if the accommodation will allow them to perform the requirements of the job. There is no limit on the types of accommodation that may be requested. Accommodation can include providing a quiet workspace for a person who is easily distracted, or permitting a person to change their break time if they are required to eat when taking medication. (Canadian Mental Health Association, 2007, p. 14)

Although workplace accommodations are very helpful, it remains true that returning to work following a period of mental health-related disability is often quite stressful. The returning employee may feel embarrassed, self-doubting, and uncomfortably aware that other employees have picked up his or her workload. While most employees are able to successfully return to work, some experience recurrence of their mental health problems, especially if they do not receive support, such as ongoing psychotherapy, during the return-to-work process.

Individuals who do not recover within a relatively short time frame may go on long-term disability, which may last many months or even years. Unless individuals are provided with intensive intervention, as well as support for recovering a sense of occupational confidence and competence, there is a risk of extended or even permanent occupational disability (Gensby et al., 2012; Tschernetzki-Neilson et al., 2007).

## Clinical Management of Work-Related Mental Health Problems

The current approach to work-related mental health problems focuses on providing the following:

*Short-term absence for individuals considered to be suffering the effects of "stress," with the assumption that simply being away from work will rectify this problem.* As discussed above, being away from work for weeks or months with no therapeutic support or recovery plan may actually intensify feelings of inadequacy, worry, and depression.

*Medical treatment, primarily pharmacological.* Medication such as antidepressants or anxiolytics can significantly reduce symptoms and are often very helpful in recovery of work function. However, in a significant minority of cases, side-effects of the medications themselves have a negative effect upon work function—for example, the level of anxiety medication needed to control obsessional worry might also cause considerable sedation, impairing the capacity of an ambulance dispatcher or airline pilot to make critical decisions.

*Counselling or psychotherapy.* This form of intervention can help individuals to overcome psychological symptoms, deal with personal issues, and solve problems in the workplace. However, if this intervention provides only reassurance, emotional exploration, or focus on childhood experiences, there may be a failure to address crucial workplace issues and teach practical strategies for coping more effectively with work and personal stresses. Current research indicates that the most effective approach to managing work-related mental health problems is a cognitive-behavioural one. This emphasizes a number of practical skills (problem solving, activation, goal setting, realistic thinking, etc.) that are highly relevant to the restoration of occupational function. To be most effective, interventions should focus on particular issues affecting this person's occupational function: deficits in coping skills, acute or chronic stressors, mismatch between employee characteristics and job requirements, and so on.

Note that we have been focusing on common mental health problems such as depression, anxiety, and substance use. But severe mental illnesses such as schizophrenia raise a different set of issues. These illnesses cause substantial impairment of work capacity while symptoms are active—it's easy to see that someone experiencing paranoid delusions would have difficulty carrying out job-related tasks or collaborating with co-workers. However, when symptoms are brought under control via treatment and rehabilitation efforts, the individual can be a highly productive employee. Alternatively, it may be necessary to help this individual find a different kind of employment that is more compatible with ongoing mental symptoms. Supported employment has proven to be a powerful intervention for individuals with severe mental illness, enabling them to contribute to society while gaining the beneficial effects of employment on self-esteem, social connection, and financial security. Other approaches to integrate people with severe mental illness have been devised. Social enterprises are initiatives in which groups of people with disabilities are assisted in operating a commercial enterprise, such as restaurants or stores. Promising efforts in developing social enterprises and other work integration activities for people with severe mental illnesses have begun in Canada, and these require increased development and exploration (Corbière et al., 2010).

# Conclusion

Stigma and discrimination play a substantial role in the suffering and exclusion experienced by people with mental health problems. The roots of stigma and prejudice may run deep, fed by fear and misinformation. It has been recommended that actions should seek to address discrimination through legal and policy means, in cohesion with efforts to protect other disabled individuals. Stigma can be diminished by increased exposure to people living with mental health problems and expanded efforts at enhancing understanding and compassion.

There is enormous potential for limiting the negative impact of mental health problems upon occupational function. This would require implementation of programs to reduce workplace stigma, enhance employee coping skills, provide sophisticated organizational and health care response to mental health problems in their early stages, improve access to clinical assessment and treatment focused on restoration of work function, and so on. Implementing these programs at a population level so that they are available to the majority of Canadian workers (rather than to the small minority employed by innovative organizations) would have measurable benefits in reducing individual suffering, increasing corporate productivity, and relieving the immense social burden of mental health-related disability.

# Glossary

**discrimination:** The making of an unjustified distinction among people on the basis of a forbidden ground, such as gender, ethnicity, age, or disability.
**microaggressions:** Everyday minor incidents and slights.
**prejudicial attitudes:** Unreasonable attitudes that are resistant to rational influence.
**stigma:** A mark or sign of disgrace, infamy, or reproach when a person is identified by a label that sets the person apart and links the person to undesirable stereotypes that result in unfair treatment and discrimination.
**workplace psychological risk factors:** Workplace characteristics shown to increase the probability that employees will develop mental health problems.

# Critical Thinking Questions

1. Describe ways in which people with mental health problems experience stigma and discrimination.
2. What are the roots of stigma and discrimination?
3. How do mental health problems manifest in the workplace?
4. Describe the three reasons motivating employers to commit to enhancing mental health in the workplace.
5. What are the current approaches to treating work-related mental health problems?

## Recommended Readings

Corrigan, P.W., Roe, D., & Tsang, H.W.H. (2011). *Challenging the Stigma of Mental Illness: Lessons for Therapists and Advocates.* Chichester, UK: John Wiley & Sons.

Gold, L.H., & Shuma, D.W. (2009). *Evaluating Mental Health Disability in the Workplace: Model, Process, and Analysis.* New York: Springer.

Mor Barak, M.E. (2013). *Managing Diversity: Toward a Globally Inclusive Workplace.* Los Angeles: SAGE Publications.

Thiederman, S.B. (2008). *Making Diversity Work: 7 Steps for Defeating Bias in the Workplace.* New York: Kaplan.

Thornicroft, G. (2006). *Shunned: Discrimination Against People with Mental Illness.* Oxford: Oxford University Press.

## Recommended Websites

Boston University Center for Psychiatric Rehabilitation. Living Well with a Psychiatric Disability in Work and School. http://cpr.bu.edu

Centre for Global Mental Health, London. Stigma and Discrimination. www.centreforglobalmentalhealth.org/index.php?option=com_content&view=article&id=62&Itemid=68

Great-West Life Centre for Mental Health in the Workplace. www.gwlcentreformental health.com/index.asp

Time to Change: Let's End Mental Health Discrimination. www.time-to-change.org.uk/

Trimbos Institute, Utrecht, The Netherlands. Mental Health in Workplace Settings. www.trimbos.org/onderwerpen/mental-health/mental-health-in-workplace-settings

## References

Baral, S.C., Kariki, D.K., & Newell, J.N. (2007). Causes of stigma and discrimination associated with tuberculosis in Nepal: A qualitative study. *BMC Public Health, 7,* 211. Retrieved from www.biomedcentral.com/1471-2458/7/211

Bilsker, D., Wiseman, S., & Gilbert, M. (2006). Managing depression-related occupational disability: A pragmatic approach. *Canadian Journal of Psychiatry, 51,* 76–83.

Canadian Mental Health Association. (2007). *Mental health works: Complex issues, clear solutions; Workplace resource.* Toronto: Canadian Mental Health Association. Retrieved from https://www.workplacestrategiesformentalhealth.com/pdf/s7_004915.pdf

Centre for Applied Research in Mental Health and Addiction. (2015). Tools and resources. Retrieved from www.sfu.ca/carmha/toolsandresources.html

Corbière, M., Lanctôt, N., Lecomte, T., Latimer, E., Goering, P., Kirsh, B., Goldner, E.M., Reinharz, D., Menear, M., Mizevich, J., & Kamagiannis, T. (2010). A pan-Canadian evaluation of supported employment programs dedicated to people with severe mental disorders. *Community Mental Health Journal, 46*(1), 44–55.

Corrigan, P.W., & O'Shaughnessy, J.R. (2007). Changing mental illness stigma as it exists in the real world. *Australian Psychologist, 42*, 90–97.

Dehar, M.A., Casswell, S., & Duignan, P. (1993). Formative and process evaluation of health promotion and disease prevention programs. *Evaluation Review, 17*(2), 204–220.

Gensby, U., Lund, T., Kowalski, K., Saidj, M., Jørgensen, A.M.K., Filges, T., Irvin, E., Amick III, B.C., & Labriola, M. (2012). Workplace disability management programs promoting return to work: A systematic review. *Campbell Systematic Reviews, 8*(17), 220–241.

Global Business and Economic Roundtable on Addictions and Mental Health. (2000). *Unheralded global business crisis: Worldwide mental health problems burning like wildfire in global economy.* Retrieved from www.mentalhealthroundtable.ca/aug_round_pdfs/Geneva%20Report%20October2.pdf

Goldney, R.D., & Fisher, L.J. (2008). Have broad-based community and professional education programs influenced mental health literacy and treatment seeking of those with major depression and suicidal ideation? *Suicide and Life-Threatening Behavior, 38*(2), 129–142.

Goffman, E. (1963). *Stigma: Notes on the management of spoiled identity.* New York: Simon and Shuster.

Guarding Minds @ Work. (2012). Guarding minds @ work: A workplace guide to psychological health and safety. Retrieved from www.guardingmindsatwork.ca/info/index

Hahn, H. (1991). Alternative views of empowerment: Social services and civil rights. *The Journal of Rehabilitation, 57*(4), 17–19.

Kirby, M.J.L., & Keon, W.J. (2006). Out of the shadows at last: Transforming mental health, mental illness and addiction services in Canada. Ottawa: The Standing Senate Committee on Social Affairs, Science and Technology.

Kolodziej, M.E., & Johnson, B.T. (1996). Interpersonal contact and acceptance of persons with psychiatric disorders: A research synthesis. *Journal of Consulting and Clinical Psychology, 64*, 387–396.

Link, B.G., & Phelan, J.C. (2001). Conceptualizing stigma. *Annual Review of Sociology, 27*(1), 363–385.

Makkonen, T. (2002). Multiple, compound and intersectional discrimination: Bringing the experiences of the most marginalized to the fore. Institute for Human Rights, Åbo Akademi University.

Mental Health Commission of Canada. (2015). National standard of Canada for psychological health and safety in the workplace (standard). Retrieved from www.mentalhealthcommission.ca/English/issues/workplace/national-standard

Mental Health International. (2013). The 5th US/Canada forum on mental health and productivity: Reference report of presentations and proceedings. Retrieved from www.mentalhealthinternational.ca/library.html

Organisation of Economic Co-operation and Development (OECD). (2015). Fit mind, fit job: From evidence to practice in mental health work. Retrieved from www.oecd.org/els/fit-mind-fit-job-9789264228283-en.htm

Pinfold, V., Thornicroft, G., Huxley, P., & Farmer, P. (2005). Active ingredients in anti-stigma programmes in mental health. *International Review of Psychiatry*, 17(2), 123–131.

Quillian, L. (1995). Prejudice as a response to perceived group threat: Population composition and anti-immigrant and racial prejudice in Europe. *American Sociological Review*, 60(4), 586–611.

Schulze, B. (2007). Stigma and mental health professionals: A review of the evidence on an intricate relationship. *International Review of Psychiatry*, 19(2), 137–155.

Siebers, T. (2008). *Disability theory*. Ann Arbor: University of Michigan Press.

Sue, D.W. (2010). *Microaggressions in everyday life: Race, gender, and sexual orientation*. Hoboken, NJ: John Wiley & Sons.

Thornicroft, G., Rose, D., & Kassam, A. (2007). Discrimination in health care against people with mental illness. *International Review of Psychiatry*, 19(2), 113–122.

Thornicroft, G., Rose, D., Kassam, A., & Sartorius A. (2007). Stigma: Ignorance, prejudice or discrimination? *British Journal of Psychiatry*, 190, 192–193.

Tschernetzki-Neilson, P.J., Brintnell, E.S., Haws, C., & Graham, K. (2007). Changing to an outcome-focused program improves return to work outcomes. *Journal of Occupational Rehabilitation*, 17(3), 473–486.

Whitley, B., & Kite, M. (2009). *The psychology of prejudice and discrimination*. Boston: Cengage Learning.

# Chapter 7

# MENTAL HEALTH AND ILLNESS AMONG CHILDREN AND YOUTH

Our greatest natural resource is the minds of our children.
—Walt Disney (American film producer and director)

## Introduction

Among the many species of the animal kingdom, it is humans, *homo sapiens*, that require the longest amount of time to reach maturity. Chimpanzees and gorillas take approximately 10 years to mature, while we require approximately twice as many years to do so. Anthropologists have found evidence indicating that our species first emerged approximately 200,000 years ago and that previous hominids, such as *homo neanderthalensis*, did not share the lengthy period of maturation that we require. Evolutionary psychologists contend that we require this lengthy period in order for our brains to develop and reach full intellectual capacity, particularly to achieve social intelligence.

Most of us have evolved to have strong protective and caring emotional responses to children. The intense joy and wonderment that some of us experience in our interactions with children are among life's deepest pleasures. Conversely, we tend to feel intense emotional pain and distress when we witness children suffering or acting in ways that we perceive to be hurtful. It has been debated by sociologists whether modern Canadian society has evolved to be one that is particularly caring to our children and youth or one that is relatively cold-hearted and prepared to neglect our young.

We will return to a discussion of the societal forces that influence children's mental health and development in Chapter 15, where we also suggest how Canadian society might better address the mental health needs of our children. In this chapter, we will examine the important periods of development and maturation occurring from the prenatal period through transition to adulthood. A number of the social determinants of health that were listed in Chapter 3 are of particular relevance during childhood

**Figure 7.1:** Chimpanzees, along with all other members of the animal kingdom, mature much more quickly than humans.

*Source:* Gary Lewis/iStockphoto

development, and we address these here. We also examine common mental health problems and mental disorders that develop during this period and consider factors that may diminish the incidence of such problems.

## Social Determinants of Health and Children's Mental Health

In order for children to be able to grow and develop the capacity for good, long-lasting mental health, they require a safe and stable physical and social environment. It may be surprising to learn that in Canada, a relatively wealthy country, many children live in poverty, and lack stable housing and other basic necessities of life. In fact, out of 17 OECD countries, Canada ranks 15th in terms of its child poverty rates (Conference Board of Canada, 2013). According to a recent report, child poverty in Canada is on the rise, with almost 20 percent of Canadian children living in poverty (Campaign 2000, 2014). Many Canadian children are homeless, and recent studies indicate that the fastest growing segments among the homeless are families with children and young people under the age of 18 (Child & Family Homelessness, 2014; Kulik et al., 2011).

## Box 7.1: Can Yuppies Bear Children?

As Germaine Greer says in her [book], *Sex and Destiny*, we in [the Western world] simply do not like kids. The birth rate is falling, and the kids we do have are born into a hostile world to the idea that children are an asset, a blessing, fun to have around.... Greer, for all her stridency, is not telling us anything we haven't seen with our own eyes.... Today in Canada, children are confined to McDonald's, Saturday-afternoon matinees, amusement parks, and schools. Before we had our children, I hadn't had a conversation with a kid since I was one. Occasionally, I'd run into one in the supermarket or on the street, but wherever I went, the environment had been carefully scrubbed of kids....

Abandoned by both Mommy and Daddy, the average Canadian kid is becoming more and more a creature of TV, of the toys he plays with, his little pals, and society at large. They're not Our kids any more, they're theirs. When we have them, which is rare in itself, we let them slip away.

I can see the signs, day after day. My boy will sit with the only adult friend he has who will talk to him for hours—his Speak and Spell—learning to spell frantically so the machine will tell him nice things such as: You are Correct. Perfect Score.

My daughter would like to know just about everything, and is not above asking all the questions, all day long. How are teddy bears made? How do you make windows? Who is the Sandman? I don't have time for these questions, so I buy her another Barbie Doll, even though I swore I'd never get one of those things. After I buy her off, it's the feeling of complacency that wells up inside like flatulence that disturbs me the most.

Who do I blame? Myself? Poor vessel that I am, I'm not capable of making such bold choices in isolation from my peers. The fundamentalists blame feminism for the breakdown of the family, but as Germaine acidly points out, no room was made for children long before the feminists got into the act.... I usually end up blaming my kids. For being too noisy, for getting up and going to bed at the wrong times. For wanting me to be with them. For wanting me to love them at least as much as I love myself. For being alive.

At least I count myself more fortunate than those sad mortals who are still trying to decide if children fit into their life-style. The answer is, of course not, dummy. But have them anyway. They're our last link, to Mother Earth....

*Source*: Excerpted from Sullivan, P. (n.d.). Can yuppies bear children? Retrieved from http://daycareinfo.net/canyup.htm. Site no longer active.

Two of the social determinants of health listed in Chapter 3 are directly pertinent to children and to the development of good mental health in Canada's population—early life and education. As stated in a WHO document on social determinants

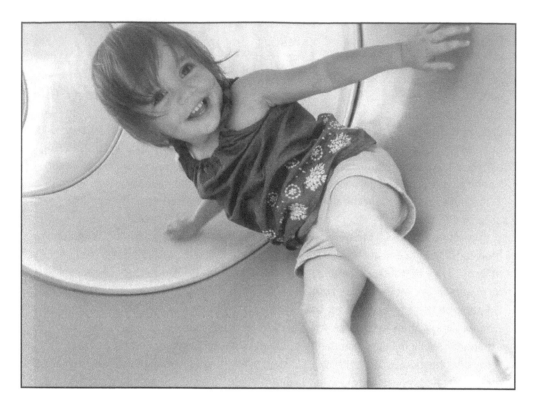

**Figure 7.2:** This little girl named Melina is having fun playing on the slide at the park. Children who are living in poverty often have less access to parks and recreational activities, which has an impact on their development and quality of life.

*Source*: Feryal Almazni, Photographer

of health, "The health impact of early development and education lasts a lifetime" (WHO, 2003, p. 14).

As a social determinant of health, early life refers to a broad range of factors that operate during prenatal development (i.e., before birth), during infancy (i.e., the first year after birth), and in early childhood. This period is of particular importance because of the neural plasticity (i.e., the capacity for the brain to undergo development and build interconnections between brain cells) during these early years and because of the potential long-standing effects on physical and mental health. Healthy prenatal development requires proper nutrition, good maternal health, and an environment that is free from toxins or exposures that could interfere with the rapid growth and development that takes place during this period. Similarly, infancy and early childhood are crucial periods for the development of physical and mental health (WHO, 2012). We will discuss these periods in human development more thoroughly later in this chapter.

Education is an important social determinant of health, and it can exert significant influence on one's life trajectory over many years (Hertzman & Power, 2006). Early childhood education includes nursery school and daycare, as well as the educational experience a child receives at home and in the community. Significant emphasis has been placed on the provision of early childhood education to young children in order to promote cognitive and emotional development during this critical period, particularly to children who are at risk due to factors such as poverty or parental mental illness or addiction. In a review of early childhood education programs in which program start, duration, and intensity were accounted for, Burger (2010) found that the majority of early education programs have substantial short-term benefits and more modest long-term effects on cognitive development. While these programs were especially advantageous for children from socio-economically disadvantaged backgrounds, these programs cannot, in and of themselves, make up for the developmental deficits experienced by children from marginalized environments (Burger, 2010).

Good education in childhood and adolescence (in fact, throughout the entire lifetime) confers lasting benefits to both physical and mental health (Hertzman & Power, 2006). In part, the benefits of education operate by opening up better opportunities for meaningful and rewarding employment and consequently enhancing income, job security, and housing options. In addition, good education leads to heightened social skills and self-esteem.

In general, people with low education levels have the worst health status (Conti, Heckman, & Urzua, 2010). Illiteracy is strongly associated with poverty, malnutrition, ill health, and increased rates of infant and child mortality (DeWalt et al., 2004). This may be exacerbated by a low degree of health literacy, making it more difficult to learn and adopt healthy lifestyle choices.

Research has found that children and young people who experience safe and supportive school environments have an increased sense of connectedness to their schools and community. In recent years, the concept of school connectedness as an important determinant of health has gained substantial traction among researchers, educators, and public health professionals. School connectedness has been described as the belief by students that adults and peers in the school setting care about them both as learners and as individuals (Centers for Disease Control [CDC], 2009; Smith et al., 2014). This sense of connectedness has been shown to be protective against a range of health issues including depression, violence, unsafe sexual activity, and substance misuse (Bond et al., 2007; Catalano et al., 2004; CDC, 2009). With this in mind, significant work has gone into developing health promotion programs to support children's mental health in the school setting.

> **Box 7.2: Theatre: A Promising Community-based Program Targeting Child and Youth Mental Health**
>
> While much of the health promotion programming that exists for children and youth takes place in school settings, there are also some innovative community-based programs that are showing great results. In Prince George, British Columbia, the Street Spirits Theatre Company brings award winning drama programs to "at-risk" youth while addressing pertinent social issues such as substance use and the sex trade. Founder Andrew Burton has stated, "I believe the greatest potential for the arts lies in the area of prevention and health promotion. Theatre work develops skills and abilities in people and awareness in the community that can influence behavior. Behavior changes can have a huge impact on community health. While there has been some recognition of this in health circles, particularly in public health, there is little awareness or acceptance in Health Services overall. In times of economic hardship like those we are dealing with now, the first services to be cut are those that promote health and wellbeing" (Arts Health Network Canada, 2014). Fun and creative health promotion and prevention programs that are responsive to children's and youths' needs and the issues that they face are an important component of a holistic approach to supporting the development of mentally healthy young people.

Given the importance of education to the health of Canadians, it follows that great expectations and responsibilities are placed on our educational system. How well is it responding to this considerable challenge? Overall, Canada's educational institutions have been found to perform strongly when compared with those of other nations (Ungerleider, Burns, & Cartwright, 2009). Of course, there is always room for improvement; there are children in Canada whose needs do not seem to be adequately met. One substantial challenge is the ability of our school systems to meet the diverse needs of our children. Howard Gardner, a psychologist, proposed the idea that there are many different components of intelligence, and consequently, education must be able to recognize and respond to these different strengths and capacities (Gardner & Hatch, 1989). Although Gardner's theory has been debated and disputed within the field of psychology, it has been embraced by many educators. The list provided in Table 7.1 will give you an idea of the different types of capacities being referred to in this theory.

Historically, our educational systems have emphasized the development of linguistic and logical-mathematical intelligence. Many educators feel that more diversity in school curricula is warranted in order to match different strengths and types of intelligence.

**Table 7.1: Different types of intelligence**

| Intelligence | End-states | Core components |
|---|---|---|
| Logical-mathematical | • scientist<br>• mathematician | Sensitivity to, and capacity to discern, logical or numerical patterns; ability to handle long chains of reasoning. |
| Linguistic | • poet<br>• journalist | Sensitivity to the sounds, rhythms, and meanings of words; sensitivity to the different functions of language. |
| Musical | • composer<br>• violinist | Abilities to produce and appreciate rhythm, pitch, and timbre; appreciation of the forms of musical expressiveness. |
| Spatial | • navigator<br>• sculptor | Capacities to perceive the visual-spatial world accurately and to perform transformations on one's initial perceptions. |
| Bodily-kinesthetic | • dancer<br>• athlete | Abilities to control one's body movements and to handle objects skillfully. |
| Interpersonal | • therapist<br>• salesman | Capacities to discern and respond appropriately to the moods, temperaments, motivations, and desires of other people. |
| Intrapersonal | • person with detailed, accurate self-knowledge | Access to one's own feelings and the ability to discriminate among them and draw upon them to guide behaviour; knowledge of one's own strengths, weaknesses, desires, and intelligences. |

*Source:* Gardner, H., & Hatch, T. (1989). Multiple intelligences go to school: Educational implications of the theory of multiple intelligences. *Educational Researcher*, 18(8), 4–10.

# Development and Mental Health

## *Prenatal Development*

Ensconced within the womb and dependent on the maternal physical environment during development, embryos (from conception to the 8th week of pregnancy) and fetuses (from the end of the 8th week until birth) are subject to various biological factors that may influence mental health. Healthy fetal development requires proper nutrition and good maternal health. Maternal malnutrition can have deleterious effects; for example, protein (essential amino acids) deprivation or glucose deprivation can result in an underdeveloped fetal brain. A tragic "natural experiment" in the 20th century allowed for study of the effects of malnutrition on mental health. From 1945 to 1946, the urban population in the Netherlands was exposed to acute starvation

## Box 7.3: Biological Embedding

Depending on your disciplinary background and own life experiences, some of you may find yourselves more closely relating to either the biological or social explanations for the development of mental health or illness. However, the two paradigms are not as separate as they may first appear. Through a process termed "biological embedding," the social factors that we are exposed to beginning in utero manage to "enter" our bodies and influence the development of our brains and central nervous system (Hertzman & Frank, 2006). A nice example of how this process occurs is illustrated through the functioning of the hypothalamic-pituitary-adrenal (HPA). The HPA axis comprises of a set of brain and endocrine structures that influence the release of cortisol, a hormone secreted in response to experiences of stress. Cortisol serves an important function in our bodies and is involved in the "fight or flight" response to stress, providing a boost in energy and immune function, and lower pain sensitivity during periods of acute stress. However, prolonged exposure to the hormone (which is common with the chronic stresses encountered in today's society) can result in damage to various organ systems, leaving us vulnerable to illness and disease (Hertzman & Frank, 2006). Of particular concern is the fact that the HPA axis is conditioned, or "programmed," early in life, permanently altering the way that our bodies respond to stress throughout the remainder of our lives! Thus, adverse social conditions or events (e.g., poor nutrition, limited parental bonding, poor access to early education, exposure to noxious substances, etc.), which are unequally distributed within society, have lifelong implications for our health and well-being and influence our vulnerability to mental disorders.

under Nazi occupation. A long-term follow-up study of children born to women who were pregnant during the famine found that they were significantly more likely to develop mental illnesses such as schizophrenia, mood disorder, and anti-social personality disorder when compared with children born at other times (Susser, Hoek, & Brown, 1998).

Some infectious illnesses that occur during pregnancy can adversely affect brain development, and various chemicals, toxins, and drugs that enter the maternal-fetal environment can also cause problems in mental development. The degree of impact of these factors ranges across a wide spectrum, from minimal effects that are difficult to detect to profound, permanent deficits in other instances.

## Box 7.4: Fetal Alcohol Spectrum Disorder (FASD)

FASD occurs as a result of damage to brain development caused by maternal alcohol use during pregnancy. Infants with FASD display irritability, jitteriness, tremors,

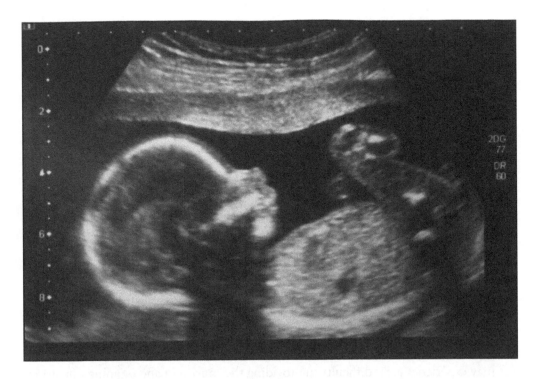

**Figure 7.3:** Good maternal health and nutrition are factors in prenatal development.

*Source:* &#169 isabelle Limbach/iStockphoto

weak sucking reflexes, problems with sleeping and eating, failure to thrive, delayed development, poor motor control, and poor habituation. In childhood, problems such as hyperactivity, attention problems, perceptual difficulties, cognitive deficits, language problems, and poor motor coordination are common. In adolescence and adulthood, the primary difficulties are memory impairments, problems with judgment and abstract reasoning, and poor adaptive functioning. How common is maternal alcohol consumption during pregnancy? Research indicates that, in countries such as Canada and the US, the prevalence of alcohol consumption during pregnancy ranges from 20 to 32 percent (May et al., 2013).

Some common secondary disabilities characteristic of adolescents and adults with FASD include being easily victimized, unfocused, and distractible. They also include difficulty handling money, problems learning from experience, trouble understanding consequences and perceiving social cues, poor frustration tolerance, inappropriate sexual behaviours, substance abuse, and trouble with the law (Brintnell et al., 2011; Rasmussen et al., 2008). The exact amount of alcohol that can cause FASD is unknown and may vary among individuals (May et al., 2013), but some research has indicated that mothers who drank as little as one drink per day have children with learning and behavioural problems (Sood et al., 2001).

## *Infancy*

Newborns interact with their environment quite differently than do most adults. Their vision is relatively undeveloped and they respond primarily to tactile (i.e., touch) and interoceptive stimuli (i.e., responses to internal stimuli such as hunger and thirst). Infants frequently let us know when something is amiss by crying, a powerful form of communication that few adults can ignore. Most of us have strong responses to crying infants and desperately want the crying to stop.

For the most part, infants are soothed when their basic needs are met (e.g., feeding them when they are hungry and changing their diapers when wet or soiled) and by touching, holding, rocking, cuddling, interacting with them, and stimulating their natural curiosity and interest in the world around them. Infants whose cries for food or comfort are ignored or produce angry and inconsistent responses by caregivers may have a difficult time trusting others and developing emotional bonds for the rest of their lives. This is reflected in Erik Erikson's theory (discussed in Chapter 3), in which he describes the first developmental stage (Trust vs. Mistrust) as the period during which infants must form loving, trusting relationships with caregivers or risk developing a sense of mistrust.

Unless supports are in place, a parent who struggles with mental illness or substance use may experience great difficulty in providing the consistent and ongoing nurturing, stimulation, and physical care that an infant or young child needs for optimal mental development. In some tragic circumstances, infants can suffer neglect and abandonment. Studies of both human and non-human primate infants have found that, when infants are separated from their parents, three stages of emotional reactions follow. First is protest, in which infants cry and refuse to be consoled by others. Second is despair, in which infants are sad and passive. Third is detachment, in which infants actively disregard and avoid the parents if they return (Robertson & Bowlby, 1952).

**Attachment theory** was developed by psychologist John Bowlby, who theorized that a newborn child is biologically programmed to seek closeness with caregivers. Bowlby was intrigued by experimental studies of infant monkeys removed from their mothers that found they preferred to spend time with soft mother-like dummies that offered no food than with dummies that provided a food source but were less pleasant to touch (Harlow & Zimmerman, 1959). A central assumption in attachment theory, as applied to human children, is that sensitive responding by the parent or caregiver to infants' needs results in infants who demonstrate secure attachment, while lack of such sensitive responding results in insecure attachment.

Infant psychiatry or infant mental health represents a multidisciplinary field in which specialists seek to foster the mental health of infants, toddlers, pre-schoolers, and their families. Often, infant mental health specialists work with families identified as "high risk" to diminish the impact of social and economic risk factors. The intervention approach may include "treatments" that are informed by the biological, psychological, or social science perspectives, however, the primary focus is typically on supporting optimal infant-caregiver relationships.

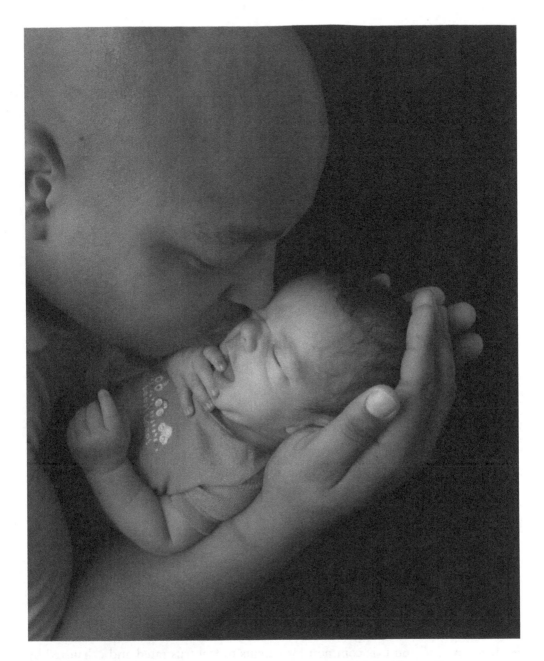

**Figure 7.4:** Infants are soothed by touch, sounds, and gentle rocking motions.

*Source:* Jani Bryson/iStockphoto

In the Canadian context, researchers at the Children's Health Policy Centre led by Dr. Charlotte Waddell at Simon Fraser University are currently evaluating an infant mental health program called the "Nurse-Family Partnership," which was originally developed in the US. The Nurse-Family Partnership program aims to provide young, first-time mothers who experience risk factors such as low income with intensive supports from the prenatal period though to the child's second birthday. Over the course of the program, these moms and their babies will meet approximately 64 times with a public health nurse who works to empower these women through education and supports required to manage parental challenges. In studies of the Nurse-Family Partnership program conducted in the US, the program has been associated with such outcomes as enhanced prenatal and early childhood mental health outcomes and decreased child and maternal mortality.

---

**Box 7.5: Infant Psychiatry**

In the past few decades, although a relatively new discipline, infant psychiatry has gained recognition as an important field. Many people tend to believe that infancy is a carefree period; however, young children can experience significant mental health problems, particularly in the contexts of early developmental processes and the parent-child relationship. Common mental health disorders in infants include crying, sleeping or feeding problems, difficulties regulating emotions or attention, and aggressive behaviour. It is important that these problems are identified early, so there is an opportunity to improve infants' developmental outcomes and promote positive parent-child relationships. One approach to treating infant mental illness is infant-parent psychotherapy, which is an attachment-based psychotherapy approach that focuses on reflective play, guidance, and aims to help parents process their emotions and caregiving experiences in relation to their interactions with their children.

---

## Childhood

In early childhood, children are developing physical skills, including walking, grasping, and rectal sphincter control. According to Erikson (1963), in the Autonomy vs. Shame and Doubt development stage, young children (from approximately 18 months to 3 years) aim to learn autonomy (i.e., ability to do certain things independently) and control, and if these developments are not handled well by caregivers, the child may internalize persistent feelings of shame and doubt. This is the period when children learn to say "no" and it is common for parents to feel frustrated and exhausted by the frequent assertions of will and temper tantrums that occur. In the subsequent stage of development identified by Erikson as Initiative vs. Guilt (approximately 3 to 6 years of age), the child continues to become more assertive and to take more initiative, but may be too forceful, leading to feelings of guilt. According to Erikson's theory, in the next stage, Industry vs. Inferiority (lasting from about 6 to 12 years of age), the child must deal with demands to learn new skills or risk a sense of inferiority, failure, and incompetence.

For most children, family members will exert the greatest influence over a child's emotional and intellectual development. Children fortunate enough to have loving, nurturing family members who invest time and effort will usually flourish. Sometimes the most important bond and primary support to a child will be someone other than a parent—possibly an older sibling or another relative or family friend. Many grandparents play a special role in this regard, and we will return to a discussion of this important intergenerational bond in Chapter 10.

**Figure 7.5:** Healthy emotional growth in childhood includes the development of a comfortable sense of autonomy, comfort in social circumstances, self-generated initiative, and capacity for industrious activity.

*Source:* BraunS/iStockphoto

While cases of child maltreatment, such as abuse or neglect, are unsettling to hear about, it is well recognized that the impact of abuse, particularly in childhood, can greatly affect the mental health of the individual in later years. There is evidence to suggest that childhood maltreatment and early stressful experiences are associated with numerous physiological changes (Teicher et al., 2002; Teicher et al., 2003). Furthermore, evidence suggests a possible causal relationship between childhood abuse and psychosis in adulthood, and child abuse and neglect is associated with an increased risk of major depressive disorder in young adulthood (Manning & Stickley, 2009; Widom, DuMont, & Czaja, 2007). Child sexual abuse is associated with increased rates of childhood and adult mental disorders (Spataro et al., 2004). While it was once believed that children who are abused become abusers as adults, research has since proven that this "cycle of abuse" is a common misperception and largely untrue (Bouvier, 2003; Salter et al., 2003).

As we have discussed earlier in this chapter, daycare settings and schools play an important role in fostering the development of social and intellectual skills, and they are important environments for the emotional growth of our children. Whether at school, home, or elsewhere, adult oversight of children's behaviour is necessary to protect them from hurting themselves or others. In Chapter 3, we introduced Kohlberg's theory of moral development that was based, in part, on observations of children's interactions and their approach to moral dilemmas. Kohlberg noted that children tend to apply quite primitive rules of behaviour in which they do not consider whether their actions are hurtful or damaging to others, often being cruel. **Bullying** is usually defined as repeated negative acts, such as hitting, kicking, teasing, or taunting, committed by one or more children against others. A real or perceived power imbalance exists between the bully and victim. Bullying has been found to be common among children in school settings and can occur in the home between siblings. In fact, in Canada, one in three young people reports having experienced bullying (Molcho et al., 2009). Tragically, the long-term harms and consequences to the mental health of victims are often severe, and recent research indicates that those who have been bullied as children have an increased risk of depression, self-harm and suicidality (Abada, Hou, & Ram, 2008; Klomek et al., 2009; McMahon et al., 2012; Saab & Klinger, 2010).

## *Adolescence*

According to Erikson (1963), an adolescent's challenge is Identity vs. Role Confusion (ages 12 to 18), during which time the youth must form a sense of identity in relation to such things as gender roles, occupational endeavours, and religious beliefs. Typically, a teenager's world is no longer centred within the family, but in the more exciting world of peers and youth culture. Adolescence has been described humorously by some parents as a brief period of "psychosis," because it is common for a previously compliant and well-behaved child to transform into an erratic, difficult, dramatic teenager. Not all young people will go through a period of intense adolescent rebellion, but almost all will identify ways to differentiate themselves from previous generations, often by their dress, preferences in music, and political or social values.

Adolescence is often a time of many firsts: first date, first love, first sexual encounter, first job, first experimentation with alcohol or drugs. The adolescent's naïveté and lack of knowledge in managing these new experiences creates risks and often produces emotional turbulence. In some families, an adolescent's risky behaviour will precipitate a crisis. Intense conflict with parents or siblings may result in the young person leaving or being ejected from the family home. The risks and negative consequences

**Figure 7.6:** In recent years, there have been a number of community efforts to bring awareness to bullying, such as this pink shirt campaign.

*Source:* Cassidy Jones, Photographer

---

**Box 7.6: Roots of Empathy**

Roots of Empathy is an evidence-based classroom program that has shown dramatic success in reducing levels of aggression among schoolchildren by raising social/ emotional competence and increasing empathy. The Roots of Empathy program fosters the development of "emotional literacy" by bringing infants into the classroom to help participants learn to understand their own and others' emotions. At the heart of the program is a neighbourhood infant and parent who visit the classroom every three weeks over the school year. A trained Roots of Empathy instructor coaches students to observe the baby's development and to label the baby's feelings. In this experiential learning, the baby is the "teacher" and becomes the conduit for the instructor to help children identify and reflect on their own feelings and the feelings of others. Emotional literacy lays the foundation for safer and more caring classrooms, where children are the "changers." They become more competent in understanding their own feelings and the feelings of others (empathy), and are therefore less likely to physically, psychologically, and emotionally hurt each other through bullying and other cruelties. In the Roots of Empathy program, children learn how to challenge cruelty and injustice. Messages of social inclusion and activities that are consensus building contribute to a culture of caring that shifts the tone of the classroom. Research results from national and international evaluations of Roots of Empathy indicate significant reductions in aggression and increases in pro-social behaviour.

*Source*: Adapted from Roots of Empathy. (2006). About our program. Retrieved from www. rootsofempathy.org/en/what-we-do.html

---

encountered by young people on the streets are very serious; prostitution, drug addiction, and violence are common, and many teens who leave home precipitously end up in a downward spiral. Therefore, the management of adolescent rebellion and family conflict is important. In Chapter 15, we shall return to a discussion of how we might prevent such negative outcomes in Canadian society.

## Transition to Adulthood

It is difficult to delineate where adolescence ends and adulthood begins. Often, young (and older) adults continue to work on developmental challenges that emerged during earlier stages of development. Studies have found that young adults in Canada are making so-called "key life transitions" (i.e., getting married and beginning full-time jobs) later and later (Statistics Canada, 2007). Some sociologists have dubbed this as a "failure to launch," and it is considered to be the result of recent social and economic changes, such as increased housing costs and fewer career opportunities. However, researchers have found that many young adults continue to move quickly

**Figure 7.7:** Adolescence is a period during which one establishes a distinctive identity and is exposed to a host of new experiences and challenges.

*Source:* ViewApart/iStockphoto

into full-time jobs and marriage, particularly those with less education. As described by Maria Kefalas,

> [these "fast-starters"] do so at a price. Young people progressing at lightning speed into adulthood accomplish this by neglecting schooling. This means fast-starters acquire the markers of adulthood on the fast track, but that they risk getting trapped between the rock and a hard place of a blue- and pink-collar labour sector where down-sizing, stagnating wages, shrinking worker's benefits, and nonexistent job mobility eat away at their chances of getting ahead. Even marriage is not as stable for this group. Fast-starters might walk down the aisle earlier in life, but their unions are more likely to end in divorce than their college educated peers. (Kefalas, 2006)

Researchers point out that spending a few extra years at university is likely to have benefits as a more educated society helps to foster economic growth, reduce crime, and promote citizenship (Milligan, Moretti, & Oreopoulos, 2005).

## Fostering Character and Social Responsibility

There has been a growing interest in understanding the development of **character**, which has been described as an individual's set of psychological characteristics that affect that person's ability and inclination to function morally (Berkowitz, 2002). Christopher Peterson and psychologist Martin Seligman (2004) have aimed to describe the core virtues that are consistently valued across cultures and across time. The main virtues identified are wisdom, courage, humanity, justice, temperance, and transcendence (see Table 7.2).

There is hope that an increased understanding of how these virtues can be fostered in childhood will lead to a more socially responsible and caring society. It appears that childhood is the critical period during which it is essential for these virtues to be relayed and incorporated into a life pattern. We will return to this topic in Chapter 15.

## Mental Disorders in Children and Youth

Although some mental health problems emerge for the first time later in life, the majority of mental disorders begin either in childhood or adolescence (National Alliance on Mental Illness, 2009). For example, depressive disorders, anxiety disorders, and anorexia nervosa typically begin before the age of 18. The most prevalent mental disorder among children and youth is depression, and its features are similar to those seen in adults and described in Chapter 4. Across Canada, studies have been conducted on children between the ages of 6 to 18, and it has been estimated that nearly 13 percent of children in this age group experience mental disorders that cause clinically significant symptoms (Waddell et al., 2014). At this point in time, prevalence estimates of mental disorders in younger children are not known. The ICD includes a block of disorders under the heading "Behavioural and emotional disorders with onset usually occurring in childhood and adolescence" (WHO, 2007). In the remainder of this chapter, we provide a brief description of the mental disorders included within this category. At the end of the chapter, we recommend additional reading for those who wish to obtain a more detailed and comprehensive understanding of mental disorders that affect children and youth.

Childhood mental disorders are sometimes distinguished as being either externalizing or internalizing. **Externalizing disorders** are those in which distress is turned outwards and directed toward others in a disruptive manner. In contrast, distress is turned inward in **internalizing disorders**, such as depression or anxiety disorder. However, many conditions affecting children cannot be placed sensibly within this simplistic dichotomy.

One group of childhood disorders described in the ICD that fits well under the category of externalizing disorders is **conduct disorders**. These disorders are "characterized by a repetitive and persistent pattern of dissocial, aggressive, or defiant conduct" (WHO, 2007). The ICD further specifies that this pattern of conduct

## Table 7.2: Character virtues and strengths

| Wisdom and knowledge |
| --- |
| 1. Curiosity/interest in the world |
| 2. Love of learning |
| 3. Judgment/critical thinking/open-mindedness |
| 4. Ingenuity/originality/practical intelligence/street smarts |
| 5. Social intelligence/personal intelligence/emotional intelligence |
| 6. Perspective |
| **Courage** |
| 7. Valour and bravery |
| 8. Perseverance/industry/diligence |
| 9. Integrity/genuineness/honesty |
| **Humanity and love** |
| 10. Kindness and generosity |
| 11. Loving and allowing oneself to be loved |
| **Justice** |
| 12. Citizenship/duty/teamwork/loyalty |
| 13. Fairness and equity |
| 14. Leadership |
| **Temperance** |
| 15. Self-control |
| 16. Prudence/discretion/caution |
| 17. Humility and modesty |
| **Transcendence** |
| 18. Appreciation of beauty and excellence |
| 19. Gratitude |
| 20. Hope/optimism/future-mindedness |
| 21. Spirituality/sense of purpose/faith/religiousness |
| 22. Forgiveness and mercy |
| 23. Playfulness and humour |
| 24. Zest/passion/enthusiasm |

*Source:* Peterson, C., & Seligman, M. (2004). *Character strengths and virtues: A handbook and classification.* New York: Oxford University Press.

must persist for more than six months and constitute severe behavioural disturbance that is well beyond ordinary mischief. The following examples are listed in the ICD: "excessive levels of fighting or bullying, cruelty to other people or animals, severe destructiveness to property, fire-setting, stealing, repeated lying, truancy from school and running away from home, unusually frequent and severe temper tantrums, and disobedience" (WHO, 2007).

Another group of disorders is labelled "hyperkinetic" and includes what is widely referred to as "**attention deficit disorder**." Children with these disorders have difficulty focusing their attention and are easily distracted. Often they experience compulsive behaviours and are hyperactive; that is, they have marked difficulty remaining still for any period. Attentional deficits associated with these disorders may persist throughout childhood and adolescence into adulthood, whereas the symptoms of hyperactivity and impulsivity tend to diminish with age. Even though many children with attention deficit disorder ultimately adjust, they are more likely to drop out of school and fare more poorly in their later careers than other children.

Most young children display some degree of separation anxiety, in which they become apprehensive when separated from their primary caregivers (usually their mothers), between the ages of 8 and 14 months. Separation anxiety disorder is diagnosed when fear of separation is unusually intense or interferes with social functioning, and persists beyond the usual age period.

Elective mutism refers to a complete lack of speech (i.e., mutism) that is believed to be volitional (i.e., willed) on the part of the child. Elective mutism may be a reaction to a traumatic event or a symptom of extreme shyness.

Another group of disorders affecting children are **tic disorders**. According to the ICD,

A tic is an involuntary, rapid, recurrent, non-rhythmic motor movement or vocal production that is of sudden onset and that serves no apparent purpose. Tics tend to be experienced as irresistible but usually they can be suppressed for varying periods of time, are exacerbated by stress, and disappear during sleep. Common simple motor tics include eye-blinking, neck-jerking, shoulder- shrugging, and facial grimacing. Common simple vocal tics include throat-clearing, barking, sniffing, and hissing. Common complex tics include hitting oneself, jumping, and hopping. Common complex vocal tics include the repetition of particular words, and sometimes the use of socially unacceptable (often obscene) words (coprolalia), and the repetition of one's own sounds or words (palilalia). (WHO, 2007)

Non-organic enuresis, more commonly called "bedwetting," involves the involuntary release of urine into bedding, clothing, or other inappropriate places by children older than five years of age. Non-organic encopresis involves repeatedly having fecal bowel movements in inappropriate places after the age when bowel control is normally expected. Psychological factors often play a role in these conditions.

Autism Spectrum Disorder (ASD) is a complex neurodevelopmental condition that results in deficits in social interaction, communication, and behaviour. Children with ASD typically also display various repetitive behaviours, odd routines, and obsessions with particular objects. Although the ICD system does not include ASD within the block of disorders titled "Behavioural and emotional disorders with onset usually occurring in childhood and adolescence" (the ICD instead classifies ASD in the block of disorders known as "Disorders of psychological development"), we feel that it is important to include some information about ASD in this chapter. The term "spectrum" is used because individuals with ASD display a wide range of symptoms with varying levels of severity, and cognitive functioning can range from severe intellectual disability to high-level intelligence. Within the spectrum of ASD, individuals who are relatively high functioning in regard to language and intellectual ability are often described as having "Asperger's syndrome." Some children with ASD have quite severe impairment of language and may be completely non-verbal. ASD can be diagnosed between the ages of 1 and 3, as symptoms are apparent even in young children. Individuals with ASD are often unable to respond appropriately in social exchanges and lack the ability to form relationships, which can be disheartening for parents, whose children may not reciprocate affection. Although the cause of ASD remains unknown, it is thought to be a neurodevelopmental disorder that involves an interaction of genetic and environmental factors. No medication is currently available to treat the primary symptoms of ASD but there are a variety of behavioural treatments that are helpful and are most beneficial if they begin as soon as a child is diagnosed; early intervention of ASD ensures the best possible prognosis. One behavioural treatment that is widely utilized is Applied Behaviour Analysis. The underlying theory promotes positive behaviour and discourages negative behaviour. As each individual with ASD is unique, outcomes of treatment vary drastically.

## Conclusion

A lengthy period of human maturation is required for the development of complex brain function and achievement of social intelligence. Social determinants that are particularly germane to the development of children's mental health are early life and education.

Many factors influence human development from the prenatal period through achievement of adulthood. Erik Erikson produced a theoretical framework that delineates specific developmental tasks considered to be central to various stages of development in infancy, childhood, adolescence, and adulthood. Currently, efforts are underway to understand the development of character and the specific virtues and strengths considered to be key components of character.

Most mental disorders begin during childhood or adolescence and the most prevalent mental conditions in children are anxiety disorders and depressive disorders. A wide range of disorders first seen in childhood are described in the ICD system.

## Glossary

**attachment theory:** Developed by John Bowlby, this theory suggests that newborn children are biologically programmed to seek closeness with caregivers.

**attention deficit disorder:** A disorder in which individuals have difficulty focusing attention and are easily distracted.

**bullying:** Repeated negative acts, such as hitting, kicking, teasing, or taunting, committed by one or more children against others.

**character:** An individual's set of psychological characteristics that affect that person's ability and inclination to function morally.

**conduct disorders:** Disorders characterized by a repetitive and persistent pattern of dissocial, aggressive, or defiant conduct.

**externalizing disorders:** Disorders in which distress is turned outward and directed toward others in a disruptive manner.

**internalizing disorders:** Disorders in which distress is turned inward, such as depression or anxiety disorder.

**tic disorders:** Disorders involving tics—involuntary, rapid, recurrent, non-rhythmic motor movements or vocal production that is of sudden onset and that serves no apparent purpose.

## Critical Thinking Questions

1. Describe the relationship between education and health. How can educational systems respond to the diverse needs of students?
2. Select one of the stages of development discussed in this chapter and describe its key features.
3. What are some of the challenges facing adolescents as they transition to adulthood?
4. What is the difference between internalizing and externalizing disorders? Provide examples of specific disorders.
5. Select a childhood/adolescent mental disorder and describe its characteristics.

## Recommended Readings

Crain, W. (2015). *Theories of Development: Concepts and Applications* (6th ed.). New Jersey: Psychology Press.

Falicov, C.J. (1988). *Family Transitions: Continuity and Change over the Life Cycle.* New York: Guilford Press.

Koocher, G., & La Greca, A. (2010). *The Parents' Guide to Psychological First Aid.* New York: Oxford University Press.

Rew, L. (2005). *Adolescent Health: A Multidisciplinary Approach to Theory, Research, and Intervention.* Thousand Oaks, CA: Sage.

## Recommended Websites

Children's Health Policy Centre. Simon Fraser University. www.childhealthpolicy. sfu.ca/

Children's Mental Health Ontario. www.kidsmentalhealth.ca/

Growing Healthy Canadians: A Guide for Positive Child Development. www. growinghealthykids.com/english/home/index.html

Taking Care: Child and Youth Mental Health. http://takingcare.knowledge.ca/

Teen Mental Health. www.teenmentalhealth.org/

## References

Abada, T., Hou, F., & Ram, B. (2008). The effects of harassment and victimization on self-rated health and mental health among Canadian adolescents. *Social Science & Medicine, 67*(4), 557–567.

Arts Health Network Canada. (2014). Street Spirits Theatre Company. Retrieved from artshealthnetwork.ca/initiatives/street-spirits-theatre-company

Berkowitz, M.W. (2002). The science of character education. In D. Damon (Ed.), *Bringing in a new era in character education* (pp. 43–64). Stanford, CA: Hoover Institution Press.

Bond, L., Butler, H., Thomas, L., Carlin, J., Glover, S., Bowes, G., & Patton, G. (2007). Social and school connectedness in early secondary school as predictors of late teenage substance use, mental health, and academic outcomes. *Journal of Adolescent Health, 40*(4), 9–18.

Bouvier, P. (2003). Child sexual abuse: Vicious circles of fate or paths to resilience? *The Lancet, 361*(9356), 446–447.

Brintnell, S., Bailey, P.G., Sawhney, A., & Kreftin, L. (2011). Understanding FASD: Disability and social supports for adult offenders. In E.P. Riley, S. Clarren, J. Weinber, & E. Jonsson (Eds.), *Fetal alcohol spectrum disorder: Management and policy perspectives of FASD* (pp. 233–247). Weinheim, Germany: Wiley.

Burger, K. (2010). How does early childhood care and education affect cognitive development? An international review of the effects of early interventions for children from different social backgrounds. *Early Childhood Research Quarterly, 25*(2), 140–165.

Campaign 2000. (2014). 2014 report card on child and family poverty in Canada. Retrieved from www.campaign2000.ca/anniversaryreport/CanadaRC2014EN.pdf

Catalano, R.F., Haggerty, K.P., Oesterle, S., Flemming, C.B., & Hawkins, J.D. (2004). The importance of bonding to school for healthy development: Findings from the social development research group. *Journal of School Health*, 74(7), 252–261.

Centers for Disease Control and Prevention. (2009). *School connectedness: Strategies for increasing protective factors among youth*. Atlanta, GA: US Department of Health and Human Services.

Child & Family Homelessness. (2014). Raising the roof. Retrieved from www.raisingtheroof.org/about-homelessness/

Conference Board of Canada. (2013). Child poverty. Retrieved from www.conferenceboard.ca/hcp/details/society/child-poverty.aspx

Conti, G., Heckman, J., & Urzua, S. (2010). The education-health gradient. *American Economic Review*, 100(2), 234–238.

DeWalt, D.A., Berkman, N.D., Sheridan, S., Lohr, K.L., & Pigone, M.P. (2004). Literacy and health outcomes. A systematic review of the literature. *Journal of General Internal Medicine*, 19(12), 1228–1239.

Erikson, E.H. (1963). *Childhood and society* (2nd ed.). New York: W.W. Norton.

Gardner, H., & Hatch, T. (1989). Multiple intelligences go to school: Educational implications of the theory of multiple intelligences. *Educational Researcher*, 18(8), 4–10.

Harlow, H.F., & Zimmerman, R.R. (1959). Affectional responses in the infant monkey. *Science*, 130(3373), 421–432.

Hertzman, C., & Frank, J. (2006). Biological pathways linking the social environment, development, and health. In J. Heymann, C. Hertzman, M.L. Barer, & R.G. Evans (Eds.), *Healthier societies: From analysis to action* (pp. 35–57). New York: Oxford University Press.

Hertzman, C., & Power, C. (2006). A life course approach to health and human development. In J. Heymann, C. Hertzman, M.L. Barer, & R.G. Evans (Eds.), *Healthier societies: From analysis to action* (pp. 83–106). New York: Oxford University Press.

Kefalas, M. (2006). Failure to launch or launching too soon? Commentary. Retrieved from www.transad.pop.upenn.edu/2006/05/failure-to-launch-or-launching-too.html

Klomek, A.B., Sourander, A., Niemelä, S., Kumpulainen, K., Piha, J., Tamminen, T., Almqvist, F., & Gould, M.S. (2009). Childhood bullying behaviors as a risk for suicide attempts and completed suicides: a population-based birth cohort study. *Journal of the American Academy of Child and Adolescent Psychiatry*, 48(3), 254–261.

Kulik, D.M., Gaetz, S. Crowe, C., & Ford-Jones, E. (2011). Homeless youth's overwhelming health burden: A review of the literature. *Paediatrics & Child Health*, 16(6), 43–47.

Manning, C., & Stickley, T. (2009). Child abuse and psychosis: A critical review of the literature. *Journal of Research in Nursing*, 14(6), 531–547.

May, P.A., Blankenship, J., Marais, A.S., Gossage, J.P., Kalberg, W.O., Joubert, B., Cloete, M., Barnard, R., De Vries, M., Hasken, J., Robinson, L.K., Adnams, C.M., Buckley, D., Manning, M., Parry, C.D., Hoyme, H.E., Tabachnick, B., & Seedat, S. (2013). Maternal alcohol consumption producing fetal alcohol spectrum disorders (FASD): Quantity, frequency, and timing of drinking. *Drug and Alcohol Dependence*, 133(2), 502–512.

McMahon, E.M., Reulbach, U., Keeley, H., Perry, I.J., & Arensman, E. (2012). Bullying victimisation, self harm and associated factors in Irish adolescent boys. *Social Science & Medicine*, 74(4), 490–497.

Milligan, K., Moretti, E., & Oreopoulos, P. (2005). Does education improve citizenship: Evidence from the U.S. and the U.K. *Journal of Money, Credit and Banking*, 88(9-10), 1667–1695.

Molcho, M., Craig, W., Due, P., Pickett, W., Harel-Fisch, Y., & Overpeck, M. (2009). Cross-national time trends in bullying behaviour 1994–2006: Findings from Europe and North America. *International Journal of Public Health*, 54(2), 225–234.

National Alliance on Mental Illness. (2009). Background and context on health reform and children and adults living with serious mental illness. Retrieved from http://www2.nami.org/namiland09/POLhcrbackground.pdf

Peterson, C., & Seligman, M. (2004). *Character strengths and virtues: A handbook and classification*. New York: Oxford University Press.

Rasmussen, C., Andrew, G., Zwaigenbaum, L., & Tough, S. (2008). Neurobehavioural outcomes of children with fetal alcohol spectrum disorders: A Canadian perspective. *Paediatrics & Child Health*, 13(3), 185–191.

Robertson, J., & Bowlby, J. (1952). Responses of young children to separation from their mothers. *Courrier du Centre International de l'Enfance*, 2, 131–142.

Saab, H., & Klinger, D. (2010). School differences in adolescent health and wellbeing: Findings from the Canadian Health Behaviour in School-Aged Children Study. *Social Science & Medicine*, 70(6), 850–858.

Salter, D., McMillan, D., Richards, M., Talbot, T., Hodges, J., Bentovim, A., Hastings, R., Stevenson, J., and Skuse, D. (2003). Development of sexually abusive behavior in sexually victimized males: A longitudinal study. *The Lancet*, 361(9356), 471–476.

Smith, A., Stewart, D., Poon, C., Peled, M., Saewyc, E., & McCreary Society. (2014) *From Hastings Street to Haida Gwaii: Provincial results of the 2013 BC Adolescent Health Survey*. Vancouver: McCreary Centre Society.

Sood, B., Delaney-Black, V., Covington, C., Nordstrom-Klee, B., Ager, J., Templin, T., Janisse, J., Martier, S., & Sokol, R.J. (2001). Prenatal alcohol exposure and childhood behavior at age 6 to 7 years: A dose-response effect. *Pediatrics*, 108(2), E34.

Spataro, J., Mullen, P.E., Burgess, P.M., Wells, D.L., & Moss, S.A. (2004). Impact of child sexual abuse on mental health. *British Journal of Psychiatry*, 184, 416–421.

Statistics Canada. (2007). Study: Delayed transitions of young adults. *The Daily*. Retrieved from www.statcan.gc.ca/daily-quotidien/070918/dq070918b-eng.htm

Susser, E., Hoek, H.W., & Brown, A. (1998). Neurodevelopmental disorders after prenatal famine: The story of the Dutch Famine Study. *American Journal of Epidemiology*, 47(3), 213–216.

Teicher, M.H., Andersen, S.L., Polcari, A., Anderson, C.M., & Navalta, C.P. (2002). Developmental neurobiology of childhood stress and trauma. *Psychiatric Clinics of North America*, 25(2), 397–426.

Teicher, M.H., Andersen, S.L., Polcari, A., Anderson, C.M., Navalta, C.P., & Kim, D.M. (2003). The neurobiological consequences of early stress and childhood maltreatment. *Neuroscience and Biobehavioral Reviews*, 27(1-2), 33–44.

Ungerleider, C., Burns, T., & Cartwright, F. (2009). The state and quality of Canadian public elementary and secondary education. In D. Raphael (Ed.), *Social determinants of health* (2nd ed., pp. 156–169). Toronto: Canadian Scholars' Press.

Waddell, C., Shepherd, C., Schwartz, C., & Barican, J. (2014). *Child and youth mental disorders: Prevalence and evidence-based interventions*. Children's Health Policy Centre, Simon Fraser University.

Widom, C.S., DuMont, K., & Czaja, S.J. (2007). A prospective investigation of major depressive disorder and comorbidity in abused and neglected children grown up. *Archives of General Psychiatry*, 64(1), 49–56.

World Health Organization. (2003). *Social determinants of health: The solid facts* (2nd ed.). Geneva: WHO.

World Health Organization. (2007). ICD-10: Version 2007. Retrieved from apps. who.int/classifications/apps/icd/icd10online/

World Health Organization. (2012). In C. Currie, C. Zannotti, A. Morgan, D. Currie, M. de Looze, C. Roberts, O. Samdal, O.R.F. Smith, & V. Barnekow (Eds.), *Social determinants of health and well-being among young people. Health behaviour in school-aged children (HBSC) study: International report from the 2009/2010 survey*. Copenhagen: WHO Regional Office for Europe.

# Chapter 8

# SEX, GENDER, AND SEXUALITY

When a man gives his opinion, he's a man, when a woman gives her opinion, she's a bitch.

—Bette Davis (American actress)

## Introduction

In this chapter, we discuss the issues related to sexual health as well as the relationship of sex and gender to mental health. Humanity has long had a preoccupation with sexual behaviour, which is likely necessary as it is the means of reproduction and propagation of our species. Advertisers and marketers have recognized this and often aim to capture our interests through sexual arousal and titillation. Nevertheless, feelings of embarrassment and shame about sexual behaviour are also rife. Paradoxically, human sexual life can be both a source of pleasure and distress. In this chapter, we examine how our gender and sexual identities and behaviour relate to the heights and depths of mental health and illness.

## Sex and Gender

Although most of us identify ourselves as either male or female, many cultures and societies recognize more than two categories and describe alternative identities (Lang & Kuhnle, 2008). The first distinction to be made is between **sex**, the biological substrate of differences between maleness and femaleness, and **gender**, the expression and modification of these differences in a social and cultural context. A definition of these terms, for research purposes, has been developed by researchers with the Canadian Institutes of Health Research (2014), who acknowledge the complexities of these concepts:

There are no single agreed-upon definitions of gender or sex, though it is fairly common to associate gender with socially constructed roles, relationships, behaviours, relative power, and other traits that societies ascribe to women and men. Sex is typically understood to refer to the biological and physiological characteristics that distinguish females from males.

The *Better Science with Sex and Gender* primer written by Johnson and colleagues (2007) offers an expanded discussion on the importance of understanding sex and gender and incorporating appropriate analyses into our research and interventions:

> Sex is a multidimensional biological construct that encompasses anatomy, physiology, genes, and hormones that together create a human "package" that affects how we are labelled. Although conceptualizing sex usually relies on the female/male binary, in reality, individuals' sex characteristics exist on a continuum. Thus, using a binary understanding of male/female cannot account for all of the breadth and variety in human sex characteristics. Still, the majority of people today, researchers included, tend to think of both animals and humans as being made up of two sexes. As our understanding of the complexities of sex increases, we will be better able to address—in both everyday life and in research—the nuances of the continuum of sex.

> Sex plays an important role in health because individuals may experience various processes differently based on their biology. For example, male and female bodies respond differently to alcohol, drugs, and therapeutics due to differences in body composition and metabolism, as well as differences in hormones. In fact, the constitution of the female body is inherently different from the male body, from cellular metabolism to blood chemistry. Indeed, some researchers now claim that "every organ in the body—not just those related to reproduction—has the capability to respond differently on the basis of sex" (Gesensway, 2001, p. 935).

> Since gender is a social construct that is culturally based and historically specific, it is constantly changing. Gender refers to the socially prescribed and experienced dimensions of "femaleness" or "maleness" in a society, and is manifested at many levels. Gender, and our experience of it, is always linked to the social world. As such, gender is also intimately connected to social and economic status where maleness is almost universally preferred over femaleness. The valuation of males over females is one way that "gender is a part of all human interactions" and "is a 'stable' form of structured inequality" (Ettorre, 2004, p. 329). These experiences and cultural values result in socially prescribed gender roles that dictate behaviours—supporting different interests, expectations, and divisions of labour for the sexes. These gender roles are further reinforced by practices and rules that affect gender identity at the individual level, gender relations at the interpersonal or group level, and institutional gender in the social realm.

## *Genetic Basis of Sex*

One's sex is determined by the karyotype (i.e., chromosomal complement) that includes sex chromosomes of either XX (female) or XY (male). The presence of one or the other of these sex chromosome configurations puts into play a series of characteristic biological differences that begin during fetal development and continue through life, such as development of different reproductive organs, external genitalia, breast growth, and hormone production. Although relatively rare, variations in sex chromosomes do exist, including: X chromosome (Turner's Syndrome), XXY (Klinefelter's Syndrome), XXX (Triple X), XYY, or other sex chromosome configurations. Usually, the presence of a Y chromosome initiates the development of male reproductive and hormonal features.

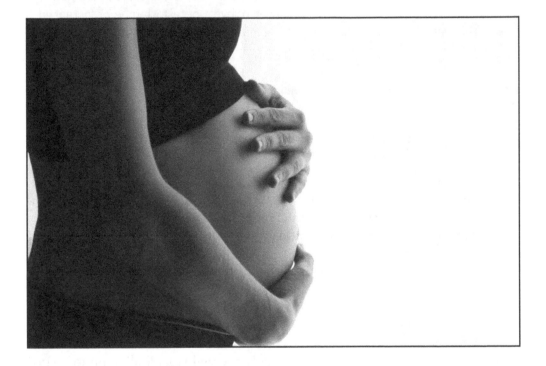

**Figure 8.1:** During fetal development, characteristic biological features of sex first begin to develop.

*Source:* suzyco/iStockphoto

Intersex is a socially constructed category that has been used to describe a person whose external genitalia looks ambiguous or "opposite" to the expected appearance, based on an individual's chromosomal karyotype. It is important to note that the "male," "female," and "intersex" categories that have been constructed lie along a

---

**Box 8.1: XYY Syndrome**

Early studies of men with XYY syndrome led to the flawed conclusion that these men were genetically predisposed to aggressive, anti-social behaviour and below-average intelligence (Price & Whatmore, 1967). The notorious case of Richard Speck, who in the 1960s murdered eight nurses in Chicago, contributed to this mistaken notion that men with XYY chromosomes have serious behavioural and personality disorders. At his criminal trial, Speck and his lawyer claimed that he was a victim of uncontrollable urges caused by his genotype. However, the jury remained unconvinced and found him guilty, sentencing him to life in prison where he eventually died. In fact, Speck did not have an XYY genotype. Recent research reports contradictory findings as to whether or not men with XYY syndrome have elevated levels of testosterone or increased levels of aggressive behaviour (Götz, Johnstone, & Ratcliffe, 1999; Theilgaard, 1984).

---

continuum and that there is great diversity in opinion regarding who falls into these different "boxes" (Intersex Society of North America, n.d.).

## *Gender Identity and Gender Role*

**Gender identity** has been defined as "how we see ourselves as masculine, feminine, or something in between and affects our feelings and behaviours. Both women and men develop their gender identity in the face of strong societal messages about the 'correct' gendered role for their presenting sex" (Johnson et al., 2007, p. 8). **Gender roles** are shaped by societal norms and involve the collection of values, attitudes, beliefs, and behaviours that are thought of as masculine and feminine.

Individuals may experience discrepancies between their gender identity and their biological sex (e.g., someone who is physically male feels a strong inner sense of being female). This incongruence between perceived gender and biological sex can cause significant emotional distress and, for many years, has been classified as a mental disorder by the ICD and the DSM. In the last several years leading up to revised versions of these diagnostic texts, experts, clinicians, and members of the transgender community advocated for the removal of "disorders" related to gender identity from the mental and behavioural disorders sections of these diagnostic manuals (De Cuypere et al., 2010). Despite the arguments put forth by these communities, who see these classifications as highly problematic, the DSM-V includes diagnostic criteria related to gender identity and the new version of the ICD is not expected until 2017.

The term "**transgender**" refers to a wide range of individuals and behaviours that differ from traditional male and female gender roles. This may be pursued through sexual reassignment surgery, by use of hormones and medications that affect hormone production, and by more superficial changes, such as to hairstyle and clothing. Not all transgendered individuals wish to undergo sexual reassignment surgery.

## Sexual Orientation

**Sexual orientation** is defined as an enduring pattern of emotional, romantic, and/or sexual attractions to men, women, or both sexes, and refers to "a person's sense of identity based on those attractions, related behaviours, and membership in a community of others who share those attractions" (American Psychological Association, 2008, p. 1). Heterosexuality involves enduring patterns of attraction to a sex/gender different from one's own, homosexuality involves stable attraction to the same sex/gender, and bisexuality denotes enduring patterns of attraction to more than one sex/gender. The term "pansexuality" is sometimes used to refer to patterns of attraction to any or all sexes/genders, while "asexuality" describes a lack of any sexual orientation, attraction, or interest overall. For many decades, any sexual orientation other than heterosexuality was considered to be a "mental disorder." This may be surprising, but it seemed obvious to psychiatrists of the 1940s and 1950s, whose views were consistent with widespread social prejudice against homosexuality and bisexuality. In the 1960s, social activists in the gay rights movement argued against the pathologizing of homosexuality and, in 1973, homosexuality was removed as a diagnosis in the prevailing psychiatric diagnostic system in North America (the DSM). There remained a diagnosis of sexual orientation disorder, defined by psychological distress over one's orientation, (i.e., those who were extremely unhappy about being homosexual would be considered to have a mental disorder and thus be appropriate for psychiatric intervention). The use of this diagnosis was based on the belief endorsed by prominent psychiatrist Dr. Robert Spitzer, who claimed that homosexuality could be cured if people were motivated. More recently, Dr. Spitzer has apologized to the lesbian, gay, bisexual, transgender and queer (LGBTQ) community and acknowledged that his studies were flawed (Carey, 2012). Note that homosexuality continued to be classified as a psychiatric disorder in the ICD system until 1993!

A number of psychiatric and psychological treatments have been applied in efforts to change homosexual orientation. None have been successful. Treatment has generally involved psychotherapy, with limited use of pharmacological agents (no anti-homosexuality drug has been discovered). But dramatic and morally questionable strategies have been tried:

> In electric shock aversion therapy, electrodes were attached to the wrist or lower leg and shocks were administered while the patient watched photographs of men and women in various stages of undress. The aim was to encourage avoidance of the shock by moving to photographs of the opposite sex. It was hoped that arousal to same sex photographs would reduce, while relief arising from shock avoidance would increase interest in opposite sex images. (Smith, Bartlett, & King, 2004, p. 2)

The historical characterization of homosexuality and bisexuality as mental disorders in psychiatric diagnostic systems (such as the ICD and the DSM) highlights the well-known difficulties regarding the validity of psychiatric diagnosis, discussed in

Chapter 4. The characterization also demonstrates the substantial role that societal norms and ideologies contribute to the way in which disorder is conceptualized. Although the mental health field does not currently view homosexual orientation as a disorder, it is associated with mental health problems, largely due to the high level of associated stigma. Homosexuality has been condemned by religious systems, vilified by societies, and portrayed by ideological movements as inferior. At the extreme, the Nazi movement in Germany massacred hundreds of thousands of individuals believed to be homosexual. Even our "enlightened" postmodern society stigmatizes homosexuality to a significant degree, with incidences of extreme violence and discrimination occurring all too often.

LGBTQ individuals may experience self-stigma as well as rejection by family or friends if they openly express their sexuality. This results in high levels of anxiety and depression as well as elevated suicide rates (Bostwick et al., 2009; Remafedi et al., 1998). In fact, recent reports identify that half of the LGBTQ youth population has considered suicide and that these young people are over four times more likely to make suicide attempts than their heterosexual peers (Dyck, 2012). It is important to realize that individuals may present to clinical services with depression or anxiety disorders without indicating the central role of stress and conflict about sexual/gender identity or orientation.

LGBTQ individuals have been the object of profound prejudice and discrimination, and as we discussed in Chapter 6, prejudice and discrimination are often rooted deep within our psyches. Cruelty and harm experienced by LGBTQ individuals often springs from ignorance, fear, and the need to feel superior to others. Through increasing education, exposure, and awareness, Canadians may gradually have become more tolerant and less stigmatizing of LGBTQ individuals. In great part, this is the result of efforts by LGBTQ communities to fight prejudice, build pride, and advocate for appropriate rights and freedoms. In Chapter 15, we return to a discussion of the importance of tolerance for diversity among the population in fostering a mentally healthy society.

Despite intensive scientific study of human development and various speculative theories that have come and gone, we have not yet been able to understand how or why individuals develop particular sexual attractions.

## Sexual Activity

Survival and continuation of the human species is dependent on large numbers of people having sexual intercourse and procreating. As a means to ensure that this happens, sexual intercourse, for most people, is experienced as highly pleasurable. Consequently, there is a strong drive for people to have sex and repeat the experience of such pleasurable sensations. There is a wide range in the particular preferences individuals may have in the type and style of sexual activity they enjoy. The old proverb "different strokes for different folks" fits well here. Variants in sexual interest range

**Figure 8.2:** The annual Gay Pride events celebrate LGBTQ culture, and they serve as venues for social activism (e.g., fighting for legal rights such as gay marriage).

*Source:* EHStock/iStockphoto

from fascination with items of clothing to sexual gratification obtained from inflicting or receiving pain. Some of these are viewed as individual traits and preferences, rather than mental disorders. They are sometimes surprising and quirky, but generally not associated with meaningful disability or harm to self or others. For example, some individuals derive sexual satisfaction from wearing furry animal costumes. However, some people have strong sexual attractions that lead to harm or result in disabling problems or circumstances, and these are considered to be mental disorders known as "**paraphilias**." These are often characterized by an inability to resist strong impulses, may involve participation of non-consenting or under-aged individuals, and may interfere with social relationships. Paraphilias, such as exhibitionism and pedophilia, frequently result in criminal charges and severe consequences.

When a suitable partner for sex is unavailable, or sometimes even when one *is* available, masturbation (i.e., stimulation of one's genitalia, usually to the point of orgasm) is a common alternative. For multiple centuries, European and North American society considered masturbation to be both sinful and harmful. Prevailing medical opinion concluded that masturbation caused "a perceptible reduction of strength, of memory and even of reason; blurred vision, all the nervous disorders, all types of gout and rheumatism, weakening of the organs of generation, blood in the urine, disturbance of the appetite, headaches and a great number of other disorders" (Tissot, 1764). Dramatic interventions were sometimes undertaken, such as the use of chastity belts and other restraining devices. Myths persist even to the present time, such as warnings that masturbation leads to blindness, hairy hands, or stunted growth. Not only have such claims been debunked, but government agencies in some countries have recently encouraged masturbation, particularly among youth, as one means to promote "safe sex" and decrease unplanned pregnancies (Grimston, 2009; Tremlett, 2009).

## Sexual Dysfunction

In classifying "[s]exual dysfunction, not caused by organic disorder or disease," the ICD system describes a variety of conditions (WHO, 2007). Some of these describe difficulties that are characterized by diminished sexual desire and lack of sexual enjoyment. This disorder has received greater clinical and research attention for women than for men. It may be that men have been more reluctant to acknowledge loss of sexual desire, given the importance of maintaining an image of sexual potency within the masculine gender role. Treatment for this disorder is usually psychological in nature (primarily Cognitive Behavioural Therapy [CBT]). Pharmacological treatments are also used in certain cases, such as medications to augment testosterone levels (Goldstein, 2007).

Other forms of sexual dysfunction are described as failure of genital response (e.g., erectile dysfunction in males and failure of lubrication in females) and orgasmic dysfunction (e.g., anorgasmia, premature ejaculation, vaginismus, and substantial delay in achieving orgasm) (WHO, 2007). Erectile dysfunction in males has received much focus in recent years with the marketing of medications such as Viagra and Cialis, which are effective treatments in about half of the cases of erectile dysfunction. However, evidence indicates that prevention of erectile dysfunction is possible through maintaining a generally positive level of overall health. This includes getting enough physical exercise, minimizing the use of tobacco, avoiding obesity, maintaining a low level of blood cholesterol, and using alcohol only in moderation. There is evidence supporting benefits of physical exercise in preventing erectile dysfunction even among men who have reached mid-life (Gupta et al., 2011). It is interesting to note that the diagnoses of sexual dysfunction are heteronormative and male-centric. For example, a "failure to lubricate" in females implies that dysfunction occurs when a woman's body does not create the appropriate response to allow for penetration by a penis. It is always good to think critically and question the ways in which we categorize and pathologize.

Sexual dysfunction is often associated with depression and anxiety, whether caused by these mental health problems (depression often triggers a reduction in desire, and anxiety can impair erectile function) or causing them (the experience of sexual dysfunction and associated discouragement or self-doubt may trigger mood

**Figure 8.3:** In recent years, medications have been marketed to treat erectile dysfunction.

*Source:* Rpsycho/iStockphoto

problems). Ironically, antidepressant medications often cause these two forms of sexual dysfunction as side effects! The rate of antidepressant-caused sexual dysfunction is in the range of 25 to 80 percent across different studies and drug types, a strikingly high rate for this problematic side effect (Serreti & Chieso, 2009).

Disorders of excessive sexual desire are also described in the ICD (WHO, 2007) and, in recent years, these are often referred to in the popular press and media as forms of "sexual addiction." However, the nature and validity of the construct of sexual addiction is neither universally accepted nor endorsed. A variety of private therapists and treatment programs have sprung up to provide treatment for sexual addiction, and various self-help groups, such as Sexaholics Anonymous, can be found in North America.

## Romantic Love, Monogamy, and Infidelity

Social psychologists have described romantic love as having components of attachment, caring, and intimacy (Rubin, 1970). Sexual attraction between individuals early in a relationship has been found to be correlated with the release of various neurochemicals in the brain. Development of longer-term intimacy, caring, and attachment is based more on the sharing of life experiences, common interests, and the formation of interpersonal bonds and loyalties. "**Monogamy**" can be defined as having only one mate, and can be further delineated as social monogamy, in which an individual lives with only one partner, and sexual monogamy, in which an individual has sex exclusively with one partner. Ethologists and other scientists who study animal behaviour have found that monogamy is relatively rare in the animal kingdom, existing primarily among birds, beavers, bats, and some primates, including gibbons, tamarins, and marmosets. Even among those animals, relationships are generally socially monogamous but not sexually monogamous. Among our closest evolutionary relatives, male gorillas fight to control a harem of females who then mate exclusively with the victorious male, whereas chimpanzees have "more of a sexual free-for-all" (Barash & Lipton, 2001).

In our evolutionary past, we *homo sapiens* were similar to our close primate relatives; our mating behaviour likely involved relationships with multiple partners. However, monogamous relationships have become the norm among most modern human societies and infidelity (i.e., unfaithfulness to a spouse) is commonly considered to be a breach

**Figure 8.4:** Prairie dogs are known for the affection they show toward one another. These animals are socially monogamous but not sexually monogamous.

*Source:* Nick Biemans/iStockphoto

of trust. Nevertheless, research surveys indicate that infidelity is common (Marín, Christensen, & Atkins, 2014); this is likely due to the fact that, in order to be faithful to a spouse, many of us must fight instinctual urges. This is a prominent example of the conflict characterized by Sigmund Freud as a battle between our instinctual drives and the values we have internalized within civilized societies (see Chapter 3).

## Gender Roles and Mental Health

Gender roles, in conjunction with biological sex, have important implications for mental health.

---

### Box 8.2: Gender Role Development in Children

Often, we see children adopt conventional, stereotypical gender roles at a young age: for example, little boys who are thrilled at banging their toy trucks together with gusto, and young girls who love to arrange their dolls to "play house." In adopting such stereotypically "masculine" or "feminine" behaviours in their play and their social interactions, or alternatively, by adopting unconventional behaviours, children internalize and establish gender identity and gender role. Much is made of characteristic differences between males and females in regard to their emotional behaviour and expressiveness. For example, researchers have found that, on average, females cry five times more often than males each month, especially before and during the menstrual cycle when crying can increase, often without obvious reasons (Frey, 1985). Interestingly, these differences in crying behaviour do not emerge until puberty; prepubertal girls and boys cry at about the same rate. Why does this difference appear at puberty? Some theories link these changes to hormonal differentiation that occurs during puberty, whereas other theories identify psychological and socio-cultural factors that may influence adolescent boys and girls to behave differently from each other.

---

Women are characterized as being more adept than men at deciphering the emotional responses of others and at expressing and communicating their own feelings, a characteristic sometimes referred to as "emotional intelligence." Widely held stereotypes of masculinity in our society often pressure men to adopt "strong and silent" behavioural styles, described in psychological studies as including the following features: autonomy (i.e., standing alone to face challenges and difficulties); achievement (i.e., placing high value in accomplishing goals in work and winning competitive ventures); aggression (i.e., responding with toughness and strength when challenged); and stoicism (i.e., maintaining composure and avoiding expressions of sadness or grief) (Jansz, 2000). Although such differences do appear to exist, on average, between men and women, it is often pointed out that there is much greater variability in behavioural styles *within* each sex/gender than exists *across* the average levels found in the two sexes/genders. There are additional factors, such as age, that have been found to impact men and women's emotional intelligence (Fernández-Berroca et al., 2012). We must be careful to avoid exaggeration of these masculine and feminine stereotypes and steer clear of pejorative characterizations that blame either men or women for supposed inadequacies.

## *Women's Mental Health*

Epidemiological studies have consistently found that women report higher prevalence rates of the most common mental disorders, that is, anxiety disorder and depression, than men. For example, a study of Ontario residents 15 years of age and older found one-year prevalence rates for depression to be 3.5 percent for males and 6.1 percent for females (Akhtar-Danesh & Landeen, 2007). This gender difference in prevalence rates might reflect, in part, a greater tendency by women to report symptoms of emotional distress, whether because they are more aware of psychological distress or other mental health symptoms, or because they are more comfortable discussing these symptoms. These differences may also reflect an absence of gender considerations in the development of diagnostic classifications and criteria, which ultimately, can influence prevalence estimates, help-seeking behaviour, diagnosis, and treatment (Johnson & Stewart, 2010). Women are almost 50 percent more likely than men to have been prescribed psychotropic medication (i.e., medications that affect mental function, such as antidepressants, sedatives, and anti-anxiety medications) (Simoni-Wastila, 2000). There is also some evidence that physicians are biased toward diagnosing depression in women over men, even when given the same symptom report (WHO, 2015). Nonetheless, factors such as reporting differences and diagnostic biases are unlikely to account entirely for prevalence rates of common mental disorders being substantially higher in women than in men. It is likely that there are true gender differences in these rates.

What aspects of the female gender role might be contributing to higher rates? Interestingly, rates of depression and anxiety disorder are similar in prepubertal boys and girls, and it is not until puberty that prevalence rates in girls increase to levels that are much higher than in boys. Arguments are made for identifying both "nature" (i.e., biological factors) and "nurture" (i.e., environmental factors) as the predominant factor in the elevation of rates of anxiety disorder and depression that appears in teenage girls. Biological factors considered to be relevant include hormonal differences in females and males that become prominent at the time of puberty. Environmental factors include the impacts of sexism and related discrimination (i.e., discrimination, both interpersonal and institutional, based on the belief that one gender is inferior to the other), experiences with violence, stress related to single parenthood, and psychological and social responses to bodily changes that occur. For example, girls may feel particularly self-conscious and vulnerable as a result of breast development and the intense attention that is often directed toward their changing body shapes and appearances. Feelings of distress and embarrassment about body shape and weight have also been identified as likely contributors to the high rates of eating disorders that emerge in teenage girls and young adult women.

Victimization as a result of domestic or sexual violence has a profound influence on women's mental health. These forms of extreme stress have far more impact on women than on men. Although both genders are affected by domestic violence, women are more vulnerable to physical harm. And most sexual violence, stalking, serious spousal assaults, and spousal homicide target women (Kessler et al., 1995). Surveys in Canada have found that the rate of sexual assault against females reported to the police was more than 10 times the rate for males, and females account for 92 percent of sexual assault victims (Statistics Canada, 2012b).

Exposure to violence strongly predicts severity of mental health problems; women who have experienced childhood sexual abuse or physical violence have rates of depression three to four times higher than women who have not been exposed to these forms of violence (WHO, 2001). Research in this area also suggests a dose-response relationship between the types and frequency of childhood trauma and occurrence of mental disorder in adulthood (Hovens et al., 2010).

Women who have experienced high levels of physical violence have increased rates of depression, anxiety, and PTSD. Violence-related PTSD is associated with chronic fear, nightmares, and flashbacks, in which the violence is re-experienced, and may result in pervasive mistrust in relationships.

Pregnancy, childbirth, and the postpartum period are often associated with mental health problems, such as depression, anxiety, or even psychosis, and this has been attributed to a couple of factors. First, there are biological/hormonal changes during and following pregnancy that may have negative impacts on mood. Second, there are psychological and behavioural changes that accompany these life events, such as the sudden increase in workload and responsibility associated with parenting, limitations on contact with friends or colleagues, and loss of workplace involvements that are central to many women's identities. In some circumstances, these losses and new stressors may be associated with a sense of shame (e.g., for not feeling unreservedly happy as a new mother) and guilt over perceived inadequacy in the parenting role.

## Men's Mental Health

Our discussion above is not meant to indicate that victimization by violence is exclusively a problem for women—in fact, most physical violence targets men. However, the mental health consequences of violence against men, typically by other men, have not been well studied. Males are more prone to take risks and this propensity for risk-taking has been linked to various health problems (Mahalik et al., 2013). Especially during adolescence and young adulthood, males engage in far higher rates of risky and impulsive behaviour, such as reckless driving, extreme sports pursuits, and illicit drug use.

Men have much higher rates of alcohol and drug abuse and dependence than do women (Statistics Canada, 2013). In association with problematic substance use, men experience a wide range of serious mental health problems, including depression, anxiety, and psychotic episodes (e.g., in the context of withdrawal). Overall, alcohol use has a direct or indirect causal role in 6 percent of men's deaths (versus 1 percent of women's deaths) (Rehm et al., 2009). Although we have a limited understanding of the reasons for men's greater propensity toward substance misuse, it may well be that the autonomous and stoical male behavioural style plays some role. If it is part of the masculine role to avoid display or acknowledgement of emotional distress to others, then the psychoactive effects of alcohol and drugs (soothing or blocking out emotional distress) may provide a psychological self-management function that men consider socially acceptable. Teaching men to expand their repertoire of strategies for managing psychological distress could have enormous health and social benefits.

While it is widely documented that men experience depression at much lower rates than women, experts in men's mental health suggest that this may be related to diagnostic criteria that do not adequately capture men's experiences of depression as well as a tendency for men to be reluctant to seek mental health care (Oliffe & Phillips, 2008). It is puzzling and concerning that, despite low reported rates of depression (a strong predictor of suicide), men have a shockingly high rate of death by suicide, compared to women (Oliffe et al., 2012). In Canada, the male suicide rate is about three times that of females (Statistics Canada, 2012a). Figure 8.5 shows the age- and gender-specific incidence of suicide in Canada, based on data from 2009 (Statistics Canada, 2013). The chart shows that male suicide rates are greater than female rates at all ages. The male suicide rate increases steadily with age until peaking among men in their late fifties. Male suicides are more likely to occur in the context of substance use disorders than are female suicides (Bilsker & White, 2011). Although men have significantly higher rates of death by suicide than do women, it should be noted that women attempt suicide more frequently than men (three to four times as often) (Statistics Canada, 2012a). Suicide is a serious health and social issue experienced by both sexes.

Suicide in men has been described by a leading suicide researcher as a "silent epidemic" (Bell, 2008). It is "epidemic" because it has a disturbingly high incidence and is a major contributor to men's mortality: between the ages of 15 and 44, suicide is among the top three causes of men's mortality. It is "silent" because there is a low degree of public awareness regarding the magnitude of this problem. Surprisingly little research has been done in this area, there are few preventive efforts specifically targeting male suicide, and men are reluctant to seek help for suicidality. In fact, men at all ages are less likely to seek help for health problems and are less likely to adopt health-protective lifestyle changes involving fitness activity or dietary modification. In comparison to women, men also tend to have a lack of social support. This has been implicated as another important factor in male suicide. An interview-based study of men who had attempted suicide suggested that social stressors (e.g., family breakdown, overwork and employment insecurity, often combined with alcohol or

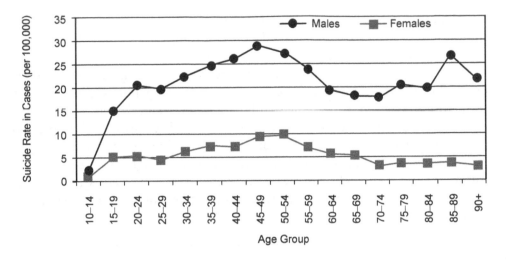

**Figure 8.5:** Suicide rates in Canada, 2001–2005

*Source:* Chart created by Elliot Goldner, based on data from the Public Health Agency of Canada.

drug abuse) are understudied contributors to male suicide (University of Western Sydney Media Unit, 2008). Interestingly, recent research exploring men's depression and suicide suggests that masculine identities related to being good providers/fathers/ partners serves as a protective mechanism against male suicide (Oliffe et al., 2012).

## *Positive Aspects of Male and Female Gender Roles*

Historically, comparisons between males and females have often tended to point out supposed inadequacies or weaknesses in one group or the other. For example, women have been characterized as being overly emotional, whereas men have been characterized as being emotionally inept. There has also tended to be a stereotyping of male and female gender roles despite the finding that the range of behaviours *within* each gender is much greater than the differences found across the average characteristics found in males and females. Increased awareness is needed of the profound diversity that exists in male and female gender roles and the complementarity of various roles and behaviours characterized as either "male" or "female."

## Conclusion

Sex and gender must be differentiated and understood as unique contributors to our identities as either males, females, or some alternative intersexual identity. Sexual identity is distinct from gender identity, and, historically, individuals who have not conformed to dominant societal norms have been subjected to profound stigma and discrimination. Efforts at increasing public awareness and education by the LGBTQ community appear to have contributed to some improvement in tolerance and acceptance of diversity.

Various forms of sexual dysfunction have been described, including disorders characterized by diminished sexual desire, problems with genital stimulation and orgasm, and problems of excessive sexual interest. Males and females tend to have different types of mental health problems, and this has been attributed, in part, to characteristic differences in male and female gender roles. Females tend to have higher rates of depression and anxiety disorder. Males tend to have higher rates of substance use disorder and are more likely to die by suicide. Nevertheless, there is a wide range and diversity of behaviour within genders, and there are complementary strengths and values that are contributed.

## Glossary

**gender:** The expression and modification of these differences in a social and cultural context.

**gender identity:** Your personal sense of knowing which gender you belong to, or the way you see yourself.

**gender roles:** The collection of values, attitudes, beliefs, and behaviours that make up the social definition of being masculine or feminine.

**monogamy:** Having only one mate.

**paraphilias:** Mental disorders involving strong sexual attraction that lead to harm or result in disabling problems or circumstances.

**sex:** The biological substrate of differences between maleness and femaleness.

**sexual orientation:** An enduring pattern of emotional, romantic, and/or sexual attractions to men, women, or both sexes and a person's sense of identity based on those attractions, related behaviours, and membership in a community of others who share those attractions.

**transgender:** A wide range of individuals and behaviours that differ from normative male and female gender roles.

## Critical Thinking Questions

1. What is the difference between sex and gender?
2. How is gender identity related to mental health?
3. Are non-heterosexual types of sexual interest viewed as mental disorders? Explain.
4. Describe several mental health problems of particular relevance to women.
5. Describe several mental health problems of particular relevance to men.

## Recommended Readings

Kornstein, S.G., & Clayton, A.H. (Eds.). (2004). *Women's Mental Health: A Comprehensive Textbook*. New York: Guildford Press.

Kreukels, B.P.C., Steensma, T.D., & de Vries, A.L.C. (Eds.) (2013). In M. Meana (Ed.), *Gender Dysphoria and Disorders of Sex Development: Progress in Care and Knowledge*. New York: Springer.

Mikulincer, M., & Goodman, G.S. (Eds.). (2006). *Dynamics of Romantic Love: Attachment, Caregiving, and Sex*. New York: Guilford Press.

Rudman, L.A., & Glick, P. (2012). *The Social Psychology of Gender: How Power and Intimacy Shape Gender Relations*. New York: Guilford Press.

## Recommended Websites

Canadian Mental Health Association. Men and Mental Illness. www.cmha.ca/public_policy/men-and-mental-illness/#.Vg7RAdZ45l8

It's Pronounced Metrosexual. http://itspronouncedmetrosexual.com/2011/11/breaking-through-the-binary-gender-explained-using-continuums

LGBTQ Mental Health Syllabus. www.aglp.org/gap/

National Alliance on Mental Illness. www.nami.org/Find-Support

Women's Health Research Network. www.cwhn.ca

World Health Organization. Gender and Women's Mental Health. www.who.int/mental_health/prevention/genderwomen/en/

## References

Akhtar-Danesh, N., & Landeen, J. (2007). Relation between depression and sociodemographic factors. *International Journal of Mental Health Systems*, 1(4).

American Psychological Association. (2008). For a better understanding of sexual orientation and homosexuality. Retrieved from www.apa.org/topics/sexuality/sorientation.pdf

Barash, D., & Lipton, J.E. (2001). *The myth of monogamy: Fidelity and infidelity in animals and people*. New York: W.H. Freeman.

Bell, D. (2008). The silent epidemic of male suicide. *BBC News*. Retrieved from news.bbc.co.uk/2/hi/uk_news/7219232.stm

Bilsker, D., & White, J.W. (2011). The silent epidemic of male suicide. *BC Medical Journal*, 53 (10), 529–533. Retrieved from www.bcmj.org/sites/default/files/BCMJ_53_Vol10_suicide.pdf

Bostwick, W.B., Boyd, C.J., Hughes, T.L., & McCabe, S.E. (2009). Dimensions of sexual orientation and the prevalence of mood and anxiety disorders in the United States. *American Journal of Public Health*, 100(3), 468–475.

Canadian Institutes of Health Research. (2014). Integrating gender and sex in health research: A tool for CIHR peer reviewers. Retrieved from www.cihr-irsc.gc.ca/e/43216.html

Carey, B. (May 18, 2012). Psychiatry giant sorry for backing gay "cure." *New York Times.*

De Cuypere, G., Knudson, G., & Bockting, W. (2010). Response of the World Professional Association for Transgender Health to the proposed DSM 5 criteria for gender incongruence. *International Journal of Transgenderism*, 12, 119–123.

Dyck, D.R. (2012). Report on outcomes and recommendations. Retrieved from egale.ca/wp-content/uploads/2013/02/YSPS-Report-online.pdf

Ettorre, E. (2004). Revisioning women and drug use: Gender sensitivity, embodiment, and reducing harm. *International Journal of Drug Policy*, 15(5–6), 327–335.

Fernández-Berroca, P., Cabello, R., Castillo, R., & Extremera, N. (2012). Gender differences in emotional intelligence: The mediating effect of age. *Behavioral Psychology*, 20(1), 77–89.

Frey, W. (1985). *Crying: The mystery of tears.* New York: HarperCollins.

Gesensway, D. (2001). Reasons for sex-specific and gender-specific study on health topics. *Annals of Internal Medicine*, 135(10), 935–938.

Goldstein, I. (2007). Current management strategies of the postmenopausal patient with sexual health problems. *Journal of Sexual Medicine*, 4(Suppl. 3), 235–253.

Götz, M.J., Johnstone, E.C., & Ratcliffe, S.G. (1999). Criminality and antisocial behavior in unselected men with sex chromosome abnormalities. *Psychological Medicine*, 29(4), 953–962.

Grimston, J. (2009). Pupils told: Sex every day keeps the GP away. *The Sunday Times* (London). Retrieved from www.thesundaytimes.co.uk/sto/news/uk_news/article177775.ece

Gupta, B.P., Murad, M.H., Clifton, M.M., Prokop, L., Nehra, A., & Kopecky, S.L. (2011). The effect of lifestyle modification and cardiovascular risk factor reduction on erectile dysfunction: A systematic review and meta-analysis. *Archives of Internal Medicine*, 171(20), 1797–1803.

Hovens, J.G.., Wiersma, J.E., Giltay, E.J., Van Oppen, P., Spinhoven, P., & Penninx, B.W. (2010). Childhood life events and childhood trauma in adult patients with depressive, anxiety and comorbid disorders vs. controls. *Acta Psychiatrica Scandinavica*, 122(1), 66–74.

Intersex Society of North America. (n.d.). What is intersex? Retrieved from www.isna.org/faq/what_is_intersex

Jansz, J. (2000). Masculine identity and restrictive emotionality. In A.H. Fischer (Ed.), *Gender and emotion* (pp. 166–186). Cambridge: Cambridge University Press.

Johnson, J.L., Greaves, L., & Repta, R. (2007). Better science with sex and gender: A primer for health research. Vancouver: Women's Health Research Network.

Johnson, J., & Stewart, D.E. (2010). DSM-V: Toward a gender sensitive approach to psychiatric diagnosis. *Archives of Women's Mental Health*, 13(1), 17–19.

Kessler, R.C., Sonnega, A., Bromet, E., Hughes, M., & Nelson, C.B. (1995). Posttraumatic stress disorder in the National Comorbidity Survey. *Archives of General Psychiatry*, 52, 1048–1060.

Lang, C., & Kuhnle, U. (2008). Intersexuality and alternative gender categories in non-Western cultures. *Hormone Research*, 69(4), 240–250.

Mahalik, J.R., Levine, C.R., McPherran, L.C., Doyle, L.A., Markowitz, A.J., & Jaffee, S.R. (2013). Changes in health risk behaviors for males and females from early adolescence through early adulthood. *Health Psychology*, 32(6), 685–694.

Marín, R.A., Christensen, A., & Atkins, D.C. (2014). Infidelity and behavioral couple therapy: Relationship outcomes over 5 years following therapy. *Couple and Family Psychology: Research and Practice*, 3(1), 1–12.

Oliffe, J.L., Ogrodniczuk, J.S., Bottorff, J.L., Johnson, J.L., & Hoyak, K. (2012). "You feel like you can't live anymore": Suicide from the perspectives of Canadian men who experience depression. *Social Science and Medicine*, 74(4), 506–514.

Oliffe, J.L., & Phillips, M.J. (2008). Men, depression, and masculinities: A review and recommendations. *Journal of Men's Health*, 5(3), 194–202.

Price, W.H., & Whatmore, P.B. (1967). Criminal behaviour and the XYY male. *Nature*, 213(5078), 815.

Rehm, J., Mathers, C.F., Popova, S., Thavorncharoensap, M., & Teerawattananon, P.J. (2009). Global burden of disease and injury and economic cost attributable to alcohol use and alcohol-use disorders. *The Lancet*, 373(9682), 2223–2233.

Remafedi, G., French, S., Story, M., Resnick, M.D., & Blum, R. (1998). The relationship between suicide risk and sexual orientation: Results of a population-based study. *American Journal of Public Health*, 88(1), 57–60.

Rubin, Z. (1970). Measurement of romantic love. *Journal of Personality and Social Psychology*, 16(2), 265–273.

Serreti, A., & Chieso, A. (2009) Treatment-emergent sexual dysfunction related to antidepressants: A meta-analysis. *Journal of Clinical Psychopharmacology*, 29(3), 259–266.

Simoni-Wastila, L. (2000). The use of abusable prescription drugs: The role of gender. *Journal of Women's Health and Gender-Based Medicine*, 9(3), 289–297.

Smith, G., Bartlett, A., & King, M. (2004). Treatments of homosexuality in Britain since the 1950s—An oral history: The experience of patients. *British Medical Journal*, 328, 427.

Statistics Canada. (2012a). Health at a glance: Mental and substance use disorders in Canada. Retrieved from www.statcan.gc.ca/pub/82-624-x/2013001/article/11855-eng.htm

Statistics Canada. (2012b). Gender differences in police-reported violent crime in Canada, 2008. Retrieved from www.statcan.gc.ca/pub/85f0033m/2010024/part-partie1-eng.htm

Statistics Canada. (2013). Suicides per 100,000, by age group and sex, Canada, 2009. Retrieved from www.statcan.gc.ca/pub/82-624-x/2012001/article/chart/11696-02-chart4-eng.htm

Theilgaard, A. (1984). A psychological study of the personalities of XYY and XXY men. *Acta Psychiatrica Scandinavica, Supplementum, 315*, 1–133.

Tissot, S.A.D. (1764). L'Onanisme: Dissertation sur les maladies produites par la masturbation. Whitefish, MT: Kessigner Publishing.

Tremlett, G. (2009). Spanish region takes hands-on approach to sex education. *The Guardian*. Retrieved from www.guardian.co.uk/world/2009/nov/12/spain-sex-education

University of Western Sydney Media Unit. (January 12, 2008). Social factors, not mental illness, to blame for high male suicide rate. Retrieved from www.uws.edu.au/mhirc/mens_health_information_and_resource_centre/press_and_media/media_releases

World Health Organization. (2001). Gender disparities in mental health. Retrieved from www.who.int/mental_health/media/en/242.pdf

World Health Organization. (2007). *International statistical classification of diseases and related health problems, 10th revision*. Retrieved from www.who.int/classifications/icd/en/

World Health Organization. (2015). Gender and women's mental health. Retrieved from www.who.int/mental_health/prevention/genderwomen/en/

# Chapter 9

# CULTURE, ETHNICITY, AND MENTAL HEALTH

I do not want my house to be walled in on all sides and my windows to be stuffed. I want the cultures of all the lands to be blown about my house as freely as possible. But I refuse to be blown off my feet by any.
—Mahatma Ghandi (political and spiritual leader in India during India's independence movement)

## Introduction

Because our mental development is influenced so strongly by the society and cultural practices in which we are immersed, it is important for us to take a careful look at the impact of cultural factors on mental health. We will find that our cultural identities can serve both to promote good mental health and expose us to certain risks of mental illness. When we develop mental health problems, our cultural identities may also shape the ways in which mental illness is expressed and experienced, and affect the manner in which we tend to heal and restore good mental health. In this chapter, we will first tackle the difficult task of defining terms such as "race," "ethnicity," and "culture," which are often confused and misapplied. We will then consider how these concepts interact with mental health and illness within Canadian society.

## Race

Although humans have been studied more intensively than any other creature, there has been profound disagreement about whether humans should be classified as a single species or as two, three, four, five, or even as sixty different races or subspecies (Darwin, [1871] 1874). Many prominent researchers, including Charles Darwin, have identified themselves to be "monogenist" on the question of race, believing that humans are of the same species and finding race to be an arbitrary distinction.

In 1776, German scientist and classical anthropologist Johann Blumenbach, in *On the Natural Varieties of Mankind*, contended that humanity could be divided into five different races. Can you guess what these might be? They were Caucasian, Negroid, Mongoloid, Malayan, and American. Blumenbach based his classification of races on skin colour, craniology (the size and shape of a person's head), and other physical characteristics.

The notion of different human races often assumes that human evolution entailed a branching of evolutionary lines and is similar to the idea of subspecies. Over recent decades, the notion of distinct races has generally been rejected and most anthropologists agree that the concept of race has no validity (Gravlee & Sweet, 2008; Gravlee, 2009). Currently, the predominant scientific notion is that human variation is distributed along a continuum, and anthropologists have generally abandoned the belief in the existence of discrete racial groups.

## Racism

Although the concept of distinct "races" has generally been rejected, the notion of racism remains important. **Racism** can be defined as a set of attitudes and behaviours in which social groups are identified, separated, treated as inferior or superior, and given differential access to power and other valued resources. Racist behaviours and attitudes exist throughout the world, and there are many notorious instances of racism that serve to remind us of the bleakest and most horrific depths to which humankind has plummeted. The kidnapping, abuse, and subjugation of African men and women for use as slaves in Europe and the Americas is an example of the extreme harm that has been committed through racist beliefs and behaviours. In Canada, First Nations, Inuit, and Metis people have suffered as a result of racist beliefs and practices, experiencing genocide and expropriation of their land and resources.

How can we explain the capacity for racist beliefs to incite large sectors of the population to condone violent and cruel behaviour to fellow human beings? In Chapter 3, we discussed how psychoanalytic theory proposed that there is a part of our minds that is unconscious, that is, hidden from our conscious awareness. One of the early psychoanalytic theorists, Alfred Adler, proposed that much of human striving can be understood as an attempt to overcome the inferiority complex and increase one's sense of personal power and self-esteem. Racism is likely a manifestation of this drive among humans to feel superior, and the lack of compassion and capacity for cruelty that is often attached to racism demonstrates the fallibility of human thought, emotion, and behaviour when influenced by these drives and motivations.

Labelling theory, which was developed as part of the discipline of criminology, states that deviance is caused when individuals who are labelled internalize the label, eventually leading them to take on the traits and behaviours that conform to the label. Thus, when people are repeatedly told that they are inferior in some way, this commonly becomes internalized and accepted as being true, even by those who have become the objects of derision.

People who are victimized by racist attitudes and behaviours may experience profound mental health problems. PTSD symptoms commonly occur, as do many other mental health problems. Later in this section, we examine how First Nations, Inuit, and Metis people in Canada have been subjected to profound and prolonged racist attitudes and behaviour, and we discuss the impact this has had on mental health and illness in these communities.

## Ethnicity

**Ethnicity** refers to a common history, language, and set of rituals that create a form of common identity shared by a group of people. The shared heritage may include preferences for music, food, clothing styles, and perceived common values. Ethnicity may be linked to a particular national origin, such as Italian, Korean, or Irish ethnicity, but may also be linked to other religious or geographical histories, such as Jewish or First Nations ethnicity.

Prominent attention to different ethnicities has often been a result of racist behaviour and attitudes, and many countries have seen tragic conflict, war, and terrible cruelty inflicted on this basis, as discussed above. However, ethnic identity can also be a source of strength and pride. In a country such as Canada, in which the population is composed of people from so many ethnic backgrounds, ethnic identity often becomes an important value to people who feel a sense of pride about the history of their families and ancestors and wish to preserve their ethnic heritage. When Canadians were asked to identify their ethnicity in the most recent Canadian census, a total of 210 different ethnic groups were listed. The 25 most commonly self-identified ethnic groups are listed in Table 9.1.

## Culture

**Culture** is broadly defined as a common heritage or set of beliefs, norms, and values that have been learned and adopted by a group of people (Kornblum, 2011). We tend to think of culture in terms of ethnic groupings, such as Chinese, Mexican, or First Nations culture, often referred to as ethnocultural groups. However, cultural groups may instead be divided into different types of social groupings such as being gay, teenaged, a devoted fan of a particular sport or music genre, or trained in a particular profession. Most of us identify with a number of such cultural groups; consequently, we usually have multiple cultural identities.

Canada is home to a multicultural society. With the highest per capita immigration rate of any country in the world, Canada has emerged to be a pluralistic nation that has embraced multiculturalism as an official policy of its government. Praised by some as "the most successful pluralist society on the face of our globe" and "a model for the world," Canada has been considered to be successful at breaking down many

**Table 9.1: Ethnocultural portrait of Canada, 2006**

| Ethnic origins | Total responses | Single responses | Multiple responses |
|---|---|---|---|
| Total population | 31,241,030 | 18,319,580 | 12,921,445 |
| Canadian | 10,066,290 | 5,748,725 | 4,317,570 |
| English | 6,570,015 | 1,367,125 | 5,202,890 |
| French | 4,941,210 | 1,230,535 | 3,710,675 |
| Scottish | 4,719,850 | 568,515 | 4,151,340 |
| Irish | 4,354,155 | 491,030 | 3,863,125 |
| German | 3,179,425 | 670,640 | 2,508,785 |
| Italian | 1,445,335 | 741,045 | 704,285 |
| Chinese | 1,346,510 | 1,135,365 | 211,145 |
| North American Indian | 1,253,615 | 512,150 | 741,470 |
| Ukrainian | 1,209,085 | 300,590 | 908,495 |
| Dutch (Netherlands) | 1,035,965 | 303,400 | 732,560 |
| Polish | 984,565 | 269,375 | 715,190 |
| East Indian | 962,665 | 780,175 | 182,495 |
| Russian | 500,600 | 98,245 | 402,355 |
| Welsh | 440,965 | 27,115 | 413,855 |
| Filipino | 436,190 | 321,390 | 114,800 |
| Norwegian | 432,515 | 44,790 | 387,725 |
| Portuguese | 410,850 | 262,230 | 148,625 |
| Metis | 409,065 | 77,295 | 331,770 |
| British Isles, n.i.e.[1] | 403,915 | 94,145 | 309,770 |
| Swedish | 334,765 | 28,445 | 306,325 |
| Spanish | 325,730 | 67,475 | 258,255 |
| American | 316,350 | 28,785 | 287,565 |
| Hungarian (Magyar) | 315,510 | 88,685 | 226,820 |
| Jewish | 315,120 | 134,045 | 181,070 |

This table includes abridged information (only the 25 most commonly listed ethnicities) from the 2006 Census survey in which surveyors answered the question: "What were the ethnic or cultural origins of this person's ancestors?" A "single" response was given when a respondent provided one ethnic origin only. A "multiple" response was given when a respondent provided two or more ethnic origins. A "total response" indicates the sum of single and multiple responses for each specific group.

[1] The abbreviation "n.i.e." means "not included elsewhere."

*Source:* Adapted from Statistics Canada. (2006). Ethnic origins, 2006 counts, for Canada, provinces and territories—20% sample data. Retrieved from www12.statcan.ca/census-recensement/2006/dp-pd/hlt/97-562/pages/page.cfm?Lang=E&Geo=PR&Code=01&Data=Count&Table=2&StartRec=1&Sort=3&Display=All&CSDFilter=5000

intercultural barriers (Stackhouse, 2013). However, not all people see Canadian multiculturalism policy as highly successful. Canadian history has been marked by tension and conflict among the three main ethnocultural groups that existed during the county's early years: Aboriginal, French, and English Canadians. As we will discuss later in this chapter, many of Canada's First Nations, Inuit, and Metis people continue to experience profound negative consequences, including mental health problems, as a result of historical intercultural conflict and racism.

## Acculturation

**Acculturation** refers to the gradual adoption of elements of the dominant culture and society by minority groups, such as by immigrants. When families immigrate to Canada from abroad, it is common for young people to acculturate at a faster rate than their parents or grandparents, due to their high adaptability and their immersion in Canadian culture at schools and among their new peers. Often, these differing rates of acculturation lead to conflict among family members. Parents may be concerned that their children will lose important traditional values and practices. Children may see their parents as being out of step with current society, and they often resent restrictions or demands placed on them to adhere to "old world" cultural practices. Generally, such tensions resolve over time as all family members move through a gradual acculturation process. However, some tensions are so severe that they create entrenched conflict, often causing depression or anxiety and, in extreme circumstances, erupting into physical fights or family breakup.

Acculturation can sometimes be particularly difficult for children and youth who feel rejected by their peers. Newly arrived immigrant youth are sometimes ridiculed or belittled on the basis of their language skills, clothing styles, or other perceived shortcomings, and they become easy targets for bullying by other youths. Some immigrant youths join street gangs as a means of building a defence against such racist behaviour. Of course, gang membership generally involves a negative and violent group identity that most often leads to greater difficulties and tragic circumstances. Many communities in Canada are developing social programs that will assist young people in the acculturation process and ease their path.

It is not only youth who experience mental health problems as a result of difficulties in their acculturation. Many adults encounter daunting challenges, such as difficulties communicating in a new language, the loss of familiar social supports, and loss of previous occupational or professional status (Beiser, 2009; Kirmayer et al., 2011). Some older adults who immigrate have particular difficulty establishing social networks and may end up isolated and depressed.

**Figure 9.1:** Some adults who immigrate experience challenges. The following is the story of a man who immigrated from Fiji as told by his granddaughter: "This is a photo of my grandfather, Manilal Gulab. He immigrated here with his wife from Fiji in 1992 after both his daughters married Canadian citizens. He had a very good life back home where he owned a shop that repaired broken watches, and he had a large and tightly knit social network. Once he moved here, he was diagnosed with Parkinson's disease, which made his transition increasingly difficult over the years as he adapted to cultural changes. Over time his level of disability heightened and impacted his mental health. His inability to gain employment greatly affected his lifestyle. This is an example of how immigrants face many challenges and are at a greater risk of mental health problems associated with life changes and unexpected challenges that may arise."

*Source*: Jessica Kumar, Photographer

# Mental Health of Immigrants and Refugees

Most new immigrants to Canada make a good adjustment and maintain good mental and physical health. A phenomenon known as the "healthy immigrant effect" refers to the long-standing finding that shows immigrants to have a better health status than the general population born in a country (Vang et al., 2015). This is thought to be the result of standard immigration policies that screen out people with illnesses, allowing only a relatively healthy group of people to be admitted. Such policies are sometimes waived in relation to individuals designated as *refugees*, who have a very high likelihood of experiencing mental health problems.

In Canada, the legal definition of the a refugee is "[a person who] owing to a well-founded fear of being persecuted for reasons of race, religion, nationality, membership of a particular social group, or political opinion, is outside the country of his nationality, and is unable to or, owing to such fear, is unwilling to avail himself of the protection of that country" (United Nations Refugee Agency, 1951). Many refugees have experienced horrific persecution, torture, and violence, including physical, psychological, or sexual abuse, before arriving in Canada. Frequently, they will suffer ongoing mental health problems and will experience chronic stress, fear, and PTSD symptoms. Such mental health problems can be long-lasting and may affect the children of refugees as well.

Well-developed, specialized mental health services are often needed to help refugees and their family members to recover. However, a report from the WHO reminds us that "[r]efugees should not be seen as helpless people who totally depend on help they are given. Refugees are often people with strong determination to survive, which is why they became refugees. People who provide help to refugees or other displaced persons should look for the capacity to survive and cope and try to help build up this positive element" (WHO, 1996).

When compared to majority groups in the Canadian population, immigrants and people belonging to ethnic minority groups are less likely to receive mental health treatment. Reasons for reduced access include language or cultural barriers, fears or feelings of shame about mental illness that deter them from seeking help, and mistrust of officials or professionals due to bad experiences in the past. Additionally, the concept of having help available for mental health problems through the health care system may be unfamiliar, and some people may be unaware of such assistance or may tend to seek help through traditional healers instead.

An ethnic minority family may go to extreme lengths to protect a mentally ill family member. However, among ethnocultural communities in which mental health problems are stigmatized, treatment by health care providers may be initiated only once there has been a profound deterioration of the ill individual's condition.

**Figure 9.2:** A boy living in a refugee camp after a major earthquake in Haiti

*Source:* Gina Kim, Photographer

## Cultural Idioms of Distress and Culture-Bound Syndromes

People of different ethnocultural backgrounds often have particular ways of experiencing, expressing, and coping with emotional distress. These are described as **idioms of distress**, and they may result in quite different types of communications being encountered across different ethnic communities. An example is somatization, the expression of distress through physical symptoms, such as complaints about headache, gastrointestinal symptoms, or dizziness. Earlier reports from Western researchers claimed that people of non-Western ethnocultural backgrounds were more likely to express psychological distress through somatic symptoms. More recent studies show that somatization is a universal form of expressing distress. However, there may be unique experiences and expressions of somatic symptoms that are culturally mediated (Kirmayer & Sartorius, 2007).

Culture-bound syndromes are defined as a combination of psychiatric and somatic symptoms that are considered to be a recognizable disease only within a specific society or culture. A notorious example of a culture-bound syndrome is *koro*, a condition noted in Southeast Asian people in which a man develops an extreme fear that his penis is retracting into his body, including the belief that this will bring about his death. Widespread *koro* symptoms have occurred as outbreaks of mass hysteria, such as in Singapore during 1967, when thousands of cases were reported.

The concept of culture-bound syndromes is often disputed, and some instances of so-called culture-bound syndromes are thought to result from misinterpretations or misperceptions on the part of observers who are outside a particular culture. For example, there is a condition that has been called "Pibloktoq" or "Arctic hysteria," first noted by explorers who travelled to the Arctic and encountered Inuit people. The condition is described as a brief and sudden disturbance among Inuit women in which they scream, tear off their clothing, and imitate the sound of animals while running wildly in the snow and ice. However, recent analyses suggest that this so-called syndrome was unlikely to have been a natural part of Inuit culture, but may have been an unusual anxiety reaction to the explorers (Dick, 1995; Steckley, 2008; Thomason, 2014).

## First Nations, Metis, and Inuit

Canada's Indigenous (also known as Aboriginal) peoples currently comprise approximately 4.3 percent of the country's total population. In some provinces and territories, Aboriginal people constitute a much larger proportion: in Manitoba (16.7 percent) and Saskatchewan (15.6 percent); in Yukon Territory, 23.1 percent; in the Northwest Territories, 51.9 percent; and in Nunavut, 86.3 percent (Statistics Canada, 2011).

Archeologists estimate that Indigenous people lived in the Americas for somewhere between 10,000 and 17,000 years before Europeans first arrived on the continent. During this lengthy period, many societies thrived and developed. Those living in the coastal areas of Canada sustained themselves by fishing the bountiful oceans, whereas inland societies oriented their lifestyle to agriculture or to hunting various indigenous animals, such as moose, caribou, and bison. Many different languages were spoken, and a wide variety of distinctive cultural groups developed, with unique artistic, linguistic, social, and musical traditions.

Following the arrival of Europeans in Canada, Aboriginal people underwent a forced colonization. **Colonialism** generally refers to a lengthy period (from the 15th to the 20th century) when a group of European nations (including Britain, France, Portugal, and Spain) built colonies in the Americas, Africa, Asia, and Oceania. Colonization was often undertaken to obtain new material resources, to extend the influence and reach of an imperial power, and to impose religious beliefs and practices on others. During this lengthy period, European colonialists considered themselves to be superior to the people they colonized, often treating indigenous people as subhuman.

Another devastating impact of the arrival of European settlers came in the form of repeated waves of disease that decimated Canada's Indigenous communities. Since they had no immunity to the infectious diseases such as smallpox, measles, influenza,

**Figure 9.3:** Canada's Aboriginal population is composed of a culturally and linguistically diverse group of peoples.

*Source:* Miranda McMurray/iStockphoto

and whooping cough transmitted by Europeans and by the animals brought by settlers, Aboriginal people succumbed in huge numbers. Without the immunological defences that Europeans had developed over centuries of exposure to these illnesses, Aboriginal people became very sick and often died when they became infected. Historical accounts describe heart-wrenching circumstances in which up to 90 percent of the population of villages and communities died over short periods of time in the areas that were most severely affected. It has been described as "the greatest human catastrophe in history, far exceeding even the disaster of the Black Death of medieval Europe" (Cook, 1998, p. 13). Such profound loss of family, friends, and community is inconceivable (Daschuk, 2013).

In the wake of these tragic historical events that harmed Indigenous people across Canada, there has been a growing strengthening and revitalization among many Aboriginal people and communities. Steps have been taken toward self-determination, and advances have been made in the negotiation of their rights and freedoms. Many First Nations, Metis, and Inuit people have become tired of the repeated recounting of the problems faced by their communities and, instead, call upon non-Aboriginal Canadians to support their strengthening and advancement. We will return to a discussion of the issues being addressed by Aboriginal people in Canada after the following brief description of the three major groupings of people who are now recognized.

## First Nations

The term "First Nations" has been in use in Canada since the 1980s, replacing the previous term "Indian band." As everyone knows, when early European explorers arrived on the shores of the Americas, they mistakenly thought they had reached the subcontinent of India and consequently called Aboriginal people "Indians." This mistaken terminology became so entrenched that many Aboriginal people continue to refer to themselves as "Indians," and the name of the main Canadian government legislation pertaining to Aboriginal people continues to be named the "Indian Act." There are more than 600 First Nations governments or bands across Canada, constituting all Aboriginal people in Canada other than Inuit and Metis people, discussed below. Table 9.2 provides a brief description of a few of the many First Nations in Canada to give a sense of their wide range of diversity.

## Inuit

The Inuit are a group of culturally similar Aboriginal people who live in the Canadian Arctic and subarctic, in the territories of Nunavut and the Northwest Territories, Yukon, and in northern areas of Quebec and Labrador. Inuit people also live in Greenland and Alaska. Previously, the term "Eskimo" was used to refer to an Inuit person. However, this term is considered pejorative by many Inuit people and consequently has fallen into disfavour.

Traditionally, the Inuit were fishers and hunters, and many Inuit still hunt seals, whales, caribou, walruses, and other animals. The inventive adaptations that Inuit people made in order to live in the climate of the far North are well known. These include the carving of ice to create igloo homes, the use of dogs to pull sleds across the snow and ice, and the creation of nimble boats using sealskins (which are now known as kayaks and, in adapted form, are used throughout the world).

## Metis

Metis are descendants of unions between persons of European origin and Aboriginal persons. Beginning in the 17th century, Metis communities began to develop through marriages of Scottish, French, and other European settlers to Cree, Ojibwa, and other Aboriginal people. Distinctive languages, traditions, and spiritual practices developed among Metis people.

Controversy exists regarding who should be considered Metis, and legal definitions have not yet been adopted. Although Canada's Constitution Act recognizes Metis

**Table 9.2: Brief description of a few First Nations across Canada**

| | |
|---|---|
| Tseshaht (pronounced see-sha-ought) | The Tseshaht people live on the west coast of Vancouver Island, British Columbia, and are one of the 14 Nations that make up the Nuu-chah-nulth Tribal Council. Historically, the Tseshaht people were whalers and fishers, and their lives revolved around their territories on both land and water. The Tseshaht First Nation reserve land is now a vibrant community with a membership of over 900 and an active and progressive natural resources–based economy, primarily with its abundant fisheries and well-developed forestry interests. The Tseshaht community is involved in many initiatives, from construction to forestry, from social development to education, from the fisheries to mental health, and is quickly moving toward self-sufficiency.<br><br>The people of Tseshaht remain proud of their heritage and work as a community to preserve their traditional values and the teachings of the past. |
| Kainai (Blood Tribe) | The Kainai are proud members of the Blackfoot Confederacy, which includes the Peigan, Siksika, and South Peigan (Blackfeet).<br><br>The Blood Tribe has a population of over 10,000 occupying approximately 549.7 square miles near the Rocky Mountains. The buffalo sustained the Kainai for untold generations. The Bloods cultivated and maintained an attitude of independence and fierce pride in their identity as Kainai. This spirit allowed them to successfully resist the efforts of governments, the churches, and other European agencies whose policies and practices could have an adverse impact on their cultural identity and legal rights. Today the Blood Tribe continues to draw strength from the past as it strives to realize a unique vision for the future. |
| Moose Cree | The Cree are the largest group of First Nations in Canada, with over 200,000 members and 135 registered bands. The Moose Cree First Nations people live on Moose Factory, an island on Ontario's James Bay. The community operates various public utilities, health and social services, education and child care, and law enforcement services, and runs a tourism wilderness program and a Cree cultural interpretative centre. |

people as one of the three groups of Aboriginal people, no description of Metis people is given. Until recently, through case law, the Supreme Court of Canada has stipulated that a person may qualify under the legal definition of Metis only when he or she can be shown to self-identify as Metis, demonstrate an ancestral connection to a historic Metis community, and provide evidence of acceptance by the Metis community. However, on April 14, 2016, the Supreme Court ruled that Metis and non-status Indians will be considered "Indians" in Canada's 1876 Indian Act. After decades of fighting with the Canadian government for recognition, the Metis people will now have the right to consult with government regarding matters that affect them, such as land rights and social benefits.

## Forced Assimilation of Aboriginal People

Over much of Canada's history, policy-driven efforts were undertaken to force the assimilation of Aboriginal people into the dominant society that was developed by European settlers in Canada. In 1998, the Minister of Indian Affairs, Jane Stewart, delivered a "statement of reconciliation," apologizing to Aboriginal people for the Canadian government's historical policies and practices:

> Attitudes of racial and cultural superiority led to a suppression of Aboriginal culture and values. As a country, we are burdened by past actions that resulted in weakening the identity of Aboriginal peoples, suppressing their languages and cultures, and outlawing spiritual practices.... The time has come to state formally that the days of paternalism and disrespect are behind us and that we are committed to changing the nature of the relationship between Aboriginal and non-Aboriginal people in Canada. (Stewart, 1998)

## Residential Schools

A particularly destructive policy and practice was enacted through the forced induction of Aboriginal children as students in residential schools. Aboriginal children were removed from their families and required to live in residence at schools that were run by religious organizations, such as the Catholic, Anglican, and Presbyterian churches of Canada. The residential schools generally took in children between the ages of 5 and 16 years of age. Adding to the harm caused to both children and parents by this forced dislocation, the children were pressured to abandon their traditions and to communicate only in English or French, consequently losing their traditional languages. Government leaders and policy-makers had the audacity to purport that separating the children from their parents and forcing religion on them was a means by which they would "civilize" First Nations people (Bombay, Matheson, & Anisman, 2014; Elias et al., 2012; Ross et al., 2015).

Tragically, children were subjected to emotional, physical, and sexual abuse in many of the schools. Residential schools were in place for approximately 100 years and established in all Canadian provinces and territories except Newfoundland, Prince Edward Island, and New Brunswick. In total, there were approximately 130 residential schools, with the last school closing its doors in 1996.

## Mental Health Consequences

Aboriginal people in Canada have high rates of mental health problems. Depression has been found to occur more often than in the general population, and the use of alcohol and other substances is often a very serious problem. Alcohol was not used

**Figure 9.4:** St. Paul's residential school in Middlechurch, Manitoba

*Source:* Library and Archives Canada/PA-182251

by Aboriginal people until contact with Europeans, who often used liquor as a trade commodity to obtain furs and other material goods from Aboriginal people. Since Aboriginal societies did not have any social conventions for handling alcohol, liquor was destructive to individuals and to many communities.

Suicide rates are elevated among Aboriginal people, and in Nunavut the suicide rate is 13.5 times the national average and one of the highest suicide rates in the world. This alarming statistic prompted a Nunavut jury to declare suicide a public health crisis in 2015 and recommend the creation of a ministry solely for suicide prevention (Canadian Press, 2015). Undoubtedly, centuries of colonization, the decimation of the population by disease, and the loss of traditional culture have created problems that undermine the mental, physical, and spiritual health of Canada's Aboriginal peoples. Cultural dislocation and the decimation of family units deprived many individuals of the healthy nurturing that would have otherwise been provided. It is remarkable that First Nations, Inuit, and Metis people have survived the centuries of subjugation and colonization. Nevertheless, these survivors carry a heavy burden. We will return to discussion of suicide prevention in Chapter 15.

**Figure 9.5**

*Source:* Andrew Penner/iStockphoto

**Figure 9.6:** Friendships can serve a particularly important role for people who are struggling with the challenges of poverty and homelessness.

*Source:* Chris Sang Yeob Park, Photographer

## Cultural Safety and Decolonization

There has been growing recognition of the importance of ensuring that Canadian health care workers are culturally competent, responsive, and respectful in their interactions with First Nations, Inuit, and Metis people. The term "**cultural safety**" was developed in New Zealand in order to emphasize the vulnerability of individuals receiving treatment in a health care system run by a dominant or colonizing culture. It draws attention to the fact that many individuals feel unsafe in the health care system due to a lack of respect for their cultural identities and calls for action to create an improved approach to health care delivery.

We conclude this section with an excerpt from Bill Mussell, who chairs the First Nations, Inuit and Metis Advisory Committee of the Mental Health Commission of Canada:

*Decolonization* refers to a process where a colonized people reclaim their traditional culture, redefine themselves as a people and reassert their distinct identity.

As a professional educator, mental health practitioner and consultant to First Nations, I see decolonization as the way to healing and restoring family and community health. The process requires:

- learning how to learn and undertaking a journey to wellness that involves self-care
- understanding forces of history that have shaped present day lifestyles
- discovering, naming and transmitting indigenous knowledge, values and ways of knowing, together with understanding selected Western ways
- applying and adapting both indigenous and Western knowledge, values and ways of knowing to address present-day challenges effectively

First Nations people must take positive control over their lives as individuals, families, and communities. They must build on who they are culturally and understand history from an indigenous perspective. Reclaiming and building on cultural strengths contributes to a secure personal and cultural identity for all First Nations and other aboriginal groups. Grieving and healing of the losses suffered through colonization is a further step toward collective wellness and self-determination. More and more First Nations leaders and workers are calling for healing, family restoration and strengthened communities of care. These people promote a renewal of cultural practices and teaching history from an indigenous perspective. They call for education and training that combines the best of mainstream and indigenous knowledge, and for building the capacity of workers to improve the quality of life in their villages. A parallel process of consciousness raising must occur within Canadian society, so stigma and discrimination against aboriginal Canadians can be eliminated, both on the personal and the structural levels of society. (Mussell, 2010)

## Conclusion

Ethnic and cultural identities play important roles in shaping experiences of mental health and illness. Racism can cause substantial mental distress, and immigrants and refugees often experience challenges in adjusting to the changes and stresses they encounter. First Nations, Inuit, and Metis people have survived profound difficulties as a result of colonization, practices of forced assimilation, and separation of families through residential school systems. Activities to build cultural safety and support decolonization of First Nations, Inuit, and Metis people are means to bring about the healing and restoration of family and community life.

## Glossary

**acculturation:** The gradual adoption of elements of the dominant culture and society by minority groups.

**colonialism:** A lengthy period when a group of European nations built colonies in the Americas, Africa, Asia, and Oceania.

**cultural safety:** A term developed in New Zealand in order to emphasize the vulnerability of individuals receiving treatment in a health care system run by a dominant or colonizing culture.

**culture:** A common heritage or set of beliefs, norms, and values that have been learned and adopted by a group of people.

**ethnicity:** A common history, language, and set of rituals that create a form of common identity and are shared by a group of people.

**idioms of distress:** The idea that people of different ethnocultural backgrounds often have particular ways of experiencing, expressing, and coping with emotional distress.

**racism:** A set of attitudes and behaviours that can been found among a population in which social groups are identified, separated, treated as inferior or superior, and given differential access to power and other valued resources.

## Critical Thinking Questions

1. What is the difference between race and ethnicity?
2. What mental health challenges can be experienced as a result of acculturation?
3. Why are immigrants and people belonging to ethnic minority groups less likely to receive mental health services?
4. How has colonization impacted the mental health of Aboriginal peoples?
5. What are some ways to build cultural safety and support decolonization of First Nations, Inuit, and Metis people?

## Recommended Readings

Fernando, S. (Ed.). (1995). *Mental Health in a Multi-Ethnic Society: A Multi-disciplinary Handbook*. London: Routledge.

Gaw, A. (Ed.). (1993). *Culture, Ethnicity, and Mental Illness*. Washington, DC: American Psychiatric Publishing.

Kirmayer, L.J., Valaskakis, G.G., & Erasmus, G.H. (2008). *Healing Traditions: The Mental Health of Aboriginal Peoples in Canada*. Vancouver: University of British Columbia Press.

Truth and Reconciliation Commission of Canada. (2015). *Executive Summary.* Retrieved from www.trc.ca/websites/trcinstitution/File/2015/Exec_Summary_ 2015_06_25_web_o.pdf

Waldram, J.B. (2004). *Revenge of the Windigo: The Construction of the Mind and Mental Health of North American Aboriginal Peoples.* Toronto: University of Toronto Press.

Waldram, J.B., Herring, D.A., & Young, T.K. (2006). *Aboriginal Health in Canada: Historical, Cultural, and Epidemiological Perspectives* (2nd ed.). Toronto: University of Toronto Press.

## Recommended Websites

Aboriginal Healing Foundation. Publications. www.ahf.ca/publications

Centre for Addiction and Mental Health. Culture Counts: Resources—Ethnocultural Communities/Cultural Competence. www.camh.net/About_CAMH/Health_ Promotion/Community_Health_Promotion/Culture_Counts_Guide/culture_ counts_ethno_resources.html

Multicultural Canada. www.multiculturalcanada.ca/

Multiculturalism. The Canadian Encyclopedia. http://www.thecanadianencyclopedia. ca/en/article/multiculturalism/

Racism. *The Canadian Encyclopedia.* www.thecanadianencyclopedia.ca/en/article/ racism/

## References

Beiser, M. (2004). Resettling refugees and safeguarding their mental health: Lessons learned from the Canadian Refugee Resettlement Project. *Transcultural Psychiatry,* 46(4), 539–583.

Bombay, A., Matheson, K., & Anisman, H. (2014). The intergenerational effects of Indian residential schools: Implications for the concept of historical trauma. *Transcultural Psychiatry,* 51(3), 320–338. doi: 10.1177/1363461513503380

Canadian Press. (September 28, 2015). Nunavut coroner agrees with inquest that suicide a public health crisis. *The Globe and Mail.*

Cook, D.N. (1998). *Born to die: Disease and new world conquest, 1492–1650.* Cambridge: Cambridge University Press.

Darwin, C. ([1871] 1874). *The descent of man* (2nd ed.). London: John Murray.

Daschuk, J.W. (2013). Clearing the plains: Disease, politics of starvation, and the loss of Aboriginal life (Vol. 65). Regina: University of Regina Press.

Dick, L. (1995). "Pibloktoq" (Arctic hysteria): A construction of European-Inuit relations? *Arctic Anthropology,* 32(2), 1–42.

Elias, B., Mignone, J., Hall, M., Hong, S.P., Hart, L., & Sareen, J. (2012). Trauma and suicide behaviour histories among a Canadian indigenous population:

An empirical exploration of the potential role of Canada's residential school system. *Social Science & Medicine,* 74(10), 1560–1569. doi: 10.1016/j. socscimed.2012.01.026

Gravlee, C.C., & Sweet, E. (2008). Race, ethnicity, and racism in medical anthropology, 1977–2002. *Medical Anthropology Quarterly,* 22(1), 27–51.

Gravlee, C.C. (2009). How race becomes biology: Embodiment of social inequality. *American Journal of Physical Anthropology,* 139(1), 47–57.

Kirmayer, L.J., Narasiah, L., Munoz, M., Rashid, M., Ryder, A.G., Guzder, J., Hassan, G., Rousseau, C., & Pottie, K. Canadian Collaboration for Immigrant and Refugee Health (CCIRH). (September 6, 2011). Common mental health problems in immigrants and refugees: General approach in primary care. *Canadian Medical Association Journal/Journal de L'Association Medicale canadienne,* 183(12), 959–967.

Kirmayer, L.J., & Sartorius, N. (January 1, 2007). Cultural models and somatic syndromes. *Psychosomatic Medicine,* 69(9), 832–840.

Kornblum, W. (2011). *Sociology in a changing world.* Boston: Nelson Education.

Mussell, B. (2010). Cultural pathways for decolonization. Here to help. Retrieved from www.heretohelp.bc.ca/publications/aboriginal-people/bck/2

Ross, A., Dion, J., Cantinotti, M., Collin-Vézina, D., & Paquette, L. (2015). Impact of residential schooling and of child abuse on substance use problem in indigenous peoples. *Addictive Behaviors,* 51, 184–192. doi: 10.1016/j.addbeh.2015.07.014

Stackhouse, J. (December 2, 2013). The 2013 Ismaili Centre Lecture. *The Globe and Mail.*

Statistics Canada. (2011). Population by age groups, sex and Aboriginal identity groups. Retrieved from www12.statcan.gc.ca/nhs-enm/2011/as-sa/99-011-x/99-011-x2011001-eng.cfm

Steckley, J. (2008). *White lies about the Inuit.* Toronto: University of Toronto Press.

Stewart, J. (1998). Minister of Indian Affairs and Northern Development on the occasion of the unveiling of *Gathering Strength—Canada's Aboriginal Action Plan.* Ottawa, ON. Retrieved from www.ainc-inac.gc.ca/ai/rqpi/apo/js_spea-eng.asp

Thomason, T. (2014). Issues in the diagnosis of Native American culture-bound syndromes. *Arizona Counseling Journal,* 30. Retrieved from http://works.bepress. com/timothy_thomason/92/

United Nations Refugee Agency. (1951). The Geneva Convention relating to the status of refugees. Retrieved from treaties.un.org/doc/Publication/MTDSG/ Volume%20I/Chapter%20V/V-2.en.pdf

Vang, Z., Sigouin, J., Flenon, A., & Gagnon, A. (2015). The Healthy Immigrant Effect in Canada: A systematic review. Population change and lifecourse strategic knowledge cluster discussion paper series/Un réseau stratégique de connaissances changements de population et parcours de vie. *Document de travail,* 3(1), 4.

World Health Organization. (1996). Mental health of refugees. Retrieved from http:// apps.who.int/disasters/repo/8699.pdf

# MENTAL HEALTH AND ILLNESS IN OLDER ADULTS

People who don't cherish their elderly have forgotten whence they came and whither they go.

—Ramsey Clark (lawyer and former US Attorney General)

## Introduction

Life expectancy in Canada is greater than ever, which is another way of saying that Canadians are living longer than ever before. With average life expectancy rates (2009 estimates) of 81.7 years (83.9 years for females and 80.0 years for males), Canada has one of the longest life expectancy rates of all countries. Worldwide, the average life expectancy is 70.5 years (73.0 years for females and 68.0 years for males), and Table 10.1 shows the shockingly wide range of life expectancy across nations of the world (WHO, 2014).

The proportion of older adults in Canada has been increasing progressively and is anticipated to continue to expand over the coming decades. In the 1930s, about 5 percent of the population was 65 years of age or older, and in 2011, approximately 14.4 percent of Canadians were 65 or older. Statistics Canada has projected that, by 2036, this proportion will be between 23 and 25 percent (Statistics Canada, 2015).

It is not uncommon for people in their seventies, eighties, and nineties to be living active and rewarding lives. Nevertheless, there are unique mental health challenges that affect older adults. In this chapter, we examine both the strengths and challenges that are common in this phase of life. We will discuss efforts that are being put in place to promote good mental health among older Canadians, while signalling important issues that are being addressed in the treatment of metal health problems within this sector of our population.

**Table 10.1: Life expectancies in selected countries**

| Rank | Country/State | Overall life expectancy | Male life expectancy | Female life expectancy |
|---|---|---|---|---|
| | World average (weighted by population) | 66.57 | 64.52 | 68.76 |
| 1 | Macau (China) | 84.36 | 81.39 | 87.47 |
| 2 | Andorra | 83.61 | 80.33 | 84.84 |
| 3 | Japan | 82.52 | 79.00 | 86.00 |
| 7 | Australia | 81.73 | 79.25 | 84.14 |
| 8 | Canada | 81.33 | 78.69 | 83.91 |
| 9 | France | 80.98 | 77.79 | 84.33 |
| 10 | Sweden | 80.86 | 78.59 | 83.26 |
| 36 | United Kingdom | 79.01 | 76.52 | 81.63 |
| 50 | United States | 78.11 | 75.65 | 80.69 |
| 105 | People's Republic of China | 73.47 | 71.61 | 75.52 |
| 145 | India | 69.89 | 67.46 | 72.61 |
| 221 | Zambia | 38.63 | 38.53 | 38.73 |
| 222 | Angola | 38.20 | 37.24 | 39.22 |
| 223 | Swaziland | 31.88 | 31.62 | 32.15 |

This table shows the shockingly wide range of life expectancy that exists in countries around the world. Ranking eighth among all countries, Canadian life expectancy is about 15 years longer than the world average. Almost all 30 nations with the lowest life expectancies are located in sub-Saharan Africa. Populations there have been suffering high rates of HIV/AIDS infection, resulting in high rates of early deaths. Also, countries with high infant mortality rates will have a lowered average life expectancy (since it is calculated from birth), but those who survive to the first year of life will have substantially higher life expectancy rates than reflected in the table.

*Source:* Adapted from CIA. (2009). Country comparisons: Life expectancy at birth. *The World Factbook.* Retrieved from www.cia.gov/library/publications/the-world-factbook/rankorder/2102rank.html

## Age, Experience, and Wisdom

One of the great benefits of advanced age is the opportunity to gain knowledge and experience that can produce wisdom. Many spiritual and cultural traditions describe historical or mythical figures who have transmitted wisdom gained through long lives or immortality, such as King Solomon, Confucius, the Norse God Odin, or the wizards and enchantresses founds in fantasy tales such as *Lord of the Rings* and the Harry Potter stories. Various cultures, including those of First Nations, Inuit, and Metis people, have long traditions of honouring and valuing the wisdom of elders.

There are many well-known examples of profound contributions to society made by individuals of advanced age. At the age of 79, Sir Winston Churchill, the famous British leader who steered his country through the challenges of the Second World War, was in his second term as prime minister when he was awarded the Nobel Prize for literature for his historical and biographical writing and for his oratory. Pierre Berton, one of Canada's best-known journalists who published 50 books on Canadiana, continued to write and publish during his eighties. As a result of having great experience and knowledge, older adults often play key roles in our organizations and societies; younger colleagues often obtain mentorship and guidance from seniors.

Within families, the role of grandparent is one of particular importance. Grandparents are often able to provide children with non-judgmental love and acceptance, thus supporting a child's important developmental and emotional needs. A child is often comforted by grandparents and obtains important feelings of safety, security, and self-esteem on the basis of being loved and attended to by caring elders. Grandparents can also help to support busy or stressed parents through providing emotional, financial, or physical support and by taking on some child care responsibilities occasionally, providing temporary relief to parents. A relationship with a grandchild gives grandparents a second opportunity to connect with children. Sometimes, accumulated wisdom and a less harried and frenetic lifestyle allow them an opportunity to improve on the parenting they were able to provide the first time around. An old Welsh proverb states: "Perfect love sometimes does not come until the first grandchild."

When parents experience extreme challenges caring for children, grandparents may end up becoming their primary providers of care and support. This often happens when parents encounter difficulties as a result of physical or mental illness or substance use problems. Grandparents may be asked by parents to step in when children are proving too difficult for parents to manage or when parents become overwhelmed by circumstances or responsibilities.

Of course, an important connection between the old and young is not exclusive to grandparents and their grandchildren. Wisdom, life experience, and love can be passed along the generations by other family members too, and by those who have no biological or familial relationship with a child. Many communities have developed programs that match older adults with children and youth who are in need of some additional support, encouragement, and love.

## Health, Illness, and Frailty among Older Adults

A large longitudinal national research study, the Canadian Study of Health and Aging, examined more than 10,000 people aged 65 or older across Canada, repeatedly obtaining information from the same group of individuals every 5 years over a 15-year period. The study found that three-quarters of these Canadians described their health as being "very good" or "pretty good" (Ebly, Hogan, & Fung, 1996).

**Figure 10.1:** Grandparents and grandchildren enjoying each other's company

*Source:* monkeybusinessimages/iStockphoto

Even those who indicated having significant disability due to heart disease, limited physical mobility, or decreased vision often rated their health to be very good. This may be because they have adjusted to such changes over time, or it could be due to a tendency of older people to minimize complaints about poor health. Nevertheless, many older Canadians experience substantial difficulties with their physical or mental health or both.

Although it is an oversimplification, older adults are described as either "fit" or "frail." Those who are fit are considered to enjoy overall good health and to have the capacity to live full and independent lives. The frail elderly are those who have significant physical or mental health problems that interfere with their independence and require them to depend on others for aspects of care and daily function. Commonly, they have lost muscle strength, are underweight, have limited physical activity, have lack of endurance, and are easily fatigued.

Health problems are more common with advanced age, and close to half of adults 65 years or older report some degree of disability, such as difficulty with mobility, vision, hearing, or performing activities of daily living. Although various aids are available to minimize disability associated with a wide range of health conditions,

**Figure 10.2:** Older adults who are considered fit enjoy overall good health and have the capacity to live full and independent lives.

*Source:* monkeybusinessImages/IStockphoto

many older adults do not access these and miss out on the benefits that could be gained. Hearing aids, walking aids, motorized wheelchairs, seat lifts for toilets, and aids for bathing can substantially improve quality of life and minimize pain and discomfort.

Some older adults experience chronic pain, which can be defined as persistent pain that does not go away for a few months. Results from the CCHS show that 27 percent of older adults living in private homes and 38 percent living in long-term health care institutions reported chronic pain. Chronic pain can impact an individual's life in numerous ways including day-to-day activities, sleep and eating patterns, and mood. Research has shown that respective of other comorbidities, older adults experiencing chronic pain are more likely to be unhappy. Additionally, chronic pain can induce feelings of irritability, make it difficult to concentrate or remember things, and can contribute to anxiety and depression.

## Loss, Loneliness, Isolation, and Elder Abuse

As people reach advanced age, it is inevitable that they will lose friends, family members, and colleagues to illness and death. Such loss takes a large toll. When one partner in a couple dies, the surviving individual often describes their experience

**Figure 10.3:** Losing one's spouse can result in profound feelings of loss and grief for the surviving individual.

*Source:* ImagesbyBarbara/iStockphoto

as "losing a part of oneself." This may be a terribly difficult adjustment for couples who have spent much of their lives together or who have formed close intellectual or emotional bonds and joint senses of identity. When couples have divided various responsibilities over many years, such as managing finances, preparing food, or managing social activities, the remaining widow or widower may find it difficult to take on unfamiliar tasks that were previously done by the deceased spouse.

Some elderly people are fortunate to have adult children, other family members, or friends who rally around them and help to ensure that their needs are being well looked after. However, many older people are estranged from family members and may not have a network of social support. In this case, they risk becoming isolated and disconnected. Marginalized older adults often have few resources, and those who have no income, retirement savings, or other material goods may be forced to rely on shelters, social housing supports, or charitable agencies such as the Salvation Army of Canada in order to survive.

Modern societies have been criticized as being **ageist**, that is, characterized by prejudice and discrimination on the basis of people's age. Intensified by advertising and mass marketing activities, the vibrancy and beauty of youth often becomes a preoccupation reinforced by frequent exposure to images of young models, actors, athletes, and celebrities. In societies like ours, which are sometimes described as being "youth obsessed," the elderly are often considered irrelevant. Older adults face discrimination in employment and are frequently passed over in favour of younger applicants. Even in their social and family relationships, they are often treated as unimportant and obsolete. For many aging individuals, the entrenched ageist attitudes and behaviours that exist in our society contribute to feelings of worthlessness (Bennett & Gaines, 2010).

Tragic and far too common occurrences of **elder abuse** have been documented in which older people may be pressured, bullied, misled, swindled, or neglected. Abuse may involve physical, emotional (such as repeated verbal aggression), financial, or other maltreatment and may involve family members as well as strangers who prey on vulnerable victims. Such abuse is considered to be criminal activity and may lead to charges and convictions.

Suicide rates are increased among older adults. Men are at higher risk, particularly those who are single or living alone (Statistics Canada, 2014). Poor physical health, social isolation, loss of social roles, and loss of independence are factors that are associated with suicide among older adults.

Erik Erikson, the psychologist known for describing developmental phases that occur sequentially through the course of human life (see the discussion of his framework in Chapter 3), considered the final developmental phase to be one that juxtaposes Ego Integrity vs. Despair. Erikson proposed that, toward the end of one's life, the inevitability of mortality must be faced, and we are impelled to review the meaningfulness of our lives, knowing that we have limited time left. Erikson's theory proposes that there is a spectrum of experience. At one end are those who feel positively about their lives, seeing themselves as being fortunate to have experienced happiness and satisfaction,

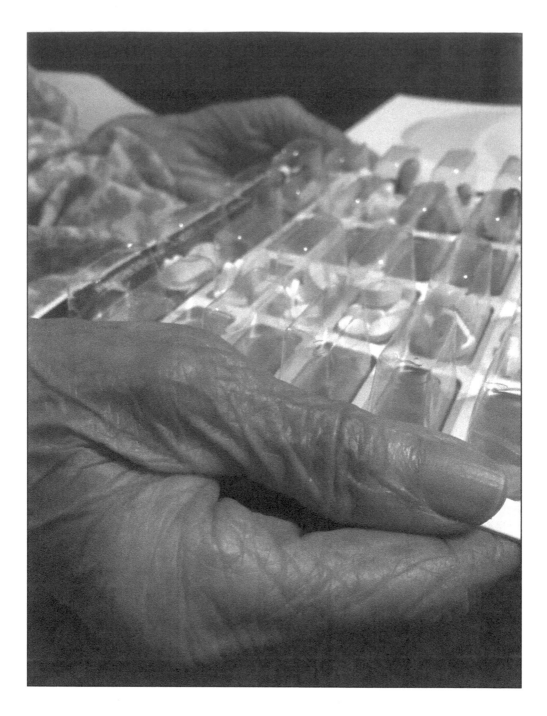

Figure 10.4: Depression occurs much more often among older adults who feel regretful about their lives, are experiencing substantial physical health problems, are isolated, or are in abusive circumstances.

*Source:* Daman Pabla, Photographer

a condition Erikson described as "ego integrity." The other extreme is despair at the lack of meaning or satisfaction that one construes when reviewing the course of one's lifetime. Although most people end up feeling positive toward the end of their lives, most will also experience a mixture of feelings that include both satisfaction and regrets.

Depression in older adults is seen much more often among those who feel regretful about their lives and in those who are experiencing substantial physical health problems or who are isolated or in abusive circumstances, such as described earlier in this section. We will discuss approaches to prevent and treat depression and other mental health problems later in this chapter.

## Death and Dying

Existential philosophers and anthropologists have brought attention to the weight carried by humans in being so aware of our own mortality. They point out that, along with the many advantages that humans have over the rest of the animal kingdom as a result of our highly developed brains, we are cursed with a serious drawback: we foresee and imagine our own deaths (Becker, 1973). Such existential angst is a frequent topic in the works of comedian and filmmaker Woody Allen, as encapsulated in the following popular quote: "I don't want to achieve immortality through my work.... I want to achieve it through not dying." Although in Canada most of us are fortunate enough to survive to a ripe old age, ultimately we all face death. As Erikson indicated, this will be easier for those who have come to terms with their lives than those who feel a nagging sense of dissatisfaction or hold many regrets.

---

### Box 10.1: The Five Stages of Grief

The model developed by psychiatrist Elisabeth Kübler-Ross for understanding how we respond to the knowledge of impending death is widely known and used in caring and supporting those who are terminally ill (Kübler-Ross, 1973). She described five stages that humans commonly experience. However, these do not necessarily follow in the order that they are typically listed, nor do all people experience each stage. Responses are highly personal and individual, although she did state that all people will experience at least two. The five stages are listed below and are accompanied by a representative statement that characterizes the thoughts and feelings that predominate in each stage:

Denial—*"This can't be happening to me."*
Anger—*"Why me? It's not fair!"*
Bargaining—*"I'll do anything for more time."*
Depression—*"I'm so sad, why bother with anything? I'm going to die."*
Acceptance—*"It's going to happen. I may as well prepare for it."*

In recent years, efforts have been made to help people die in comfortable surroundings. Where possible, most people would prefer to be in their homes or usual residences rather than in hospital. This can be supported by physicians and other health care professionals, sometimes working together as a team, and delivering care to dying people in their homes. However, in some circumstances, hospital or institutional care is necessary. Palliative care units and hospices are designed to be responsive to the emotional and spiritual needs of people who are dying and allow individuals to avoid unnecessary medical procedures. When cure is not possible, and often it is not, then a primary goal of health care should be to relieve suffering. Thankfully, advances in pharmacotherapy and new anaesthetic techniques, such as nerve blocks and spinal anaesthetics, often provide highly effective methods to remove

**Figure 10.5:** When a person is facing death, it is a very important time for family members. This photograph was taken by a student whose grandmother was facing death. Her comments about this photograph are as follows: "This is a picture of my grandma a couple of days before she died of leukemia. She was 90 years old and a healthy and strong woman who lived as a widow for 20+ years. She used to wear black almost every day to show her mourning and grief of my grandpa being gone. When she knew she was passing away she decided that she wanted to be removed from the hospital setting and just come home because she would rather die there than in a hospital bed. In this picture, I wanted to take her out and show her my favourite park that she had never seen before. I wanted to spend some time with her because I knew she didn't have much time left to live. I remember she said, 'Oh my, look at all those ducks, this is so lovely Jeanelle, thank you so much.' I will always remember this day and never forget it."

*Source:* Jeanelle Aldaba, Photographer

or diminish pain. Consequently, most people with advanced or invasive disease can be helped to live their final days without profound physical suffering or discomfort.

## Cognitive Impairment and Memory Loss in Older Adults

The degree to which older people experience or exhibit problems with cognitive functions or memory loss varies widely. Many people maintain very sharp mental faculties well into their eighties and nineties. Some continue to engage in complex and challenging computational or linguistic activities, demonstrate formidable debating skills, and show little if any signs of limitations when compared to young whippersnappers. However, some older people complain that certain memory functions are not as sharp as they once were. The evidence for structural changes in the brain causing difficulties in memory associated with aging is still being studied and analyzed by researchers. Changes in structure of the grey or white matter of the brain have been associated with memory loss in some studies (Silbert et al., 2009), and it is found that conditions such as hypertension (high blood pressure) may put some people at risk for repeated vascular and structural damage that impairs brain function over time (Cohen, 2007). Excessive use of alcohol or other substances may lead to profound memory problems and other cognitive disturbances in older age as a result of physiological changes that occur in the brain.

Although older people sometimes worry when they notice themselves being forgetful or misplacing keys, studies have found that mild memory loss symptoms such as these are not a sign of impending dementia for most individuals (Erber, 2012). Many of the memory problems that older people experience have been found to have a psychological basis and may be a consequence of stress, mild depression, or being overtired.

More serious memory problems affect the ability to carry out everyday life activities. When older people are getting lost in familiar places; becoming confused about time, dates, people, or places; or forgetting to eat regularly, a careful determination of their cognitive and memory functions is needed and measures to ensure their safety are essential. Progressive memory problems and other cognitive deficits in older adults may be caused by various medical conditions, such as hypothyroidism, HIV illness, or Parkinson's disease, but are commonly associated with the development of dementia.

### Dementia in Older Adults

**Dementia** is a clinical syndrome that is characterized by general and irreversible loss of mental capabilities, such as memory, reasoning, judgment, and the ability to communicate. The Canadian Study of Aging and Health estimated that most older adults do not have any signs of dementia; of those 65 years or older, only 8.9 percent were estimated to meet criteria for a diagnosis of dementia (Public Health Agency of Canada, 2010). However, the likelihood of having dementia increases progressively

**Figure 10.6:** The degree to which older people experience or exhibit problems with cognitive functions or memory loss varies widely. Many older people are able to participate in activities that demand concentration and intact cognitive abilities.

*Source:* Jacob Wackerhausen/iStockphoto

with advancing age. For example, 7 percent of individuals over the age of 60 years, and 49 percent of individuals over 90 years were estimated to meet criteria for dementia (Alzheimer Society Canada, 2010).

There are many potential causes of dementia, with pathological mechanisms that vary considerably. The most common cause of dementia is **Alzheimer's disease**. This disease is associated with characteristic structural changes to the brain, including **plaques** (i.e., small, dense deposits that accumulate in the spaces between brain cells, scattered throughout the brain) and **tangles**, (i.e., twisted strands of protein that are found within brain cells). As brain cells degenerate and die, the brain shrinks markedly in some regions. Researchers are working to understand the mechanisms that underlie Alzheimer's disease and their relationship to the structural changes.

Other types of dementia include those that are caused by vascular problems, infections, brain injury, excessive use of alcohol or other substances, and nutritional deficiencies. Vascular dementias develop as a result of repeated losses of brain cells when blood vessels in the brain are damaged as a result of stroke, hypertension

**Figure 10.7:** Symptoms of dementia often appear very gradually, and early symptoms may only be apparent in hindsight. It is not until the late stages of dementia that memory loss often becomes so severe that individuals can no longer recognize close family members or friends.

*Source:* Rich Legg/iStockphoto

(high blood pressure), or other problems that interfere with the supply of oxygen to brain cells.

## *Stages and Progression of Dementia*

Irrespective of cause, dementia is sometimes classified into a series of stages according to the severity of cognitive disturbance that is present. The rate of progression varies substantially among various individuals and, on average, it will take about 10 years for progression from early, mild symptoms to the development of severe dementia and profound disability.

The appearance of symptoms of dementia is often very gradual, and early symptoms may only be apparent in hindsight. In early stages of dementia, people may become apathetic and unable to adapt to changes. Memory problems may become evident through frequent repetition of questions, misplaced items, or confusion about events. Some people may appear to become more self-centred and less concerned with the feelings of others, or become more irritable or upset when things do not go smoothly.

In moderate stages of dementia, symptoms are more disabling. Memory problems generally become significant with more frequent and extensive forgetfulness and confusion about time, people, or events. If away from familiar surroundings, an individual may become lost. In this stage, it is not unusual for people to wander out of their residences, walking aimlessly and unable to find their way home. Irritability and difficulties in behaviour may increase, and it is not uncommon for people to neglect their food intake and hygiene.

With severe dementia, disability becomes profound. Memory loss often becomes so severe that individuals can no longer recognize close family members or friends. Some individuals may become aggressive or combative, and many become incontinent and unable to feed or dress themselves.

It is essential to carry out careful assessments of the ability of people with dementia to perform activities of daily living to ensure their safety and proper care. Structured assessments have been developed to assess the ability to undertake activities such as meal preparation, shopping, telephone use, handling personal finances, travelling alone by car or public transportation, dressing, grooming, bathing, and toileting. Such assessments are carried out by occupational therapists (OTs) or other health care workers and are used to determine the level of care and support needed.

---

### Box 10.2: Music Therapy

In recent years, there has been growing recognition of the therapeutic and healing nature of music for individuals with Alzheimer's or other forms of dementia. Rhythmic responses while listening to music require little cognitive processing, as they are controlled by the motor centre of the brain. This means that a person with dementia can actively engage in music even during late stages of the disease. Music is used to create positive moods and emotions, initiate social interaction, manage stress and agitation, and, perhaps most profoundly, stimulate memory recall. Many individuals tend to associate music with life events, memories, and emotions—whether they be good or bad. Music therapists will play music that is familiar to the individual from an era that is previous to their dementia, to which there has been an overwhelmingly positive response. Some people will recall memories that they associate with the music, others will sing or dance, and some have even remembered how to play instruments and can accompany the performer. For those who are able to dance, music therapy has increased physical activity, which can have tremendous health benefits for those who are generally otherwise sedentary. Worldwide, there has been an increase in non-profit organizations and music students volunteering to perform in long-term residential care facilities, as evidence grows for this non-pharmaceutical alternative approach to managing dementia.

---

**Box 10.3: A New Alzheimer's Treatment?**

Although there is currently no cure for Alzheimer's disease, a recent preliminary study performed on mice has rendered promising results. It is currently believed that Alzheimer's is a result of a buildup of amyloid plaque that interferes with the function of neurons and causes brain cells to die. Researchers in the study injected microbubbles into the brains of the mice; they disturb the blood-brain barrier when activated with an ultrasound. This then allows molecules to enter the brain and stimulate cells that reduce amyloid plaque. In mice, this resulted in an elimination of amyloid plaque in 75 percent of treated mice. After treatment, mice responded better on memory tests and object recognition. It is currently unknown whether such a treatment would be effective in humans. The human brain is much more complex than those of mice, and it is unclear whether amyloid plaque truly does cause Alzheimer's, though there is a strong association. However, this study provides interesting insight into possible future treatments for this degenerative disease.

---

# Health Promotion, Illness Prevention, and Treatment

In this section, we will discuss treatments and interventions that can be put into place to help people with dementia and other mental health problems. Before doing so, however, we will describe some of the population and public health approaches that can help to promote good mental health and prevent mental health problems among older adults.

## *Mental Health Promotion and Illness Prevention Strategies*

The development of healthy practices and patterns of behaviour early in one's life may prove to be important in promoting one's mental health in later years. For example, healthy nutritional intake, moderation in the use of alcohol, physical exercise patterns, and social skills that are developed when someone is young may contribute to good mental health later in life. Wearing helmets when cycling or participating in sports that involve a risk of head injury is a good practice that can prevent mental problems later in life.

There are also valuable health promotion and illness prevention strategies that can be put in place later in life. Programs that keep older adults physically and mentally active will help them maintain cognitive abilities and social function, and enjoy a higher quality of life. Work has also been done to help people who must cope with chronic physical health conditions by providing them with effective strategies to prevent depression and other negative consequences. Relief of pain, improvement of mobility, and social connectedness can have a strong impact on preventing depression and despair. Another beneficial strategy is to target preventive interventions to

**Figure 10.8:** The development of healthy practices and patterns of behaviour early in life may prove to be important in promoting mental health in later years. Exercise is a practice that promotes both mental and physical health.

*Source:* &#169 al wekelo/iStockphoto

help older adults who are at particular risk of experiencing mental health problems because of recent circumstances, such as the loss of a job or death of a spouse. Group programs and activities that connect people who have had similar experiences provide an excellent means of preventing illness through mutual support and other benefits of social networks.

## *Independence, Support, and Institutionalization*

Various aids, support services, and home care workers can be put in place to help older adults continue to live at home, even when they require regular care and support. Services and supports may be available through the health care system, social services, and agencies such as the Alzheimer Society Canada. Often, however, much of the care of older adults falls to a spouse, adult children, friends, or other family members. If the person who needs care has severe physical or mental disability, then the burden on the caregiver can become great. It is not uncommon for one member of an older couple to become exhausted and overwhelmed by the continuous burden of providing care to a spouse.

**Figure 10.9:** Much of the care of older adults falls to family members or friends. If the person who needs care has severe physical or mental disability, then the burden on the caregiver can be significant.

*Source:* iofoto/iStockphoto

Since family members so often play a key role in caring for and supporting the care of older adults, health care service providers must work closely with family members and work collaboratively with them. Frequently, educational sessions or materials are made available to help family members gain the best possible knowledge about how to provide good quality support.

As described earlier, many older adults are left without family members or friends to help them. Such individuals are at high risk and can easily "fall through the cracks" unless there is a dedicated effort by health care workers to address their needs.

It is not uncommon to discover that an older adult is experiencing so much disability that institutional care is required in order to manage health concerns and protect physical safety. Such care is provided in various facilities referred to as "long-term care facilities," "nursing homes," or "homes for the aged." They provide 24-hour personal care, nursing care, and medical attention, and they generally include social and recreational opportunities for residents.

## Caring for People with Dementia

Individuals with dementia are often unable to recognize their own cognitive difficulties. Sometimes this will lead to conflict or disputes with family members, friends, or caregivers who perceive them as requiring additional care or institutional treatment. In the early stages of dementia, people will often struggle with memory problems. Some forms of dementia, such as Alzheimer's disease, can sometimes be slowed in the early-to-intermediate stages with cholinesterase inhibitor medications. Although the medical and physical are important components of the care of people with more advanced dementia, the quality of interpersonal and environmental support that is made available is an important factor in determining how well or poorly individuals manage. At times, facilities and services for people with dementia may find it difficult to recruit skilled staff, and financial cutbacks may result in staffing levels that are insufficient to provide quality time to residents and patients (Walent, 2003). Ideally, frequent human contact and warm, caring interactions will form a substantial component of the care provided to people with dementia.

## Treatment of Depression and Grief in Older Adults

As discussed in Chapter 4, depressive illnesses are among the most prevalent mental disorders experienced throughout the lifespan. Among older adults, depression can be a substantial problem that requires careful attention and treatment. Depression is more common among older adults who are facing substantial physical health problems, are socially isolated, and have experienced substantial loss, such as the death of loved ones or the loss of employment or housing.

As in other phases of life, the treatment of depression is often multi-modal and may require intervention to help solve specific problems that are contributing to

---

**Box 10.4: Managing Memory Difficulties**

The following approaches are useful in helping individuals with dementia to manage memory difficulties that might otherwise create problems and cause individuals to feel excessive distress:

1. *Diminish stress and distraction.* Memory problems are intensified with stress and in distracting situations where there is a lot of noise or activity. It helps to provide quieter and more relaxed surroundings where it is easier to concentrate on one thing at a time.
2. *Provide orienting information and avoid challenging questions.* It helps to provide cues and assistance to help people remember and orient themselves to people and places. For example, it is helpful to say "Look, your niece, Susan, has come to visit you" rather than "Do you remember who this is?"
3. *Instill a regular routine.* A regular routine around meals, bathing, exercise, and other activities often helps people to feel more secure and makes it easier to remember daily activities.
4. *Use memory aids.* Lists and clearly written instructions can help stimulate an individual's memory and help him or her carry out daily activities.

---

one's depression (such as social isolation or physical disability) as well as counselling, psychotherapy, and use of medications or other physical treatments.

Antidepressant medications may be effective treatments for depression among older adults. However, more caution is required with their use in this age group due to potential side effects, interactions with other medications, and other difficulties that older people may have in metabolizing or tolerating antidepressant medications. In Chapter 12, we discuss the treatment known as "electroconvulsive therapy" (ECT) in which electrical current is passed through electrodes placed on an individual's head, resulting in a seizure of electrical activity throughout the brain. Although this sounds dangerous and odd, ECT appears to be a relatively safe and effective treatment for severe depression (Oudman, 2012; Rapinesi et al., 2013). Whereas the use of antidepressants are associated with substantial risks of medical complications, ECT can often be used safely, and consequently it is quite frequently used as a treatment for depression in older adults.

## Responding to the Growing Older Adult Population

As mentioned at the beginning of this chapter, the proportion of older adults in Canada is increasing. With this rise, a recent study anticipates a doubling in the rate

**Figure 10.10:** Older adults who have poor physical health, are socially isolated, and have experienced significant loss are more likely to experience depression than their peers who are not facing these challenges.

*Source*: David Sucsy/iStockphoto

of dementia over the next 25 years (Alzheimer Society Canada, 2010). How will our health and social service systems respond to the needs of older adults as they grow in numbers? Efforts are being put in place to develop innovative approaches to health-promoting and preventive and early intervention activities that will keep older people healthier and more independent in the future. There is also increased training of health care and social service staff to develop the skills and knowledge needed to provide good care for older people, including thoughtful attention to their mental health needs. Nevertheless, the challenges faced by our "greying population" are significant ones, and we must continue to ensure that we pay attention to the needs of our elders' mental health.

## Conclusion

Older age often brings wisdom and experience that is shared with younger generations, and most older Canadians enjoy good mental health, despite the inevitable aches and pains and the increased likelihood of various physical health problems and disabilities. Many older adults experience loss of loved ones, and some will end up lonely and socially isolated. They are at risk of suffering economic hardships and often end up marginalized in our communities, dependent on social services and supports. Various services and supports have been developed to help older adults live fuller, more active lives. Treatments to address depression and improve care of people with dementia are available. Additionally, palliative care has been developed to help people at the end of their lives to experience more comfort and dignity. Increased attention to health promotion and illness prevention throughout the lifecourse appears to foster good mental health in later life.

## Glossary

**ageist:** Characterized by prejudice and discrimination on the basis of a person's age.
**Alzheimer's disease:** The most common cause of dementia; associated with characteristic structural changes to the brain.
**dementia:** A clinical syndrome characterized by general and irreversible loss of mental capabilities such as memory, reasoning, judgment, and the ability to communicate.
**elder abuse:** Abuse against older adults that may include being pressured, bullied, misled, swindled, or neglected.
**plaques:** Small, dense deposits that accumulate in the spaces between brain cells, scattered throughout the brain.
**tangles:** Twisted strands of protein that are found within brain cells.

## Critical Thinking Questions

1. What are some of the unique mental health problems that affect older adults?
2. Is modern society an ageist society? Support your answer with examples.
3. Describe the stages of dementia.
4. Select a mental health promotion or mental disorder prevention strategy. Briefly describe the strategy and explain how it can benefit the mental health of older adults.
5. What are key factors to consider when caring for older adults with dementia or other mental health problems?

## Recommended Readings

Blazer, D.J., & Steffens, D.C. (2009). *The American Psychiatric Publishing Textbook of Geriatric Psychiatry* (4th ed.). Arlington, VA: American Psychiatric Publishing.
Erber, J.T. (2012). *Aging and Older Adulthood*. Chichester, UK: John Wiley & Sons.

Prohaska, T.R., Anderson, L.A., & Binstock, R.H. (2012). *Public Health for an Aging Society* (3rd ed.). Baltimore, MD: Johns Hopkins University Press.

Zarit, S.H., & Zarit, J.M. (2012). *Mental Disorders in Older Adults: Fundamentals of Assessment and Treatment* (2nd ed.). New York: Guilford Press.

## Recommended Websites

Alzheimer Society Canada. www.alzheimer.ca

Canadian Coalition for Seniors' Mental Health. www.ccsmh.ca/en/default.cfm

The Canadian Network for the Prevention of Elder Abuse. www.cnpea.ca/

Health Canada. Just for You—Seniors. www.hc-sc.gc.ca/hl-vs/jfy-spv/seniors-aines-eng.php

Public Health Agency of Canada. Healthy Aging in Canada: A New Vision, A New Investment—A Discussion Brief. www.phac-aspc.gc.ca/seniors-aines/publications/public/healthy-sante/vision/vision-bref/index-eng.php

## References

Alzheimer Society Canada. (2010). *Rising tide: The impact of dementia on Canadian society*. Toronto: Alzheimer Society Canada.

Becker, E. (1973). *The denial of death*. New York: Free Press.

Bennett, T., & Gaines, J. (2010). Believing what you hear: The impact of aging stereotypes upon the old. *Educational Gerontology*, 36(5), 435–445.

Cohen, R.A. (2007). Hypertension and cerebral blood flow: Implications for the development of vascular cognitive impairment in the elderly. *Stroke*, 38(6), 1766–1773.

Ebly, E.M., Hogan, D.B., & Fung, T.S. (1996). Correlates of self-rated health in persons aged 85 and over: Results from the Canadian Study of Health and Aging. *Canadian Journal of Public Health/Revue Canadienne De Santé Publique*, 87(1), 28–31.

Erber, J.T. (2012). *Aging and older adulthood*. Chichester, UK: John Wiley & Sons.

Kübler-Ross, E. (1973). *On death and dying*. London: Routledge.

Oudman, E. (2012). Is electroconvulsive therapy (ECT) effective and safe for treatment of depression in dementia?: A short review. *The Journal of ECT*, 28(1), 34–38.

Public Health Agency of Canada. (2010). *The Chief Public Health Officer's report on the state of public health in Canada 2010*. Retrieved from www.phac-aspc.gc.ca/cphorsphc-respcacsp/2010/fr-rc/cphorsphc-respcacsp-06-eng.php#c3-3

Rapinesi, C., Kotzalidis, G.D., Serata, D., Del Casale, A., Scatena, P., Mazzarini, L., Caccia, F., Brugnoli, R., Carbonetti, P., Fensore, C., & Girardi, P. (2013).

Prevention of relapse with maintenance electroconvulsive therapy in elderly patients with major depressive episode. *The Journal of ECT, 29*(1), 61–64.

Silbert, L.C., Howieson, D.B., Dodge, H., & Kaye, J. (2009). Cognitive impairment risk: White matter hyperintensity progression matters. *Neurology, 73*(2), 120–125.

Statistics Canada. (2014). Suicide and suicide rate, by sex and by age group. Retrieved from www.statcan.gc.ca/tables-tableaux/sum-som/l01/cst01/hlth66d-eng.htm

Statistics Canada. (2015). Population projections for Canada, provinces and territories. Retrieved from http://www.statcan.gc.ca/pub/91-520-x/91-520-x2010001-eng.htm

Walent, R. (2003). On time, money and caring. *Journal of Gerontological Nursing, 29*(6), 3.

World Health Organization. (2014). World health statistics. Retrieved from www.who.int/mediacentre/news/releases/2014/world-health-statistics-2014/en/

# Chapter 11

# RESPONDING TO MENTAL HEALTH CRISIS, EMERGENCY, AND DISASTER

I have left orders to be awakened at any time in case of national emergency, even if I'm in a cabinet meeting.

—Ronald Reagan (40th US President)

## Introduction

In this chapter and those that follow, we discuss how various systems and services in Canada respond to mental health problems. When distress associated with mental health problems increases to unmanageable levels or puts individuals at risk of harm, a mental health problem can become a **crisis** or emergency. It is particularly important to respond well to such crises and emergencies, both because risk of harm must be averted and because the handling of such crises can leave long-standing impressions on someone who has experienced a mental health crisis. If a person feels that he or she was treated unfairly or inappropriately, this negative impression of treatment systems and services can be difficult to change. Consequently, a person who has had a bad experience during a mental health crisis or emergency may be reluctant to receive services in the future. In some circumstances, this can detract from opportunities to obtain meaningful support and recovery.

## Coping

Among the most powerful approaches to the understanding of human behaviour is the Coping Model (Lazarus, 1993). This model is concerned with the ways people deal with life challenges, with how they overcome obstacles to achieve their goals. **Coping** can be defined as finding ways to accomplish goals despite obstacles and challenges. Each of us has goals to accomplish from the very beginnings of our lives, whether or not we can articulate them. Infants cannot articulate their goals, and yet they must accomplish goals of considerable difficulty—learning to walk, acquiring language, and dealing with the frustrating and inconsistent behaviours of adults. These are formidable challenges! With maturation, goals change, as do the obstacles to their attainment, and the person finds new ways to overcome obstacles and (mostly) attain goals. Over time, goals become increasingly individualized—one person seeks excellence in a sport, another seeks popularity in a certain social group, another seeks financial success, and so forth.

For most of the world's population, coping is often focused on the need to remain adequately fed, clothed, and sheltered. For most of us living in higher income countries, such as Canada, goals and needs mostly involve the struggle to be loved, esteemed, and successful. A useful way to think about these different levels of needs and goals is in terms of Abraham Maslow's Hierarchy of Needs (see Figure 11.1). Each of these needs, at each level, represents important goals that require a different set of cognitive and behavioural skills and approaches, that is, different **coping strategies** (Carver, Scheier, & Weintraub, 1989).

Individuals develop unique ways of accomplishing goals: habitual behaviours, modes of problem solving, forms of social interaction, and so on. These characteristic ways of thinking and acting in order to accomplish goals can be described as "coping styles." Each of us has a characteristic coping style, our own way of making a path through this difficult life to reach the goals important to us. For example, one person

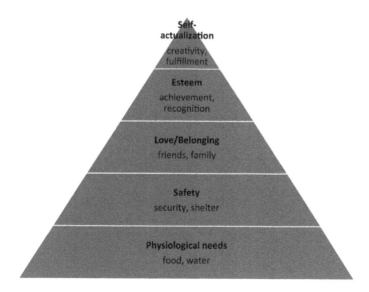

**Figure 11.1:** In Maslow's Hierarchy of Needs, the greatest and most fundamental needs occur at the bottom of the pyramid and must be achieved before the individual will be able to rise up the pyramid toward the ultimate goal of achieving his or her potential, or *self-actualization*.

will approach a looming deadline for a term paper mainly through problem-focused coping, cancelling other activities to focus on the paper, or applying for an extension. Another person will respond with emotion-focused coping, seeking reassurance from friends or convincing oneself that the term paper doesn't really mean that much (Folkman & Lazarus, 1985). If you think about people you know, you can see how each has a characteristic coping style. When under stress, one person will increase exercise, another will increase social activities, another will spend more time alone, and another will drink more alcohol. They all have coping styles that mostly work, most of the time.

An interesting way to classify coping styles is by reference to the personality categories of diagnostic systems, such as the WHO's ICD (described in Chapter 4). Although these categories are meant to define psychopathology, they actually describe coping styles that become problematic only when they are exaggerated, self-destructive, or overly fixed. For example, someone with a histrionic coping style will be dramatic, highly expressive, attention-seeking, and impulsive. This coping style can be quite successful in a wide range of social situations and occupational settings; only if it becomes extreme or very troublesome might we describe it as a "mental health problem." Similarly, someone with an obsessive-compulsive coping style will be quite reserved, have a high need to organize and control situations, and will focus on a narrow range of concerns in a persistent manner. This coping style can also be quite successful in the right context, unless it is done in an extreme or inappropriate way (Strack & Millon, 2007).

## Stress

When the demands and challenges of your life situation exceed your capacity to manage them while satisfying your basic needs and goals, you will experience **stress**. Here's a good definition: "Stress has been defined as the result of a relationship with the environment that the person appraises as significant for his or her well-being, and in which demands tax or exceed available coping resources" (Montero-Marin et al., 2014). There are many definitions of stress, but they all share the basic concept of an imbalance between environmental challenges and coping capacity. When environmental challenges operate in this way, taxing or overtaxing an individual's coping ability, they are described as "**stressors.**" Note that a situation perceived by one person as highly stressful may be perceived by another as minimally stressful, depending on each person's particular coping style and goals. For example, if it is extremely important to be perceived as self-reliant, then asking for directions will be a significant stressor; for someone who does not place such a high value on a self-reliant image, asking for directions will not be stressful at all.

Most of us deal with a certain degree of stress as we grapple with problematic life situations and challenges. It's just part of being human. Ideally, we will put our own internal resources into play effectively and, if needed, obtain help from friends, family members, health professionals, and others. But sometimes the level of stress becomes unmanageable and our coping resources are exhausted. At those times, we may enter a state of crisis.

## Crisis

In the crisis state, we feel overwhelmed by our life situation—we experience ourselves as unable to cope with important challenges and unable to achieve crucial goals. Our usual means of maintaining balance are unsuccessful and we feel a sense of disequilibrium or even chaos (Kanel, 2014). When we have difficulty coping, we tend to increase our efforts and shift to a mode of "urgent coping" in order to regain control—perhaps turning to family members for extra support or taking time away from work or school activities. It is when these attempts to regain equilibrium fail that we can find ourselves in a state of crisis.

Crisis states have been defined as follows:

> limited time periods of upset in the psychosocial functioning of individuals, precipitated by current exposure to environmental stressors, which appear to be turning points in the development of mental disorder. (Caplan, 1989, p. 3)

This brings us to one of the key elements of crisis states: Someone may have a coping style that works quite well in his or her usual life situation—but then the situation changes. Perhaps the level of stress increases dramatically or a different kind of stress emerges. Picture someone with an obsessive-compulsive style of coping, comfortable with a high level of predictability in work and personal life, who is suddenly given a new kind of work project that is unpredictable and quite novel. That person might find the new project to be exceedingly difficult. His or her natural tendency would be to impose organization upon the situation—but if this is unsuccessful, he or she may become increasingly anxious and unhappy, feeling inadequate. Furthermore, if this person receives negative feedback about his or her handling of the situation, he or she might begin to experience stress effects such as poor sleep, excessive worry, or anxiety. As this continues, this person might go into a state of crisis—this might include becoming depressed due to the feeling of helplessness and the failure of his or her usual coping style.

Another key element of crisis is that individuals may do "more of the same"— that is, show an exaggerated form of their usual coping style—and perhaps make the situation worse. The obsessive-compulsive individual might become even more obsessive-compulsive, desperately trying to organize every aspect of the situation and make it entirely predictable (which might elicit resentment from others and worsen the situation); a histrionic individual might express a high level of unhappiness to anyone who will listen, magnifying the intensity of his or her suffering (which might elicit irritation and withdrawal by others, once again worsening the situation); and so on. Or consider individuals who tend to become indignant and slightly aggressive when others do not comply with their wishes—this behaviour may trigger resentment and resistance on the part of others, which in turn may trigger increased anger and indignation, triggering more resistance, and so forth. If that spiral of ineffective coping continues long enough, they might find themselves in a state of crisis. It is common for individuals to enter a state of crisis through this kind of vicious spiral, with situational difficulties being handled by relatively ineffective coping mechanisms, leading to more frustration and an increase of the same ineffective coping, leading to a worsened situation (see Figure 11.2).

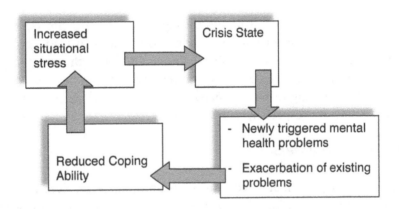

**Figure 11.2:** Vicious cycle of crises

## *Mental Health and Crisis*

The state of crisis relates to mental health problems in several interesting ways. First, it may be that an individual has a long-standing mental health condition that reduces his or her ability to cope with life challenges and therefore makes this person more vulnerable to crisis. In this case, the mental health condition would represent a vulnerability to stress and a risk factor for crisis (Devylder et al., 2013). Second, a long-standing mental health condition may in itself represent a substantial source of stress—for example, if a chronic psychotic condition causes an individual to be evicted from housing and become homeless. Homelessness represents an extraordinarily stressful life situation, sufficient to overwhelm anyone's coping skills and cast him or her into crisis. Furthermore, a stressful situation may exacerbate a pre-existing mental health condition, making its symptoms acutely worse in the context of the crisis state. For example, an individual with bipolar disorder might find that a situation of unusual stress triggers the onset of manic symptoms—needless to say, the presence of manic symptoms will make it harder to cope with the stressful situation. This can feed into the kind of vicious spiral we described above. Third, high situational stress and loss of control associated with a crisis state may trigger mental health symptoms, especially depression or anxiety. It is not uncommon for depressed individuals to describe themselves as feeling helpless and unable to deal with life challenges, in effect, as feeling "defeated" by their lives. This state of feeling unable to cope has been described as "learned helplessness" (Seligman, 1972) and is viewed as a crucial feature of depression. Alternatively, the sense of overwhelming fear or apprehension often associated with crisis may give rise to anxiety symptoms, such as panic or obsessive worry.

## Mental Health Emergencies

If a crisis state is not resolved (whether through extra coping efforts, lessening of situational stress, or additional support from others) and instead becomes more intense, then this person may transition to a mental health emergency. In the emergency state, there are acute issues of safety, whether because of dangerously poor self-care (e.g., failing to eat adequately, exposing oneself to physical risks, etc.) or self-harm behaviour (especially, risk of suicide).

### *First-Contact Providers*

Police officers and paramedics working with ambulance services are frequently summoned to address situations that involve erratic behaviour by people with mental disorders and are often the first point of contact when someone is acutely mentally ill.

It may be that police are telephoned when an individual who is experiencing psychosis begins yelling on the street or when an individual expresses suicidal intent. Police officers are often placed in difficult situations, sometimes working outside of their range of training and comfort. On occasion, this may result in a higher level of physical aggression being used by police than would have been required if a mental health care provider were involved. There has been a shift toward including mental health workers in police response units, working alongside police to defuse situations with the least possible violence. Increasingly, police training conveys knowledge and skill about how to best intervene and "de-escalate" situations when approaching someone who is acutely delusional, agitated, or depressed.

### *The Mental Health Act*

When police or paramedics suspect that a person may be suffering with a mental illness, they are empowered to transport that individual to a hospital or other facility under the **Mental Health Act**, a piece of legislation that governs such circumstances. Each province and territory has a unique Mental Health Act, so there is variation across the country in regard to various details, such as the length of time that someone may be detained or hospitalized on an involuntary basis. Typically, an assessment by one or more physicians is required within a certain time period. If an individual is judged by physicians to absolutely require hospitalization because of mental health reasons, the individual may be required to stay in a "designated mental health facility," typically a hospital, on an involuntary basis. When the Mental Health Act is applied in this way, the procedure is referred to as "committal."

One of the key issues that arises with hospitalizations due to mental health problems is that of balancing the goal of ensuring safety (protecting the individual from causing harm to self or others) with the goal of ensuring that rights are respected (imposing the least possible restriction on the individual). In line with the first goal, hospitals will typically rely on legal certification or committal procedures, gaining the authority to hold the individual in hospital with or without his or her consent. This does not mean that hospitals now have a free hand in administering treatments—the legislation governing committal defines the sorts of treatment that may be administered against the patient's will and those that may not be administered without permission (permission is given by the patient or by a designated representative of the patient). Typically, individuals who have been committed to a facility have the right to ask that this decision be reconsidered within a fixed period of time by a review board. These individuals must be clinically evaluated, and committal must be formally renewed at legally fixed intervals.

When a patient refuses prescribed treatment, such as antipsychotic medication, a number of complex procedures come into play. One is the evaluation of the patient's competence with regard to making treatment decisions. If the patient is judged by a physician to be incompetent to make treatment decisions, a "substitute decision-maker" may be appointed, either a person who has been selected by the patient, the nearest relative, the Public Guardian, or another individual identified by provincial legislation (Psychiatric Patient Advocate Office, 2009). Note that if individuals have been judged incompetent to make treatment decisions, they also cannot agree to accept recommended treatment.

A fairly recent variation on committal is the community treatment order, which requires the individual to accept specific treatment or support in the community for a specified period of time. A supervisor will be designated to oversee this order and ensure that the individual is receiving the required care; for example, appearing for community clinic follow-up visits. The community treatment order can be enforced, that is, the supervising physician can authorize a police officer to apprehend the individual, who can be taken to a designated facility for examination. A police officer can take measures to apprehend the individual, such as going into his or her home and/or using physical restraint (Canadian Mental Health Association, 2012).

When it comes to involuntary hospitalization, clinical and legal worlds meet in a way that causes much anxiety and potential conflict for health care providers, family members, and, of course, individuals experiencing mental health emergencies.

## Hospital Emergency Departments

Hospitals have emergency departments to which individuals suffering mental health emergencies can be brought for immediate protection and urgent care. Yet, hospital emergency departments are hectic places; individuals suffering mental health emergencies often have a difficult time dealing with that environment. Furthermore, emergency departments are more geared to dealing with physical emergencies than mental ones, and staff often find it challenging to work with people with mental health problems. Consequently, mental health emergencies are ideally handled in hospital units specialized for this kind of work. Over the last 20 years, hospitals across North America have developed various kinds of intensive and brief stay units focused on rapid assessment and treatment of mental health emergencies.

## Crisis Lines, Shelters, and Other Crisis Services

Not all mental health crises or emergencies are dealt with in hospital emergency departments or other health care settings. Some are averted and addressed through crisis lines, which generally provide quick access to advice, information, and referral over the telephone. Staff may respond by steering a person to appropriate help and by helping to de-escalate crises. Crisis lines may be staffed by volunteers or paid workers and are often operated by non-profit organizations and societies. Similar services can also be provided face-to-face or through mobile services, delivered by individuals or small teams of mental health professionals who travel (usually by car) immediately to meet with an individual in crisis and provide help (Guo et al., 2014). Mobile services provide a critical connection between individuals experiencing mental health emergencies and other elements of the system of mental health response (hospitals, community health care providers, family members, police, etc.). Some of the advantages of mobile services include the ability to assess a patient's support system in context, a better grasp of the perspective of the patient and other caregivers, and increased effectiveness compared to out-patient or in-patient services in preserving the patient's sense of autonomy.

Shelters provide short-term accommodation for people who are homeless or who are experiencing crises that have interrupted their living arrangements. Shelters are often needed by individuals who have been the subject of domestic violence or who have been ejected as a result of a dispute, including youth who have left home precipitously. Many of these crises involve various mental health problems. The Canadian government estimated that there were more than 27,000 shelter beds operating each night in Canada in 2012 (Employment and Social Development Canada, 2016). Nevertheless, shelter beds are often in short supply.

## Acute Hospitalization

Following an assessment in a hospital emergency department (or in other settings), health care professionals may conclude that a person requires in-patient hospital treatment for an acute mental health problem. Typically, this is done to ensure a safe environment for acute treatment, but it may also be recommended when it is judged that a person needs very intensive treatment interventions that could not be

**Figure 11.3:** Salvation Army mat program, Fort McMurray, Canada. The Salvation Army provides shelter for up to 32 homeless people from September through the winter months with a mat program. At 5 p.m. it is first-come, first-served for the mats laid out in the basement of the Salvation Army building.

*Source*: GetStock/Peter Essick

provided on an out-patient basis. Hospital treatment for mental health conditions is generally provided in psychiatric in-patient units that are staffed and designed to address specific needs. These include the need for safety, which is commonly a concern among people who are acutely suicidal or experiencing intense psychotic symptoms. Treatment services often include medication management, crisis management, and counselling or therapy, which may be undertaken both in individual and group settings. In-patient psychiatric hospitalization tends to be relatively brief (averaging approximately two weeks) and efforts are made to make follow-up arrangements to continue treatment following discharge.

## Acute Withdrawal Management and Detoxification Services

As discussed in Chapter 5, people who have become dependent on alcohol and various other substances often experience profound withdrawal symptoms when their use is stopped or interrupted. Withdrawal from alcohol, opiates, barbiturates, and other substances can involve extreme physical illness and discomfort; in some cases, death may result due to strain on the heart or other organs. Withdrawal management services primarily address the physical health problems that people experience when they are going through withdrawal; these services are also known as "detoxification," commonly abbreviated to "detox" services. **Withdrawal management** or detoxification services can occasionally be provided in hospitals but are more often delivered in specific short-term shelters run by health care systems or by non-profit organizations, such as the Salvation Army. Home detoxification involves services to assist individuals to undergo withdrawal within their home settings. Withdrawal management and detoxification may involve treatment with various medications to block or diminish physical symptoms of withdrawal, reduce adverse physical health complications and, ideally, these include supportive care, counselling, or therapy.

## Common Mental Health Emergencies

There are many mental health emergency situations, but the most frequent situations are the suicidal, psychotic, and substance use emergencies described in the following sections. These situations often overlap; mental health emergencies frequently involve combinations of suicidality, acute psychosis, and substance use. Individuals with concurrent disorders (i.e., substance use in combination with another mental disorder) are at particularly high risk of serious difficulties that overwhelm coping mechanisms and lead to emergency situations.

Regardless of the type of problem that results in a mental health crisis or emergency, it is important that health care professionals and others who respond to crises do their utmost to minimize the distress that people experience when they are in the midst of a mental health emergency. Compassionate treatment that avoids the use of force or physical restraint and maintains a respectful approach will help to create a sense of trust that may have long-lasting benefits. A person who feels he or she has been treated roughly or inappropriately by hospital staff, police, or others during a mental health crisis may develop an enduring mistrust and avoidance of mental health care, and this may contribute to poor outcomes.

### *The Suicidal Emergency*

When a person's coping abilities are overwhelmed, often triggered by increased stress or mental health problems, suicidal thoughts and behaviours may develop. Health care providers will first aim to determine the level of suicide risk, which requires the assessment of a number of key factors. These include whether the person has made an active plan to commit suicide, the dangerousness of any such plans, access to potentially lethal means of self-harm, any previous self-harming behaviour, situational factors that could precipitate further crises, the presence or absence of specific mental disorders or substance use problems that could influence suicidal behaviour, and the presence or absence of social supports.

The next major task is to help the person become less suicidal, that is, to address suicidality as a clinical problem. Various interventions can be put in place to help reduce suicide risk on the basis of the particular situation and circumstances being faced by the individual. Treatment of outstanding mental health and substance use problems may help to diminish suicidal ideas and impulses. Often, it is helpful to provide the suicidal individual with a different way of thinking about problems that have seemed impossible to fix. A useful explanatory model helps people to recognize that serious suicidal thoughts often arise when they feel that their lives have the following three characteristics:

- *Intolerable* (meaning their life situation is so painful that it seems unbearable)
- *Interminable* (it seems like it's going to go on like this forever)
- *Inescapable* (it seems like nothing they've tried has changed or will change their experience).

The next task is to help strengthen coping mechanisms, including increased tolerance for distressing emotions, modification of unrealistic and discouraging thoughts, and systematic problem-solving activities. The individual is helped to implement positive coping skills used previously. This is done by examining situations that have been handled successfully in the past, and then applying some of the same skills. A safety plan is developed collaboratively with the individual. This consists of a written plan to help them stay safe in the short term, for example, by removing means of self-harm and helping to find means of self-soothing and getting support from others. The person is supported in sharing the safety plan with his or her support network, including health care providers, family members, and friends. Significant others are involved (friends, family members, and so on) to help the individual build up a network for ongoing support after hospitalization.

## *The Psychotic Emergency*

Individuals in this kind of emergency state are experiencing a severe disturbance of the capacity to distinguish reality and to think in a rational manner. Often, they have confused and frightening thoughts that can sometimes lead to behaviours that place them or others at significant risk. For example, a man who believes that other people are conspiring against him may "protect" himself by physically assaulting strangers or may refuse to eat in case the food is poisoned. Psychotic emergencies can occur with mental disorders such as schizophrenic disorders or bipolar disorder if psychotic symptoms such as delusions or hallucinations are prominent.

The first priority of health care professionals and first-contact providers will be to calm the individual and provide a safe environment so that there is not an immediate risk of harm. This often involves a strategy known as "rapid tranquilization" and it typically relies upon medications with antipsychotic or sedating properties (Nordstrom & Allen, 2007). Once this initial risk reduction phase has been completed, clinical attention will focus on pharmacological treatment of the individual in order to reduce delusions and hallucinations.

More recently, there has been a shift in the standard approach to the short-term management of violent behaviour associated with psychiatric disorders. This involves a transition from reliance on restrictive interventions such as physical restraint or seclusion to reliance instead on "skills, methods and techniques to reduce or avert imminent violence and defuse aggression when it arises (for example, verbal de-escalation)" (National Institute for Health and Care Excellence, 2015). In this new approach, restrictive interventions are implemented only after efforts to de-escalate or defuse a situation have failed. Note that this approach requires considerable training to enhance staff skill in sophisticated behavioural management techniques. Should a mental health service impose an expectation of non-restrictive management without adequate staff training, an unintended consequence might be that of exposing staff to increased risk of physical and psychological harm.

Once there has been a meaningful degree of improvement in symptoms and safety, clinical focus will shift to ensuring that the individual has community resources in place (housing, financial support, clinical services and supports, and so on) to make a successful transition out of hospital and prevent recurrence of the problems that led up to the emergency situation.

## *The Substance Use Emergency*

Individuals dependent upon psychoactive substances such as alcohol, cocaine, and methamphetamine may develop significant mental health problems. For example, an individual who is intoxicated on methamphetamine may become disorganized and agitated and be brought to hospital by police or paramedics. Measures to prevent harm may be required, such as providing a safe environment or administering medications to diminish agitation. As the drug-induced state subsides over one or several days, the individual typically returns to baseline function and is discharged.

As discussed earlier, individuals who are in withdrawal from substance use may develop acute physical problems involving damage or dysfunction of bodily organs and may require withdrawal management (also known as "detoxification") services. Depression, psychosis, or other symptoms of mental disorder may occur as part of the withdrawal process.

Those who have experienced a crisis or emergency due to substance use should be helped to access treatment services and supports once the crisis has passed. Tragically, this does not usually occur. One contributor to this gap in service is the inadequate availability of treatment services for substance use disorders. Although some high-quality treatment programs exist in Canada, they are not widely available and many are not covered by our public health insurance plans. Therefore, unless an individual or family is able to pay "out of pocket" for such treatment programs or has special benefits through their employers that will cover such services, treatment may be inaccessible. Another contributor to the service gap is the poor integration and communication among various systems or services that deal with the needs of individuals with substance use problems. A recent report on substance use treatment in Canada noted: "People who may have significant health problems, at a time of great personal strain, must navigate a complex and ever-changing labyrinth of services and supports" (National Treatment Strategy Working Group, 2008, p. 1).

Also, people with substance use problems are typically ambivalent about obtaining treatment. Because of the nature of substance use dependence and addiction, impulses to resume using are extraordinarily difficult to overcome even when there is a desperate wish to escape the vicious cycle of addiction. There is often a good window of opportunity to engage someone in treatment after a substance use emergency has occurred and immediately following detoxification; however, the window usually closes quickly. Since treatment services for substance use are in short supply, there are few opportunities for people to gain immediate access to treatment. Consequently, most people will resume the pattern of substance use dependence that led to the crisis, resulting in a repetitive cycle of crisis, illness, and disability and a "revolving door" in and out of emergency services.

## Management of Trauma

Occasionally, individuals experience extremely stressful events, such as those that threaten their survival (physical or psychological). These include events in which someone is attacked, assaulted, or victimized, and situations in which an individual witnesses a horrific event, such as a violent death. Such circumstances are referred to as "trauma," and they may overwhelm the individual's coping capacities so quickly and intensely that lasting psychological harm occurs. The resulting condition is known as PTSD, and it typically includes symptoms such as flashbacks or frightening dreams related to the traumatic event, a sense of emotional numbness, angry outbursts, and avoidance of thoughts or situations reminiscent of the event. An individual suffering from PTSD is effectively in a sort of ongoing crisis and has been unable to fully process the frightening event in order to restore a sense of effective coping and competence.

The most effective intervention for PTSD involves the use of exposure therapy, a form of CBT in which the individual is led in a safe and structured way to gradually re-experience aspects of the frightening event while using new coping methods, taught in the therapy, to cope with the experience in a healthier way.

Another approach is critical incident stress debriefing (CISD), which is carried out very soon after an individual has been exposed to a traumatic event, sometimes in a work or school setting where the event occurred. Individuals involved in this event are brought together to talk about what happened and their feelings about the event in a safe and confidential context, with the discussion typically being guided by a professional or peer counsellor. There has been considerable debate about the impact of CISD. Proponents consider it an important tool in preventing the onset of PTSD: for example, a study by Boscarino, Adams, and Figley (2005) found CISD to reduce rates of depression and PTSD in individuals who had experienced the 9/11 attack on the New York World Trade Center. Meanwhile, critics cite a number of research trials that indicate no benefit or even increased rates of PTSD in individuals who receive CISD (Adler et al., 2008; Feldner, Monson, & Friedman, 2007). Furthermore, it has been argued that CISD cannot be evaluated as a single intervention but must be implemented as one component of a full spectrum of crisis interventions, including individual counselling, family intervention, and availability of formal assessment or psychotherapy for individuals requiring this level of service (Blacklock, 2012; Everly & Lating, 2013).

## Responding to Disasters

Disasters may occur as a result of "natural" environmental events (e.g., floods, earthquakes, and tsunamis); large-scale accidents (e.g., industrial fires and explosions, plane crashes); and terrorist and wartime attacks and violence. In addition to the toll of death and injury, such disasters result in profound trauma that often affects the mental health of large groups of people simultaneously.

Much has been learned about the nature of disaster response and approaches to enhance individuals coping with the aftermath of disaster since the 9/11 terrorist attack in the US (Park et al., 2008; Updegraff, Silver, & Holman, 2008). Fortunately, most individuals are able to survive disasters with only transitory symptoms that do not result in persistent psychological consequences and do not require formal intervention to restore mental health (National Institute of Mental Health, 2002; Norris, Tracy, & Galea, 2009). However, a substantial proportion of those who survive disasters develop persistent PTSD (Srinivasa Murthy, 2007); it has been found that those who provide emergency response services are at particular risk. A key development in this field has been the recognition that individuals respond very differently to disasters. By applying their particular coping styles and capacities, individuals handle the extreme psychological stress in unique ways.

Three stages have been described in the response to disasters: the preparedness phase, the response phase, and the recovery phase (Laurendeau, Labarre, & Senécal, 2007). The preparedness phase involves the advance planning and preparation of actions, communications, and leadership roles, including the training of individuals who will be responsible for various aspects of disaster response. The response phase refers to the period immediately following the disaster, when re-establishment of feelings of safety, confidence, competence, and social cohesion among the population is of paramount importance. Clear communication of information to the general public is needed during this phase and supersedes the need for psychological intervention. The recovery phase involves the extended period following the disaster. It is during this phase that mental health interventions are needed to diminish incidence of PTSD and other difficulties.

**Figure 11.4:** Sichuan earthquake, China. Earthquakes and other disasters have significant impacts on the psychological health of survivors.

*Source*: youding xie/iStockphoto

## Conclusion

When usual coping mechanisms are overwhelmed, individuals may experience mental health crises or emergencies. An initial response to mental health emergencies and crises may be undertaken by police, paramedics, and other first-responders; they will often transport people who are in crisis to hospital emergency departments for assessment. Crisis lines, emergency shelters, and other services can help to avert problems, provide temporary support, and assist people in obtaining additional help.

Common mental health emergencies include suicidal, psychotic, and substance use emergencies. Following assessment, people who are determined to require in-patient admission are hospitalized in order to receive treatment that usually includes medications and individual or group counselling or therapy. Withdrawal management, also known as "detoxification" services, may be provided to individuals who are experiencing substantial physical and mental health problems during acute withdrawal from psychoactive substances.

Studies of the psychological outcomes of people who experience traumatic events and disasters have found that most people have only transient problems, but some will experience persistent PTSD and other mental health problems. Negative psychological outcomes can be minimized through good preparedness, well-organized responses immediately following disasters, and provision of appropriate interventions during the longer-term recovery phase.

## Glossary

**coping:** Finding ways to accomplish goals despite obstacles and challenges.
**coping trategies:** A set of cognitive and behavioural skills and approaches used to meet goals and needs.
**crisis:** Limited time periods of upset in the psychological functioning of individuals, precipitated by current exposure to environmental stressors, which appear to be turning points in the development of mental disorder.
**Mental Health Act:** A piece of legislation that regulates involuntary transportation and admission to psychiatric services for individuals suspected of suffering from mental illness.
**stress:** Occurs when the perceived pressure exceeds one's perceived ability to cope.
**stressors:** Environmental challenges that tax or overtax an individual's coping ability.
**withdrawal management:** Services that primarily address the physical health problems that people experience when they are going through withdrawal.

## Critical Thinking Questions

1. What are the key elements of a crisis?
2. What are the three ways in which a state of crisis relates to mental health?
3. What is the Mental Health Act and what issues arise with hospitalization due to mental health problems?
4. Select one type of common mental health emergency and describe the tasks involved in addressing it.
5. What are the three stages in response to disaster? Briefly describe each stage.

## Recommended Readings

Allen, M.H. (Ed.). (2008). *Emergency Psychiatry* (Vol. 21). Arlington, VA: American Psychiatric Publishing.

Chiles, J.A, & Strosahl, K.D. (2008). *Clinical Manual for Assessment and Treatment of Suicidal Patients.* Washington, DC: American Psychiatric Publishing.

Clark, C., & Classen, C.C. (2014). *Treating the Trauma Survivor: An Essential Guide to Trauma-informed Care.* New York: Routledge.

Lazarus, R. (2006). *Stress and Emotion: A New Synthesis.* New York: Springer.

Paton, D., & Johnston, D. (2006). *Disaster Resilience: An Integrated Approach.* Springfield, IL: Charles C. Thomas.

## Recommended Websites

American Association for Emergency Psychiatry. www.emergencypsychiatry.org/

Canadian Mental Health Association. Coping with Stress. toronto.cmha.ca/mental_health/stress/#.Vg7aJNZ45l8

Centres for Disease Control and Prevention. Emergency Preparedness and Response. www.bt.cdc.gov/mentalhealth/primer.asp

Substance Abuse and Mental Health Services Administration. National Centre for Trauma-Informed Care and Alternatives to Seclusion and Restraint. www.samhsa.gov/nctic

US National Institute of Mental Health. Coping with Traumatic Events. www.nimh.nih.gov/health/topics/coping-with-traumatic-events/index.shtml

## References

Adler, A.B., Litz, B.T., Castro, C.A., Suvak, M., Thomas, L., Burrell, L., McGurk, D., Wright, K.M., & Bliese, P.D. (2008). A group randomized trial of critical incident stress debriefing provided to U.S. peacekeepers. *Journal of Traumatic Stress*, 21(3), 253–263.

Blacklock, E. (2012). Interventions following a critical incident: Developing a critical incident stress management team. *Archives of Psychiatric Nursing*, 26(1), 2–8.

Boscarino, J.A., Adams, R.E., & Figley, C.R. (2005). A prospective cohort study of the effectiveness of employer-sponsored crisis interventions after a major disaster. *International Journal of Emergency Mental Health*, 7(1), 9–22.

Canadian Mental Health Association. (2012). Community committal. Retrieved from www.cmha.ca/public_policy/community-committal/

Caplan, G. (1989). Recent developments in crisis intervention and the promotion of support services. *Journal of Primary Prevention*, 10(1), 3–25.

Carver, C.S., Scheier, M.F., & Weintraub, J.K. (1989). Assessing coping strategies: A theoretically based approach. *Journal of Personality and Social Psychology*, 56(2), 267–283.

Devylder, J.E., Ben-David, S., Schobel, S.A., Kimhy, D., Malaspina, D., & Corcoran, C.M. (2013). Temporal association of stress sensitivity and symptoms in individuals at clinical high risk for psychosis. *Psychological Medicine*, 43(2), 259–268.

Employment and Social Development Canada. (2016). Housing—Homeless shelters and beds. Retrieved from well-being.esdc.gc.ca/misme-iowb/.3ndic.1t.4r@-eng.jsp?iid=44

Everly, Jr., G.S., & Lating, J.M. (2013). Crisis intervention and psychological first aid. In *A clinical guide to the treatment of the human stress response* (pp. 427–436). New York: Springer.

Feldner, M.T., Monson, C.M., & Friedman, M.J. (2007). A critical analysis of approaches to targeted PTSD prevention: Current status and theoretically derived future directions. *Behavior Modification*, 31(1), 80–116.

Folkman, S., & Lazarus, R.S. (1985). If it changes it must be a process: Study of emotion and coping during three stages of a college examination. *Journal of Personality and Social Psychology*, 48(1), 150–170.

Guo, S., Biegel, D.E., Johnsen, J.A., & Dyches, H. (2014). Assessing the impact of community-based mobile crisis services on preventing hospitalization. *Psychiatric Services,* 52(2), 223–228.

Kanel, K. (2014). *A guide to crisis intervention.* Stamford, CT: Cengage Learning.

Laurendeau, M.C., Labarre, L., & Senécal, G. (2007). The psychosocial dimension of health and social service interventions in emergency situations. *Open Medicine*, 1(2), 102–106. Retrieved from www.openmedicine.ca/article/viewArticle/100/57

Lazarus, R.S. (1993). Coping theory and research: Past, present, and future. *Psychosomatic Medicine*, 55(3), 234–247.

Montero-Marin, J., Prado-Abril, J., Demarzo, M.M.P., Gascon, S., & García-Campayo, J. (January 1, 2014). Coping with stress and types of burnout: Explanatory power of different coping strategies. *PLoS One*, 9, 2.

National Institute for Health and Care Excellence. (2015). Violence and aggression: Short-term management in mental health, health and community settings. Retrieved from nice.org.uk/guidance/ng10

National Institute of Mental Health. (2002). *Mental health and mass violence.* Washington, DC: US Government Printing Office.

National Treatment Strategy Working Group. (2008). A systems approach to substance use in Canada: Recommendations for a national treatment strategy. Retrieved from http://www.ccsa.ca/Resource%20Library/nts-systems-approach-substance-abuse-canada-2008-en.pdf

Nordstrom, K., & Allen, M.H. (2007). Managing the acutely agitated and psychotic patient. *CNS Spectrums*, 12(S17), 5–11.

Norris, F.H., Tracy, M., & Galea, S. (2009). Looking for resilience: Understanding the longitudinal trajectories of responses to stress. *Social Science & Medicine*, 68(12), 2190–2198.

Park, C.L., Aldwin, C.M., Fenster, J.R., & Snyder, L.B. (2008). Pathways to posttraumatic growth versus posttraumatic stress: Coping and emotional reactions following the September 11, 2001, terrorist attacks. *American Journal of Orthopsychiatry*, 78(3), 300–312.

Psychiatric Patient Advocate Office. (January 2009). Substitute decision makers: What is an SDM? Retrieved from www.ppao.gov.on.ca

Seligman, M. (1972). Learned helplessness. *Annual Review of Medicine*, 23(1), 407–412.

Srinivasa Murthy, R. (2007). Mass violence and mental health: Recent epidemiological findings. *International Review of Psychiatry*, 19(3), 183–192.

Strack, S., & Millon, T. (2007). Contributions to the dimensional assessment of personality disorders using Millon's model and the Millon Clinical Multiaxial Inventory (MCMI–III). *Journal of Personality Assessment*, 89(1), 56–69.

Updegraff, J.A., Silver, R.C., & Holman, E.A. (2008). Searching for and finding meaning in collective trauma: Results from a national longitudinal study of the 9/11 terrorist attacks. *Journal of Personality and Social Psychology*, 95(3), 709–722.

# Chapter 12

# TREATMENT FOR MENTAL DISORDERS AND SUBSTANCE USE DISORDER

Respond intelligently even to unintelligent treatment.
—Laozi (Chinese philosopher, writing in the 6th century BC)

## Introduction

The range of approaches commonly utilized in the treatment of mental disorders and substance use disorders may be classified broadly as biological, psychological, or spiritual. In this chapter, we provide a brief overview of the major treatments currently used in the treatment of mental illness. Biological treatments include the use of medications, ECT, magnetic seizure therapy, neurostimulation, and psychosurgery. Psychological approaches include CBT, psychoanalytic psychotherapies, play therapy, family therapy, and motivational interviewing. Spiritual approaches to finding meaning in the experience of mental illness include those provided by organized religions, distinct cultural traditions, meditative practices, or other unique spiritual practices and paths.

At the end of the chapter, we have listed recommendations for further reading, so that you may obtain more complete information about the treatments listed here and others that are not included. We also provide a self-help section aimed at helping you to cope with stress and enhance mental health; this is written with *students* in mind (since readers of this book will often be students), but it is applicable to people in all walks of life.

## Psychopharmacotherapy

The advent of psychopharmacotherapy, that is, the use of medications in the treatment of psychiatric symptoms, occurred during the 1950s when chlorpromazine (now known as an antipsychotic medication) was first marketed for the treatment of psychotic symptoms. Since that time, pharmacotherapy has become the predominant mode of treatment in psychiatry and other medical settings. The main classes of psychiatric medications and their established uses are described below, but note that medications are sometimes prescribed "off label" (i.e., used in the treatment of disorders for which the medication has not been approved by the official regulatory body, Health Canada).

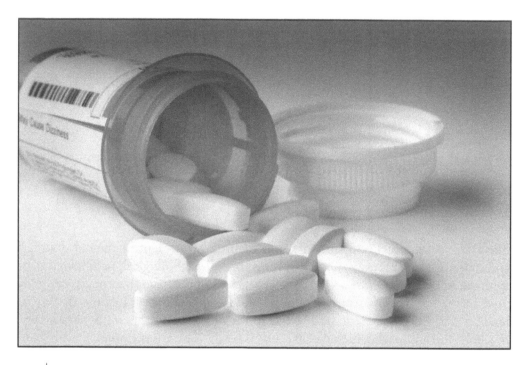

**Figure 12.1:** Psychopharmacological treatment is commonly prescribed by physicians for mental disorders.

*Source:* YinYang/iStockphoto

## *Antipsychotic Medications*

The discovery of chlorpromazine as an effective treatment for psychotic symptoms (i.e., delusions and hallucinations) changed the course of psychiatric therapy. It was a surgeon in France, Henri Laborit, who was studying the potential use of chlorpromazine in anaesthesia, and who wondered whether it might soothe agitated patients in psychiatric wards. The improvements that psychiatrists saw in patients who were administered the new medication were so profound that they considered chlorpromazine to be a miracle drug that ushered in the rapid development and marketing of antipsychotic medications (Ban, 2007). The group of psychopharmaceuticals, known as "antipsychotics," include chlorpromazine and a variety of similar medications. The discovery of this first-generation of antipsychotic medications significantly improved the prognosis for individuals with psychotic illnesses and is partly responsible for the deinstitutionalization policies that swept across Canada. These and many of the more recently developed antipsychotic medications appear to act by blocking dopamine receptors in various areas of the brain. Over the past 20 years, first-generation antipsychotics have lost favour as treatments for psychosis, partly because of the side effects associated with these medications. The side effects include: (1) extrapyramidal symptoms, which are movement disorders that develop as a result of the inhibition of dopamine activity by antipsychotic medication and include dystonia (i.e., muscle spasms resulting in distorted or twisted body positions), akathisia (i.e., restlessness and inability to sit still), and parkinsonism (slowed movements, stiff posture, and emotionless facial expression); (2) tardive dyskinesia, sometimes irreversible and consisting of unusual involuntary movements (e.g., lip-smacking, and "pill-rolling" finger movements); and (3) oculogyric crisis, which is a medical emergency involving a fixed upward stare of the eyes lasting for several minutes to an hour, sometimes treated with intramuscular injections of anticholinergic medications.

Second-generation antipsychotics have become the standard treatment of psychosis. The first of these so-called "atypical" antipsychotic medications, clozapine, was patented in the 1960s. Unfortunately, a very serious side effect called agranulocytosis (i.e., dangerously low levels of white blood cells that result in an increased risk for acquiring life-threatening infections) was found to the associated with this medication. Clozapine use declined, but its effectiveness in treating psychotic symptoms in patients not responding to other treatments led to its reintroduction to clinical practice, although with extra monitoring. Second-generation antipsychotics are recommended as an initial treatment for psychosis because they are less likely to induce the side effects listed above. However, a harmful side effect of these medications has been identified: metabolic syndrome, in which individuals experience substantial weight gain and are at a significantly increased risk of diabetes mellitus.

## Antidepressant Medications

Antidepressant medications are used in the treatment of mood disorders, such as major depression and dysthymic disorder (i.e., a chronic form of depression with less severe symptoms than major depression) and several anxiety disorders, (e.g., panic disorder and obsessive-compulsive disorder). The first group of antidepressant medications used widely were tricyclic antidepressants, but they are now prescribed infrequently due to their poor side effect profile and high level of lethality in overdose. Monoamine oxidase inhibitors are also infrequently prescribed due to their side effects and potential for dangerous interaction with certain foods and other drugs. Selective serotonin reuptake inhibitors (SSRIs) are currently the most frequently prescribed antidepressants. Antidepressant medication is generally considered to be effective for individuals with moderate to severe forms of depression. However, the effectiveness of antidepressant medications has been called into question by recent reviews of clinical trials, suggesting that antidepressant medication may be no more effective than a placebo for many individuals with major depression, showing true effectiveness only for the most severely depressed individuals (Fournier, DeRubeis, & Hollon, 2010). This finding is controversial and subject to ongoing debate (Horder, Matthews, & Waldmann, 2010). What we do know is that antidepressant medication is over-prescribed for mild depression, where it does not seem effective (Barbui et al., 2011; Baumeister, 2012).

## Mood Stabilizers

Mood stabilizers are prescribed for patients diagnosed with bipolar disorder, and these medications help to control abnormally high mood states. Lithium carbonate was the first medication approved for this purpose and continues to be widely used. Commonly used mood stabilizers include divalproex sodium and topiramate. Antipsychotics are also used to treat the manic symptoms of bipolar disorder. The depressive episodes of this disorder can be long-lasting and are particularly difficult to treat: antidepressant medications often result in limited benefit (Nivoli et al., 2011).

## Sedatives

Sedative medications include a number of types of drugs that cause drowsiness when given in higher does. They can be used to induce sleep or to reduce agitation and anxiety. Of the different classes of sedative drugs available, the benzodiazepines are the most commonly used in treatment of symptoms such as anxiety or agitation. Although safe for short-term use, extended use of benzodiazepines can lead to dependence and withdrawal.

## Substitution Therapy for Substance Use Dependence

Substitution therapy refers to replacing illicit drugs with less harmful prescription drugs to prevent withdrawal symptoms and reduce the harmful effects of drug use. This approach has been used most commonly in the treatment of opiate dependence in which people who are dependent on injections of heroin, morphine, or other opiates are prescribed methadone and buprenorphine. These substitution drugs are taken orally, sharply reducing the rates of infection associated with injections.

## Issues in Psychopharmacotherapy

In recent years, the biological approach has become the dominant form of treatment provided for those with mental health problems (Kazdin & Blase, 2011; Schwartz,

2006). This has occurred for a number of reasons, including the introduction of relatively effective medication therapies for certain mental disorders, the development of new technologies with the promise of greater understanding of hypothesized relationships between neurochemistry and mental illness, and the effective use of marketing strategies by the pharmaceutical industry (Schwartz, 2006). Although psychopharmacotherapies benefit many individuals, enthusiasm must also be balanced by appropriate prudence in the use of medications outside the bounds of current knowledge. Medications can be combined in a "pharmacological cocktail" to address various symptoms and enhance response (Mojtabai & Olfson, 2010). However, **polypharmacy** increases the risk of significant side effects, and the effectiveness of some frequently used medication combinations is questionable (Honer et al., 2009). Side effects and other potential harms that may be caused by psychiatric medications must be prevented wherever possible. Another important concern is that psychopharmacologic treatment has become so predominant among medical practitioners that other evidence-based treatments have been underutilized (Barker & Buchanan-Barker, 2004), with negative consequences for the quality of mental health care.

## Electroconvulsive Therapy and Magnetic Seizure Therapy

**Electroconvulsive therapy** (ECT), first developed in the 1930s, is perhaps the most controversial treatment to be used commonly in modern psychiatry. ECT involves passing an electric current through the brain to induce a seizure. It is used primarily in the treatment of severe depression. The mechanism of action is not understood, but it is hypothesized to involve an increase in release of specific neurotransmitters. In its early use, ECT was somewhat barbaric, as seizures were induced without anesthesia, often resulting in convulsions and causing substantial discomfort or injury. In current practice, a very brief-acting anesthetic agent is given in preparation for ECT to induce sedation and block muscular response (thereby reducing the physical impact of seizures). ECT is considered effective for the treatment of depression. It has been proposed that ECT may be safer than medication for elderly or medically ill individuals. However, this claim is controversial and is currently being investigated (Brown University Psychopharmacology Update, 2015; van der Wurff et al., 2003). Some patients receive maintenance ECT, regular treatments intended to reduce relapse. Side effects include short-term memory loss and confusion, and some ECT recipients report lasting impairment of their memory (Meeter et al., 2011; Reisner, 2003).

Recently, a new form of convulsive therapy, magnetic seizure therapy, has been developed and may prove to be a safer alternative to ECT (Zyss et al., 2010). Since evoking a seizure by using magnetic stimulation allows more control of seizure activity, it is hoped that there may be fewer cognitive side effects with this new approach.

**Box 12.1: Thalidomide**

**Figure 12.2:** Thalidomide caused birth defects resulting in short, unformed limbs.

*Source:* GetStock

There is often pressure to quickly introduce medications with the potential for improving mental health problems (Light, 2010). But the need for caution is highlighted by the case of thalidomide, a medication prescribed to thousands of pregnant women during the late 1950s and early 1960s as a treatment for anxiety as well as morning sickness (Kim & Scialli, 2011). It was learned too late that thalidomide use during pregnancy can cause birth defects. As many as 20,000 children were born with severe physical deformities as a result of exposure to this medication in utero. The birth defects associated with thalidomide use are characterized by short, unformed limbs. In response to this tragedy, the process for developing, testing, and marketing new medications became stricter and more closely regulated in the hope of preventing such a disaster in the future.

# Neurostimulation

There has been a surge of interest in the potential utility of various new treatment approaches for mental disorders that deliver more focal stimulation to discrete areas of the brain. These modalities include transcranial magnetic stimulation (TMS), vagus nerve stimulation (VNS), trigeminal nerve stimulation (TNS), and deep-brain stimulation (DBS). In TMS, a magnetic coil is placed over a specific area of the patient's scalp while the patient is awake and a magnetic field is induced that passes directly through the skull unimpeded. Thus, brain cells directly beneath the skull are depolarized to a depth of approximately two centimetres, which is at the junction of the grey and white matter of the cerebral cortex. For the most part, TMS is used as a second-line treatment for patients with depression who have not responded to first-line treatments, and it is generally delivered over the area of the dorsolateral prefrontal cortex. TMS has been studied as a potential treatment in a wide range of mental and neurological disorders (Wassermann & Zimmermann, 2012). VNS involves placement of an electrode in the neck that stimulates the vagus nerve repeatedly through use of a pacemaker, and is thought to transmit stimulation to subcortical brain areas. VNS has previously been used extensively to treat epilepsy but is now being examined as a potential treatment for depression and other mental disorders (Beekwilder & Beems, 2010). TNS similarly transmits neurostimulation to the brain, but does so through implantation of an electrode that stimulates the trigeminal nerve, which is located in the cranial area. In DBS, a surgical procedure is undertaken to place an electrode in a specific location in the brain; through use of a pacemaker, the implanted electrode will deliver repetitive stimulation to deep brain structures. This experimental procedure has been studied in patients with severe disorders that have not responded to conventional treatment. To date, the relative benefits and risks of DBS remain unclear (Fitzgerald & Segrave, 2015).

# Psychosurgery

**Psychosurgery** (i.e., brain surgery for psychiatric benefit) was popularized in the 1950s when American psychiatrist Walter Freeman developed a procedure called the "ice pick lobotomy." This procedure was grisly, involving the use of a hammer and an ice pick, which was inserted just above the tear duct of the eye and manipulated to sever certain connections in the patient's brain. Psychosurgery was first introduced by Egan Moniz in the 1930s (and he won a Nobel prize for it) (Jansson, 1998). The popularity of psychosurgery declined, and it was recognized that this procedure was inhumane and ineffective. Currently, psychosurgery is rarely undertaken and uses proper neurosurgical procedures. Its use is reserved for unusual and extremely severe conditions that have not responded to any other interventions. DBS (described above) has generally replaced previous ablative psychosurgical approaches and current research

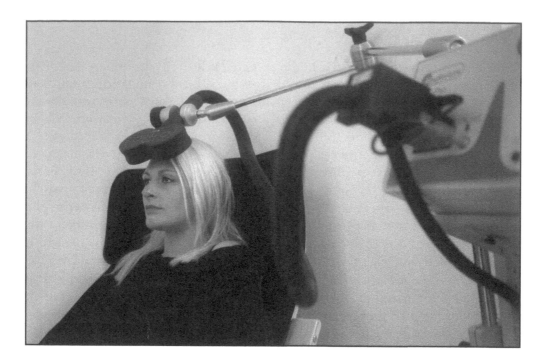

**Figure 12.3:** Transcranial magnetic stimulation (TMS)

*Source:* GetStock/AMELIE-BENOIST/BSIP

continues to explore the benefits and risks of DBS for intractable or treatment-resistant conditions (Luigjes, et al., 2013).

# Psychotherapy and Other Psychologically Oriented Treatments

Psychotherapy and other psychologically oriented treatments have been developed in line with a series of ideas and theories about mental function. Although there is good evidence that such approaches result in substantial improvements, there remains substantial debate about particular approaches being more effective than others. There are hundreds of psychotherapy methods that have been develop and applied. In the following, we discuss a few commonly used approaches, beginning with a discussion of psychological self-management.

## *Self-Management and Peer Support*

Prior to seeking any form of professional consultation or treatment for mental health problems, many people seek "self-help" resources—they want to manage their own mental health problems. There are books, tool kits, movies, groups, and websites, all devoted to helping people make changes for themselves. Furthermore, it is estimated that two-thirds of Internet users seek mental health information—a Google search for "self-help mental health" turns up thousands of sites devoted to providing mental health information and resources.

So, are mental health self-management resources effective? The simple answer is: yes, reasonably so. Research has demonstrated moderate effectiveness of self-management programs when compared to no-treatment, wait-list, and placebo control groups (Cuijpers, 2010; McKendree-Smith, Floyd, & Scogin, 2003). Many individuals report that self-help books have played an important part in their psychological improvement, and psychologists often recommend self-help books or groups to their patients (Campbell & Smith, 2003). Self-management resources are also inexpensive, compared to professional treatment. Many people fear stigma and discrimination when seeking professional treatment, while self-management resources offer privacy and anonymity.

But we shouldn't be putting mental health professionals out to pasture just yet. Self-help does not work for everyone; there are many cases where a mental problem is so severe that immediate professional help is necessary. Furthermore, self-help tools are more effective when accompanied by coaching and support (Corrigan & Mueser, 2012; Cuijpers et al., 2010), which brings us to **supported self-management** (SSM).

SSM involves a workbook or online program that teaches the individual skills for coping more effectively with mental health problems, usually based on CBT principles, and coaching and encouragement provided by a health care provider, family member, or peer counsellor. It is a "low-intensity" intervention suitable for a broad range of common mental health problems, including depression, anxiety, and eating disorders. SSM focuses on such skills as setting goals to become more behaviourally active, systematic problem solving, thinking in a fairer and more realistic way, managing worry or physical tension, and identifying warning signs of relapse. SSM builds upon individuals' own coping strengths and enhances their sense of personal competence; in this way, it helps to address issues of stigma and disempowerment. SSM has performed well in controlled research: for example, it is effective in mildly to moderately depressed individuals. But note that SSM requires active participation in the recovery process, which may not be possible for very ill individuals.

Peer support refers to a support that is provided by individuals who themselves have had lived experience of mental illness. Peer support is provided in both formal and informal settings and, in some jurisdictions, peer support workers are hired as a part of the mental health treatment team (Mahlke et al., 2014). Probably the best-known approach to providing peer support in a group format is that of Alcoholics Anonymous (AA) and its allied 12-step programs, such as Narcotics Anonymous (NA). These groups are extraordinarily well distributed throughout North America and provide an accessible form of support for those who want to gain control of their substance use. The "12-Step Program," a sequence of tasks the individual seeks to complete on the path to recovery, includes admitting one does not have control over the substance dependence and making amends for harms done to others. AA/NA groups may be helpful for those who maintain a commitment to following its principles, but the overall effectiveness of these groups remains uncertain (Ferri, Amato, & Davoli, 2006; Kaskutas, 2009). Peer support groups are also available for many other mental health problems such as depression, eating disorders, and psychosis. Groups are also available to provide support to friends and family members as they cope with the mental health issues of loved ones.

## Cognitive Behavioural Therapy

CBT is the form of psychotherapy that has the strongest evidence for its effectiveness in the treatment of a wide variety of conditions. CBT represents a merger of "old-school" behavioural therapy (focused on the use of situational rewards to increase the frequency of adaptive behaviours and decrease maladaptive ones) and cognitive therapy (focused on helping individuals to identify unrealistic/unfair thinking patterns and replace them with more beneficial ones). It has been shown to be effective in the treatment of a wide variety of mental disorders including: major depression, substance dependence, panic disorder, and bulimia nervosa (Zinbarg et al., 2010). Through individual or group CBT sessions, clients are taught to recognize maladaptive behaviours (such as withdrawal from social contact when feeling depressed) and distorted thought patterns (such as harshly critical self-labelling) and given skills to change these habits of thought and behaviour. Homework is assigned between sessions to try out new ways of acting or thinking in different situations. In fact, most therapeutic progress is made via these "behavioural experiments" outside of the clinical sessions.

Crucial features of CBT are (1) a focus on the present, how someone is thinking and acting in the current situation; (2) an emphasis on the collaborative relationship between therapist and client; (3) treatment goals that are concrete, specific, and measurable (e.g., "rate mood as 20 percent improved"; "participate in fitness activity for 15 minutes, three times each week"); and (4) time-limited intervention, working within 6 to 12 sessions for most common mental health problems.

A distinct form of CBT-derived therapy, dialectical behaviour therapy (DBT), emerged as an intervention for individuals suffering from borderline personality disorder, who are among the most challenging patients. It is described as follows:

> DBT evolved from standard cognitive-behavioral therapy as a treatment for [borderline personality disorder], particularly for recurrently suicidal, severely dysfunctional individuals. The theoretical orientation to treatment is a blend of three theoretical positions: behavioral science, dialectical philosophy, and Zen practice. Behavioral science, the principles of behavior change, is countered by acceptance of the client (with techniques drawn both from Zen and from Western contemplative practice); these poles are balanced within the dialectical framework. (Barlow, 2008, p. 369)

DBT has spread rapidly in the mental health system. It is considered to be the definitive treatment for borderline personality disorder, despite the fact that DBT is only mildly to moderately effective for that disorder. The wide dissemination of DBT has been attributed to the lack of any other plausible treatment for borderline personality disorder, its sophisticated theoretical model, and the practical strategies it provides for helping this very challenging patient group (Swenson, Torrey, & Koerner, 2002).

## Psychoanalytic Therapies

Psychoanalytic therapies refer to psychotherapeutic approaches that apply the theories of Sigmund Freud and the many other theorists who further developed and extended the original ideas of psychoanalysis. We have discussed psychoanalytic theory earlier in the book (Chapter 3); it aims to solve deep-seated conflicts that are purported to operate unconsciously (without our awareness). Once the most common approach to psychotherapy, psychoanalytic therapies have decreased in popularity as a result of their perceived impracticality as brief interventions and their inconclusive demonstrations of effectiveness in reducing symptoms (Paris, 2005). However, there continues to be considerable interest in structured forms of psychoanalytic therapy that have been developed, known as "brief dynamic therapy" and "short-term psychodynamic psychotherapy." Such approaches to dynamic therapy are of shorter duration than traditional psychoanalytic treatment and have shown reasonable effectiveness in the treatment of certain conditions (Abbas et al., 2013; Driessen et al., 2015).

## Play Therapy

Typically used with children between the ages of 3 and 12, play therapy allows children to express thoughts and feelings in a way that is natural and familiar to them—through play. The assumption behind play therapy is that children who are allowed to play freely will engage in play that reveals the issues with which they are struggling. Play therapy has been used effectively to treat a broad range of children's mental health problems, including anxiety, aggressive behaviour, abuse, and trauma (Seligman & Reichenberg, 2011), and can be combined with other approaches, such as CBT. Parents and caregivers are typically the first to initiate contact with a play therapist, who conducts a number of one-on-one sessions using toys, art, games, and stories to communicate with the child. For example, the therapist and child might role-play a game of "house" to explore family relationships and the home environment, or a therapist might ask the child to use toy cars to show what happened in a car accident.

**Figure 12.4:** A counsellor taking notes during a therapy session.

*Source:* Brad Killer/iStockphoto

## Family Therapy

Although various family therapy approaches have been developed, they all consider the involvement of "families" in treatment to be beneficial. In addition to relatives, "families" may include close friends and others in an individual's social network. The theoretical frameworks that inform family therapy have had a rich history and many creative applications have been developed, including structural, systems, intergenerational, solution-focused, and narrative therapies. Family therapy may occur as a stand-alone intervention, or alongside other forms of mental health treatment (Eisler et al., 2005; Hooper et al., 2012).

## Motivational Interviewing

Motivational Interviewing is a psychotherapy approach that was developed initially to address substance use disorders and was later applied more widely to address a variety of mental health problems (Miller & Rose, 2009). A central feature is a focus on helping clients to consider their current situations and envisage the changes they would like to put in place. This is undertaken through

**Figure 12.5:** Play therapy has been shown to enhance children's self-concepts, accelerate cognitive development, reduce anxiety, and improve social skills. Here, a young girl uses playdough to express her feelings during play therapy.

*Source:* GeorgeBurba/iStockphoto

a non-judgmental and non-adversarial approach. Motivational interviewing acknowledges that individuals are at various states of readiness for change and seeks to meet people "where they are."

## Religious, Spiritual, and Meditative Approaches

Many people consider mental health problems in a religious or spiritual context and may seek support from religious or spiritual advisors. Group prayer, meditation, pastoral counselling, traditional ritual practices, and other activities may be recommended. Mental health professionals are sometimes criticized as being antagonistic toward spiritual practices that are adopted by many people who experience mental illness or substance use disorders. Recently, there has been an increased awareness of the importance of spirituality in mental health (Barker & Buchanan-Barker, 2004; Koenig, 2009).

**Figure 12.6:** There is increased awareness of the importance of spirituality in mental health. Group prayer, meditation, pastoral counselling, and traditional ritual practices are being employed to promote and maintain mental well-being.

*Source:* Redrockschool/iStockphoto

## *Mindfulness*

An approach to mental health problems that has emerged recently is **mindfulness**, which has its roots in Buddhist meditation and has been combined with CBT principles. It involves a set of skills designed to increase one's capacity to be clearly aware of one's immediate situation, ongoing thoughts, and bodily sensations without feeling the need to "fix" them. The aim of this approach is to be "present" in a non-judgmental way, observing the flow of thoughts and feelings without getting caught up in these experiences. It represents a form of awareness practice that promotes acceptance and openness, which in turn helps to relieve psychological symptoms and improve one's ability to manage psychological pain. A growing body of research supports the effectiveness of this therapeutic approach for anxiety and depression (Kim et al., 2009; Kuyken et al., 2008; Vøllestad, Birkeland Nielsen, & Høstmark Nielsen, 2012).

## Combining Treatments

When it comes to the application of treatments to an individual's mental health or substance use problems, there is no "one-size-fits-all" approach. Selecting the most appropriate treatment depends on the pattern, duration, and severity of the problem; the availability of social or financial supports in the person's life; the presence of other physical or mental disorders; and other factors. Commonly, there is value in combining various treatment approaches, whether biological, psychological, or spiritual.

## Personal Mental Health Tool Kit

Self-care—why is this important? At various times in our lives, we all deal with high levels of stress, whether in school, when we are busy learning difficult material, meeting deadlines, making friends, planning seriously for the future, and preparing for exams; at work, when we are carrying responsibilities and working alongside others who may be difficult to deal with; or with families or friends, when our relationships may become rocky or upsetting. When stress becomes difficult to manage, any of us are liable to experience some psychological difficulty, whether this manifests in worry, poor sleep, low mood, excessive drinking, drug use, or irritability. Sometimes you have a trusted friend, family member, or counsellor you can talk to, but mostly you must work it out on your own. Here are some strategies to help you deal with the stress of life. But remember, if you think you might be having serious difficulties with depression, anxiety, or substance use, contact the student counselling and health services or talk to your family physician. This self-care guide is not a replacement for getting treatment when you need it.

### *Learning to Set Action Goals*

Dealing with stress in a healthy manner involves setting goals for trying out new ways of coping, then practising and sustaining these new coping behaviours over time. You need to learn how to set goals in the most effective way. Often people set goals that aren't likely to be carried forward and achieved. Let's say a friend of yours sets an ambitious goal to begin a fitness program, determined to go from no exercise to working out for an hour every day at the local fitness centre. This is not very effective goal setting because it is just too ambitious: your friend will probably attend fitness class for a couple of days, then miss one or two, then feel guilty, then find reasons for not going—and end up not only failing to improve his or her fitness, but also feeling discouraged.

An effective goal has three characteristics: it is *specific* (states exactly what you are going to do), *realistic* (within your capability and likely to be carried out), and *scheduled* (you write down when and how often you are planning to do it). Table 12.1 offers an example of an effective goal.

**Box 12.2: Stand Up for Mental Health**

Figure 12.7: David Granirer, a Vancouver-based counsellor and comedian, combines both his careers to help people with mental health issues use comedy to deal with their problems.

*Source:* GetStock/Rick Madonik

Someone wise once said "Laughter is the best medicine," and Vancouver counsellor David Granirer took it to heart. Granirer developed a unique and innovative program for individuals with mental illness called "Stand Up for Mental Health." The program, which helps participants to develop stand-up comedy routines, has been found to have therapeutic results. In fact, students and researchers from Western University in Ontario are currently studying the quantitative benefits of participating in the Stand Up for Mental Health program. The program has had such a positive response that Granirer is unable to accommodate everyone wanting to participate. If only all therapy could be so much fun! In a recent interview, Granirer laughingly joked, "People don't want to hear from a stand-up comic that's happy and well adjusted.... That would be really boring" (Carletti, 2010, p. 4).

**Table 12.1: Example of an effective goal**

| What I'm going to do | When |
|---|---|
| 30-minute workout at the fitness centre | Mondays and Wednesdays, after my last class |

## *Finding a Means to Ground and Balance Yourself*

It is helpful to find an approach to grounding, balancing, or centring yourself—whatever that may be that you do regularly as a source of pleasure and health promotion. It may be an activity like yoga, an exercise class, a martial art, a sport, swimming, running, cycling, hiking, dance, music, or artwork. One such activity should likely be physical, and you should find one that you truly enjoy and want to do at least once every week, even if it is for a brief period of time. Ensure that the activity you choose really is one that is calming, grounding, and promotes feelings of happiness. At times of high stress, it is particularly important to find a way to ensure that you are engaging in your grounding activity.

## *Relaxation*

Knowing how to relax yourself mentally and physically is one of the most useful things you can learn. One way to do so is through a systematic relaxation method and, to make this easier, we've posted a free online audio file (download at www.sfu.ca/carmha/publications/positive-coping-with-health-conditions.html) to guide you. It shows you how to let go of tension and calm anxious thoughts. Find a quiet spot and listen to the audio file. The relaxation procedure is about 17 minutes long. Each time you listen to the relaxation procedure, you'll learn more about how to relax yourself. Perhaps start by setting a goal of listening twice per week for the next several weeks. After a few weeks, it will be time to find a portable relaxation method, a short version of the relaxation procedure that you can do in any setting. One method of developing this portable method is to use the part of the relaxation procedure where you slowly say "deeply relaxing" to yourself while breathing out. You can then continue this with each out-breath. We call this procedure the "slow breathing method." You might also figure out your own portable relaxation method, using the relaxation audio file or other mental strategies that help you relax. Perhaps there is a particular image that has always been calming for you, such as a sunny beach or a cool pond. Go with whatever works for you, as long as it helps you to relax and it can be used easily in different situations.

## Worry Management

You might have a worry issue if you worry so much about problems that it interferes with other activities, always imagine the worst possible outcome, frequently experience a high level of anxiety, or have difficulty falling asleep, or wake frequently because of worry. If this is an issue for you, start by writing down a problem about which you've been worrying, along with the "worry thoughts" that are making you anxious. For example, perhaps you've been worrying about an impending exam for a course called "Mental Health in Canada," and having the "worry thought": "I'll never be able to learn this stuff. I'll fail the course and the program and I'll never get a job." Then use the reality questions in the left-hand column of Table 12.2 to rethink the situation and come up with more calming and realistic thoughts about the exam, the course, and your employment prospects.

**Table 12.2: Questions to help manage worry**

| | |
|---|---|
| *Can I get more evidence, maybe by asking someone about the situation?* | It's often helpful to get another person's opinion about the situation. |
| *Would most people agree with this thought? If not, what would most people think?* | Just by imagining how most people would react to a "worry thought," you might be able to come up with a fair and realistic way of thinking. |
| *What would I say to a friend if my friend were in a similar situation?* | If a friend of yours were worrying too much, what would you say to him or her? It's likely that you would be able to help your friend think about the situation more fairly by looking at it in a more balanced way. |
| *What will happen if I continue to think this way?* | It's important to understand what results are likely if you continue to worry excessively. Consider the effect of worry on your enjoyment of time with other people, willingness to try activities, ability to get restful sleep, physical symptoms, etc. What might be the results for you and others if you continue to worry excessively? |
| *What is a more encouraging or useful way of thinking?* | Can you come up with another thought that would have better results? Is there a way of thinking that would be more encouraging and helpful in improving the situation? |

Once you've used these questions to come up with thoughts that are more calming and realistic, you'll need to deliberately practise them. Whenever you notice yourself starting to worry too much about a problem, deliberately practise calm and realistic thinking. Tell yourself how to look at the situation, advising yourself just as you might a friend. Talk back to the worry thinking. Every time you talk back, you make the worry thinking weaker and the realistic thinking stronger.

A big problem with worry is that it happens while you're trying to do something else—watch a movie, talk with a friend, or concentrate on a book. Two things happen: first, it's hard to enjoy these activities or do them properly; and, second, you can't focus on the problems you're worrying about because you're so distracted! Trying to force yourself to "stop thinking it" doesn't usually work. But what you can do is schedule a particular time during the week when you will concentrate on worrying about your problems. During this "worry time," you're not allowed to do anything that would distract you from worrying. Write it into your schedule and make sure you won't be interrupted.

The aim of this scheduled worry time is to allow you to worry toward a solution instead of in circles. In order to fully benefit from this time, set yourself up in a comfortable spot, maybe at a desk in a quiet area, and make sure you have paper and pen or a computer—whatever helps you to think about problems and solutions. A useful way to organize your worry time is by using structured problem solving, outlined below.

## Structured Problem Solving

First, write down a particular problem you've been dealing with—don't start with a huge problem, but a relatively small one. Next, write down three actions you might take that would help you get closer to a solution, though not necessarily solve it. For each of the actions, write down its advantages and disadvantages. Choose one of these actions to try out, the best or least bad of the three. Table 12.3 offers an example of structured problem solving.

Now make a goal, in the way we've described above, to carry out the action you have selected.

## Identify a Social Support Network

It helps to have one or more people who you can trust in order to get support when you are facing problems in your life. This can be a friend, a life partner, a relative, a teacher or professor, a coach, a counsellor or therapist, or members of a peer support group. Our problems often become more burdensome and difficult when we keep them to ourselves. Aim to keep up connections with people whom you find to be helpful, non-judgmental, and uplifting, and don't be shy about reaching out to such people and sharing your personal concerns and struggles. They may also call on you when they are facing their own life stresses—we all face such times. There may be times when it is harder to identify good sources of social support, such as when you

**Table 12.3: Examples of structured problem solving**

Problem: I have a big exam coming up, and I've been worrying so much that I'm sleeping badly.

| Possible actions | Advantages | Disadvantages |
|---|---|---|
| Have three or four drinks each night to calm me down so I can sleep. | • It seems to help me sleep.<br>• It calms my worrying. | • I've been suffering from hangovers, so I haven't been concentrating very well.<br>• If I keep relying on this kind of drinking to sleep, I'll become dependent—now I've started worrying about my drinking.<br>• I've been told that this kind of drinking only works for a short while, then it makes anxiety and sleep even worse.<br>• I don't like to need this kind of crutch to sleep. |
| Get some sleep medication from my family doctor. | • It would help me sleep and relax at night. | • Sleep medication is to be used only for a short while; just like with alcohol, I might become physically and mentally dependent.<br>• Also like alcohol, I might still feel the effects in the morning and have trouble concentrating. |
| Use relaxation and worry management to deal with my anxiety. | • This would help my worry and sleep.<br>• There is no risk of physical or mental dependence.<br>• There are no hangovers in the mornings. | • I'll need to practice these new skills. |

have been in a close relationship that has broken up, or when you are travelling or have moved to a different environment. These are times when it can be helpful to find a support group or see a therapist or counsellor.

### *Check Out Our Free Online Self-Care Workbooks*

You can learn more about mental health self-care by downloading one of our free workbooks at www.sfu.ca/carmha/toolsandresources.html.

## Conclusion

Mental health problems may be addressed by biological, psychological, or spiritual approaches. In Western society, the biological approach has become dominant, typically involving the use of medications to reduce mental symptoms and suffering. Commonly used medications include antidepressants, mood stabilizers, sedatives, and antipsychotics; a non-medicinal form of biological treatment is that of ECT, used mainly for severe depression. Biological treatments have also included frontal lobotomy and thalidomide; these were dark chapters in the history of mental health treatment, alerting us to the importance of carefully evaluating treatments before implementing them widely. Psychological interventions include self-help approaches, such as workbooks or online programs (most effective when supported by a health care provider or coach) and various kinds of psychotherapy. Various psychotherapeutic approaches have been devised to address mental health and substance use problems. There has recently been an increased openness by mental health professionals to the use of spiritual practices and a mindfulness approach. Combined treatments are often beneficial.

## Glossary

**cognitive behavioural therapy (CBT):** A widely practised form of psychotherapy that merges behavioural therapy and cognitive therapy to provide a goal-oriented therapy.

**electroconvulsive therapy (ECT):** An invasive treatment that involves electrically induced seizures to treat a variety of mental disorders.

**mindfulness:** A set of skills designed to increase one's capacity to be clearly aware of one's immediate situation, ongoing thoughts, and bodily sensations without feeling the need to "fix" them.

**polypharmacy:** The use of multiple medications of various sorts to address varied symptoms and hopefully enhance response.

**psychosurgery:** Brain surgery for psychiatric benefit.

**supported self-management (SSM):** A low-intensity intervention that involves a program to teach individual skills for coping more effectively with mental health problems, in addition to coaching and encouragement provided by a health care provider, family member, or peer counsellor.

## Critical Thinking Questions

1. Describe a form of psychotherapy discussed in this chapter.
2. Compare and contrast typical and atypical antipsychotic medications. Be sure to provide an example for each.
3. What happened in the thalidomide tragedy, and what lessons were learned?
4. What are the three main types of interventions for substance abuse?
5. Why is self-care for students important? What are some specific strategies that might be effective in helping you deal with the stress of student life?

## Recommended Readings

Goldbloom, D.S. (2010). *Psychiatric Clinical Skills*. St. Louis, MO: Centre for Addiction and Mental Health.

Goldenberg, I., & Goldenberg, H. (2012). *Family Therapy: An Overview* (8th ed.). Belmont, CA: Nelson Education.

Nathan, P.E., & Gorman, J.M. (Eds.). (2007). *A Guide to Treatments That Work* (3rd ed.). New York: Oxford University Press.

Stahl, S.M. (2013). *Stahl's Essential Psychopharmacology: Neuroscientific Basis and Practical Applications* (4th ed.). New York: Cambridge University Press.

## Recommended Websites

Centre for Addiction and Mental Health. www.camh.net/

Mental Health Commission of Canada. www.mentalhealthcommission.ca

US National Institute of Mental Health. www.nimh.nih.gov/

UK National Health Survey. National Institute for Health and Clinical Excellence. http://guidance.nice.org.uk/

World Health Organization. www.who.int/mental_health/en/

## References

Abbass, A.A., Rabung, S., Leichsenring, F., Refseth, J.S., & Midgley, N. (2013). Psychodynamic psychotherapy for children and adolescents: A meta-analysis of short-term psychodynamic models. *Journal of the American Academy of Child & Adolescent Psychiatry,* 52(8), 863–875. doi: 10.1016/j.jaac.2013.05.014

Ban, T.A. (2007). Fifty years chlorpromazine: A historical perspective. *Neuropsychiatric Disease and Treatment,* 3(4), 495–500.

Barbui, C., Cipriani, A., Patel, V., Ayuso-Mateos, J., & van Ommeren, M. (2011). Efficacy of antidepressants and benzodiazepines in minor depression: Systematic review and meta-analysis. *The British Journal of Psychiatry*, 198(1), 11–16. doi: 10.1192/bjp.bp.109.076448

Barker, P., & Buchanan-Barker, P. (Eds.). (2004). *Spirituality and mental health: Breakthrough*. London: Whurr Publishers.

Barlow, D. (2008). *Clinical handbook of psychological disorders: A step-by-step treatment manual* (4th ed.). New York: Guilford Press.

Baumeister, H. (2012). Inappropriate prescriptions of antidepressant drugs in patients with subthreshold to mild depression: Time for the evidence to become practice. *Journal of Affective Disorders*, 139(3), 240–243. doi: 10.1016/j.jad.2011.05.025

Beekwilder, J.P., & Beems, T. (2010). Overview of the clinical applications of vagus nerve stimulation. *Journal of Clinical Neurophysiology: Official Publication of the American Electroencephalographic Society,* 27(2), 130–138. doi: 10.1097/WNP.0b013e3181d64d8a

Brown University Psychopharmacology Update. (2015). ECT yields faster remission in elderly with depression. *Brown University Psychopharmacology Update,* 26(4), 7–8.

Campbell, L.F., & Smith, T.P. (2003). Integrating self-help books into psychotherapy. *Journal of Clinical Psychology,* 59, 177–186.

Carletti, F. (2010). A funny thing happened to me on the way to mental illness. Retrieved from thetyee.ca/News/2010/03/01/CarlettiLaugherMedicine/

Corrigan, P.W., & Mueser, K.T. (2012). *Principles and practice of psychiatric rehabilitation: An empirical approach.* New York: Guildford Press.

Cuijpers, P., Donker, T., van Straten, A., Li, J., & Andersson, G. (2010). Is guided self-help as effective as face-to-face psychotherapy for depression and anxiety disorders? A systematic review and meta-analysis of comparative outcome studies. *Psychological Medicine,* 40(12), 1943–1957. doi: 10.1017/S0033291710000772

Driessen, E., Hegelmaier, L.M., Abbass, A.A., Barber, J.P., Dekker, J.J., Van, H.L., Jansma, E.P., & Cuijpers, P. (2015). The efficacy of short-term psychodynamic psychotherapy for depression: A meta-analysis update. *Clinical Psychology Review,* 42, 1–15. doi: 10.1016/j.cpr.2015.07.004

Eisler, I., Dare, C., Hodes, M., Russell, G., Dodge, E., & Le Grange, D. (2005). Family therapy for adolescent anorexia nervosa: The results of a controlled comparison of two family interventions. *Focus,* 3, 629–640.

Ferri, M,. Amato, J., & Davoli, M. (2006). Alcoholics Anonymous and other 12-step programmes for alcohol dependence. *Cochrane Database of Systematic Reviews,* 19(3), CD005032.

Fitzgerald, P.B., & Segrave, R.A. (2015). Deep brain stimulation in mental health: Review of evidence for clinical efficacy. *The Australian and New Zealand Journal of Psychiatry,* 49(11), 979–993.

Fournier, J.C., DeRubeis, R.J., & Hollon, S.D. (2010). Antidepressant drug effects and depression severity: A patient-level meta-analysis. *Journal of the American Medical Association,* 303(1), 47–53.

Honer, W.G., Procyshyn, R.M., Chen, E.Y., MacEwan, G.W., & Barr, A.H. (2009). A translational research approach to court treatment response in patients with schizophrenia: Clozapine-antipsychotic polypharmacy. *Journal of Psychiatry and Neuroscience,* 34(6), 433–442.

Hooper, C., Thompson, M., Laver-Bradbury, C., & Gale, C. (2012). *Child and adolescent mental health: Theory and practice* (2nd ed.). Boca Ratan, FL: Taylor & Francis Group.

Horder, J., Matthews, P., & Waldmann, R. (2011). Placebo, Prozac and PloS: Significant lessons for psychopharmacology. *Journal of Psychopharmacology,* 25(10), 1277–1288. doi: 10.1177/0269881110372544

Jansson, B. (1998). Controversial psychosurgery resulted in a Nobel Prize. *Nobelprize. org*. Retrieved from nobelprize.org/nobel_prizes/medicine/laureates/1949/moniz-article.html

Kaskutas, L.A. (2009). Alcoholics anonymous effectiveness: Faith meets science. *Journal of Addictive Diseases*, 28(2), 145–157. doi: 10.1080/10550880902772464

Kazdin, A.E., & Blase, S.L. (2011). Rebooting psychotherapy research and practice to reduce the burden of mental illness. *Perspectives on Psychological Science*, 6(1), 21–37. doi: 10.1177/1745691610393527

Kim, J.H., & Scialli, A.R. (2011). Thalidomide: The tragedy of birth defects and the effective treatment of disease. *Toxicological Sciences*, 122(1), 1–6.

Kim, Y.W., Lee, S.H., Choi, T.K., Suh, S.Y., Kim, B., Kim, C.M., Cho, S.J., Kim, M.J., Yook, K., Ryu, M., Song, S.K., & Yook, K.H. (2009). Effectiveness of mindfulness-based cognitive therapy as an adjuvant to pharmacotherapy in patients with panic disorder or generalized anxiety disorder. *Depression and Anxiety*, 26(7), 601–606.

Koenig, H.G. (2009). Research on religion, spirituality, and mental health: A review. *Canadian Journal of Psychiatry*, 54(5), 283–291.

Kuyken, W., Byford, S., Taylor, R.S., Watkins, E., Holden, E., White, K., Barrett, B., Byng, R., Evans, A., Mullan, E., & Teasdale, J.D. (2008). Mindfulness-based cognitive therapy to prevent relapse in recurrent depression. *Journal of Consulting and Clinical Psychology*, 76(6), 966–978.

Light, D. (2010). *The risk of prescription drugs*. New York: Columbia University Press.

Luigjes, J., de Kwaasteniet, B.P., de Koning, P.P., Oudijn, M.S., van den Munckhof, P., Schuurman, P.R., & Denys, D. (2013). Surgery for psychiatric disorders. *World Neurosurgery*, 80(3-4), S31.e17–28. doi: 10.1016/j.wneu.2012.03.009

Mahlke, C.I., Krämer, U.M., Becker, T., & Bocka, T. (2014). Peer support in mental health services. *Current Opinion in Psychiatry*, 27(4), 267–281. doi: 10.1097/YCO.0000000000000074

McKendree-Smith, N.L., Floyd, M., & Scogin, F.R. (2003). Self-administered treatments for depression: A review. *Journal of Clinical Psychology*, 59, 275–278.

Meeter, M., Murre, J.M.J., Janssen, S.M.J., Birkenhager, T., & van den Broek, W. (2011). Retrograde amnesia after electroconvulsive therapy: A temporary effect? *Journal of Affective Disorders*, 132(1), 216–222. doi: 10.1016/j.jad.2011.02.026

Miller, W.R., & Rose, G.S. (2009). Toward a theory of motivational interviewing. *American Psychologist*, 64(6), 527–537. doi: 10.1037/a0016830

Mojtabai, R., & Olfson, M. (2010). National trends in psychotropic medication polypharmacy in office-based psychiatry. *Archives of General Psychiatry*, 67(1), 26–36.

Nivoli, A.M., Colom, C.F., Murru, A., Pacchiarotti, I., Castro-Loli, P., Gonzalez-Pinto, A., Fountoulakis, K.N., & Vieta, E. (2011). New treatment guidelines for acute bipolar depression: A systematic review. *Journal of Affective Disorders*, 129(1-3), 14–26.

Paris, J. (2005). *The fall of an icon: Psychoanalysis and academic psychiatry*. Toronto: University of Toronto Press.

Reisner, A.D. (2003). The electroconvulsive therapy controversy: Evidence and ethics. *Neuropsychology Review*, 13(4), 199–219.

Schwartz, S. (2006). Biological approaches to psychiatric disorders. In A.V. Horwitz & T.L. Scheid (Eds.), *A handbook for the study of mental health* (pp. 79–102). New York: Cambridge University Press.

Seligman, L., & Reichenberg, L.W. (2011). *Selecting effective treatments: A comprehensive, systematic guide to treating mental disorders*. Hoboken, NJ: John Wiley & Sons.

Sharav, V.H. (2003). The impact of the Food and Drug Administration Modernization Act on the recruitment of children for research. *Ethical Human Sciences and Services*, 5(2), 83–108.

Swenson, C.R., Torrey, W.C., & Koerner, K. (2002). Implementing dialectical behavior therapy. *Psychiatric Services*, 53(2), 171–178.

van der Wurff, F.B., Stek, M.L., Hoogendijk, W.J., & Beekman, A.T. (2003). The efficacy and safety of ECT in depressed older adults: A literature review. *International Journal of Geriatric Psychiatry*, 18(10), 894–904.

Vøllestad, J., Birkeland Nielsen, M., & Høstmark Nielsen, G. (2012). Mindfulness- and acceptance-based interventions for anxiety disorders: A systematic review and meta-analysis. *British Journal of Clinical Psychology*, 51(3), 239–260. doi: 10.1111/j.2044-8260.2011.02024.x

Wassermann, E.M., & Zimmermann, T. (2012). Transcranial magnetic brain stimulation: Therapeutic promises and scientific gaps. *Pharmacology & Therapeutics*, 133(1), 98–107. doi: 10.1016/j.pharmthera.2011.09.003

Zinbarg, R.E., Mashal, N.M., Black, D.A., & Flückiger, C. (2010). The future and promise of cognitive behavioral therapy: A commentary. *Psychiatric Clinics of North America*, 33(3), 711–727. doi: 10.1016/j.psc.2010.04.003

Zyss, T., Zieba, A., Hese, R.T., Dudek, D., Grabski, B., Gorczyca, P., & Modrzejewska, R. (2010). Magnetic seizure therapy (MST): A safer method for evoking seizure activity than current therapy with a confirmed antidepressant efficacy. *Neuro Endocrinology Letters*, 31(4), 425–437.

# Chapter 13

# MENTAL HEALTH SERVICES IN CANADA

The moral test of government is how it treats those who are in the dawn of life, the children; those who are in the twilight of life, the aged; and those who are in the shadows of life, the sick, the needy and the handicapped.
—Hubert H. Humphrey (38th US Vice-President)

## Introduction

In this chapter, we examine the services that are provided in Canada to address mental health and illness within the health care system. Although it is common to discuss the Canadian mental health "system," it is often pointed out that services are rarely woven together to form an integrated system. Instead, there is a patchwork of different programs and services that is not completely integrated or interconnected (and, in some circumstances, may be badly disintegrated) (Kirby & Keon, 2006). In order to understand mental health services in Canada, we first discuss the overall organization of health care delivery in the country and then describe how mental health services fit into this larger framework. An important focus of this chapter will be a description of efforts that have been put in place to strengthen and improve mental health services in Canada, including the recent work by the Mental Health Commission of Canada with its role as "a catalyst for improving the mental health system and changing the attitudes and behaviours of Canadians around mental health issues" (Mental Health Commission of Canada, 2015). We end the chapter with a brief comparison of the Canadian mental health system with those of other countries.

# The Structure and Organization of Canada's Health Care Services

Since this book focuses on *Canada's* approach to mental health, we have asked ourselves: What is distinctive about Canada and its services? In his poem "We are More," delivered at the opening ceremonies of the 2010 Winter Olympics, Shane Koyczan (2010) offers the following image:

> And some say what defines us
> Is something as simple as "please" and "thank you"
> And as for "you're welcome," well, we say that, too
> But we are more than genteel or civilized
> We are an idea in the process of being realized
> We are young, we are cultures strung together then woven into a tapestry
> And the design is what makes us more than the sum total of our history
> We are an experiment going right for a change

Canada has a national health care insurance scheme that supports egalitarian principles, which means that effort is made to ensure that all Canadian residents are able to obtain good quality health care, regardless of their social or economic status. Historically, Canadians have been proud of this commitment, often considering our approach to be more humane than that taken in many other countries where only the wealthy can access good quality health care services.

## *Canada Health Act*

To some degree, health care services in Canada are shaped by the **Canada Health Act**, a piece of federal legislation that stipulates key characteristics of the health care insurance coverage provided by Canada's provinces and territories (Minister of Justice, 2009). The five principles of the Canada Health Act are universality, accessibility, portability, comprehensiveness, and public administration, each described below. If a province or territory does not comply with these principles, the federal government may impose a penalty by withholding funds that would otherwise have been transferred to the province or territory for health care services.

The principle of universality stipulates that *all* Canadian residents are entitled to receive coverage for health care services—a principle that, as mentioned above, has been a source of pride for many Canadians.

The principle of accessibility indicates that all Canadians should have access to services, regardless of their geographical location. Of course, with Canada's vast size and dispersed population, there are enormous challenges in providing services to people living in remote areas. Nevertheless, it is expected that mechanisms will be in place to arrange access to health care services for all residents, including emergency and ambulance responses serving all corners of a province or territory.

**Figure 13.1:** Tommy Douglas is credited as the "founding father of Medicare" (our national health insurance program).

*Source:* GetStock/Barry Philp

The principle of portability stipulates that health care insurance coverage should remain intact when a Canadian travels or moves from one province or territory to another (or requires urgent health care when travelling in another country).

The principle of comprehensiveness refers to coverage of all "medically necessary" health care services. However, there is substantial dispute as to which health care services are included or excluded in this definition. There is a common misconception that, in Canada, all health care services are covered by the national health insurance scheme. In fact, it is estimated that approximately 30 percent of health care services received in Canada are not covered by government and people must pay "out of pocket" for many of those services that are not covered (Canadian Institute for Health Information, 2013). For example, dental care is generally not covered. Some Canadians will have jobs with private benefits that cover some portion of their dental bills (and their employers may also provide similar benefits that cover other health care bills for themselves, their spouse, and children). However, a person without a private health care plan and without the means to pay for dental care may have to go without treatment for even serious dental problems, such as infections, cavities, and broken teeth. Similarly, Canadians will often have to cover the costs of medications, many of which are very expensive.

Finally, the principle of public administration denotes that the provincial/territorial health care insurance plan must be administered "publicly"; that is, as a non-profit enterprise undertaken by governments. Not all health care services in Canada are publicly administered, and some services operate under "private" administration for profit. In recent years, there has been substantial debate about whether governments should relax some of the restrictions against the operation of private, for-profit health care services in Canada. Those in favour argue that these could improve the quality and availability of services and would not detract from publicly funded health care services. Those who are opposed warn that increased privatization would inevitably advantage wealthy Canadians and reduce access to and the quality of health care services for those who are poor and vulnerable (Angell, 2008). For those interested in this debate, we have recommended some additional reading at the end of this chapter.

## *Thirteen Health Care Insurance Plans and Delivery Systems*

Although often referred to as a "national" health insurance plan, Canada's system is actually composed of 13 different plans that cover the costs of health care services— one in each Canadian province or territory, covering all residents. These are funded primarily through taxes that our governments collect each year. In fact, the health care portion is by far the largest portion of the government budget covered by our taxes. We are each issued a health care card that identifies us as having insurance coverage, and we each have a unique personal health care number that is recorded for billing purposes whenever we obtain services at a hospital, doctor's office, or other setting. Although most health care services are covered, some are not (e.g., dental care, prescription eyeglasses, out-patient medications, and various out-patient psychological

**Figure 13.2:** Map of Canada showing the 13 provinces and territories. The provincial and territorial governments play a strong role in the delivery and direction of health care services.

*Source:* GetStock/Indos82

services). Employers may provide some additional health care benefits that cover such services and perquisites ("perks"), such as private hospital rooms.

Health care services in Canada are structured differently than those in most other countries. Primarily, health care services are the responsibility of individual provinces and territories. Consequently, decisions about most activities, policies, and priorities are made within each province/territory, rather than at the national level. The strong role of provincial/territorial governments in Canadian health care services can make it difficult to implement national initiatives or policies. To some extent, each province/territory is likely to "march to its own drummer," pursuing different goals and often unaware of activities and developments in other parts of the country.

Responsibility for the delivery of services within a province or territory is often further divided among a number of smaller administrative regions, known as Health Authorities in British Columbia, Local Health Integration Networks in Ontario, and Health and Social Services Centres in Quebec. No matter what their designated name, these authorities are generally responsible for the delivery of health care services within a defined geographical region of the province or territory, including all in-patient and out-patient hospital care, diagnostic laboratories, emergency services, various clinics, long-term care facilities, and home care services. These health authorities are often headed by chief executive officers and groups of executive managers. Although they may vary considerably in the size of the population they serve, many are very large enterprises with annual operating budgets in the billions of dollars and they often employ more people than any other business or company within a region.

Another feature of Canadian health care services is the separate administration of physician services, which are not under the direct control of health authorities but operate through agreements negotiated by physician associations directly with provincial or territorial governments. Because physicians are generally not employed or managed by health authorities, there can be challenges in coordinating physician practice with policies and practices undertaken by health authorities.

There are a number of federally funded components of Canada's health care "system," and these include national agencies with responsibility for health research, evaluation, and public health activities. Table 13.1 provides a brief description of the roles of a number of these agencies. At times, the federal and provincial/territorial governments and agencies may disagree on policies and activities, and it is sometimes difficult to achieve effective and harmonious co-operation of these different health care components. Later in this chapter, we will return to a discussion of the Mental Health Commission of Canada and its unique role in catalyzing improvements to mental health services in Canada. The federal government also holds responsibility for delivery of health services to particular groups in Canada, including some First Nations, Inuit, and Metis groups and inmates of federal correctional facilities.

Many mental health services in Canada are covered by our "national" health insurance plans, including treatment delivered in hospitals, emergency services, and out-patient treatment provided by family physicians and psychiatrists. In addition, some community treatment services delivered by various other health professionals are available for people who meet certain diagnostic criteria for mental disorder. However, these services are generally reserved for people with the most serious and acute (i.e., urgent) mental disorders. One study found that 25 percent of all acute care hospital days used in Canada involved patients diagnosed with mental illnesses (Statistics Canada, 2012). People with less severe mental health problems often have difficulty obtaining access to appropriate treatment through the public health system (Institute of Health Economics, 2008). Many mental health services in Canada require people to pay "out of pocket" and may be too expensive for many people to afford. These include many psychological treatments for depression, anxiety, and other common mental health problems, marital or family therapy, and specialized treatment for substance use problems.

**Table 13.1: Select list of federally funded agencies relevant to mental health in Canada**

| Name of agency | Mission and purpose |
|---|---|
| Public Health Agency of Canada (PHAC) | Goals are to: promote health; prevent and control chronic diseases and injuries; prevent and control infectious diseases; prepare for and respond to public health emergencies; and strengthen public health capacity |
| Canadian Institutes of Health Research (CIHR) | Responsible for funding health research in Canada with goals to: fund more research on targeted priority areas; build research capacity in underdeveloped areas such as population health and health services research; train the next generation of health researchers; and focus on knowledge translation, so that the results of research are transformed into policies, practices, procedures, products, and services |
| Health Canada | Federal department responsible for helping the people of Canada maintain and improve their health |
| Statistics Canada | Produces statistics about many issues that help Canadians better understand their country—its population, resources, economy, society, and culture; health statistics are one of many sets of statistics that are produced regularly |
| Canadian Centre on Substance Abuse (CCSA) | Goal is to: provide national leadership and evidence-informed analysis and advice to mobilize collaborative efforts to reduce alcohol- and other drug-related harms |
| Mental Health Commission of Canada | Goal is to: help bring into being an integrated mental health system that places people living with mental illness at its centre |

# Delivery of Mental Health Care Services

A large spectrum of services is called into play to address mental health problems, provided by a host of professional and non-professional workers and volunteers. These include family physicians, nurses, psychiatrists, and other medical specialists, psychologists, social workers, occupational therapists, child care workers, counsellors, family and marital therapists, peer support workers, pharmacists, dieticians, and housing and employment support workers. Figure 13.3 depicts how mental health services operate at various levels. Services at the bottom of the figure are low-intensity interventions, are easily available, and are used by a large number of individuals. In contrast, services at the top of the triangle are high-intensity interventions suited to a much smaller number of people who require intense treatment. An example of a low-intensity service is a group session in which education about how to recover from depression is delivered by a nurse to a large number of people with depression, along with their family members and friends. An example of a high-intensity intervention is an in-patient hospital treatment program for people with severe depression and suicidality that includes a combination of medications and psychosocial treatments delivered by a team of health care professionals.

## *Stepped-Care*

When mental health care systems are well designed, they ensure that the high-intensity treatments are reserved for those people who truly need them by applying a **stepped-care approach** (see Figure 13.3). This means that the system generally aims to provide low-intensity treatment for most people, and will *step up* the intensity of treatments if needed (Richards et al., 2012). Since many people will respond well to the low-intensity intervention, it would be a mistake to provide them with more intensive treatments for two important reasons. First, limited money and resources must be utilized to help as many people as possible. Second, intrusiveness should be minimized. We know that more intensive interventions, such as hospital treatments in which individuals may receive multiple medications and other treatments, come with the risk of complications and side effects. Therefore, we should avoid intruding with medical or psychiatric care unless there is a strong imperative for doing so. In the delivery of mental health services, interventions can have a negative impact—even when health care providers intend to be helpful. This negative impact can be due to side effects and complications of treatments, and other indirect effects, such as intense self-stigmatization following diagnosis or treatment for mental illness (see Chapter 6) or difficulty reintegrating into "normal" life after removal from one's normal environment of school, friends, and family. Such negative outcomes as a result of medical or health care intervention are known as **iatrogenic** (i.e., caused by medical care).

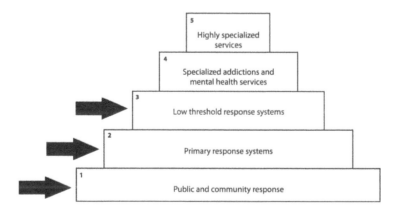

**Figure 13.3:** The stepped-care model showing that larger numbers of people are served by "lower steps" (involving less resource-intensive services). Individuals who require more intensive levels of care may move up (and later back down) these steps, accessing the minimum resource-intensity care required. This preserves resources for people who need them most and avoids imposition of intensive care upon those who do not require it.

## *Early Intervention*

One approach to enhancing the effectiveness of mental health care is to provide intervention at an early stage in the course of the mental health condition. By intervening early, it is hoped that symptoms will be effectively addressed and functional impairment prevented. An exemplar of this approach is the provision of early intervention for psychosis. Early intervention for psychotic disorders generally involves the use of medication, cognitive behavioural therapy (CBT), and/or family therapy specifically tailored to individuals dealing with psychotic symptoms. A CBT approach to early intervention might include psychoeducation about the disorder, strategies for improving social function and self-esteem, coping strategies for managing psychotic symptomatology, and methods for relapse prevention (Addington & Gleeson, 2005). A family therapy intervention, delivered to family members as well as diagnosed individuals, might incorporate psychoeducation about the disorder, communicational strategies to reduce criticism and negative affect, problem-solving techniques, and methods for expanding social support (Falloon, Boyd, & McGill, 1984; Leff, 1994).

One systematic review concluded that the effectiveness of early intervention for psychotic disorders had yet to be empirically proven, describing the evidence as "emerging but as yet inconclusive" (Marshall & Rathbone, 2011). However, another systematic review, conducted for the main clinical guidelines unit in the UK, reached a more positive conclusion. This review concluded that "early intervention services appear to have clinically important benefits over standard care", with benefits including lower rates of relapse and hospital admission, reduced symptoms severity, and enhanced treatment participation (Bird et al., 2010). Although further research is needed to definitively establish the effectiveness of early intervention for psychosis, it remains a very promising innovation in the field of mental health services.

## *Primary, Secondary, and Tertiary Health Care*

**Primary health care** services refer to the initial, entry-level services that one receives when accessing health care. In Canada, this level of care is generally provided by family physicians and other general health care professionals. As the first contact for a health care problem, primary health care services are designed to provide an initial diagnosis and treatment and, ideally, will be able to resolve the problem without the need for further treatment. However, in many cases, primary health care may be the start of a referral pathway to other services. When it comes to mental health care, family physicians have limited time, and they complain of a lack of available specialists who could accept referrals. The Canadian National Physician Survey showed that 66 percent of family practitioners rated accessibility for their patients to psychiatrists as fair or poor, and 52 percent rated access to psychosocial support as fair or poor (National Physician Survey, 2007). The rating showed that family physicians rated access to psychiatrists to be worse than to any other medical specialists.

Another step in accessing health care consists of low-barrier services, that is, services that are relatively easy to access and require little in the way of formal referral procedures. Low-barrier services are found to be important in facilitating access to services that may otherwise never be received by those who would benefit from them. For example, access to low-barrier services for the homeless and for people with substance use problems increases the likelihood that treatment will be utilized (Tsemberis, Gulcur, & Nakae, 2004). In Canada, various low-barrier services are often provided by NGOs (non-governmental organizations) and non-profit agencies. Such organizations often provide important components of care to many people with mental health and substance use problems. A description of such an agency is provided later in this chapter.

**Secondary health care** is the service provided by specialists, such as out-patient treatment by psychiatrists and hospital care by teams of health care professionals. **Tertiary health care** includes specialized long-term treatment services, such as in a long-stay psychiatric facility, as well as highly specialized treatment for rare, complex, or treatment-resistant conditions. Generally, tertiary services are provided by teams with special staffing levels to meet the specific needs of their clientele.

## Use of Existing Treatment Services

Figure 13.4 provides information compiled by the Public Health Agency of Canada about the use of formal health services (i.e., those provided by the publicly funded services, such as family physicians, psychiatrists, and hospitals) for mental illness in Canada across the lifespan. Note that for individuals 15 years of age and older females use mental health services more frequently than males. You may remember the discussion in Chapter 8 describing that men experience greater challenges in requesting assistance when they experience mental health issues such as depression (Johnson et al., 2012; Olliffe & Phillips, 2008). Males also report that they view help-seeking behaviour as a feminine characteristic that exposes personal weakness and vulnerability (Chambers & Murphy, 2011). Men will often ignore or deny serious symptoms, may have limited knowledge about their bodies and health care, and consider it necessary to endure high degrees of pain and conceal mental health issues (O'Brien, Hunt, & Hart, 2005).

In contrast, Figure 13.4 shows that boys in the younger age groups are more likely than girls to receive health services for mental health problems. This is likely due, in part, to higher rates of various childhood mental disorders, such as conduct disorder and attention deficit disorder, among boys (Public Health Agency of Canada, 2015).

## Services and Involvement of Peers and Caregivers

It is widely accepted that people with lived experience of mental illness should be involved in the review, planning, and delivery of services. Peer support services are those in which individuals who are in recovery from mental illness or substance

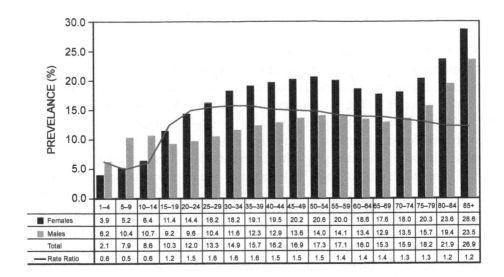

**Figure 13.4:** Age-specific annual prevalence (%) of the use of health services for mental illness among people aged 1 year and older by sex, Canada, 2009/10.

use disorder assist others in their recovery efforts by sharing knowledge and skills, and providing support. Caregivers, including family members and friends, can also play an important role in supporting the recovery of people with mental disorders (Canadian Mental Health Association, 2012). Means and mechanisms to allow peers and caregivers to play an active and meaningful role in mental health care have only been developed to a small degree in Canada, and there is a need to increase the development of peer support and caregiver-based services.

## *Forensic Mental Health Services*

Since people with mental health conditions may commit criminal behaviour, specialized **forensic mental health services** have been set up to provide appropriate assessment and treatment. These include in-patient facilities where individuals are held for assessment or treatment and out-patient services that often provide ongoing follow-up treatment.

If someone who commits a crime is suspected of having a mental illness, the court may order a determination of the individual's **fitness to stand trial**. This involves an examination by psychiatrists and other professionals to determine whether the individual understands the nature of the trial and the possible consequences, and whether he or she is able to communicate effectively with a lawyer. If an individual is deemed unfit to stand trial, hearings will be delayed until the individual is deemed fit.

The Criminal Code of Canada stipulates that an individual may be deemed not criminally responsible for reason of mental disorder: "No person is criminally responsible for an act committed or an omission made while suffering from a mental disorder that rendered the person incapable of appreciating the nature and quality of the act or omission or of knowing that it was wrong" (Section 16). Individuals who have committed crimes but are found to be not criminally responsible for reason of mental disorder are generally required to submit to treatment provided through forensic mental health services. Each province and territory has a review board that is given the responsibility to monitor the progress of individuals who are receiving forensic mental health services and decide when they are ready for discharge.

Correctional facilities across Canada have a disproportionate number of inmates with significant mental disorders. In fact, some have stated that correctional facilities have become "*de facto* mental health services" in Canada and have registered concerns about poor conditions that inmates with mental health conditions may endure (Arboleda-Florez, 2004; Sapers, 2008).

**Figure 13.5:** Have corrections facilities become "*de facto* mental health services"?

*Source:* Hélène Vallée/iStockphoto

## Improving Mental Health Services

The 2006 Canadian Senate Report, *Out of the Shadows at Last*, recommended creation of the Mental Health Commission of Canada with the following rationale: "It remains that the whole complex, pervasive problem of mental illness and addiction in Canadian society continues to be neglected. The Canadian Mental Health Commission will provide a much needed national (*not federal*) focal point that will keep mental health issues in the mainstream of public policy debates in Canada and accelerate the development and implementation of effective solutions to the long-standing problems of this sector" (Kirby & Keon, 2006, p. 435). The Mental Health Commission of Canada was initiated in 2008, with the following mission:

- Act as a facilitator, enabler and supporter of a national approach to mental health issues;
- Be catalyst for reform of mental health policies and improvements in service delivery;
- Provide a national focal point for objective, evidence-based information on all aspects of mental health and mental illness;
- Be a source of information to governments, stakeholders and the public on mental health and mental illness;
- Educate all Canadians about mental health and increase mental health literacy among them, particularly among those who are in leadership roles such as employers, members of the health professions, teachers, etc;
- Eliminate the stigma and discrimination faced by Canadians living with a mental illness, and their families. (Mental Health Commission of Canada, 2010)

One of the activities of the Commission has been the creation of the Mental Health Strategy for Canada, identified through an extensive public consultation across the country. The Strategy is reproduced in Box 13.1.

## Comparison with Other Nations

It is difficult to undertake an objective comparison of the quality of mental health services in Canada with those delivered in other nations. Varied funding structures, organization of health care systems, and cultural and political contexts are but a few of the factors that make an objective comparison challenging. Furthermore, nations may be at different stages in the transformation and change process of their health care systems.

In recent years, a number of other nations have undertaken substantial efforts to reform and improve their mental health systems. (Appleby, 2007; New Freedom Commission, 2003; New Zealand Ministry of Health, 2010; Sainsbury Center for Mental Health, 2005; Whiteford & Buckingham, 2005). A review of seven countries

## Box 13.1: Changing Directions, Changing Lives: The Mental Health Strategy for Canada

We know what needs to be done. Drawing on the best available evidence and on input from thousands of people across Canada, *Changing Directions, Changing Lives* translates this vision into recommendations for action. The scope of the *strategy* is broad and its recommendations are grouped into six key Strategic Directions. Each Strategic Direction focuses on one critical dimension and together they combine to provide a comprehensive blueprint for change. The six Strategic Directions are as follows:

1. **Promote mental health across the lifespan in homes, schools, and workplaces, and prevent mental illness and suicide wherever possible.** Reducing the impact of mental health problems and illnesses and improving the mental health of the population require promotion and prevention efforts in everyday settings where the potential impact is greatest.
2. **Foster recovery and well-being for people of all ages living with mental health problems and illnesses, and uphold their rights.** The key to recovery is helping people to find the right combination of services, treatments and supports and eliminating discrimination by removing barriers to full participation in work, education and community life.
3. **Provide access to the right combination of services, treatments and supports, when and where people need them.** A full range of services, treatments and supports includes primary health care, community-based and specialized mental health services, peer support, and supported housing, education and employment.
4. **Reduce disparities in risk factors and access to mental health services, and strengthen the response to the needs of diverse communities and Northerners.** Mental health should be taken into account when acting to improve overall living conditions and addressing the specific needs of groups such as new Canadians and people in northern and remote communities.
5. **Work with First Nations, Inuit, and Métis to address their mental health needs, acknowledging their distinct circumstances, rights and cultures.** By calling for access to a full continuum of culturally safe mental health services, the *Mental Health Strategy for Canada* can contribute to truth, reconciliation, and healing from intergenerational trauma.
6. **Mobilize leadership, improve knowledge, and foster collaboration at all levels.** Change will not be possible without a whole-of-government approach to mental health policy, without fostering the leadership roles of people living with mental health problems and illnesses, and their families, and without building strong infrastructure to support data collection, research, and human resource development.

*Changing Directions, Changing Lives* calls on all Canadians to play a role in improving the mental health system. Not all of the recommendations in the *Strategy* can be accomplished at once, and, in a country as diverse as Canada, there will never be a 'one size fits all' approach to the complex task of transforming the mental health system. Despite the broad consensus on the key directions for change, there will never be universal agreement on everything that needs to be done or on what should be done in what order.

Mental health is also not the concern of the health sector alone. The policies and practices of multiple government departments (including education, justice, corrections, social services and finance) have a major impact on people's mental health and well-being. Beyond government, it is clear that workplaces, non-government organizations, the media, and many others all have a role to play.

It will be up to people in each region of the country and at every level of government to create their own plans for acting on the *Strategy*'s recommendations, in keeping with their particular circumstances. In this way, *Changing Directions, Changing Lives* offers an opportunity for everyone's efforts—large and small, both inside and outside the formal mental health system—to help bring about change.

It will take time to implement the recommendations in this *Strategy*, and it will take sustained commitment and leadership at many levels. The *Strategy* calls for:

- people living with mental health problems and illnesses and their families to become more engaged in the planning, organization, delivery and evaluation of mental health services, treatments and supports;
- mental health service providers to work with planners, funders, and users of the system to examine what changes are required in the way that they work in order to create a system that is better integrated around people's needs and fosters recovery;
- governments to take a comprehensive approach to addressing mental health needs, to re-focus spending on improving outcomes, and to correct years of underfunding of mental health;
- senior executives in both the public and private sectors to create workplaces that are as mentally healthy as possible, and to actively support the broader movement for improved mental health;
- all Canadians to promote mental health in everyday settings and reduce stigma by recognizing how much we all have in common—there is no 'us' and 'them' when it comes to mental health and well-being.

Strategic investment, clear indicators of progress, and a strong social movement are needed to drive change. *Changing Directions, Changing Lives* presents an ambitious plan, but it is one that can be achieved step-by-step. It identifies directions for change while building on the many excellent initiatives already underway across the country. Many of its recommendations point to ways to maximize the benefits derived from existing resources.

*Source*: Excerpted from the Mental Health Commission of Canada. (2012). *Changing Directions, Changing Lives: The Mental Health Strategy for Canada*. Ottawa, Ontario. Retrieved April 20, 2016 from http://strategy.mentalhealthcommission.ca/pdf/strategy-images-en.pdf

(Australia, Canada, England, Italy, New Zealand, Scotland, and the United States) in the process of reforming their mental health systems reveals similar identified problems, policy direction, prioritization of issues, and strategies for change, despite having significant differences in policy, organization, finance, and delivery of mental health services (Adams, Daniels, & Compagni, 2009). Across these nations, some of the identified problems included the lack of mental health in the public policy agenda, inadequate system capacity and work force resources, and high levels of variability in service provision. Interestingly, all seven nations identified the lack of a recovery orientation as one of the main underlying problems in their mental health care systems; a recovery paradigm has been included in reform agendas (Adams, Daniels, & Compagni, 2009). In terms of vision, six major common themes across the nations were identified: relevance and parity, responsiveness, involvement and recovery-orientation, person-centredness, integration and multidisciplinary approaches, and evidence-based effective care and accountability for outcomes (Adams, Daniels, & Compagni, 2009).

## Conclusion

The unique structure and organization of health services in Canada affects many features of service delivery. A consequence of the prominent role given to provinces and territories in governing health care is a system that may vary across the country's 13 geographical jurisdictions despite a number of common principles guided by the Canada Health Act, a piece of federal legislation that stipulates key characteristics of health care insurance coverage provided to Canadian residents.

Mental health services in Canada are delivered by a wide variety of health professionals, and ideally they are implemented using a stepped-care model that reserves costlier and more intense services for those who require them. In addition to formal health care services delivered in hospitals and various community-based programs, many non-health care services and supports contribute to the recovery of people with mental health problems. Services supplied with peer and caregiver support are also valuable components of a comprehensive mental health system.

The Mental Health Commission of Canada is a national initiative with a mandate to facilitate a national approach to mental health and be a catalyst for improvements in service delivery. A mental health strategy for Canada has been created with six strategic directions. Although it is difficult to compare Canada's mental health system with those of other nations, many of the same challenges appear to be in place in other countries that have recently undertaken efforts to improve their mental health services.

## Glossary

**Canada Health Act:** Federal legislation that stipulates key characteristics of the health care insurance coverage provided by Canada's provinces and territories.

**fitness to stand trial:** An examination to determine whether an individual understands the nature of the trial and the possible consequences and whether he or she is able to communicate effectively with a lawyer.

**forensic mental health services:** Appropriate assessment and treatment for people who have mental illness who commit criminal behaviour.

**iatrogenic:** Negative outcomes as a result of medical or health care intervention.

**primary health care:** Services provided by family physicians and other general health care professionals designed to provide an initial diagnosis and treatment, and may be the start of a referral pathway to other services.

**secondary health care:** Services provided by specialists who generally do not have first contact with patients, such as out-patient treatment by psychiatrists and hospital care by teams of health care professionals.

**stepped-care approach:** An approach where the system generally aims to provide low-intensity treatment for most people, and will step up the intensity of treatments, as needed.

**tertiary health care:** Specialized long-term treatment services, such as a long-stay psychiatric facility, including highly specialized treatment for rare, complex, or treatment-resistant conditions.

---

## Critical Thinking Questions

1. Briefly describe each of the five principles of the Canada Health Act.
2. How is the Canadian health care system structured?
3. What is a stepped-care model, and why is it important to mental health services?
4. What role do peers and caregivers play in the delivery of mental health services?
5. Briefly describe the six strategic directions of the Mental Health Strategy for Canada developed by the Mental Health Commission of Canada. How do these strategic directions aim to improve the mental health of Canadians?

---

## Recommended Readings

Fellin, P. (1996). *Mental Health and Mental Illness: Policies, Programs and Services.* Belmont, CA: Brooks/Cole.

Gray, J.E., Shone, M.A., & Liddle, P.F. (2000). *Canadian Mental Health Law and Policy.* Toronto: Butterworths Canada.

Kirby, M.J.L., & Keon, W.J. (2006). *Out of the Shadows at Last: Highlights and Recommendations.* The Standing Senate Committee on Social Affairs, Science and Technology. Retrieved from http://www.parl.gc.ca/39/1/parlbus/commbus/senate/com-e/soci-e/rep-e/pdf/rep02may06high-e.pdf

Knudsen, H.C., & Thornicroft, G. (Eds.). (1996). *Mental Health Service Evaluation.* Cambridge: Cambridge University Press.

Olson, R.P. (Ed.). (2006). *Mental Health Systems Compared.* Springfield, IL: Charles C. Thomas.

## Recommended Websites

The Canadian Association for Health Services and Policy Research. www.cahspr.ca/
Health Canada—Health Care System. www.hc-sc.gc.ca/hcs-sss/index-eng.php
The Mental Health Commission of Canada.
www.mentalhealthcommission.ca/english/pages/default.aspx
The World Health Organization—Health Systems. www.who.int/topics/health_
systems/en/

## References

Adams, N., Daniels, A., & Compagni, A. (2009). International pathways to mental health transformation. *International Journal of Mental Health*, 38(1), 30–45.

Addington, J., & Gleeson, J. (2005). Implementing cognitive-behavioural therapy for first-episode psychosis. *The British Journal of Psychiatry*, 187(48), s72–ds76.

Angell, M. (2008). Privatizing health care is not the answer: Lessons from the United States. *Canadian Medical Association Journal,* 179(9), 916–919. doi: 10.1503/cmaj.081177

Appleby, L. (2007). Mental health ten years on: Progress on mental health care reform. Department of Health. Retrieved from www.dh.gov.uk/en/Publicationsandstatistics/Publications/PublicationsPolic

Arboleda-Florez, J. (2004). On the evolution of mental health systems. *Forensic Psychiatry*, 17(5), 377–380.

Bird, V., Premkumar, P., Kendall, T., Whittington, C., Mitchell, J., & Kuipers, E. (2010). Early intervention services, cognitive-behavioural therapy and family intervention in early psychosis: Systematic review. *The British Journal of Psychiatry*, 197(5), 350–356. doi: 10.1192/bjp.bp.109.074526

Canadian Institute for Health Information. (2013). National health expenditure trends, 1975 to 2013. Ottawa: Author.

Canadian Mental Health Association. (2012). Family and caregiver support. Retrieved from www.cmha.ca/mental-health/find-help/family-and-caregiver-support/

Chambers, D, & Murphy, F. (2011). *Learning to reach out: Young people, mental health literacy and the Internet.* Dublin: Inspire Ireland Foundation.

Falloon, I.R.H., Boyd, J.L., & McGill, C.W. (1984). *Family care of schizophrenia: A problem solving approach to the treatment of mental illness.* New York: Guilford Press.

Institute of Health Economics. (2008). Consensus statement on depression in adults: How to improve prevention, diagnosis and treatment. Retrieved from www.ihe.

ca/publications/consensus-statement-on-depression-in-adults-how-to-improve-prevention-diagnosis-and-treatment

Johnson, J.L., Oliffe, J.L., Kelly, M.T., Galdas, P., & Ogrodniczuk, J.S. (2012). Men's discourses of help-seeking in the context of depression. *Sociology of Health & Illness,* 34(3), 345–361.

Kirby, M.J.L., & Keon, W.J. (2006). Out of the shadows at last: Transforming mental health, mental illness and addiction services in Canada. The Standing Senate Committee on Social Affairs, Science and Technology. Retrieved from parl.gc.ca/39/1/parlbus/commbus/senate/Com-e/SOCI-E/rep-e/pdf/rep02may06part1-e.pdf

Koyczan, S. (2010). We are more. Retrieved from www.vancouverisawesome.com/2010/02/12/shane-koyczans-we-are-more/

Leff, J. (1994). Working with families of schizophrenic patients. *British Journal of Psychiatry,* 164(Suppl. 23), 71–76.

Marshall, M., & Rathbone, J. (2011). Early intervention for psychosis. *Schizophrenia Bulletin,* 37(6), 1111–1114. doi: 10.1093/schbul/sbr110

Mental Health Commission of Canada. (2010). Retrieved from www.mentalhealthcommission.ca

Mental Health Commission of Canada. (2015). About MHCC. Retrieved from mentalhealthcommission.ca/English/who-we-are

Minister of Justice. (2009). Consolidation: Canada Health Act—Chapter C-6. Retrieved from http://laws-lois.justice.gc.ca/PDF/C-6.pdf

National Physician Survey. (2007). 2007 survey results. Retrieved from http://nationalphysiciansurvey.ca/surveys/2007-survey/2007-results/

New Freedom Commission. (2003). President's New Freedom Commission on mental health. Retrieved from www.cartercentre.org/documents/1701.pdf

New Zealand Ministry of Health. (2010). Mental health. Retrieved from www.moh.govt.nz/moh.nsf/indexmh/mentalhealth-resources-publications

O'Brien, R., Hunt, K., & Hart, G. (2005). "It's caveman stuff, but that is to a certain extent how guys still operate": Men's accounts of masculinity and help seeking. *Social Science & Medicine,* 61(3), 503–516.

Olliffe, J.L., & Phillips, M.J. (2008). Men, depression and masculinities: A review and recommendations. *Journal of Men's Health,* 5(9), 194–202.

Public Health Agency of Canada. (2015). Report from the Canadian chronic disease surveillance system: Mental illness in Canada, 2015 (No. 140526). Ottawa: Author.

Richards, D.A., Bower, P., Pagel, C., Weaver, A., Utley, M., Cape, J., Pilling, S., Lovell, K., Gilbody, S., Leibowitz, J., Owens, L., Paxton, R., Hennessy, S., Simpson, A., Gallivan, S., Tomson, D., & Vasilakis, C. (2012). Delivering stepped care: An analysis of implementation in routine practice. *Implementation Science,* 7(3). doi: 10.1186/1748-5908-7-3.

Sainsbury Center for Mental Health. (2005). The neglected majority: Developing intermediate mental health in primary care. Retrieved from www.nwppn.nhs.uk/attachments/article/14/SainsburyCentreforMH2005TheNeglectedMajorityPolicyPaper.pdf

Sapers, H. (2008). A preventable death. Office of the Correctional Investigator. Retrieved from http://www.oci-bec.gc.ca/cnt/rpt/pdf/oth-aut/oth-aut20080620-eng.pdf

Statistics Canada. (2012). Acute care hospital days and mental diagnoses by Helen Johansen and Philippe Finès. Catalogue no. 82-003-XPE. Health Reports, Vol. 23, no. 4, December 2012. Retrieved from www.statcan.gc.ca/pub/82-003-x/2012004/article/11761-eng.pdf

Tsemberis, S., Gulcur, L., & Nakae, M. (2004). Housing first, consumer choice, and harm reduction for homeless individuals with a dual diagnosis. *American Journal of Public Health*, 94(4), 651–656.

Whiteford, H.A., & Buckingham, W.J. (2005). Ten years of mental health service reform in Australia: Are we getting it right? *Medical Journal of Australia*, 182(8), 396–400.

# Chapter 14

# MENTAL HEALTH
# PROFESSIONS AND PRACTICES

Individually, we are one drop. Together, we are an ocean.
—Ryunosuke Satoro (Japanese poet)

## Introduction

In this chapter, we discuss the roles and contributions of the many different health care professionals involved in Canada's mental health "system." **Clinical service providers** are drawn from a variety of health care professions (medicine, nursing, social work, psychology, occupational therapy, and so forth), and they include **peer support workers** (i.e., people with lived experience of mental illness who provide clinical support to others), and others who provide services and supports. These different groups often have different types of training, experience, and educational backgrounds and they bring unique perspectives and strengths (and occasionally biases) to the delivery of clinical assessment, prevention, and treatment.

In addition to clinical service providers, there are others who play key roles in the functioning of the mental health system, including managers and administrators, politicians and government bureaucrats, and researchers and educators. In this chapter, we discuss the challenges that exist in integrating the activities of the many different health care professionals working within the mental health system in Canada, and we outline promising approaches to the integration and harmonization of these efforts.

## Clinical Service Providers

### Family Physicians

Of all clinical service providers, family physicians see the largest numbers of people who are experiencing mental illness in Canada. This is because they see such a large percentage of the general population each year (approximately 80 percent) (Statistics Canada, 2013), many of whom have some type of mental disorder. Since mental health problems are highly prevalent, family physicians devote a relatively large portion of their time attending to mental health care issues.

In Canada, family physicians deliver primary mental health care in which they undertake assessments, initiate treatment, and, in theory, make referrals to other health professionals when they consider a problem to require more specialized treatment. However, family physicians often find that they cannot adequately access mental health specialists. For example, the most common response by Canadian family physicians to a survey question about access to psychiatrists was that it is "poor" and significantly worse than access to other medical specialists (National Physician Survey, 2007). Time constraints also present challenges to the provision of mental health care by family doctors. Despite these difficulties, family physicians are often involved in the treatment of the highly prevalent mental disorders (Oyama et al., 2012; Fleury et al., 2012), such as anxiety disorders, depression, somatization disorders, and dementia.

## Nurses

Nurses undertake many different roles in the delivery of mental health care. They play a prominent role in hospital treatment settings, such as emergency departments and in-patient psychiatric units, and in a multitude of community-based settings where specialized mental health care is provided. These include clinics, outreach programs, home care services, specialized housing services, and residential treatment settings. Most often, nurses work as members of an interdisciplinary team, however, there is a small proportion of nurses who focus on providing psychotherapy or counselling. Nurse Practitioners are a relatively new group to Canadian clinical service providers. These nurses have advanced training in assessment, diagnosis, and disease management, and are often involved in delivering primary care services.

Although many nurses work in hospital and community services that are focused on medical or surgical treatment, rather than on mental health care, they will often encounter people with mental health problems in those settings. Mental disorders and physical illnesses are commonly comorbid (i.e., occurring simultaneously), and nurses bring skills in both medical and emotional care.

## Psychiatrists

Psychiatrists are medical doctors who have received advanced specialty training in the care of individuals with mental disorders. Some psychiatrists further subspecialize in child psychiatry or geriatric psychiatry, and many develop specialized interests and experience in the treatment of particular problems or conditions (e.g., schizophrenic disorders, eating disorders, or personality disorders). Psychiatrists work in various settings and organize their practices in many different ways. Some work individually, whereas others act as members of interdisciplinary teams; often, psychiatrists

**Figure 14.1:** Nurses take on a variety of roles in a multitude of settings. Here, a nurse provides at-home care.

*Source:* killerb10/iStockphoto

undertake a combination of such activities in their overall practice. As physicians, they are licensed to prescribe medications, and generally assume a leadership role in the selection, prescription, and monitoring of psychiatric medications such as antipsychotics, antidepressants, and mood stabilizers.

## Clinical Psychologists

Although training and licensing requirements vary across Canada, most clinical psychologists complete doctoral training (i.e., a PhD) in clinical psychology, intern, and undergo supervision in order to obtain licensure. Psychologists also have widely varying practices, including "private practice," in which psychotherapy and other services may be delivered. They may work in private or public organizations, including hospitals, schools, forensic services, and correctional facilities. Psychologists also conduct psychological testing, which assists in the assessment of cognitive problems, learning difficulties, and brain injuries and helps to reach sound diagnoses and treatment plans for individuals who have complex problems that are difficult to discern. The degree to which psychologists are accessed for mental health services varies across Canada; when utilization rates are compared

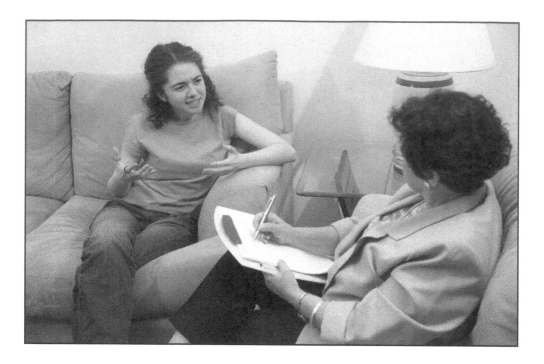

**Figure 14.2:** Psychologists play a variety of roles in the treatment of individuals with mental health issues. While some provide therapy, others are involved in psychological testing, assessment of cognitive problems and learning difficulties, and various other roles.

*Source:* Lisa F. Young/iStockphoto

across the country, psychologists are accessed much more commonly in Quebec than in other provinces (Lesage et al., 2006).

## Social Workers

Social workers work with people who have been socially excluded and those who are in social, financial, or emotional crises. A large proportion of social work is directed toward helping young people and their families negotiate difficulties. Social workers play an important role in assessing and protecting the safety of children and youth who are thought to be in peril as the result of abuse, neglect, or insufficient care. Although it may be necessary to apprehend children who are in acute risk (i.e., apply child protection and child welfare law to remove children from the custody of their parents or legal guardians), efforts are generally directed toward supporting parents and families by helping them to resolve problems and maintain family cohesion. Social workers work to protect the welfare of many other vulnerable people in society, including those who are elderly, physically ill, mentally ill, or developmentally disabled.

Social workers practice in various settings, including hospital and community programs and "private practice," where they may deliver individual, group, or family therapy or other services. Some social workers function as "navigators" to connect people with a host of services, including shelter and housing, employment assistance, and financial support. The importance of helping people to access such services and supports cannot be overemphasized; housing, financial supports, and employment support often result in profound improvements to mental health problems. Currently, the educational requirements to become a registered social worker are moving toward graduate-level degree preparation, and many provinces now require a master's degree for entry to the profession.

## Counsellors

Although counsellors generally provide advice and assistance geared at solving problems or achieving specific goals, there is not a single or widely accepted definition of the role. In some provinces, regulatory bodies oversee registration and practice, but in others there are no regulations or requirements placed upon individuals who advertise themselves as counsellors. Many focus on helping individuals with personal growth or mental health, but counsellors may also address spiritual, financial, occupational, or other concerns as focal points. Counsellors may focus on particular problems (e.g., addiction or marital difficulties) and may adopt particular modalities or therapies (e.g., art therapy, music therapy, or family therapy).

## Occupational Therapists

OTs are involved in promoting meaningful involvement in "occupations" when we use the word in its broadest sense (i.e., to describe participation in employment, leisure activities, physical activity, and self-care, among others). The philosophy of occupational therapy is that the ability to engage in activities of daily life promotes health and well-being. OTs assist people to engage in a wide range of activities, from using computers to attending to daily needs, such as dressing, cooking, and eating. When working with people who have cognitive disturbances or memory problems, OTs may help with the development of time-management skills, budgeting, shopping, homemaking, and use of public transportation. Various community-based services and hospital programs that provide care for people with mental health problems include OTs as members of interdisciplinary teams.

## Other Health Care Professionals

There are many other groups of health care professionals whose services are utilized in addressing mental health and illness in Canada. Medical specialists, including pediatricians and geriatricians, often devote substantial attention to mental health problems in the young and old, respectively, and occupational physicians have become increasingly involved in addressing the prevention and treatment of mental illness within the workplace setting. Pharmacists provide expertise regarding the optimal use and safety of a long list of psychiatric medications. Dieticians are involved in

**Figure 14.3:** Occupational therapists assist people to engage in a wide range of activities, including attending to daily needs.

*Source:* orangelinemedia/iStockphoto

helping patients with specific nutritional needs that may be related to mental health problems. In particular, they are involved in the treatment of people with eating disorders (e.g., anorexia nervosa), and they provide assistance to people with mental health problems who are at risk of excessive weight gain and diabetes mellitus as side effects of certain medications.

## Application of the Recovery Model

The **Recovery Model** is a paradigm of care and service delivery that focuses on helping people with mental health issues achieve "a way of living a satisfying, hopeful, and contributing life even with the limitations caused by illness" (Anthony, 1993, p. 527). At the centre of the Recovery Model are the concepts of *hope* and *empowerment*, which are believed to be essential to achieving health. Traditionally, the term "recovery" may have been viewed as synonymous with remission, that is, the absence of clinical symptoms. However, recovery, as used in conceptualizing this model, refers to the "process of growth and transformation as the person moves beyond acute distress often associated with mental health problems or illness and develops new-found strengths and new ways of being" (Mental Health Commission of Canada, 2009, p. 28). In fact, the Recovery Model has nothing to do with achieving a "cure," but rather with achieving a full and productive life and optimal function.

The Recovery Model first emerged within the field of addictions within the 12-step AA program, where it remained until the late 1980s (Deegan, 1988). At that time, the process of deinstitutionalization was well underway, and mental health services that had previously operated within institutions were being established in the community. With this move into the community, many of the inadequacies of the mental health system became more evident; the mental health "system" and society often failed to achieve the social inclusion of people with mental illnesses. People living with mental illness rose to meet this adversity by demanding a shift in services and approach, advocating for the incorporation of the Recovery Model in mental health policy and service delivery (Deegan, 1988). Subsequently, the Recovery Model has been gradually embraced by various sectors in a number of countries as a component of their efforts to reform mental health systems. In Canada, the *Out of the Shadows at Last* report advocated for recovery to be "placed at the centre of mental health reform" (Kirby & Keon, 2006, p. 42), a call that has since been embraced by the Mental Health Commission of Canada in its strategy framework (Mental Health Commission of Canada, 2009) (see Chapter 13).

One of the appealing aspects of the recovery approach is that it puts emphasis on the importance of valuing every person's individuality and unique life experience. Within this model, care providers and health care services are oriented toward supporting clients in achieving health. Health providers learn that they can promote recovery "by helping a person to understand their experience, while strengthening their sense of meaning and purpose" (Mental Health Commission of Canada, 2009, p. 29).

The Mental Health Commission of Canada (2009, p. 28) has summarized the key components of recovery as:

- Finding, maintaining, and repairing hope: believing in oneself; having a sense of being able to accomplish things; being optimistic about the future.
- Re-establishing a positive identity: finding a new identity which incorporates illness but retains a core, positive sense of self.
- Building a meaningful life: making sense of illness; finding a meaning in life, despite illness; being engaged in life and involved in the community.
- Taking responsibility and control: feeling in control of illness and in control of life.

Figure 14.4 displays 10 fundamental components that have been included in the Recovery Model. Although various health professionals have embraced this paradigm of care, additional effort will be required to achieve a more complete adoption of these principles and practices throughout mental health and addiction services in Canada.

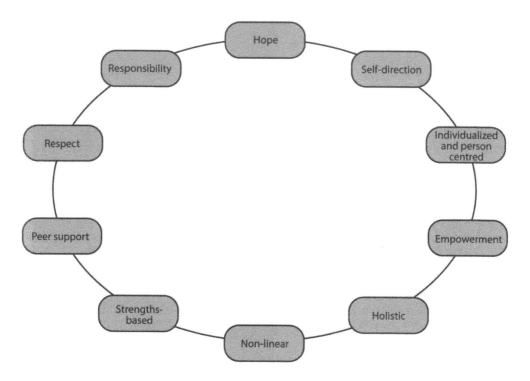

**Figure 14.4:** Components of recovery

*Source:* Substance Abuse and Mental Health Services Administration. (n.d.) National consensus statement on mental health recovery. Retrieved from http://store.samhsa.gov/shin/content/SMA05-4129/SMA05-4129.pdf

## Client-Centred Care and the Therapeutic Relationship

Client-centred care, or "patient-centred care" as it is termed in some circles, aims to ensure that the client is at the core of all therapeutic efforts, emphasizing the "centrality of the patient experience; the need for respect and the expressions of values and beliefs; the need to take an integrated approach to care; to communicate effectively; and to share in decision-making processes" (Kitson et al., 2012, p. 9). In the Canadian context, this approach to care was spearheaded in the 1990s by Moira Stewart with a focus on improving outcomes in primary care through enhanced physician-client relationships. One way to strengthen a culture of client-centred care is through inclusion of peer support workers and family caregivers in the delivery of mental health care services. More broadly, professionals must work to ensure that the wishes and concerns of clients and family members are respected and addressed.

The development of **therapeutic relationships** with clients and family members has been described as the formation of an alliance and sense of trust in pursuing common goals (Peplau, 1962). However, not all professional-client relationships are successful; factors such as unrealistic expectations on behalf of the client or professional, inconsistency in the relationship, and the limited availability of the health professional have been found to hinder the therapeutic relationship, resulting in frustration and impeding progress (Cahill, Paley, & Hardy, 2013; Forchuk et al., 2000). The phases that have been identified in the development of therapeutic and non-therapeutic relationships are depicted in Figure 14.5. Therapeutic relationships also promote the client's sense of empowerment and self-esteem, which as discussed earlier is a central tenet of the Recovery Model, and have been found to enhance treatment outcomes (Forchuk, 1995).

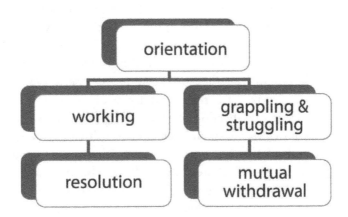

**Figure 14.5:** Phases of therapeutic and non-therapeutic relationships

*Source*: Forchuk, C., Westwell, J., Martin, M.L., Bamber-Azzapardi, W., Kosterewa-Tolman, D., & Hux, M. (2000). The developing nurse-client relationship: Nurses' perspectives. *Journal of the American Psychiatric Nurses Association*, 6(1), 3–10.

## Occupational Stress, Burnout, Moral Distress, and Misconduct

Helping people with mental health problems can be a very rewarding experience, especially when you are witness to recovery and wellness. However, the work can also be very frustrating and stressful; health care professionals can become overwhelmed and emotionally exhausted by constant exposure to sadness, crisis, or disability. Compassion fatigue, first described by Joinson (1992), refers to the loss of empathy and the development of a pervasive negative attitude and hopelessness that sometimes develops among health care professionals in these circumstances. A related concept, "burnout," has been defined as a state of emotional, mental, and physical exhaustion caused by excessive and prolonged stress, and it is described by some mental health professionals as a hazard of their occupations.

While compassion fatigue and burnout are seen to result from exposure to the stresses of working in an environment where extreme sorrow and trauma are commonplace, the concept of "moral distress" has emerged in the recent scientific literature and describes the suffering experienced by health care professionals when they "[lack] the necessary resources to provide attentive, competent, and ethical care" (Musto & Schreiber, 2012, p. 138). The situations that are seen to constrain moral action and contribute to moral distress include the perceived lack of support from managers secondary to budget limitations, feeling unheard by colleagues, and having concerns left unaddressed—situations which, unfortunately, are prevalent in mental health settings, as they are often underfunded and undervalued (Mental Health Commission of Canada, 2012).

Individuals who provide mental health care services need a sound understanding of the impact that the work has on their own mental health and require coping strategies to deal with the stress that accompanies the role. Ideally, health care professionals put provisions in place for their own support, including regular contacts with colleagues and mentors. Professional associations often provide confidential services and supports to help members who are experiencing difficulties. Unfortunately, some health care professionals are reluctant to disclose mental health problems, due to concerns that they could lose credibility or have their privileges to practise suspended.

Health care professionals are regulated by professional colleges that are responsible for evaluating qualifications and awarding licensure to those who meet all requirements. In order to maintain licensure, health care professionals may be required to demonstrate that they have undertaken adequate continuing education and maintained their skill level. Professional colleges also monitor and investigate complaints and may discipline professional members who are found to have acted unethically or to have not met acceptable standards of practice.

## Organizational Health and Leadership

Many mental health care professionals work within health care facilities or organizations, such as a hospitals, clinics, or agencies. Ideally, health care organizations provide supportive working environments and maintain healthy organizational cultures that foster open communication and positive relationships among management and staff members. Good leadership has been found to be an important factor in high-functioning organizations. Table 14.1 describes four characteristics of leadership associated with high-functioning organizations (Krause & Weekly, 2005).

**Table 14.1: Four dimensions of transformational leadership**

| Challenging | Providing a flow of challenging new ideas aimed at rethinking old ways of doing things; challenging dysfunctional paradigms; promoting rationality and careful problem solving. |
| --- | --- |
| Engaging | Helping others to commit to the desired direction, including the ability to coach, mentor, provide feedback and personal attention, and link the individual's needs to the organization's mission. |
| Inspiring | Setting high standards; using symbols to focus effort; modelling new standards; and communicating a vision and translating it into language that resonates with individuals at all levels of the organization. |
| Influencing | Building a sense of mission and commitment to the vision; gaining respect and trust; increasing optimism and instilling pride. |

*Source:* Chart created by Elliot Goldner and based on Krause, T.R., & Weekly, T. (2005). A four-factor model for establishing a high-functioning organization. *Professional Safety*, 50(11), 31–41.

When organizations are strained as a result of economic pressures, restructuring, or difficulties in leadership, the negative impact is often felt by all members. For mental health care professionals who are coping with the emotional stresses of their work, difficult organizational environments can further challenge their abilities to cope and increase the likelihood of burnout.

## Collaborative Mental Health Care

Ideally, the many health care professionals involved in the delivery of services to people with mental health problems would work together in a coordinated and harmonious manner. Commonly, this does not occur—the Senate Committee that undertook an intensive study of Canada's mental health services found a complex array that are delivered in "silos," that is, not in integrated or coordinated ways (Kirby & Keon, 2006).

A movement to build collaborative mental health care services (also known as "shared care" and "collaborative care") has been in place in Canada in recent decades, initiated and championed by a psychiatrist, Nick Kates, and a family physician, Marilyn Craven, who brought the delivery of specialized mental health to the offices of family physicians in the Hamilton, Ontario, area. Subsequently, collaborative mental health care has grown to become a broadened effort to bring together different health care professionals, people with lived experience, family members, and other caregivers (Gagné, 2005). Nevertheless, uptake of this model has been patchy. Incentives and supports may be required in order to foster such coordinated mental health care services.

---

**Box 14.1: Teamwork**

**Figure 14.6:** In order to play the game successfully, hockey players must work together as a team.

*Source*: technotr/iStockphoto

A famous football coach, Vince Lombardi, is quoted as saying, "Individual commitment to a group effort—that is what makes a team work, a company work, a society work, a civilization work." Many Canadians love hockey, a game that demands teamwork. To be successful, hockey players must learn (often reluctantly) to pass the puck and let other players be the ones to score the big goal. Novice hockey players are instilled with messages from their coaches, such as "There is no 'I' in TEAM," and they are guided repeatedly to work as a well-coordinated and synchronized group until this becomes second nature. In contrast, health care professionals receive little training to work in a coordinated manner. Yet, good quality mental health care requires the coordinated activity of various players just as much as any successful hockey team.

**Interprofessional collaboration** in the health care setting refers to the interaction and co-operation of agents from different professional groups in "an effort to integrate and translate, at least to some degree, themes and schemes shared by several professions" (D'Amour et al., 2005, p. 120). Professionals who are able to work effectively in providing interprofessional care are able to see beyond their professional egos and respect the value of others' expertise. Further, these professionals are more flexible in their roles and are able to share responsibilities with other care providers.

Despite research indicating that interprofessional collaboration is necessary and effective (San Martin-Rodriguez et al., 2005), it is often very difficult to accomplish. It is simply not as easy as gathering a group of professionals and telling them to work together—a number of additional factors are necessary, including trust, effective communication, and negotiation (D'Amour et al., 2005). One of the issues that further contributes to the difficulties encountered in enacting interprofessional collaboration is that educational programs are largely focused on training professionals to be effective in one paradigm of treatment and care (Baldwin, 2007). Little emphasis is put on preparing these professional groups to work together effectively, and efforts are needed to change the education of health care professionals to foster such collaboration.

**Figure 14.7:** Interprofessional collaboration is a necessary and effective strategy for achieving optimal health outcomes for our population.

*Source:* iStockphoto

## *Communities of Practice*

The term "community of practice" was coined by educational theorists to describe a group of people who share an interest, a craft, and/or a profession (Lave & Wenger, 1991). Often such groups will evolve naturally as a result of the common interests in a particular field, or they can be created purposely with the goals of sharing and gaining knowledge related to their field. Communities of practice often constitute important social networks for professionals and others who work in mental health or who share an interest or passion about certain topics. Often, communities of practice form in relation to a particular diagnosis or problem, such as childhood autism, dementia, homelessness among people with mental illness, and many other issues of interest. Communities of practice often include professionals of many types, and may involve people with lived experience, family members, and others as participants. Such opportunities to exchange knowledge, share perspectives, and build relationships are of great benefit. These networks, which are often informal, also serve to provide mutual support, encouragement, and inspiration to their members.

## Insider Knowledge, Lived Experience, and Family Caregivers

The term "insider knowledge" can be used to refer to the privileged understanding that is often gained by people who have extensive first-hand experience in various circumstances. This notion is also captured in the term "lived experience," further signifying the unique perspectives that are gained by people exposed to life experiences that most people do not encounter. Such insider knowledge and lived experience can be applied to help others with less experience. This approach has been applied for a long time in the field of addiction, where therapists and counsellors have often recovered from their own difficulties with substance use and apply their personal experiences when guiding others. Similarly, 12-step peer support groups (see Chapter 12) utilize insider knowledge and lived experience to help people negotiate the path toward recovery. Often, individuals who are new to 12-step groups will pair up with others who are already in recovery; the more experienced of the pair becomes the "sponsor," providing additional guidance and support on the basis of his or her personal experience and knowledge.

The knowledge and wisdom gained through lived experience of addiction or mental illness has not always been recognized by mental health care professionals. Historically, many people have felt excluded from meaningful participation in decisions because only those with professional training and credentials were acknowledged as having expertise (Chamberlin, 2005). In recent years, there has been more recognition of the important contributions to be made by people with lived experience. The inclusion of peer support workers as legitimate members on health care provider teams constitutes a step in this direction; however, there remain many instances in which people with lived experience are excluded from meaningful participation.

Another group of people with insider knowledge and lived experience are family members of those with mental illnesses and substance use disorders. Often, family members and other caregivers provide the lion's share of support and assistance to a person who is unwell; in many instances, the provision of necessary support may become the full-time occupation of a family member. He or she may become the principle holder of information about the history, treatment response, medication regimen, allergies, sensitivities, and other facets of clinical care. Yet, family members often feel excluded, unrecognized, and unsupported by health care professionals. At times, they are informed that privacy concerns prevent treatment providers from sharing information with them. Often, busy clinicians do not make a priority of spending time with family members, despite the value that would be added. For example, studies have found that the inclusion of family members in treatment programs for people with schizophrenic disorders results in better outcomes, including reduced hospitalization (Dyck et al., 2002).

## Roles of Other Key Stakeholders

In addition to clinical service providers, individuals with lived experience, family members, and other caregivers, there are other "stakeholders" (i.e., individuals who affect the system or who can be affected by it) with key roles that are necessary for the mental health "system" to function.

Managers and administrators have the responsibility of ensuring that services are organized properly and staffed appropriately and must often deal with financial pressures and directives from above to cut operating budgets and trim expenses. People in these positions often feel under intense pressure. Many have moved from clinical roles into management and may feel particularly torn when they are required to implement decisions that will cause distress to clients or clinicians under their charge. Such positions are commonly "high pressure zones" due to endless crises, deadlines, problems, and directives that occur within health care organizations.

Politicians and government bureaucrats who address decisions related to mental health and substance use issues also operate under great pressure much of the time. These individuals hold the heavy responsible for making, implementing, and overseeing key policies and decisions about a wide range of issues in Canadian society. When something goes awry, they are often criticized mercilessly by disgruntled citizens and may be skewered by journalists, advocates, or members of other political parties. Politicians are often called upon by their constituency to address problems related to mental health care, such as increased housing for people who are homeless and ill or improved care for people who have substance use disorders. In the process, they often encounter the "not-in-my-backyard" syndrome, or NIMBYism (i.e., outcries from local citizens who do not want these services in their neighbourhoods). In turn, politicians (e.g., premiers, ministers, mayors, councillors) often put intense pressure on members of the bureaucracy (e.g., deputy ministers, assistant deputy members, and other civil servants) to solve complex problems. It is not surprising that those who work within government bureaucracies often maintain a barrier between themselves and people who are outside of government as a means of protecting themselves from impossible demands and dilemmas.

**Figure 14.8:** Politicians play an important role in making, implementing, and overseeing key policies and decisions that impact mental health and substance use issues.

*Source:* Rich Legg/iStockphoto

The creation and exchange of new knowledge that can improve prevention and treatment, including evaluation of novel approaches and new treatments, often falls within the domain of researchers. Historically, the scientific research community was considered to be too restrictive in its definitions of "knowledge" and "evidence." More recently, expanded dimensions of research activity have enriched knowledge about mental health and substance use (see Chapter 15). Further, research paradigms such as participatory action research and integrated knowledge translation emphasize the importance of including people with lived experience, health care practitioners, family members, and policy-makers throughout the entire research process, from conception of the research questions through to the dissemination of findings.

Another important contribution is made by educators, who prepare professional practitioners and others to apply expert knowledge and skills and adopt ethical practices that respect and support the values held by our society. Earlier in the chapter, we mentioned that the long separation of various professional groups from each other during their educational training may contribute to the difficulties experienced in the collaboration and integration of services. Increased attention to interdisciplinary education is needed, including opportunities for professionals to learn to work well with those who have different training, expertise, and experience.

## Conclusion

A group of people with a wide range of expertise and experience is involved in the provision and maintenance of services and supports to address mental health and substance use problems. This includes health care professionals who have been trained in a variety of disciplinary backgrounds, people with lived experience, family members and other caregivers, managers and administrators, politicians and bureaucrats, researchers, and educators. The Recovery Model is a paradigm that has been identified as being important in achieving enhanced mental health care. Client-centred care and the development of therapeutic alliances between professionals and clients have also been emphasized. Fostering collaboration among the many stakeholders in the mental health system is a challenge that needs ongoing attention and may require incentives and supports developed through government policy and financing. Such development may be helped by interdisciplinary education and through greater recognition of the potential benefits of a better integrated mental health "system."

## Glossary

**clinical service providers:** Professionals from a variety of health care professions, such as medicine, nursing, and social work, who provide clinical services.

**interprofessional collaboration:** The interaction and co-operation of agents from different professional groups in an effort to integrate and provide holistic, effective care.

**peer support workers:** People with lived experience of mental illness who provide clinical support to others.

**recovery model:** A paradigm of care and service delivery that focuses on helping clients through a process of growth and transformation by supporting their individual potential for recovery.

**therapeutic relationships:** The important relationships between nurses and clients aimed at improving client care and outcomes—both nurses and clients are contributors to the relationships.

## Critical Thinking Questions

1.  Why do you think a diverse group of professionals from many different backgrounds is required to provide mental health services?
2.  Select one type of clinical service provider. What role do these professionals play in the delivery of mental health services?
3.  What are the strengths and challenges of providing interprofessional mental health services?
4.  Why are therapeutic relationships so important to promoting optimal health in the mental health care setting?
5.  Describe the key components of the Recovery Model.

## Recommended Readings

Corey, G., Corey, M.S., & Callanan, P. (2010). *Issues and Ethics in the Helping Professions* (8th ed.). Belmont, CA: Cengage Learning.

Klitzman, R. (2012). *In a House of Dreams and Glass: Becoming a Psychiatrist.* New York: Simon and Schuster.

Kramer, P.D. (1997). *Listening to Prozac: The Landmark Book about Antidepressants and the Remaking of the Self* (Rev. ed.). New York: Penguin.

Slade, M. (2009). *Personal Recovery and Mental Illness: A Guide for Mental Health Professionals.* New York: Cambridge University Press.

Wegeneck, A.R., & Buskist, W. (2010). *The Insider's Guide to the Psychology Major: Everything You Need to Know about the Degree and the Profession.* Washington, DC: American Psychological Association.

## Recommended Websites

Canadian Mental Health Association. Recovery. www.ontario.cmha.ca/about_mental_health.asp?cID=7667

Canadian Interprofessional Health Collaborative. www.cihc.ca/

Helpguide.org. Preventing Burnout. www.helpguide.org/articles/stress/preventing-burnout.htm

National Coalition for Mental Health Recovery. www.ncmhr.org/

## References

Anthony, W.A. (1993). Recovery from mental illness: The guiding vision of the mental health service system in the 1990s. *Psychosocial Rehabilitation Journal,* 16(4), 11–23.

Baldwin, Jr., D.C. (2007). Some historical notes on interdisciplinary and interprofessional education and practice in health care in the USA. *Journal of Interprofessional Care*, 21(S1), 23–27.

Cahill, J., Paley, G., & Hardy, G. (2013). What do patients find helpful in psychotherapy? Implications for the therapeutic relationship in mental health nursing. *Journal of Psychiatric & Mental Health Nursing*, 20(9), 782–791. doi: 10.1111/jpm.12015

Chamberlin, J. (2005). User/consumer involvement in mental health service delivery. *Epidemiologica e Psichiatria Sociale*, 14(1), 10–14.

D'Amour, D., Ferrada-Videla, M., San Martin Rodriguez, L., & Beaulieu, M.D. (2005). The conceptual basis for interprofessional collaboration: Core concepts and theoretical frameworks. *Journal of Interprofessional Care*, 19(S1), 116–131.

Deegan, P.E. (1988). Recovery: The lived experience of rehabilitation. *Psychosocial Rehabilitation Journal*, 11(4), 11–19.

Dyck, D.G., Hendryx, M.S., Short, R.A., Voss, W.D., & McFarlane, W.R. (2002). Service use among patients with schizophrenia in psychoeducational multiple-family group treatment. *Psychiatric Services*, 53, 749–754.

Fleury, M., Imboua, A., Aubé, D., Farand, L., & Lambert, Y. (2012). General practitioners' management of mental disorders: A rewarding practice with considerable obstacles. *BMC Family Practice*, (13), 19. doi: 10.1186/1471-2296-13-19

Forchuk, C. (1995). Development of nurse-client relationships: What helps? *Journal of the American Psychiatric Nurses Association*, 1(5), 146–153.

Forchuk, C., Westwell, J., Martin, M.L., Bamber-Azzapardi, W., Kosterewa-Tolman, D., & Hux, M. (2000). The developing nurse-client relationship: Nurses' perspectives. *Journal of the American Psychiatric Nurses Association*, 6(1), 3–10.

Gagné, M.A. (2005). *What is collaborative mental health care? An introduction to the collaborative mental health care framework*. Mississauga, ON: Canadian Collaborative Mental Health Initiative. Retrieved from www.cpa-apc.org/media.php?mid=195

Joinson, C. (1992). Coping with compassion fatigue. *Nursing*, 22(4), 116–122.

Kirby, M.J.L., & Keon, W.J. (2006). *Out of the shadows at last: Transforming mental health, mental illness and addiction services in Canada*. The Standing Senate Committee on Social Affairs, Science and Technology. Retrieved from parl.gc.ca/39/1/parlbus/commbus/senate/Com-e/SOCI-E/rep-e/pdf/rep02may06part1-e.pdf

Kitson, A., Marshall, A., Bassett, K., & Zeitz, K. (2012).What are the core elements of patient-centred care? A narrative review and synthesis of the literature from health policy, medicine and nursing. *Journal of Advanced Nursing*, 69(1), 4–15.

Krause, T.R., & Weekly, T. (2005). A four-factor model for establishing a high-functioning organization. *Professional Safety*, 50(11), 34–41. Retrieved from http://campus.murraystate.edu/academic/faculty/dfender/OSH650/readings/Krause--Safety%20Leadership.pdf

Lave, J., & Wenger, E. (1991). *Situated learning: Legitimate peripheral participation*. Cambridge: Cambridge University Press.

Lesage A., Vasiliadis, H.M., Gagné, M.A., Dudgeon S., Kasman N., & Hay C. (2006). Prevalence of mental illnesses and related service utilization in Canada: An analysis of the Canadian Collaborative Mental Health Initiative. (2006). *Canadian community health survey: Final report*. Mississauga, ON: Canadian Collaborative Mental Health Initiative. Retrieved from www.cpa-apc.org/media.php?mid=245

Mental Health Commission of Canada. (2009). Toward recovery and well-being: A framework for a mental health strategy for Canada. Retrieved from www.mentalhealthcommission.ca/English/document/241/toward-recovery-and-well-being

Mental Health Commission of Canada. (2012). *Changing directions, changing lives: The mental health strategy for Canada*. Calgary, AB: Author.

Musto, L., & Schreiber, R.S. (2012). Doing the best I can do: Moral distress in adolescent mental health nursing. *Issues in Mental Health Nursing*, 33, 137–144.

National Physician Survey. (2007). 2007 survey results. Retrieved from http://nationalphysiciansurvey.ca/surveys/2007-survey/2007-results

Oyama, O., Burg, M.A., Fraser, K., & Kosch, S.G. (2012). Mental health treatment by family physicians: Current practices and preferences. *Family Medicine*, 44(10), 704–711.

Peplau, H.E. (1962). Interpersonal techniques: The crux of psychiatric nursing. *The American Journal of Nursing*, 62(6), 50–54.

San Martin-Rodriguez, L., Beaulieu, M-D., D'Amour, D., & Ferrada-Videla, M. (2005). The determinants of successful collaboration: A review of theoretical and empirical studies. *Journal of Interprofessional Care*, 19(S1), 132–147.

Statistics Canada. (2013). Access to a regular medical doctor, 2013. Retrieved from www.statcan.gc.ca/pub/82-625-x/2014001/article/14013-eng.htm

# Chapter 15

# MENTAL HEALTH
# AND SUBSTANCE USE

## Opportunities to Improve
## Population and Public Health

Prevention is better than cure.
>    —Desiderius Erasmus (Dutch Renaissance humanist and theologian)

## Introduction

In this final chapter, we draw together many of the elements discussed throughout the book and address the question "How can we improve the mental health of our population?" This turns out to be a question of critical importance because good mental health is strongly associated with so many key characteristics that are desirable in human society; happiness, productivity, good physical health, and satisfaction with life are all strongly correlated with good mental health. It has been pointed out that there can be "no *health* without *mental health*" (Prince et al., 2007, p. 859) because of the intricate relationship between mental and physical health.

In this chapter, we will discuss opportunities to bring about meaningful improvements, and we hope to inspire you to participate in actions that will enhance the mental health of our society. We begin the chapter by describing the population and public health approach and then discussing the application of this paradigm to mental health in Canada.

## Population and Public Health Paradigm

In Canada, the field of **public health** has been combined with a more recent **population health** approach to create the population and public health paradigm. Public health dates back many centuries and initially addressed sanitation conditions, including efforts to provide clean water, adequate waste control, and other measures to prevent and control the spread of infectious disease (measures that resulted in better health outcomes for populations). In modern times, one of the most significant contributions to public health was the development of vaccines to prevent and virtually eradicate some of the most deadly infectious diseases that, in earlier times, ravaged human life. The public health approach emphasizes prevention of illness and promotion of health. A public health approach is now applied far more broadly and is just as important to mental health and substance use as it is to infectious disease.

The population health approach emphasizes social determinants, such as poverty, education, and housing, as key factors influencing the health of populations (see Chapter 3). This paradigm brings attention to the social gradient in health; that is, the consistent finding that health within a population moves along a gradient in association with socio-economic status; those who are poor also have poor health. This is certainly true with regard to mental health. Although mental illness can affect all people, irrespective of their wealth, people who are poor are far more likely to have mental health problems at a population level (Saraceno & Barbui, 1997).

The relationship between poverty and poor mental health is bi-directional. Those who live below the poverty line are likely to experience increased stresses and have fewer resources and supports, often leading to increased levels of anxiety, depression, and substance use. Conversely, people with mental health problems often encounter barriers to employment, housing, and income security due to both disability and the resultant stigma and discrimination. Consequently, they are less likely to be able to escape poverty.

In combining the public health and population health traditions to create a population and public health approach, a number of principles have emerged as central features.

1. *An emphasis on illness prevention.* This principle focuses attention on the benefit of stopping the development of illnesses before they start, or at least very early in their course (referred to as "upstream" rather than "downstream").
2. *An emphasis on health promotion.* This focuses efforts on resilience-building activities that will strengthen a population's resistance and diminish susceptibility to health problems.
3. *A perspective focused on the population rather than the individual.* This perspective recognizes the importance of understanding the characteristics of populations (since a focus on individuals may "miss the big picture"), fostering actions that will benefit a large proportion of society.
4. *An effort to address health equity.* Social determinants such as poverty, education, and housing are recognized as key factors influencing the health of populations and an effort is made to improve the health of populations that suffer due to the social gradient.

Population and public health efforts have not focused attention on mental health, historically. However, an increasing awareness that positive mental health contributes to both individual and societal well-being has led to an increased focus

**Figure 15.1:** Poverty is one of the social determinants of health. Vancouver's Downtown Eastside community is one of the most impoverished neighbourhoods in North America.

*Source:* Chris Sang Yeob Park, Photographer

on improvements to mental health at a population level. One implication of this is heightened attention to the laws and public policies made by government and society that will have a broad impact on the mental health of the population.

## Laws and Public Policies Addressing Mental Health and Substance Use

Laws and public policies are developed and implemented to prevent harm, to promote health and safety of the population, and to promote the smooth functioning of society. Laws are binding rules of conduct meant to enforce justice in society, carrying penalties for those who refuse or fail to obey. Public policies are often defined as the decisions of government about particular issues and problems. Public policies may encompass laws and other regulatory measures enacted by government, but may also be put in place by decisions regarding government spending and support for particular societal issues. Ultimately, laws and public policies seek to enact ideas about how to best address key issues we face and common goals we seek as a society. A good law or public policy can transform knowledge, values, and ideals into adopted practices and social structures that benefit many people. However, a bad law or public policy can lead to great harms. We empower governments and legislators to create public policies and laws that are in the best interests of our citizens. In democratic societies, complex electoral processes have been put in place to determine which parties and leaders will be given the authority (and heavy responsibility) to steer public policy and address legislation (i.e., creating public policies and enacting laws).

Canadian governments engage in a great deal of legislative and public policy efforts, including those directed toward health. Laws and public policies are often debated when complex health issues surface or manage to capture government or public interest. In the following sections, we will discuss laws and public policies that address mental health and substance use in Canada, topics that are often surrounded by great controversy. We will also describe efforts that focus on mental health promotion and mental illness prevention, as we consider these to be important facets of a population and public health approach to improving mental health in Canada.

### *Mental Health Law and Public Policy*

Laws, acts, and statutes that are relevant to mental health may govern key decisions about detainment and involuntary hospitalization, responsibility for criminal acts, incarceration, and other penalties for substance use and other issues. They also direct certain actions of health professionals, police, judges, and others who may have a substantial impact on people who experience mental health problems. In Chapter 11, we discussed the Mental Health Act, provincial legislation that stipulates how individuals who are thought to have mental illness may be detained or admitted to hospital on an involuntary basis. Existing legislation also governs how people are treated when they commit criminal acts and their capacity for rational behaviour has been impaired by mental illness, as discussed in Chapter 13.

A key issue is one of human rights. Particular care and attention is required to ensure that the rights of people with mental health problems are upheld and respected. Some people with mental illnesses are vulnerable due to the incapacity they may experience as a result of illness and the stigma that people with mental illness face within society.

In addition to the laws that have been put in place to define the rights of people with mental illness, there are many relevant public policies that influence the health and quality of life of people with mental health problems and their families. The WHO has highlighted the following three recommendations for policy regarding the organization of mental health services: (1) deinstitutionalize mental health care; (2) integrate mental health into general health care; and (3) develop community mental health services (WHO, 2008). In addition to government policies that address the delivery of mental health services, there are many other essential policy issues that influence mental health. Public policy addressing social determinants of mental health, such as income, housing, education, and early childhood development, are of critical importance.

---

**Box 15.1: Headlines Theatre's** *After Homelessness*

Working to influence policy can be a lot of hard work, but not all of it needs to be tedious and boring. In 2009, Headlines Theatre began its production of *After Homelessness*, a show that features actors who have personal experience with homelessness and mental illness. This production, like others produced by Headlines Theatre, is crafted to influence policy. Unlike traditional theatre performances, Headlines Theatre presents two shows every night. The first showcases the screenplay written by the participating actors, while the second allows members of the audience to "interject" and join the stage in order to model how they would like to see the issues handled. This unique process allows for collaboration between actors, community members, advocates, local government officials, health care professionals, and others to help shape strategies to address important issues. At the conclusion of the production, audience suggestions are compiled and presented to local officials to incorporate into future policy development.

---

## Substance Use Laws and Public Policies

The most extreme substance use control policies are those of **prohibition**, in which the possession, selling, or marketing of a substance is made illegal. In Canada, heroin, opium, cocaine, cannabis, amphetamines, and various other drugs are prohibited through the Controlled Drugs and Substances Act. The legislation includes maximum penalties for possession, trafficking, exportation, and production of different groups of drugs. However, prohibition does not effectively eliminate all use; even when severe punishments are in place, illegal drug use continues. Canada is one of a number of countries that attempted to prohibit alcohol use but later abandoned such efforts when this proved to be unsuccessful.

Currently, extreme control policies, such as prohibition, have been replaced with more moderate policies to diminish harms caused by alcohol use in Canada. These include limits on the minimum age for drinking and purchase of alcohol, laws governing alcohol use and operation of motor vehicles, limits on the hours of sale of alcohol, and liquor taxes. There is now very good scientific evidence that shows that policy and legislation such as these are very effective at diminishing alcohol-related harms (Stockwell et al., 2005). Among the most successful targeted interventions are deterrence-based policies directed at drinking and driving. The imposition of blood alcohol concentration limits for drivers, strongly enforced through highly visible sobriety checkpoints and breath testing by police, can have a sustained effect on reducing alcohol-related motor vehicle accidents, injuries, and deaths (Rehm et al., 2008).

The policies that have been put in place to address substance use vary dramatically around the world. In some countries, use of certain substances is prohibited under criminal law and draws serious punishment; in others, use of these substances may be tolerated or accepted. The degree to which control policies are adopted in a country is often related to its type of government (e.g., countries with authoritarian governments are more likely to impose strict and extreme prohibitory policies, laws, and practices).

A useful classification of substance use policies makes use of the notion that there is both a demand for and a supply of drugs. **Supply reduction** efforts are those that aim to decrease the availability of drugs through means such as seizures of illegal drug shipments, and arrest and prosecution of drug suppliers. **Demand reduction** refers to efforts to reduce the desire and preparedness to obtain and use drugs by potential consumers, including education, prevention and treatment programs, and social pressures and deterrents.

Debate about policies to address the use of cannabis has been prominent in Canada. Despite its status as an illegal drug, cannabis was reported to have been used by approximately 24.4 percent of Canadians 15 years of age and older in 2013, while about 40 percent reported having used cannabis in their lifetimes, making it the most commonly used illicit drug in Canada (Canadian Centre on Substance Abuse, 2015; Health Canada, 2005). Opinion is divided as to whether it remains a sensible policy to maintain cannabis as an illegal drug when it is used by so many people with seemingly minimal harm. Many advocate for the decriminalization of cannabis use (i.e., the removal of legal sanctions for personal use and possession), arguing that its status as an illegal drug causes more harm to Canadian citizens (through inappropriate criminalization and creation of black market trade) than access to the drug itself. A large group of Canadians call for legalization of cannabis along the lines of tobacco and alcohol.

## Box 15.2: Prohibition

In the early 20th century, most regions of Canada instituted prohibition, under which the use and sale of alcohol was illegal. To a large degree, prohibition was brought about through the efforts of the women's temperance movement and by religious groups that had become concerned about the frequent violence and havoc prominent in and around Canada's many bars and drinking establishments. However, prohibition was short-lived in Canada, and most provinces repealed the legislation soon after it was initiated. In the United States, prohibition lasted for a longer period and was not repealed until 1933. What was the outcome of this experiment? Prohibition was intended to diminish alcohol use and, as a result, reduce crime, solve social problems, and improve the health of Americans. Instead, alcohol use became more popular under prohibition and created a huge black market for alcohol. Canada became the source of much of the alcohol smuggled into the United States and a thriving underground economy of booze smuggling became prominent. Most considered prohibition in North America to be a profound failure (Thornton, 1991).

**Figure 15.2:** Members of the women's temperance movement advocate the return of prohibition, c. 1945.

*Source:* Adapted from the Canadian Institutes of Health Research.

**Figure 15.3:** Driving while under the influence of intoxicants causes a significant number of injuries and deaths each year in Canada.

*Source:* tillsonburg/iStockphoto

Many argue that cannabis can confer health benefits, including reduction of nausea following chemotherapy and reduction of pain caused by chronic illness. The use of medical marijuana (i.e., marijuana prescribed for medical purposes) has become more common in Canada along with the creation of "compassion clubs" and the recent proliferation of marijuana dispensaries that provide marijuana for ostensibly "medical purposes." Although such provision of marijuana remains illegal, the current government is considering reforms to laws governing the sale and possession of marijuana. Membership in compassion clubs generally requires a note from a physician.

Various policies and programs have been introduced across Canada to reduce harms that result from injection drug use. **Harm-reduction** policies aim to reduce the harmful consequences of drug use. Examples of harm-reduction efforts include needle-exchange programs, in which clean needles and syringes are distributed freely in areas where people who inject illicit drugs often congregate and used needles and syringes are collected and disposed of safely. Such programs sharply decrease the transmission of serious blood-borne infections. Other harm-reduction programs include supervised injection sites and the distribution of free condoms to sex trade workers in order to prevent the spread of sexually transmitted infectious diseases.

Harm-reduction efforts have also been implemented to address the potential risks associated with non-injection drug use. Encouragement of the use of vaporizers for cannabis and free ride programs for people who have been drinking are examples of harm-reduction activities.

Critics of harm reduction object on the basis that the approach may convey that illicit drugs can be used safely; they are concerned that such policies may give the wrong messages to young people, namely, that illicit substance use is non-preventable and should be accepted as a feasible lifestyle. What is certain on the basis of repeated evidence is that harm-reduction activities, such as those in the examples given above, are effective at reducing rates of HIV illness, hepatitis C, and other infectious diseases, injuries, and death (European Monitoring Centre for Drugs and Drug Addiction, 2010).

---

**Box 15.3: Vancouver's Insite Program**

People living in the Downtown Eastside of Vancouver have very high rates of illicit substance use. Some of the consequences are high rates of infectious disease transmission (e.g., it is estimated that 99 percent of Vancouver's Downtown Eastside drug-using population is infected with the hepatitis C virus), overdose and death, and drug-related crime. There are many tragic stories and much suffering among residents of this neighbourhood, although these are accompanied by instances of great courage and humanity. Insite, Vancouver's supervised injection site, is a service that operates within the Downtown Eastside, providing clean needles, syringes, water, and other items needed to inject drugs (such as heroin or cocaine), and nurses who are available to help monitor and intervene in emergencies. This service, which is provided free to people who meet certain criteria, has been operating since 2003, despite being highly controversial and politically inflammatory. It operates through a constitutional exception to the Controlled Drugs and Substances Act. Canada's Federal Minister of Health previously refused to renew the program's exemption, which would have forced its closure, but this decision was overturned by a Supreme Court of Canada, ruling that application of the act would be unconstitutional. Hence, Insite has been permitted to continue its operations.

---

## Mental Health Promotion

Efforts to bring attention to the importance of mental health promotion have become more prominent in recent years. This follows the general trend of health promotion, recognizing that opportunities to build strong foundations for good health can be sound investments, resulting in less illness and a healthier society in the long term. Mental health promotion is enacted through policies and programs that aim to increase psychological well-being, competence, and resilience among individuals and communities.

**Figure 15.4:** Inside the Insite "shooting gallery"—Vancouver's supervised injection site

*Source:* Vancouver Coastal Health

Mental health promotion activities include parenting programs, in which parents are empowered in their child-rearing roles through access to knowledge and support; community-based recreational programs that provide youth with enjoyable extracurricular opportunities; community activities for older adults aimed at maintaining good physical and mental health; and initiatives that build social connectedness among residents of neighbourhoods and communities. Other mental health promotion activities mentioned earlier in this text include a program geared to build empathy in schoolchildren through regular contact with infants (Chapter 7) and programs that pair older adults with children (Chapter 10).

In the past, most activities in the field of mental health have focused almost exclusively on addressing illness, pathology, and disability. Recently, there has been a movement to address positive facets of mental health; more attention is now given to the support of individuals in their efforts to strengthen nascent skills and abilities. It has been recognized that humanity has long had the ability to overcome great adversity. Strengths refer to characteristics that help a person cope with difficulties, making life more fulfilling for oneself and others. Examples include the use of humour to deal with difficult situations, perseverance in the face of adversity, and the ability to form social relationships that provide support and comfort.

**Figure 15.5:** Parenting is an important skill for promoting lifelong health and well-being.

*Source:* Feryal Almazni, Photographer

As discussed in Chapter 7, Peterson and Seligman (2004) identified six main groups of core virtues that are consistently valued across cultures and across time: wisdom, courage, humanity, justice, temperance, and transcendence. Though Peterson and Seligman's virtues emerged as part of a new field of positive psychology, the shift in the mental health field to a focus on strengths has occurred in other clinical disciplines, such as social work and nursing. It is consistent with a population and public health paradigm in which efforts work toward the development of resistance and resilience, building long-standing capacity for protection against key risk factors. Resistance refers to the ability of individuals (or social organizations) to withstand very stressful events or ongoing stressful situations. Resilience refers to the ability of these individuals and organizations to rebound from very stressful events.

The term "mental capital" has been used to refer to "a person's cognitive and emotional resources. It includes their cognitive ability, how flexible and efficient

## Box 15.4: Physical Activity as Mental Health Promotion

**Figure 15.6:** Regular physical activity is one of the most effective mental health promotion activities, helping to decrease stress and depression and sharpen mental function.

*Source:* Alana Pineault, Photographer

Physical activity is one of the most effective mental health promotion activities a person can do. Regular physical activity—whether it is yoga, exercise class, hockey, wrestling, running, swimming, cycling, hiking, soccer, tennis, martial arts, horseback riding, football, skating, badminton, or some other activity—has been found to reduce stress, anxiety, and depression and bring about many mental health benefits. Various explanations have been proposed, including neurotransmitter release, increased blood flow to the brain, release and distraction from unpleasant thoughts or preoccupations, and increased social contact. In a modified form, physical activity is also possible for those with physical disabilities and for older adults. Although it is recommended that Canadians should engage in at least 150 minutes per week of moderate-to-vigorous physical activity, accumulated in bouts lasting at least 10 minutes, only a small proportion of Canadians do so. A Statistics Canada survey found that only 15 percent of adults (17 percent of men and 14 percent of women) meet that minimum—most of us are far too sedentary. How about you? Do you meet this minimum recommended standard? If not, we recommend that you find a way to fit in some type of regular physical activity every week. It will improve both your physical and mental health!

**Figure 15.7:** Two of the qualities we recommend for addressing the social determinants of mental health and changing public policy are playfulness and humour.

*Source:* Chris Sang Yeon Park, Photographer

they are at learning, and their 'emotional intelligence,' such as their social skills and resilience in the face of stress. It therefore conditions how well an individual is able to contribute effectively to society, and also to experience a high personal quality of life" (Jenkins et al., 2008, p. 2). Use of the word "capital" is meant to denote the similarity to financial capital, which can either be squandered or invested wisely.

## Prevention of Mental Illness and Substance Use Disorder

Efforts to prevent mental disorders and substance use disorder aim at reducing the incidence, prevalence, and recurrence of these disorders and associated harms. Some preventive strategies focus on physiological risk factors for developing mental disorders. For example, the use of folic acid (also known as vitamin B9) supplements by women who are planning to become pregnant can prevent problems in fetal brain development. Consequently, the Public Health Agency of Canada recommends that all women who could become pregnant take a multivitamin daily that contains 0.4 mg of folic acid and continue to do so throughout the first three months of pregnancy (Public Health Agency of Canada, 2008). The addition of iodine to table salt in many countries (including Canada) has effectively prevented iodine deficiency, the leading preventable cause of developmental disability (Delange et al., 2001). Prevention and early treatment of infectious diseases, such as syphilis, has greatly reduced neuro-psychiatric conditions that were once much more common (Tramont, 1995).

Effective mental illness prevention has also been accomplished by fostering changes in behaviour through laws and policies and by introducing education and programs in schools and other venues. For example, laws requiring the wearing of seat belts and helmets have decreased brain injuries (Centres for Disease Control and Prevention, 1995; Freedman, 1984), and a child- and family-focused group intervention program has been found to be effective at preventing anxiety disorders among children identified as at-risk through a school-based screening program (Dadds et al., 1999).

Prevention strategies have been classified according to the group of people being targeted by the prevention effort. **Universal prevention** strategies target entire populations; for example, a television commercial that is aimed at all viewers and conveys a message about the dangers of excessive alcohol use. **Selective prevention** targets subgroups of the population whose risk of developing mental disorders is significantly higher than average. Higher risk may be determined on the basis of a variety of factors, such as family history, socio-economic status, age, or exposure to trauma. An example of selective prevention would be a prevention program that aims to prevent the development of depression and other mental health problems in children who have been victimized by abuse. **Indicated prevention** strategies are those targeted at high-risk individuals who do not meet diagnostic criteria for mental disorders or substance use disorder, but are identified as having minimal but detectable signs or symptoms. For example, the Fast Track program was developed to help young children at risk for anti-social behaviour and includes a classroom-wide educational component, social skills training, tutoring, and parenting and home training (Conduct Problems Prevention Research Group, 2000).

Table 15.1 lists examples of various risk factors and protective factors that are relevant to the prevention of mental disorders and substance use disorder.

Although efforts to promote good mental health and to prevent mental illness and substance use disorder are valuable at *all* stages of life, it is particularly important to implement policies and strategies aimed at helping children and youth. Early in human life, there is great opportunity to shape the course for the lifetime. An important value for our society calls on us to recognize the importance of the mental health and well-being of our children and youth and invest great efforts in support of parenting, education, and policies that protect children against poverty, homelessness, and other negative impacts.

In Chapter 7, we used the example of teens who leave home precipitously due to family conflict and who end up on the streets in a downward spiral of depression, drug use, and prostitution. Such a situation is an opportunity for prevention. The provision of supports to adolescents and their families can help them effectively traverse this period, and survive adolescent rebellion and family conflict without dire consequences. There are many other opportunities for mental illness prevention that can contribute to better lives for future generations.

**Table 15.1: Risk factors and protective factors for mental and substance use disorders**

| Risk factors | Protective factors |
|---|---|
| Maternal malnutrition during pregnancy | Social and conflict management skills |
| Child abuse and neglect | Adaptability |
| Chronic pain | Self-esteem |
| Academic failure | Skills for life |
| Elder abuse | Literacy |
| Excessive substance use | Good parenting |
| Loneliness | Exercise |
| Low social class | Feelings of security |
| Low birth weight | Feelings of mastery and control |
| Poor work skills and habits | Positive parent-child interaction |
| Social incompetence | Socio-emotional growth |
| Stressful life events | Stress management |
| Emotional immaturity | Social support of family and friends |
| Family conflict | Early cognitive stimulation |
| Medical illness | Stable housing |
| Personal loss—bereavement | Good-quality education |
| Reading disabilities | Positive relationships with peers |

Chapter 12 was devoted to a discussion of mental health treatment and, in Chapter 13, we discussed the organization and delivery of mental health services in Canada. Important goals include delivery of effective treatment on a more timely basis through early intervention approaches and better coordination of primary and secondary mental health care services.

## Suicide Prevention

An important focus of prevention efforts is the prevention of suicide, and these efforts are often directed toward youth. Many high schools, colleges, and universities are working to implement programs that will address campus mental health and prevent suicide, and such efforts are being promoted by different levels of Canadian governments. For example, the Province of Ontario recently committed $27 million to address mental health issues on college and university campuses as a response to concerns about suicides on campuses (Brown, 2013). Most programs tend to utilize a combination of awareness/education curricula and gatekeeper training. Awareness/ education curricula and skills training tend to be delivered as universal interventions, whereas screening, gatekeeper training, and peer leadership are geared toward selected or indicated prevention approaches (Robinson et al., 2013). A review of community-based suicide prevention programs found strong evidence for the effectiveness of student curriculum, combined student curriculum and gatekeeper training, and competence programs (York et al., 2013). Concerns have been raised that awareness/ education curricula in schools focusing on suicide prevention may increase knowledge about suicide among students but there may be potential for students who are already distressed to be negatively affected by the program content (Shaffer & Gould, 2008).

**Figure 15.8:** Early in human life, there is great opportunity to shape health and social outcomes throughout the lifecourse.

*Source:* Feryal Almazni, Photographer

---

### Box 15.5: Preventing Suicide in Inuit Communities

As mentioned in Chapter 9, suicide is a public health issue that disproportionately affects Aboriginal people in Nunavut. The suicide rate in Nunavut, a territory that has a predominately Inuit population, is 13.5 times higher than the average suicide rate in Canada. This distressingly high statistic prompted the territory of Nunavut to declare suicide a public health emergency in 2015. The high suicide rate among the Inuit people is partially due to socio-economic factors, such as the high poverty rate, low levels of education, housing issues, and the high rate of unemployment. However, factors that are specific to the Inuit population have also been identified, including intergenerational trauma due to historical events within the community and a lack of coping skills. In order to prevent suicide within the Inuit community, programs and strategies must be culturally relevant and sensitive to the specific and diverse needs of this population. Drawing from the traditional knowledge of elders in Inuit communities, the National Aboriginal Health Organization Ajunnginig Centre identified coping skills that are particularly important in Inuit culture. These include helping others as a way of promoting connection and a sense of purpose; paying attention to each other's needs; being productive, active, and healthy; talking things out and solving conflicts with others; and accepting that life is not always easy but that tomorrow can be better. Elders in the Inuit community believe that, along with these coping and resilience skills, values used in the community in the past including patience, perseverance, caring, communication, awareness of self and others, and respect for others are still relevant to the community (Inuit Tapiriit Kanatami, 2015).

## Science and Research

Science and research provide us with the important means to create and test new knowledge, including the identification and understanding of effective approaches to build resilience, prevent and treat illness, reduce harm, and use our societal resources in the most effective and efficient ways possible. Neuroscientists study the brain and the many fascinating mental functions (discussed in Chapter 2), including wakefulness/arousal, sensation and perception, thought, memory, and so forth. Despite the daunting challenge of making sense of what may be the most complex and elegant apparatus in existence, neuroscientists continue to make strides in revealing the fascinating mysteries of the human brain. A host of scientists work to expand our understanding of the intricate biological mechanisms that are involved in mental function and physiological responses to psychoactive substances, focusing on anatomy, physiology, chemistry, pharmacology, molecular biology, genetics, and other biological sciences. However, scientific research relevant to mental health and substance use goes beyond laboratory studies done by scientists in white coats using microscopes and test tubes. Social scientists, applying many approaches and disciplinary traditions, such as psychology, sociology, anthropology, criminology, and others, also contribute important knowledge; only a brief survey of some of the more prominent findings by social scientists relevant to mental health were presented in Chapter 3.

The Canadian Institutes of Health Research, which is the Government of Canada agency responsible for funding health research in Canada, recognizes four pillars of research. Table 15.2 lists these four pillars and notes examples of the type of research that may be conducted. Basic and biomedical research produces findings about the fundamental mechanisms that are involved in mental function. Although most basic research studies are incremental, slowly adding small pieces of information to solve a large jigsaw puzzle, such research has the potential to occasionally create breakthroughs with the potential to eliminate disease and create radical improvements. Clinical research is needed to make advances in treatment and often focuses on the development and evaluation of new treatments for various conditions, such as depression, anxiety disorders, schizophrenic disorders, dementia, and so on. In recent decades, clinical research in mental health has tended to focus excessively on pharmacological studies, and we return to discuss a re-balancing of this bias later in this chapter. Health services and policy research produces knowledge about improved approaches to the delivery of services and the advancement of policies that govern our collective efforts. Population health research addresses the determinants of health and attitudes and provides understanding of how various social systems relate to health, often drawing on social science, public health, and epidemiological research traditions.

**Table 15.2: The four pillars of research**

| Research pillar | Examples of type of research |
|---|---|
| Basic science/biomedical | Molecular studies; neuropharmacological studies |
| Clinical | Clinical trials; clinical conceptual studies |
| Health services and policy | Examination of costs and outcomes of service; evaluation of efforts to improve access to and delivery of services |
| Population health | Social and cultural impacts on the health of the population; preventive strategies |

*Source:* Adapted from the Canadian Institutes of Health Research.

In conducting scientific research of any kind, careful attention to ethics is of great importance. Since some people with mental health problems may be vulnerable due to emotional distress or difficulties in thinking or perception, ethical conduct of research that involves such individuals is of particular concern. Research studies associated with universities and other public institutions are required to undergo ethical review and obtain approval by research ethics boards.

An important advance in mental health research has been the development of participatory action research and the recognition and inclusion of lived experience as an important contributor to advances in understanding mental health and illness. In the past, research tended to be undertaken on "subjects" who played a passive role and had no opportunity to contribute meaningfully to the design of research studies or the analysis or interpretation of research findings. Many community-based research activities are participatory and action-based and emphasize full involvement of people with lived experience of mental illness in the creation of new knowledge.

Scientific research provides valuable evidence to inform good policy decisions and improvements that governments and health care systems might adopt. In addition, researchers are continually providing new knowledge that can help clinicians to provide better treatment, and to inform people with mental health problems, and their family members, about how to optimize recovery.

## Knowledge Translation and Mobilization

**Knowledge translation and mobilization** can be defined as "closing the gap between what we know and what we do" (Graham & Tetroe, 2009, p. 46). The concepts of "push" and "pull" are also important in understanding knowledge translation and mobilization. "Push" refers to efforts to enhance the movement of knowledge from those who generate knowledge outward to those who may be able to benefit from its utilization. It involves gathering, synthesizing, and funnelling high quality information. Push strategies may involve scientific publications, reports, systematic reviews, guidelines, online materials, conference presentations, courses, webinars, educational outreach, prompts, social marketing efforts, financial incentives, and media campaigns. Knowledge is "pulled" when health care providers, policy-makers, or patients seek out the knowledge that is needed to guide their actions. Such efforts can be facilitated by effective search tools that can locate high quality information, access to knowledge syntheses and databases, training in the identification and application of research findings in decision making, critical appraisal skill development, and creation of rapid response units and government-university liaisons (Goldner, 2014).

An important aspect of knowledge translation and mobilization involves fostering health literacy, that is, the ability of individuals to access and use health information to make appropriate health decisions to maintain good health. This has been identified as a critical factor for improved health outcomes (Canadian Council on Learning, 2007) and is consistent with the Recovery Model that has been identified as a valuable framework for mental health (see Chapter 14).

## Advocacy and Involvement

We believe that excellent opportunities exist to improve Canada's mental health "system" and mental health globally; however, many people will need to contribute. We also believe that each of us has unique strengths and abilities to contribute, regardless of our age, education, experience, or background. In the following, we list a series of opportunities for advocacy (i.e., active support of an idea, cause, or issue); these are different ways in which you might become involved. You may be interested in more than one of these activities.

1.  *Help address the social determinants of mental health—poverty, housing, education, and so on.* Despite Canada's status as a relatively wealthy country, there are many groups of people who are marginalized and living in poverty. Recognizing the social gradient that exists within Canadian society in regard to mental health, we need to help individuals in need. Since, as a whole, we are a relatively wealthy and fortunate group of people in Canada, we also have a social responsibility as global citizens to help populations of low-income countries. Canadians have a social responsibility to share the considerable expertise we have gained in research, education, and other service delivery.

2.  *Contribute to public policy activities related to mental health and substance use.* This can be accomplished either through political activities and advocacy efforts, such as lobbying decision-makers, or by working or volunteering within government or other organizations that contribute to policy development and implementation.

3.  *Help address human rights and other legal issues relevant to mental health and substance use.* Opportunities exist to become involved in legal societies and human rights activities that are geared to help people who may be vulnerable on the basis of mental illness or substance use.

4.  *Contribute to mental health promotion or to prevention or treatment of mental illness or substance use disorder.* There are various ways to become involved in such activities, either as part of the formal health care work force or through more informal or volunteer efforts. A wide range of skills and talents can be put to use, with particular roles drawing on certain strengths and virtues.

5.  *Contribute to research endeavours.* A wide range of research activities are underway and there are many contributions to be made by people with various skills, whether these are related to expanding knowledge through biological, social, or other scientific traditions or through research that applies lived experience.

6.  *Become active in knowledge translation and mobilization.* There are unlimited opportunities to exchange valuable knowledge about mental health and help move knowledge to action that results in improvements to mental health. Once again, such activities can be done as part of formal organizational activities or undertaken in more informal, individual efforts.

We hope you will find some areas that excite your interest and enthusiasm and that you will become engaged in action to enhance mental health outcomes in Canada. The Mental Health Commission of Canada intends to create more opportunities for people across Canada to become involved and we hope you will do so!

# Conclusion

In Chapter 1, we signalled the value of a broad approach to mental health in Canada, one that goes "from synapse to society" and avoids the reductionism that often undermines successful collaborative efforts. The population and public health perspective focuses on opportunities to make improvements at the population level, including those that focus on policies, laws, and government-supported initiatives. A strengths-based approach is consistent with a health promotion perspective; such an approach constitutes a significant shift to the delivery of mental health services that, in the past, has tended to focus on pathology and illness. We have described opportunities to foster improvements in Canada's mental health system by addressing social determinants of mental health; contributing to public policy activities; addressing human rights and other legal issues; contributing to mental health promotion, and to prevention and treatment of mental health problems; contributing to research; and becoming involved in knowledge exchange.

---

# Glossary

**demand reduction:** Efforts to reduce the desire and preparedness to obtain and use drugs by potential consumers, including education, prevention and treatment programs, and social pressures, and deterrents.

**harm reduction:** An approach aimed at reducing the harmful consequences of drug use and other high-risk activities.

**indicated prevention:** Prevention strategies targeted at high-risk individuals who are identified as having minimal but detectable signs or symptoms.

**knowledge translation and mobilization:** Refers to the *push* and *pull* found in the multiple directional movement of data, information, and knowledge between individuals and groups for mutual benefit.

**population health:** The health of the population, as measured by health status indicators, and as influenced by social, economic, and physical environments, personal health practices, individual capacity and coping skills, human biology, early childhood development, health services, and gender and culture.

**prohibition:** Policy in which the possession, selling, or marketing of a substance is made illegal.

**public health:** The science and art of preventing disease, prolonging life, and promoting health through the organized efforts and informed choices of society, organizations, communities, and individuals.

**selective prevention:** Prevention strategies that target subgroups of the population whose risk of developing a mental disorder is significantly higher than average.

**supply reduction:** Efforts to decrease the availability of drugs through means such as the arrest and prosecution of drug suppliers.

**universal prevention:** Prevention strategies that target entire populations.

## Critical Thinking Questions

1. Identify ways in which public policy can address mental health and substance use.
2. What is harm reduction, and why has it been a controversial approach?
3. Using the classified prevention strategies discussed in this chapter, highlight ways in which mental illness and substance use can be prevented.
4. Citing specific examples, explain why science and research is important in improving mental health systems and service delivery.
5. How can we improve the mental health system and the mental health of our population?

## Recommended Readings

Babor, T.F., Caulkins, J.P., Edwards, G., Fischer, B., Foxcroft, D.R., Humphreys, K., Obot, I.S., Rehm, J., Reuter, P., Room, R., Rossow, I., & Strang, J. (2010). *Drug Policy and the Public Good*. New York: Oxford University Press.

Jenkins, R., Meltzer, H., Jones, P.B., Brugha, T., Bebbington, P., Farrell, M., Crepaz Keay, D., & Knapp, M. (2008). *Mental Capital and Wellbeing: Making the Most of Ourselves in the 21st Century*. London: Government Office for Science.

Tengland, P.A. (2013). *Mental Health: A Philosophical Analysis*. New York: Springer Science & Business Media.

World Health Organization. *The WHO Mental Health Policy and Service Guidance Package*. Retrieved from www.who.int/mental_health/policy/essentialpackage1/en/index.html

World Health Organization. (2005). *The WHO Resource Book on Mental Health, Human Rights and Legislation*. Geneva: WHO. Retrieved from http://www.who.int/mental_health/policy/legislation/Resource%20Book_Eng2_WEB_07%20(2).pdf

## Recommended Websites

Canadian Mental Health Association. Mental Health Promotion Toolkit. www.cmha.ca/download.php?docid=270

Canadian Mental Health Association of Ontario. Legislation. www.ontario.cmha.ca/legislation.asp

Mental Health Commission of Canada. www.mentalhealthcommission.ca/

UK Mental Health Policy. www.mentalhealth.freeuk.com/uk.htm

World Health Organization. Mental Health. www.who.int/mental_health/en/

# References

Brown, L. (2013). Queen's Park earmarks $27 million to tackle mental health issues on Ontario campuses. *The Toronto Star*.

Canadian Centre on Substance Abuse. (2015). Canadian drug summary: Cannabis. Retrieved from www.ccsa.ca/Resource Library/CCSA-Canadian-Drug-Summary-Cannabis-2015-en.pdf

Canadian Council on Learning. (2007). *Health literacy in Canada: Initial results from the International Adult Literacy and Skills Survey 2007*. Ottawa: Author.

Centres for Disease Control and Prevention. (1995). Injury-control recommendations: Bicycle helmets. *Morbidity and Mortality Weekly Report*, 44, 1–18.

Conduct Problems Prevention Research Group. (2000). Merging universal and indicated prevention programs: The Fast Track Model. *Addictive Behaviors*, 25, 913–927.

Dadds, M.R., Holland, D., Barrett, P.M., Laurens, K., & Spence, S. (1999). Early intervention and prevention of anxiety disorders in children: Results at 2-year follow-up. *Journal of Consulting and Clinical Psychology*, 67(1), 145–150.

Delange, F., de Benoist, B., Pretell, E., & Dunn, J.T. (2001). Iodine deficiency in the world: Where do we stand at the turn of the century? *Thyroid*, 11(5), 437–447.

European Monitoring Centre for Drugs and Drug Addiction. (2010). Harm reduction: Evidence, impacts and challenges. Retrieved from www.emcdda.europa.eu/publications/monographs/harm-reduction

Freedman, L.S. (1984). Initial assessment of the effect of the compulsory use of seat belts on car occupants' injuries, and the trauma department work-load. *Injury*, 16(1), 60–62.

Graham, I.D., & Tetroe, J.M. (2009). Getting evidence into policy and practice: Perspective of a health research funder. *Journal of the Canadian Academy of Child and Adolescent Psychiatry*, 18(1), 46–50.

Goldner, E.M. (2014). Knowledge translation. In K.L. Bassil & D.M. Zabkiewicz (Eds.), *Health research methods: A Canadian perspective* (pp. 251–278). Don Mills, ON: Oxford University Press.

Health Canada. (2005). Canadian addiction survey: A national survey of Canadians' use of alcohol and other drugs. Retrieved from http://www.ccsa.ca/Resource%20Library/ccsa-004028-2005.pdf

Inuit Tapiriit Kanatami. (2015). Inuit approaches to suicide prevention. Retrieved from www.itk.ca/inuit-approaches-suicide-prevention

Jenkins, R., Meltzer, H., Jones, P.B., Brugha, T., Bebbington, P., Farrell, M., Crepaz Keay, D., &

Peterson, C., & Seligman, M. (2004). *Character strengths and virtues: A handbook and classification*. New York: Oxford University Press.

Prince, M., Patel, V., Saxena, S., Maj, M., Maselko, J., Phillips, M.R., & Raham, A. (2007). No health without mental health. *The Lancet*, 370(9590), 859–877.

Public Health Agency of Canada. (2008). Folic acid and prevention of neural tube defects. Retrieved from www.phac-aspc.gc.ca/fa-af/fa-af08-eng.php

Rehm, J., Gnam, W.H., Popova, S., Patra, J., & Sarnocinska-Hart, A. (2008). Avoidable costs of alcohol abuse in Canada 2002. Centre for Addiction and Mental Health. Retrieved from www.researchgate.net/publication/49676020_Avoidable_Cost_of_Alcohol_Abuse_in_Canada

Robinson, J., Cox, G., Malone, A., Williamson, M., Baldwin, G., Fletcher, K., & O'Brien, M. (2013). A systematic review of school-based interventions aimed at preventing, treating, and responding to suicide-related behavior in young people. *Crisis: The Journal of Crisis Intervention and Suicide Prevention, 34*(3), 164–182.

Saraceno, B., & Barbui, C. (1997). Poverty and mental illness. *Canadian Journal of Psychiatry, 42*, 285–290.

Shaffer, D., & Gould, M. (2008). Suicide prevention in schools. In K. Hawton & K. van Heeringen (Eds.), *The international handbook of suicide and attempted suicide.* West Sussex, England: John Wiley & Sons. doi: 10.1002/9780470698976.ch37

Stockwell, T., Gruenewald, P., Toumbourou, J., & Loxley, W. (Eds.). (2005). *Preventing harmful substance use.* Hoboken, NJ: John Wiley & Sons.

Thornton, T. (1991). Alcohol prohibition was a failure. *Cato Institute Policy Analysis, 157,* 1–12. Retrieved from www.cato.org/pub_display.php?pub_id=1017

Tramont, E.C. (1995). Syphilis in adults: From Christopher Columbus to Sir Alexander Fleming to AIDS. *Clinical Infectious Diseases, 21,* 1361–1369.

World Health Organization. (2008). Integrating mental health into primary care: A global perspective. Retrieved from www.who.int/mental_health/policy/Integratingmhintoprimarycare2008_lastversion.pdf

York, J., Lamis, D.A., Friedman, L., Berman, A.L., Joiner, T.E., Mcintosh, J.L., Silverman, M.M, Konick, L., Gutierrez, P.M., & Pearson, J., (2013). A systematic review process to evaluate suicide prevention programs: A sample case of community-based programs. *Journal of Community Psychology, 41*(1), 35–51.

# COPYRIGHT
# ACKNOWLEDGEMENTS

## Figures

Figure 1.1: © zmeel / iStockphoto

Figure 1.3: © Judy Waytiuk / Alamy

Figure 1.4: © Charline Xia / GetStock

Figure 1.5: © topham Picture Point / GetStock

Figure 1.6: Republished with permission of © SAGE publications, from Lesage, A.D., Morissette, R., Fortier, L., Reinharz, D., & Contandriopoulos, A-P. (2000). Downsizing psychiatric hospitals: Needs for care and services of current and discharged longstay inpatients. *Canadian Journal of Psychiatry*, 45(6), 526–531; permission conveyed through Copyright Clearance Center, Inc.

Figure 1.7: © Statistics Canada. (2015). Table 105-0592—*Health indicator profile, annual estimates, by age group and sex, Canada, provinces, territories, health regions (2013–2014 boundaries) and peer groups, occasional*, CANSIM (database). Retrieved from http://www5.statcan.gc.ca/cansim/a26?lang=eng&retrLang=eng&id=1050592&&pattern=&stByVal=1&p1=1&p2=31&tabMode=dataTable&csid=

Figure 1.8-1.10: © Mental Health Commission of Canada. (2013). Making the case for investing in mental health in Canada, p. 8. Retrieved from www.mentalhealthcommission.ca/English/ system/files/private/document/Investing_in_Mental_Health_FINAL_Version_ENG.pdf

Figure 2.1: © Nucleus Medical Art Inc / GetStock

Figure 2.2: © Xiaofeng Luo / iStockphoto

Figure 2.3: © ktsimage / iStockphoto

Figure 2.4: © Nicky Gordon / iStockphoto

Figure 2.5: Republished with permission of © John Wiley & Sons, Inc, from Tortora, G., & Grabowski, S.R. (2002). *Principles of anatomy and physiology* (10th ed.). Hoboken, NJ: John Wiley & Sons, 508.

Figure 2.7: © luismmolina / iStockphoto

Figure 2.8: Martini, F.H. (2004). *Fundamentals of anatomy and physiology* (6th ed.). San Francisco, CA: Pearson Education Inc. (Benjamin Cummings), 59. Copyright © Pearson Education Inc.

Figure 2.9: © Brenden Westman
Figure 3.1: © Joe Cicak / iStockphoto
Figure 3.2: © Nicole S. Young / iStockphoto
Figure 3.3: © skynesher / iStockphoto
Figure 3.4: © iStockphoto
Figure 3.5: Republished with permission of © Proceedings of the National Academy of Sciences of the United States of America, from Kahneman, D., & Deaton, A. (2010). High income improves evaluation of life but not emotional well-being. *Proceedings of the National Academy of Sciences of the United States of America*, 107(38), 16489–16493. doi: 10.1073/pnas.1011492107.
Figure 3.6: © Steve Geer / iStockphoto
Figure 3.7: Adapted from Street to Home Foundation. (2014). *Street to Home 2014 Annual Report*. Vancouver: Street to Home Foundation, p. 4. Data from 2014 City of Vancouver Homeless Count. Retrieved March 31, 2016 from http://streetohome.org/about-streetohome/annual-report. Copyright © Metro Vancouver.
Figure 3.8: © Soroush Moallef
Figure 4.1: © Wikimedia Commons / gruntzooki
Figure 4.2: © Chris Sang Yeon Park
Figure 4.3: © BraunS / iStockphoto
Figure 4.4: © Ximagination / iStockphoto
Figure 4.5: © iulianvalentin / iStockphoto
Figure 4.6: © Maks08 / iStockphoto
Figure 5.1: © Martin McCarthy / iStockphoto
Figure 5.2: © Stephanie Horrocks / iStockphoto
Figure 5.4: © Palangsi / GetStock
Figure 5.5: © Chris Sang Yeon Park
Figure 5.6: © Brasil2 / iStockphoto
Figure 5.7: © Mlenny / iStockphoto
Figure 5.8: © KarenMower / iStockphoto
Figure 5.9: © ermingut / iStockphoto
Figure 5.10: © ANKORS, from www.ankorsvolunteer.com
Figure 6.1: © Sheffield Newspapers, from *The Star* (2004)
Figure 6.2: © Overture Films.
Figure 6.3: © topham Picture Point / GetStock
Figure 6.4: © David H. Lewis / iStockphoto
Figure 7.1: © Gary Wales / iStockphoto
Figure 7.2: © Feryal Almazni
Figure 7.3: © &#169 isabelle Limbach / iStockphoto
Figure 7.4: © Jani Bryson / iStockphoto
Figure 7.5: © BraunS / iStockphoto
Figure 7.6: © Cassidy Jones
Figure 7.7: © ViewApart / iStockphoto

perspectives (p. 9). Journal of the American Psychiatric Nurses Association, 6(1), 3–10.

Figure 14.6: © technotr / iStockphoto

Figure 14.7: © iStockphoto

Figure 14.8: © Rich Legg / iStockphoto

Figure 15.1: © Chris Sang Yeon Park

Figure 15.2: © Archives of Ontario

Figure 15.3: © tillsonburg / iStockphoto

Figure 15.4: © Vancouver Coastal Health

Figure 15.5: © Feryal Almanzi

Figure 15.6: © Alana Pineault

Figure 15.7: © Chris Sang Yeon Park

Figure 15.8: © Feryal Almanzi

## Tables

Table 3.1: Cramer, C., Flynn, B. and LaFave, A. (1997). Erik Erikson's 8 Stages of Psychosocial Development: Summary Chart. Retrieved November 23, 2010 from: http://web.cortland.edu/andersmd/ERIK/sum.HTML

Table 3.3: Sareen, J., Afifi, T. O., McMillan, K. A., & Asmundson, G. J. G. (2011). Relationship between household income and mental disorders: Findings from a population-based longitudinal study. *Archives of General Psychiatry*, 68(4), 419-426. doi:10.1001/archgenpsychiatry.2011.15

Table 4.1: Adapted from © World Health Organization. (1992). The ICD 10 classification of mental and behavioural disorders. Retrieved June 24, 2010, from www.who.int/classifications/icd/en/GRNBOOK.pdf

Table 5.1: Adapted from Csiernik, R. (2016). *Substance Use and Abuse: Everything Matters*. Second edition. Copyright © Canadian Scholars' Press.

Table 7.1: Gardner, H., & Hatch, T. (1989). Multiple intelligences go to school: Educational implications of the theory of multiple intelligences (p. 6). *Educational Researcher*, 18(8), 4–10.

Table 7.2: Peterson, C., & Seligman, M. (2004). *Character Strengths and Virtues: A Handbook and Classification*. New York: Oxford University Press.

Table 9.1: Adapted from © Statistics Canada. (2006). Ethnic origins, 2006 counts, for Canada, provinces and territories—20% sample data. Retrieved from www12.statcan.ca/census-recensement/2006/dp-pd/hlt/97562/pages/page.cfm?Lang=E&Geo=PR&Code=01&
Data=Count&Table=2&StartRec=1&Sort=3&Display=All&CSDFilter=5000

Table 10.1: Adapted from © Central Intelligence Agency (2009). Country comparisons: Life expectancy at birth. *The World Factbook*. Retrieved from www.cia.gov/library/publications/the-world-factbook/rankorder/2102rank.html

Table 14.1: Chart created by Elliot Goldner and based on information from article by Krause, T.R. & Weekly, T. (2005). A four-factor model for establishing a high-functioning organization. *Professional Safety*, 50(11), 31-41.
Table 15.2: Adapted from © Canadian Institutes of Health Research.

## Boxes

Box 4.2: © *The Globe and Mail*, June 20, 2008
Box 6.1: Kirby, M. J. L. & Keon, W. J. (2006). Out of the shadows at last: Transforming mental health, mental illness and addiction services in Canada. Copyright © The Standing Senate Committee on Social Affairs, Science and Technology.
Box 6.2: Copyright © Guarding Minds @ Work. Gilbert, Bilsker, Shain & Samra, 2012.
Box 7.1: Excerpted from Sullivan, P. (n.d.). Can yuppies bear children? Retrieved April 12, 2015 from http://daycareinfo.net/canyup.htm. Site no longer active.
Box 7.6: Adapted from © Roots of Empathy. (2016). About our program. Retrieved April 20, 2016, from http://www.rootsofempathy.org/en/what-we-do.html
Box 13.1: Excerpted from © Mental Health Commission of Canada. (2012). *Changing Directions, Changing Lives: The Mental Health Strategy for Canada*. Ottawa, Ontario. Retrieved April 20, 2016 from http://strategy.mentalhealthcommission.ca/pdf/strategy-images-en.pdf

# INDEX

AA. *See* Alcoholics Anonymous
Aboriginal peoples, 7–8, 197–205
  alcohol and, 104, 201–202
  assimilation of, 201
  colonialism and, 197
  depression and, 201
  discrimination toward, 129
  disease and, 197–198.
  elders, 210
  mental health of, 201–202
  residential schools and, 57
  solvent use and, 112
  spiritual and philosophical framework
    of, 78
  substance use and, 201
  suicide and, 202
  tobacco and, 104
Aboriginal status, as social determinant of
  health, 59
absenteeism, 131
absolute deprivation theory, 60
absolute-deprivation hypothesis, 49
abuse
  of children, 155–156, 302
  elder, 215, 229
  emotional, 215
  financial, 215
  physical, 215
  sexual, 155, 181
accessibility, principle of, 280
accidents, large-scale, 246
accommodations, workplace, 136
acculturation, 193–194, 206
achievement, men and, 179–180

action goals, 267
adaptive learning, 50
addiction, 101, 119, 245, 303
  vicious cycle of, 245
adenosine triphosphate (ATP), 36–37
adjustment disorders, 85
Adler, Alfred, 48, 126, 190
administrators, role of, 313
adolescence
  behavioural problems in, 90
  cannabis use and, 88
  depression in, 332
  as developmental stage, 52–53, 156–158
  education and, 147
  neurodevelopment and, 24
  as "psychosis," 156
  risks of, 156
adrenal glands, 40–41
adrenaline, 40
adulthood
  as developmental stage, 52–53
  transition to, 158
advocacy, 337–339
affective disorders, 84
Afghanistan, 57
Africa, sub-Saharan, life expectancy in, 210
African Americans, 126
age
  benefits of, 210–211
  discrimination on basis of, 124
  stereotypes based on, 126
aged, homes for, 226
ageism, 215, 229
aggression, men and, 179

agoraphobia, 85
agranulocytosis, 255
AIDS, 210
akathisia, 255
alcohol
    Aboriginal peoples and, 104, 201–202
    black market in, 325
    burden of disease and, 16
    dependence on, 244
    divergent opinions about, 103
    driving and, 326
    effects of on brain, 96
    genetic factors and, 104
    harms caused by, 324
    legal status of, 324
    men and, 182
    metabolism of, 104
    minimum age for, 324
    modest use of, 96
    morbidity, 103
    prohibition of, 103, 323–325
    risks and harms of, 103
    taxes for, 324
    use of, 4, 24, 55, 99, 104, 115, 135,
        219, 220
    withdrawal from, 241
alcohol consumption, in pregnancy, 150
Alcoholics Anonymous (AA), 261, 305
aldehyde dehydrogenase, 104
alkaloids, 97
Allen, Woody, 169, 215
Alzheimer's disease, 27, 80, 220, 226, 229
    treatment of, 222–223
Alzheimer's Society of Canada, 224
American Psychiatric Association, 74
amobarbital, 111
amphetamines, prohibition of, 323
anandamide, 105
Anderssen, Erin, "The Son Who
    Vanished," 82–84
animals, research on, 49
ANKORS Harm-Reduction Services, 114
anomie, 55, 66
anorexia nervosa, 86, 87, 305
anorgasmia, 176

anosognosia, 32
anthropology, 190, 336
anti-anxiety medication, 119
    women and, 180
Antidepressant Skills @ Work, 135
antidepressants, 24, 137, 255–256, 301
    elderly and, 227
    over-prescription of, 256
    sexual dysfunction and, 177
    side effects of, 180
    tricyclic, 255
    women and, 180
anti-discrimination, 129
anti-psychiatry protests, 59–60
antipsychotic medications, 12, 24, 239,
    243, 254–255, 301
    "atypical," 255
    first-generation, 254–255
    second-generation, 255
    side effects of, 255
anti-Semitism, 128
anti-social personality disorder, 87
    prenatal development and, 150
anti-social tendencies, 44, 332
anxiety, 1, 12, 41, 48, 55, 80, 131, 135, 137
    men and, 182
    poverty and, 320
    prevalence of, 14–15
    sexual dysfunction and, 176
    sexual orientation and,142
    stress and, 236
    treatment for, 256, 258, 284
    women and, 180–181
    in youth, 160
anxiety disorder, 43, 56
anxiety disorders, 16, 85, 300, 336
    children and, 332
    treatment for, 255
anxiolytics, 111, 137
Applied Behaviour Analysis, 163
archetypes, 48
Arctic hysteria, 197
arithmetic impairment, 90
arousal, 27–28
art therapy, 303

Asia
    alcohol use in, 87
    suicide in, 56
Asperger's syndrome, 163
assimilation, 201
asylums, residential, 9, 10
At Home/Chez Soi, 63
ATP. *See* adenosine triphosphate
attachment theory, 152, 164
attention deficit disorder, 78, 162, 164
attitude, workplace, 131
Australia, mental health care services in,
    294
Autism Spectrum Disorder (ASD), 27, 90,
    162
    childhood, 311
autonomy, 155, 240, 307
    men and, 179
    vs. shame/doubt, 52, 155
avoidance behaviour, 101
avoidant personality disorder, 87

B vitamins, 39
Baby Boomers, 56
balance, workplace, 133
barbiturates, 111
    withdrawal from, 241
bedwetting, 162
behaviour
    individual and group, 47–51
    "normal," 54
    patterns of, 32–33
    suicidal, 48
behaviour therapy, 49–50
behavioural disorders, 87–89
    in childhood and adolescence, 90, 160
    physiological/physical, 86–87
    substance use and, 80–81
benzodiazepines, 111, 256
    dependence and withdrawal, 256
Berton, Pierre, 211
Bhutan, 62–63, 63
Bigelow, Jesse, 82–84
bigotry, 128
binary, 170
binge eating disorder, 86

bingeing, 115
biological embedding, 150
biological foundations, 23–37
biological perspective, 6
biological sex, 172
biological theories, 116
biology, influence of, 5
bipolar, 15
bipolar disorder, 84, 87, 237, 243
    prevalence of, 14–15
    treatment of, 256
birth cohorts, 56, 66
bisexuality, 173
blood glucose, 37
blood pressure, high. *See* hypertension
blood-alcohol concentration, 324
blood-brain barrier, 37, 43, 96
Blumenbach, Johann, *On the Natural
    Varieties of Mankind*, 190
bodily changes, women and, 180–181
bodily-kinesthetic intelligence, 149
body shape and weight, women and, 181
bondage, 88
borderline personality disorder, 263
Bowlby, John, 152
brain, 23–26
    abnormalities of, 9
    alcohol and, 96
    amygdala, 31–32
    cannabis and, 105
    cellular activity in, 36
    cerebellum, 31
    cerebral cortex, 29, 80
    cerebral hemispheres, 30–31, 43
    cingulate gyrus, 31
    cocaine and, 132
    as computer hardware, 4
    damage to, 78
    dementia and, 220
    functions of, 24–30
    hippocampus, 31–32
    hypothalamus, 23, 31, 40
    injury to, 301, 332
    left and right halves of, 42
    limbic system, 31
    memory loss and, 219

mind vs., 4–5
motor cortex, 30
neuroscientists and, 335
nucleus accumbens, 31
nutrients of, 37
opium and, 96
plaques in, 220, 229
plasticity of, 42–43, 146
pregnancy and, 150
psychoactive substances and, 96
regenerativity of, 42
reticular formation, 27
shock absorbers in, 39
tangles in, 220, 229
thalamus, 31
tobacco and, 87
brain disorders, 27
Brain Research through Advancing
  Innovative Neurotechnologies
  (BRAIN), 27
Brasfield, Charles, 57
breathing, regulation of, 29
brief dynamic therapy, 263
British Columbia, health authorities in, 284
Buddhism, 266
bulimia nervosa, 86
  treatment for, 262
bullying, 156, 164
buprenorphine, 256
burden of disease, 15, 16
bureaucrats, role of, 313–314
burnout, 131, 308–309, 309
Burton, Andrew, 148

caffeine, 28, 31, 106
  high use of, 106
Cameron, Dr. Ewen, 112
Canada
  armed forces, substance use in, 57
  Constitution Act, 199
  Controlled Drugs and Substances Act,
    323, 327
  educational institutions in, 148
  elderly people, proportion of in, 209,
    227–228
  Federal Tobacco Control Strategy, 105

federally funded mental health services,
  282–285
health care insurance plans and delivery
  systems in, 282–285
impact of substance use in, 116–118
Indian Act, 199
life expectancy in, 209
mental health services in, 279–294
mental health strategy for, 291–293
Minister of Health, 327
political and economic stability of, 56
prohibition in, 103
provincial and territorial health care
  services, 282–284
Senate Standing Committee report on
  mental health, 2, 309
structure of health care services in,
  280–285
suicide rates in, 183
Supreme Court, 200, 327
Canada Health Act, 280–282, 295
Canadian Centre on Substance Abuse
  (CCSA), 285
Canadian Community Health Survey
  (CCHS), 15
Canadian Institutes for Health Research
  (CIHR), 169, 285, 336
Canadian Mental Health Association, 123
Canadian National Physician Survey, 287
Canadian Public Health Association, 104
Canadian Study of Health and Aging
  (CSHA), 211, 219
cannabis, 105–106
  black market in, 324
  criminalization of, 324
  decriminalization of, 324
  harms, 105
  prohibition of, 323
  rates of use of, 105
  risks and benefits of, 106
  use of, 324
caregivers, 224–225, 288, 312–313
Carey, Henry Charles, 47
CBT. See Cognitive Behavioural Therapy
CCSA. See Canadian Centre on Substance
  Abuse

Centre for Addiction and Mental Health
    (Toronto), 83
cerebral hemispheres, 32
cerebrospinal fluid, 39
*Changing Directions, Changing Lives:*
    *The Mental Health Strategy for Canada,*
    292–294
character, 160, 164
    virtues of, 160, 328–329
Charles, Ray, 111
chemotherapy, 326
child mortality, 147
child poverty, rates in Canada, 144
child protection/welfare law, 302
childbirth, mental health and, 181
childhood, as developmental stage, 154–156
childhood/children
    abuse in, 155–156
    acculturation and, 193
    behavioural problems in, 90
    homelessness and, 146
    influence of, 5, 51
    maltreatment of, 155–156
    mental disorders in, 150–132
    mental health and illness in, 143–163
    poverty and, 147
    preventive strategies for, 332
    safety of, 302
    sexual abuse in, 156, 181
    social determinants of health and,
        144–149
    treatment for, 263
Children's Health Policy Centre, 153
chimpanzees, 143
    sexuality and, 178
China, opium addiction in, 110
chlorpromazine, 253, 254, 254
cholinesterase inhibitors, 226
chromosomes, 171–172
chronic pain, in older adults, 213
Churchill, Sir Winston, 211
Cialis, 176
CIHR. *See* Canadian Institutes for Health
    Research
CISD. *See* critical incident stress debriefing
Clark, Ramsey, 209

classical conditioning, 49–50, 66
client-centred care, 307–309
clinical psychologists, 301–302
clinical service providers, 300, 315
Clinton, Bill, 123
clozapine, 255
club drugs, 113
Cobain, Kurt, 111
coca plant, 107
Coca-Cola, 107
cocaine, 24, 31, 107–108
    crack, 108
    dependence on, 244
    freebase, 108
    health problems from, 108
    prohibition of, 323
codeine, 109
Cognitive Behavioural Therapy (CBT), 50,
    261, 262–263, 263, 266, 273
    post-traumatic stress disorder and, 245
    sexual dysfunction and, 144
    work-related mental health problems,
        136, 137
cognitive development, 147
cognitive impairment
    cannabis and, 106
    elderly and, 219–223
cognitive problems, 302
cohesion, family, 54
collaborative mental health care, 309–310
collective unconscious, 48–49, 66
Collins, Patricia Hill, 59
colonialism, 197, 202, 206
coma, 27
comedy, as therapy, 268
committal. *See* hospitalization, involuntary
communication, family, 54
communities of practice, 312
community treatment order, 239
community treatment services, 284
community-based recreational programs, 328
community-based research activities, 337
community-based services, 13, 303, 323
comorbidity, 303
compassion clubs, 326
compassion fatigue, 308, 308

comprehensiveness, principle of, 282
compulsive behaviours, 84, 162
concurrent disorders, 81, 242
conditioning
    classical, 50, 66
    instrumental, 50, 66
conduct disorder, 160, 164, 191
conflict
    family, 158
    workplace, 131
conventional morality, 53–54
convulsive therapy, 257
coping, 233–235, 248
    difficulties with, 236
Coping Model, 233
coping strategies, 234–235, 243, 248
    histrionic, 235
    obsessive-compulsive, 235, 236
correctional facilities, 290
cortisol, 41, 150–131
counselling, 137, 242, 300
    elderly and, 227
    pastoral, 265
    trauma management and, 246
courage, as character virtue, 160, 329
Craven, Marilyn, 309
Crazies, The, 127
Cree, 199, 200
Criminal Code of Canada, 289–290
criminal responsibility, 290, 322
criminology, 74, 190, 336
crisis, 233, 236–238, 248
    mental health and, 237–238
    vicious cycles of, 237
crisis interventions, 246
crisis lines, 240
crisis management, 241
crisis services, 240
crisis states, 236–237
    definition of, 236
critical incident stress debriefing (CISD), 246
crowds, madness of, 51
CSHA. See Canadian Study of Health and
    Aging
cultural idioms of distress, 196–197, 206

cultural relativity, 78
cultural safety, 204–205, 206
culture, 191, 206
    influence of, 5
culture-bound syndromes, 196–197
cyanocobalanin (vitamin B12), 39

DALY. See Disability Adjusted Life Years
darkness, 41
Darwin, Charles, 189
date rape drug, 111
DBT. See dialectical behaviour therapy
death, 217–218
    premature, 15
decision making, 307
decolonization, 204–205
deep brain stimulation, 259
deinstitutionalization, 11–12, 12–13, 255,
    305, 323
delirium, 80
delusional disorders, 82
delusions, 31, 82, 85, 244
    grandiose, 82
    paranoid, 82
    religious, 82
    schizophrenia and, 32
    treatment for, 254
demand reduction, 295, 324
dementia, 16, 80, 229, 300, 312, 336
    care for people with, 226
    causes of, 220
    in elderly, 219–222, 227–228
    prevalence of, 14–15, 16
    stages and progression of, 221–222
    vascular, 220
dental care, 282
dependence, 28, 82, 99, 119, 245
    physiological vs. psychological, 87, 101
depression, 1, 6–7, 12, 15, 16, 27, 56, 59,
    80, 131, 136, 137, 300, 336
    Aboriginal peoples and, 201
    burden of disease and, 16
    ECT and, 257
    elderly and, 217, 219, 227
    gender difference in prevalence rates, 180

men and, 182
poverty and, 320
prevalence of, 13
prevention of, 223
rates in men, 184
sexual dysfunction and, 176–145
sexual orientation and, 142
stigma and discrimination and, 126
stress and, 238
treatment of, 255–256, 261–262, 284
unipolar, 84
withdrawal and, 245–246
women and, 180–181
YLD and, 15
in youth, 160, 332
depressive disorder, 77
    major, 84, 87
    in youth, 160
"depth psychology," 48–49
despair, ego integrity vs., 52, 215
detainment, 322
detoxification (detox), 241, 244–245
    home, 242
development, mental health and, 51–54, 149–159
developmental disability, 89
developmental problems, 59
developmental stages, Erikson's, 52–53. See also Erikson, Erik
deviance, 78, 190
diabetes mellitus, 255, 305
diacetylmorphine hydrochloride. See heroin
Diagnostic and Statistical Manual of Mental Disorders (DSM), 74, 78
diagnostic categories, 78–79
diagnostic classification
    concerns about, 59–60
    consistency of, 60
    cultural relativity and, 78
    labelling and, 77–78
    political and economic misuses of, 78
    reliability of, 76–77
    systems of, 74
    validity of, 76–77
dialectical behaviour therapy (DBT), 262

diazepam, 111
dieticians, 303
disability
    aging and, 212–213, 227
    costs of, 130
    developmental, 302, 332
    discrimination on basis of, 124, 320
    focus on, 328
    stereotypes based on, 126
    workplace and, 107
Disability Adjusted Life Years (DALY), 15–16
"disabling environment," 132
disasters, responding to, 246–247
discrimination, 74, 78, 123–130, 138
    ageist, 215
    causes of, 126–129
    combating, 129–130
    definition of, 99
    foci of, 129
    gender, 180
    vs. non-discrimination, 124
    treatment and, 261
    in workplace, 130
disease, Aboriginal people and, 197–198 170
dissociatives, 95
distress, cultural idioms of, 196–197, 206
divalproex sodium, 256
DNA, 35–36
dogs, research on, 49
dopamine, 24, 107
    blocking of receptors in brain, 254–255
Douglas, Tommy, 281
drug purity test, 114
drug use, 55, 96. See also substance use
    adolescence and, 158
    injection, 326
    men and, 181
    non-injection, 327
drunkenness. See intoxication
Dufresne, Phillip, 125
Durkheim, Emile, 54–55
dying, death and, 217–218
dysthymic disorder, 255

dystonia, 255

early childhood development, 323
early childhood education, 147
early life, as social determinant of health,
    59, 147
eating disorders, 86, 300, 305
    prevalence of, 14–15
    treatment of, 261–262
    women and, 181
economy, influence of, 5, 56–58, 78
ecstasy, 109
ECT. *See* electroconvulsive therapy
education, 146–149, 154, 320, 323, 332,
    338
    benefits of, 147
    as social determinant of health, 59
educators, role of, 314
ego integrity vs. despair, 52, 217
elder abuse, 215, 229
elderly. *See* older adults
elders, Aboriginal, 210
elective mutism, 162
electroconvulsive therapy (ECT), 227,
    257, 273
    maintenance, 257
    side effects of, 257
emergency, 233
    mental health, 238–245
    psychotic, 243
    substance use, 244–245
    suicidal, 242–243
emergency departments, 300
emergency services, 284
emotion, 31–32
    women and, 179, 183
emotional well-being, 60–61
employment. *See also* workplace
    barriers to, 320
    discrimination in, 130, 215
    as social determinant of health, 59
    support for, 303
engagement, workplace, 133
England, mental health care services in, 294
entheogens, 112
environment

gender and, 180
    role of, 4
epidemiology, 14–18
    estimate of in Canada, 14–15
epigenetics, 35, 43
erectile dysfunction, 176
ergot, 112
Erikson, Erik, developmental stages of,
    52–53, 152, 154–155, 156, 215, 217
"Eskimo," use of term, 199
estrogen, 40
ethanol. *See* alcohol
ethics, 336
ethnic minorities, 195
ethnicity, 191, 206
    discrimination on basis of, 124
ethnocultural groups, 191
ethnocultural portrait of Canada, 192
exhibitionism, 88, 175
existential angst, 217
experience
    age and, 210–211
    lived, 313, 336
exposure therapy, 245
expropriation, 190
externalizing disorders, 160, 164
extrapyramidal symptoms, 254–255
extraversion, 33

"failure to launch," 158
families
    influence of, 5
    mental health and, 51–54
    support for, 302–303
    three dimensions of, 54
family caregivers, 312–313
family cohesion, 54
family communication, 54
family flexibility, 54
family intervention, 246
family physicians, 299–300, 309
family therapy, 264, 284, 303
FASD. *See* fetal alcohol spectrum disorder
Fast Track program, 332
fear, 29, 125
feminine stereotypes, 179–180, 180

feminist theory, 59
fentanyl, 151
fetal alcohol spectrum disorder (FASD), 150–151
fetal development, 149, 171, 331
fetishism, 88
fire-setting, pathological, 87
First Nations peoples, 7–8, 78, 104, 199–200, 202–205. *See also* Aboriginal peoples
  elders, 210
  health services for, 284
  racism and, 190–191
fitness to stand trial, 289, 295
flunitrazepam, 111
folic acid, 331
food security, as social determinant of health, 59
forensic mental health services, 289–290, 295
frailty, among older adults, 212–213
France, colonization by, 197
Francis, Allen, 75
free ride programs, 327
Freeman, Walter, 259
Freud, Sigmund, 10, 47–48, 179, 263
frontal lobe, 32
functional mental disorders, 75, 79

gambling, 84
  pathological, 87
gamma hydroxybutyrate (GHB), 111
gang membership, 193
ganja, 105
Gardner, Howard, 148
gay, lesbian, bisexual, and transgendered (GLBT) community, 175
Gay Pride events, 175
gay rights movement, 173–174
gay society, methamphetamine in, 109
gender, 169–184, 180, 184
  discrimination on basis of, 124
  vs. sex, 169–170
  as social determinant of health, 59
  stereotypes based on, 126

  variation within vs. variation across, 180
gender identity, 170, 172, 184
gender identity disorders, 88, 172
gender roles, 170, 172, 172, 184
  men and, 181–183
  mental health and, 179–183
  positive aspects of, 183
  women and, 180–181
generalized anxiety disorder, 15, 85
Generation X, 56
generativity vs. stagnation, 52
genes, 35
genetics, 35
  alcohol use and, 87
genital response, failure of, 176
genocide, 190
geriatricians, 303
GLBT. *See* gay, lesbian, bisexual, and transgendered community
glucose, 37
  deprivation, 149
  low blood, 39
glutamate, 24
goals, setting of, 267
good boy-nice girl orientation, 53–54
gorillas, 143
  sexuality and, 178
government bureaucrats, role of, 313–314
grandiose delusions, 82
grandparents, role of, 155, 211
Granirer, David, 268
Great Britain, colonization by, 197
Greece, rates of suicide in, 56
Greenland, 199
Greer, Germain, *Sex and Destiny*, 145
"greying population," 228
grief, elderly and, 226–227
Gross Domestic Product, 50
Gross National Happiness, 62–63
group behaviour, 47–51
group intervention programs, 332
Guarding Minds @ Work, 134
guilt, initiative vs., 52, 154

habit disorders, 87

Haiti, refugee camp in, 196
hallucinations, 82, 85, 113, 243
    schizophrenia and, 32
    treatment for, 254
harm prevention, 322
harm reduction, 295, 326–327
    critics of, 326–327
harm reductions, 114
hashish, 105
Headlines Theatre, *After Homelessness*, 323
health. *See also* health care services
    among elderly, 212–213, 227
    social determinants of, 58–59, 320,
        323, 336, 338
    social gradient in, 321, 338
health authorities, provincial and
    territorial, 282–284
Health Canada, 254, 285
health care insurance, 280
health care services. *See also* mental health
    care services
        federally funded services, 282–285
        as portion of government budget, 282
        primary, 287–288, 295, 300, 333
        provincial and territorial, 282–284
        secondary, 288, 295, 333
        as social determinant of health, 59
        structure of in Canada, 280–285
        tertiary, 288, 295
health literacy, 147, 337
health promotion, 223–227, 322
health status, mental illness and, 13
hearing, difficulties with, 213
heart disease, 212
heart rate
    changes in, 1
    regulation of, 29
Hendrix, Jimi, 111
hepatitis C, 327
herd behaviour, 50, 66
heroin, 109, 256
    prohibition of, 323
heterosexuality, 173
high-intensity interventions, 285
hippocampus, 43
HIV/AIDS, 210, 219

reduction in rates of, 327
hockey, teamwork and, 310
Hoffmann, Albert, 112
Holocaust, Nazi, 128
home-care services, 300
homelessness, 50–51, 237, 312, 323, 332
    chronic, 63
    stress and, 237
    substance use and, 84
    in Vancouver, 64
*homo neanderthalensis*, 143
*homo sapiens*, 143
homosexuality, 173–174
    condemnation of, 174
    discrimination and prejudice against,
        173–174
    as disorder, 174
    pathologization of, 174
    stigmatization of, 173–174
    "treatment" of, 174
homunculus, somatosensory, 29
hope, as central part of Recovery Model, 305
hormones, 1, 40–41, 44
    gender differences and, 172
    pregnancy and, 181
hospital emergency departments, 239–240
hospitalization
    acute, 240–241
    involuntary, 239, 322
housing
    barriers to, 320
    as social determinant of health, 59, 61,
        64, 320, 323, 338
housing services, 300
HPA axis. *See* hypothalamic-pituitary-
    adrenal axis
human rights, 57, 322, 338
humanity, as character virtue, 160, 329
Humber College (Toronto), 10
humour, role of, 328
hydrocodone, 91
hydromorphone, 110, 115
hyperactivity, 59, 162
hyperkinetic disorders, 162
hypersomnia, 87
hypertension, 219, 220

hypomania, 84
hypothalamic-pituitary-adrenal (HPA) axis, 150
hypothalamus, 23, 32, 40–41
hypothyroidism, 219
hypoxia, 39

iatrogenic outcomes, 286, 295
ICD. *See International Classification of Diseases*
"ice pick lobotomy," 259
id, 48
identical (monozygotic) twins, 35
identity development, 52–53
identity vs. role confusion, 52, 156
idioms of distress, cultural, 196–197, 206
illicit psychoactive substances, 115, 119
illiteracy, 147
illness prevention, 223–227, 320
immigrants, mental health of, 195
immigration policies, 193
immortality, 210
impulse disorders, 87
incarceration, 322
incidence, 13, 15
income, as social determinant of health, 59, 323
income security, barriers to, 320
independence, 224–226
    loss of, 215
"Indians," use of term, 199
indicated prevention, 295, 332
Indigenous peoples. *See* Aboriginal peoples
individual behaviour, 47–51
industry vs. inferiority, 52, 154
infancy, 146, 153–154
infant mental health, 152–154
infant mortality, 147, 210
infant psychiatry, 152–154
infectious disease, 320, 327
inferiority, 126
    industry vs., 52, 154
inferiority complex, 48, 67, 190
in-group/out-group dynamics, 126
inhalants, 95
initiative vs. guilt, 52, 154

injection sites, supervised, 326, 328
ink-blot tests, 3
in-patient psychiatric services, 300
insider knowledge, 313–270
Insite, 328
insomnia, 87
instinctual drives, 48
institutionalization, 9. *See also* residential asylums
    elderly and, 224–226
instrumental conditioning, 50, 67
instrumental relativist orientation, 53–54
integrity, ego, 52–53
intellectual disability, 89, 163
intelligence, Gardner's components of, 148
Intelligence Quotient (IQ), 90
intelligence testing, 90
internalizing disorders, 160, 164
*International Classification of Diseases* (ICD), 74, 78, 95–96
    diagnosis blocks, 75
    ICD-10, 74, 160–163, 173, 176–145, 235
interpersonal intelligence, 149
interprofessional collaboration, 311, 315
intersectionality, 59
intersex, 171
intersexuality, 171
interventions, low-intensity vs. high-intensity, 285
intimacy vs. isolation, 52
intoxication
    accidents caused by, 103
    cannabis, 106
    psychological and environmental factors affecting, 97
intrapersonal intelligence, 149
intravenous drug use, 99, 101
introversion, 33, 126
intrusiveness, minimization of, 286
Inuit, 7, 78, 104, 197, 199, 202–205
    elders, 210
    health services for, 284
    racism and, 190–191
involvement, 337–339
    and influence, 133

iodine, 331
iodine deficiency, 332
isolation, 217, 227
    intimacy vs., 52
    social, 215
Italy, mental health care services in, 294

jails, influx of mentally ill to, 13
Jews, hatred of, 128
Johnson, Ruth, 124
Joplin, Janis, 111
Jung, Carl, 48–49
justice, as character virtue, 160, 329

Kainai First Nation, 200
karyotype, 171–172
Kates, Nick, 309
Kefalas, Maria, 159
ketamine, 112
"key life transitions," 158
Kirby, Michael, 124
kleptomania, 87
Klinefelter's Syndrome, 171
knowledge translation and mobilization,
    295, 337, 338
Kohlberg, Lawrence, 6
    stages of moral development, 53–54, 156
koro, 197
Koyczan, Shane, "We are More," 280
Kübler-Ross, Elisabeth, 217

labelling, effects of, 77–78
labelling theory, 77–78, 91, 190, 206
laboratory animals, 49
Laborit, Henri, 254
Labrador, Inuit in, 199
language impairment, 90
latency stage, 52
law and order orientation, 53–54
laws addressing mental health and
    substance use, 322–335
leadership
    dimensions of transformational, 309
    organizational, 308–309
learned helplessness, 238

learning problems, 302
Lennon, John, 111
LGBTQ, 173
licensure, 308
licit psychoactive substances, 115, 119
life expectancy
    in Canada, 209
    internationally, 210
    in men, 209
    in women, 209
    world average, 210
light, 41
limbic system, 31–32, 44
linguistic intelligence, 149
lithium carbonate, 256
lived experience, 313–270, 336
lobotomy, 10
locomotor stage, 52
logical-mathematical intelligence, 149
Lombardi, Vince, 310
loneliness, elderly and, 213
long-term care facilities, 222
Long-Term Disability, 136
long-term residential care, 10
lorazepam, 111
loss, elderly and, 213, 224, 228
low-barrier services, 287–288
low-intensity interventions, 286
LSD (lysergic acid diethylamide), 112
lubrication, failure of, 176
Luechauer, Dr. David, 63

magic mushrooms, 112
magnetic seizure therapy, 257
major depressive disorder, 84, 87
    child abuse and, 155
Makkonen, Timo, 129–130
maladaptive learning, 50
malnutrition, 84
    illiteracy and, 147
    maternal, 149
maltreatment, child, 155–156
managers, role of, 313
mania, 80, 84
manic depressive illness, 84

Manitoba, Aboriginal population of, 197
marijuana, 24, 81, 105
    medical use of, 326
marital therapy, 285, 303
masculine stereotypes, 179–180
Maslow, Abraham, hierarchy of needs, 234
masochism, 89
masturbation, 88, 175
    encouragement of, 176
    prevention of, 176
maturation
    in chimpanzees and gorillas, 143
    in humans, 143
maturity stage, 52–53
MDMA. *See* ecstasy
media, stereotyping in, 126
medically necessary services, 282
medications, 12, 136, 227, 301
    anti-anxiety, 98, 180
    antidepressant, 180, 227, 255–256
    antipsychotic, 12, 77, 239, 243,
        254–255, 301
    dementia and, 226
    diagnosis and sale of, 78
    hormones and, 172
    management of, 243
    mood stabilizing, 256
    off label, 254
    over-the-counter, 108
    as pharmacological cocktail, 257
    prescription, 115, 256
    psychiatric, 253, 301
    sedative, 256
    sexual dysfunction and, 176
    side effects of, 136, 285
    for treatment of workplace mental
        health problems, 136
meditation, 265
    Buddhist, 266
memory, 31–32
    ECT and impairment of, 257
    long-term, 32
    loss of, 80, 219–223
    management of difficulties with, 227
    progressive loss of, 219

men
    life expectancy of, 209
    mental health of, 181–183
meninges, 39, 44
mental capital, 329
mental disorders, 91
    categories of, 78–90
    in children and youth, 160–163
    definition of, 91
mental health, 1–2, 19
    Aboriginal peoples and, 201–202
    among children and youth, 143–163
    biological foundations of, 23–37
    brain function and, 24–30
    of Canadians, 13–15
    cross-sectional view of, 4
    definition of, 1–2
    development and, 51–54, 149–159
    emergencies of, 238–245
    epidemiology and, 14–18
    gender roles and, 179–183
    genetics and epigenetics of, 35
    historical view of, 7–12
    hormones and, 40–41
    laws and public policies addressing,
        322–335
    light, darkness, and, 41
    men and, 181–183
    older adults and, 209–229
    population level and, 2
    positive facets of, 328
    professions and practices, 299–315
    promotion of, 224
    services in Canada, 279–294
    social groups and, 51
    social sciences and, 47–67
    society and, 54–61
    substance use and, 319–339
    tests or measures of, 1, 2–4
    tool kit for, 268–271
    traditional, 7–8
    treatment and, 253–273
    women and, 180–181
    workplace and, 131–137
Mental Health Act, 239, 248, 322

mental health care services, 279–294
  collaborative, 310
  comparison of with other nations, 291
  delivery of, 285–290
  forensic, 289–290
  improvements to, 291
  integration of into general health care,
    323
  professions and practices, 299–315
Mental Health Commission of Canada,
  16, 124, 124, 284, 305, 338
  creation of, 291
  First Nations, Inuit and Métis Advisory
    Committee, 204
  framework for a mental health strategy,
    291–293
  goals of, 291–293
  mission of, 279, 291
mental health law and public policy,
  322–323
mental health problems, 91
  definition of, 91
mental health promotion programs, 148,
  327–331, 338
mental illness, 75, 78, 91
  among children and youth, 143–163
  communities of practice and, 312
  deinstitutionalization and, 11–12
  discrimination and, 123, 126
  illusory, 78
  lived experience and, 288, 299, 313–
    270, 337
  medications for, 12
  neurochemistry and, 257
  prevention of, 331–333
  shame and, 195
  treatment of, 8–9
  violence and, 104
  in workplace, 130
mental retardation, 89–90
mental status examination, 2–3, 19
mescaline, 112
metabolic syndrome, 255
metabolites, 37
methadone, 110, 256

methamphetamine, 31, 108, 108
  addictive nature of, 108
  dependence on, 244
methylenedioxymethamphetamine
  (MDMA). See ecstasy
methylphenidate. See Ritalin
Métis, 7, 78, 104, 200, 202–205
  elders, 210
  federal health services for, 284
  racism and, 190–191
microaggressions, 126, 138
Millenials, 56
Milton, John, 1
Mimico Lunatic Asylum, 10
mind
  brain vs., 4–5
  conflict between aspects of, 48
  as construct, 4
  health of, 4–7
  influences on development of, 4–5
  unconscious, 48, 67
mindfulness, 266, 273
minority groups, labelling of, 77
misconduct, occupational, 308
mistrust, trust vs., 52, 152
mobile services, 240
mobility
  improvement of, 223
  limited, 212–213
Moniz, Egan, 259
monoamine oxidase inhibitors, 255
monoamines, 24
monogamy, 177–178, 184
  animals and, 177–178
  sexual vs. social, 178
monogenist, 189
monozygotic twins. See identical twins
Monteith, Cory, 111
mood, 32, 44
  problems, 80, 136
mood disorder, 15, 43
mood disorders, 84
  prenatal development and, 150
mood stabilizers, 256, 301
Moose Cree First Nation, 200

moral development, Kohlberg's stages of, 53–54, 156
moral model, 116
morality, 53–54
morphine, 97, 109, 256
Morrison, Jim, 111
mortality, 215
    awareness of our own, 217
    infant, 147, 210
    premature, 15
motivational interviewing, 265
movement, 30–31
mu receptors, 97
multiculturalism, 191
muscular-anal stage, 52
music therapy, 222, 303
musical intelligence, 149
Mussell, Bill, 204–205
mutism, elective, 162

Narcotics Anonymous (NA), 261
National Standard on Psychological Health and Safety in the Workplace, 134
natural disasters, 246–247
nature vs. nurture, 180
navigators, social workers as, 303
Nazi Germany, 128, 174
nerve pathways, excitatory vs. inhibitory, 96
nervous system activity, 1
Netherlands, Nazi occupation of, 150
neurochemistry, mental illness and, 257
neurodevelopmental disorder, 163
neurogenesis, 43
neurons, 24, 24, 32, 36–37, 43, 44, 80
neuroscientists, 335
neurostimulation, 257
neurotic disorders, 85
neurotransmitters, 6, 24, 24, 32, 44, 105, 257
    substance use and, 87, 100–101, 107, 108
New Brunswick, 201
new knowledge, creation and exchange of, 314
New Zealand, 204
    mental health care services in, 291
Newfoundland, 201

NGOs. See non-governmental organizations
niacin (vitamin B3), 39
nicotine, 87
night terrors, 87
nightmares, 87
NIMBYism ("not-in-my-backyard" syndrome), 313
9/11 attacks, 246
non-governmental organizations (NGOs), 288
non-organic dyspareunia, 87
non-organic encopresis, 162
non-organic enuresis, 162
non-therapeutic relationships, phases of, 307
norepinephrine, 24
Northwest Territories
    Aboriginal population of, 197
    Inuit in, 199
Nunavut
    Aboriginal population of, 197
    Inuit in, 199
    suicide in, 15, 202
nurse practitioners, 300
Nurse-Family Partnership, 153
nursing, 48, 300, 329
nursing homes, 226, 299
nutritional deprivation, 101

obsessive worry, 238
obsessive-compulsive disorder, 85
    treatment for, 255
occupational burnout, 309
occupational stress, 309
occupational therapists (OTs), 303
oculogyric crisis, 255
Ojibwa, 199
older adults
    cognitive impairment and memory loss in, 219–223
    community activities for, 328
    dementia in, 219–222
    health, illness, and frailty among, 212–213
    mental health and illness in, 209–229

responding to growth in population of, 226–227

treatment of depression and grief in, 226–227

Ontario, Local Health Integration Networks in, 284

opiates, 29
  dependence on, 256
  withdrawal from, 241

opioids, 24, 109
  prescription, 115

opium, 109–111
  addiction to, 110
  effects of, 97
  prohibition of, 323

oppression, 48

oral-sensory stage, 52

organic mental disorders, 79–80, 91

organizational culture, 133

organizational health, 308–309

organizational leadership, 308–309

orgasmic dysfunction, 176

Osbourne, Ozzy, 95

OTs. See occupational therapists

"out of pocket" payment, 282, 284

Out of the Shadows at Last, 124, 291, 305

out-group dynamics. See in-group/out-group dynamics

out-patient services, 284, 289

overdose, 115

overeating, 55

oxycodone, 110, 115

oxygen, 37, 221


pain reduction/relief, 223, 326

palliative care, 218

panic, 238

panic disorder, 85
  treatment for, 255, 261

pansexuality, 173

paranoid delusions, 82

paraphilias, 175, 184

parenting, 181, 332–333

parenting programs, 328

parietal lobe, 32

parkinsonism, 255

Parkinson's disease, 219

participatory-action research, 337

pastoral counselling, 265

pathological disorders, 87

pathology, focus on, 328

Pavlov, Ivan, 49

pediatricians, 303

pedophilia, 88, 175

peer support, 260

peer support workers, 261–262, 299, 307, 315
  12-step groups, 312

pendulum swings, 6–7, 12

perception, 29–30

perseverance, 328

personality, 32–33, 44, 235
  changes in, 80
  disorders of, 87–89, 300

Peterson, Christopher, 160, 329

peyote cactus, 112

PHAC. See Public Health Agency of Canada

pharmaceutical industry, 78
  marketing strategies of, 257

pharmacists, 303

"pharmacological cocktail," 257

pharmacological studies, 336

pharmacological substances, impact of, 6

pharmacological treatment, 137

phencyclidine (PCP), 113

phobic anxiety disorder, 85

physical activity, mental health and, 330

physical health problems, quality of life and, 2

physical science, social sciences vs., 6–7

physician services, administration of, 284

physicians, family, 200–300, 309

physiological dependence, 87, 101

Pibloktoq, 197

pink shirt campaign, 157

pituitary gland, 40–41

plaques, 220, 229

play therapy, 263, 263

police, 238, 240

politicians, role of, 313–314

politics, influence of, 5, 46–47, 78

polypharmacy, 257, 273
poppies, 98
population and public health paradigm,
    319–322
population health, 295, 319–322
    opportunities to improve, 319–339
portability, principle of, 282
Porter, Nathaniel, 73
Portugal, colonization by, 197
post-conventional morality, 53–54
postpartum depression, 87, 181
post-traumatic stress disorder (PTSD), 57,
    85, 181, 191, 245–246, 246
potentiation, long-term, 32
poverty, 48–49
    children and, 147
    illiteracy and, 147
    impact on mental health, 59
    mental illness and, 320–321
    as social determinant of health, 320,
        332, 338
power, personal, 190
prayer, 265
pre-conventional morality, 53–54
pregnancy
    folic acid and, 331
    infectious illnesses in, 150
    mental health and, 181
prejudicial attitudes, 123, 123, 126–128,
    138, 138, 215
premature ejaculation, 87, 176
prenatal development, 149, 149–151
preparedness phase, 246
prescription drug use, 115, 115
presenteeism, 131
prevalence, 13, 14–15, 19
    of mental disorders, 16–18
prevention strategies, 332–289
    indicated, 295, 332
    selective, 295, 332
    universal, 295, 332
preventive interventions, 223
primary health care services, 258, 287–
    288, 295, 333
Prince Edward Island, 201

private health care, 282
private practice, 302
privatization, 282
problem solving, structured, 271–233
professional associations, 308
professional "colleges," 308
progesterone, 40
prohibition, 116, 295, 323–325
prospective surveys, 15
prostitution, 158
    adolescence and, 332
protective factors, risk factors and, 332
protein deprivation, 149
protests, 126
provincial health care services, 282–284
psilocybin mushrooms, 112
psychiatric diagnosis, 74–93. See also
    diagnostic classification
psychiatric hospitals, 9
    number of beds in, 12
psychiatric medication, 301
psychiatric profession, 78
psychiatric therapy, 254
psychiatry, 10, 48, 300
    accessibility to, 300
    child, 300
    geriatric, 300
psychoactive drugs, 10, 24, 56
psychoactive substances. See substance use
psychoanalysis, 10, 263
psychoanalytic therapies, 263
psychological activity, regulation of, 29
psychological dependence, 87, 101, 119
psychological development, disorders of,
    73
psychological health and safety, workplace,
    133–135
psychological risk factors, workplace,
    131–135, 138
psychological testing, 3, 302
psychological theories, 116
psychology, 48, 336
    clinical, 301–302
    "depth," 48–49
psychopathology, 235

psychopharmacology, 12
psychopharmacotherapy, 253–257
    issues in, 256
    side effects of, 257
psychosis, 12, 55, 80
    acute, 242
    adolescence and, 156
    cannabis and, 106
    childhood abuse and, 155–156
    cocaine and, 107
    men and, 181
    puerperal, 87
    treatment of, 253–255, 262
    withdrawal and, 244
    women and, 181
    youth and, 106
psychosocial ideas and therapies, 11–12
psychosocial stress, 61
psychosocial support, access to, 289
psychosurgery, 259, 273
psychotherapy, 137, 227, 246, 260–265, 300
    use and acceptance of, 10–11
psychotic emergency, 243
PTSD. See post-traumatic stress disorder
public administration, principle of, 282
public health, 295, 319–322
    opportunities to improve, 319–339
Public Health Agency of Canada (PHAC),
    289, 331
public policies addressing mental health
    and substance use, 322–335, 339
puer aeternus, 48
puerperal psychosis, 87
puerpurium, disorders of, 87
punishment-obedience orientation, 53–54
pyromania, 87

quality of life, 2
Quebec
    Health and Social Services Centres in, 284
    Inuit in, 199
    psychiatric beds in, 12
    rates of access to psychologists in, 302

race, 189–190
    lack of validity of, 190

stereotypes based on, 126
racism, 190, 190–159, 206
Raphael, Dennis, 59
rapid tranquilization, 243
Reagan, Ronald, 233
recognition and reward, 133
recovery
    components of, 306
    remission and, 305–306
Recovery Model, 305–306, 315, 337
recovery phase, 246
reductionistic thinking, 5, 6
refugees, 57
    definition of, 195
    mental health of, 195
relative deprivation theory, 60–61
relaxation, 269
reliability, diagnostic, 76–77, 91
religion, stereotypes based on, 126
religious approaches to treatment, 265
religious delusions, 82
remission, recovery and, 305–306
repression, 48
research
    four pillars of, 336–337
    science and, 335–337
research activity, scientific, 314, 335–337,
    338
residential asylums, 9
residential school syndrome, 57, 67
residential schools, 57, 200
residential treatment services. See nursing
    homes
resilience, 331
resistance, 329
respiration
    changes in, 1
    regulation of, 29
response phase, 246
retrospective surveys, 15
return to work (RTW), 136
review boards, 239, 290
riots, 51
risk factors, 329, 332
    preventive factors and, 331
risk taking, men and, 181

Ritalin (methylphenidate), 78
Rohypnol, 111
role confusion, identity vs., 52, 156
romantic love, 177–178
roofies, 111
Roots of Empathy, 158
Rorschach tests, 3
Rosenhan, David, 77
RTW. *See* return to work

SAD. *See* Seasonal Affective Disorder
sadism, 89
sadomasochism, 89
Salvation Army, 215, 241, 242
salvia divinorum, 113
sanitation, 319
Saskatchewan, Aboriginal population of, 197
Satoro, Ryunosuke, 299
schizophrenia, 16, 27, 35, 43, 60, 80,
    82–67, 243
    cannabis and, 106
    negative symptoms of, 82
    positive symptoms of, 82–66
    prenatal development and, 150
    prodromal symptoms of, 82
    stigma of, 129
schizophrenia spectrum disorder,
    prevalence of, 14–15
schizophrenic disorders, 82–67, 300, 336
schizotypal disorders, 82
school connectedness, 147
science, research and, 335–337
scientific research community, 314
Scotland, mental health care services in, 294
Seasonal Affective Disorder (SAD), 41–42
secobarbital, 111
Second World War, 128
secondary health care services, 288, 295, 333
sedatives, 29, 95, 111, 243, 256
    women and, 180
segregation, 9
selective prevention, 295, 332
selective serotonin uptake inhibitors
    (SSRIs), 255
self-care, workbooks for, 272
self-determination, 198

self-discrimination, 126
self-esteem, 126, 190
self-help resources, 261
self-image, 55
self-isolation, 126
self-management, 261
self-stigma, 126, 286
self-worth, lack of, 126
Seligman, Martin, 160, 329
sensation, 29–30
    proprioceptive, 29
sensory perception, 29–30
separation anxiety, 90, 162
serotonin, 24, 107
sex, 169–184, 184
    as a construct, 170
    vs. gender, 169–170
    variation within vs. variation across, 180
sex trade workers, free condoms for, 326
Sexaholics Anonymous, 177
sexism, 180
sexual activity, 174
sexual addiction, 177
sexual assault, 115
sexual aversion, 87
sexual behaviour, compulsive, 84
sexual desire
    excessive, 87, 177
    lack or loss of, 87, 176
sexual dysfunction, 87, 176–177
sexual identity ,138–139
sexual intercourse, 174
sexual orientation, 173–174, 184
sexual preference, disorders of, 88
sexual reassignment surgery, 172, 172
sexuality, 169–184
    stereotypes based on, 126
Seymour Hoffman, Philip, 110
Shambhala Music Festival, 115
shame/doubt, autonomy vs., 52, 154
shared care. *See* collaborative mental health care
shelters, 240
short-term disability, 135–136
Sichuan earthquake, 247
"silos," delivery of mental health services
    in, 309

Singapore, 197
skin tone, stereotypes based on, 126
slavery, 190
sleep, 29
    disturbances, 87
sleeping pills, 111
sleep-wake cycle, disorder of, 87
sleepwalking, 87
Slow Breathing Method, 270
social connectedness, 223
social constructionism, 54, 56, 57
social contract orientation, 53–54
social determinants of health, 58–59, 67,
    320, 323, 336
    children's mental health and, 144–149
social enterprises, 137
social exclusion, as social determinant of
    health, 59
social gradient in health, 320, 338
social networks, connections to, 55, 224
social responsibility, 160
social roles, loss of, 215
social safety net, as social determinant of
    health, 59
social sciences
    mental health and, 47–67, 336
    physical science vs., 6–7
social support network, 271
social work, 48, 302–303, 329
societal norms, 48
society, mental health and, 54–61
sociological theories, 116
sociology, 51, 77, 336
solvents, 112–113
somatization, 196
somatization disorders, 300
somatoform disorders, 85
soporifics, 111
Spain, colonization by, 197
spatial intelligence, 149
Speck, Richard, 172
spiritual approaches to treatment, 265
spiritual practices, 7–8
Spitzer, Dr. Robert, 173
sponsors, 312

SSRIs. See selective serotonin uptake
    inhibitors
stagnation, generativity vs., 52
stakeholders, roles of, 313
"Stand Up for Mental Health," 268
Statistics Canada, 13, 14–16, 285
stealing, pathological, 87
stepped-care approach, 286, 295
stereotyping, 123, 126, 129
Stewart, Jane, 200
stigma, 123–130, 138, 323
    causes of, 126–129
    combating, 129–130
    definition of, 123
    disability and, 320
    ethnocultural groups and, 195
    foci of, 129
    treatment and, 261
    in workplace, 130
stimulants, use of, 31, 106–109
stoicism, men and, 179
Street Spirits Theatre Company, 148
Street to Home Foundation, 66
stress, 235–236, 248
    definition of, 242
    memory loss and, 219
    occupational, 308
    social, 182
    women and, 180
    workplace, 131–132, 135, 137
stress reactions, 85
stressors, 235, 248
    role of, 4
    social, 182
stress-related disorders, 85
stroke, 32, 220
structured problem solving, 271–233
students, mental health tool kit for,
    268–271
substance abuse, prevalence of, 14–15
substance dependence, prevalence of,
    14–15
substance use, 4, 31, 32, 95, 131, 137,
    219, 220, 284
    Aboriginal peoples and, 201
    dependence and, 80, 99, 101, 106, 119

harmful use, 80
impact of in Canada, 116–118
laws and public policies addressing, 322–335
licit vs. illicit, 95, 119
low-barrier services and, 288
men and, 182
mental and behavioural disorders due to, 80–81
mental health and, 319–339
psychosis and, 80
range of in Canada, 126–141
risks and harms of, 101–102
spectrum of, 96
stigma of, 129
substitution therapy for, 256
tolerance and, 101, 119
treatment for, 244, 261
withdrawal and, 80, 101, 119, 242
substance use disorder, 15, 16, 56, 95–96, 119
    prevention of, 332–289
substance use emergency, 245
substitute decision-makers, 239
substitution therapy, 256
suicidal emergency, 242–243
suicide
    Aboriginal peoples and, 202
    anomie and, 55
    in Asia, 45
    bullying and, 156
    elderly and, 215
    gender differences in, 182–183
    men and, 182–183
    in Nunavut, 15
    poverty and, 48
    rates in Nunavut, 202
    a "silent epidemic," 182
    substance use and, 182
suicide prevention, 333–335
    in Inuit communities, 335
superego, 48
supervised injection sites, 326, 328
supply reduction, 295, 324
supported employment, 137

supported self-management (SSM), 261–262, 273
sweat lodge ritual, 8
symptomatic mental disorders, 79–80
syphilis, 332
systems theory, 54

tangles, 220, 229
tardive dyskinesia, 255
teamwork, 310
technology, development of, 257
temperance
    as character virtue, 160, 329
    women's movement, 325
territorial health care services, 282–284
terrorist attacks, 246
tertiary health care services, 288, 295
testosterone, 40
    medication to augment levels of, 176
tetrahydrocannabinol (THC), 105
thalidomide, 258
THC. See tetrahydrocannabinol
therapeutic relationships, 307, 315
    phases of, 307
thiamine (vitamin B1), 39
Thornicroft, Graham, 129
thought, 31–32
thyroid gland, 39
tic disorders, 90, 162, 164
tobacco, 95, 104–105
    Aboriginal peoples and, 104–105
    control of in Canada, 104–105
    harms of, 104–105
    legal status of, 324
    morbidity, 103
    widespread use of, 104–105
tolerance, 101, 119
topiramate, 256
traditional mental health, 7–8
traditional ritual practices, 265
transcendence, as character virtue, 160, 329
transcranial magnetic stimulation (TMS), 259
transexualism, 88
transgender, 88, 172, 184
transinstitutionalization, 13, 39

transsexualism, 88, 91
transvestitism, 88
    dual-role, 88
trauma, management of, 245–246
traumatic brain injury, 27
treatment, 8–9, 253–273
    combination of, 266
    for dementia and related problems,
        223–227
    psychopharmacotherapy, 253–257
    psychotherapy, 257–265
    refusal of, 239
    religious, spiritual, and meditative
        approaches, 265–266
    side effects of, 284
trigeminal nerive stimulation (TNS), 259
Triple X syndrome, 171
trust vs. mistrust, 52, 152
Tseshaht First Nation, 200
Turner's Syndrome, 171
"12 Step Program," 261, 305
12-step facilitation, 261

unconscious, collective, 48–49, 67
unconscious mind, 48, 67
unemployment, as social determinant of
    health, 48
unipolar depression, 84
United States
    health care in, 294
    mental health care services in, 294
    prohibition in, 325
    racist attitudes in, 126
universal ethical principle orientation, 53–54
universal prevention, 295, 332
universality, principle of, 280
unspecified mental disorder, 74
"upstream" vs. "downstream," 320

vaccines, development of, 320
vaginismus, 176
vagus nerve stimulation (VNS), 259
validity, diagnostic, 76–77, 91
Vancouver, homelessness, 64
Vancouver, Downtown Eastside, 51, 321,
    327

Viagra, 176
victimization
    violent criminal, 13
    women and, 181
violence, 158
    domestic, 181
    men and, 181
    sexual, 181
    women and, 180–181
violent behaviour, 244
vision, difficulties with, 212
visuo-spatial impairment, 90
vitamins, 39, 331
voyeurism, 88
vulnerability, 323

Waddell, Dr. Charlotte, 153
"wake and bake," 4
wakefulness, 27–28
Wangchuck, Jigme Singye, 62–63
war, mental health and, 56
War on Drugs, 116
wartime attacks, 246
waste control, 319
weight, stereotypes based on, 126
weight gain, 305
wisdom
    age and, 210–211
    as character virtue, 160, 329
    lived experience and, 312
withdrawal, 80, 101, 119, 182, 242, 256
withdrawal management, 242, 244–245, 248
    acute, 241–242
women
    as heterogeneous group, 48
    life expectancy of, 209
    mental health of, 180–181
    temperance movement, 325
work integration activities, 137
workload management, 133
workplace
    accommodations in, 136
    clinical management of mental health
        problems in, 136–137
    costs vs. benefits of absence from,
        135–136

mental health and, 131–137, 303
positive features of, 132
protective factors for psychological
   health and safety in, 133
psychological risk factors in, 131–135,
   138
stereotyping and, 123
stigma and discrimination in, 130
World Health Organization (WHO), 1–2,
14, 48, 74, 103, 195, 323
worry management, 270–271

X chromosomes, 171
XYY syndrome, 171–172

Y chromosomes, 171
Years Lived with Disability (YLD), 15, 20
Years of Life Lost (YLL), 15, 20
YLD. *See* Years Lived with Disability
YLL. *See* Years of Life Lost
youth
   acculturation and, 193
   ageism and, 215
   immigrant, 193
   marijuana and, 4
   mental disorders in, 160–163
   mental health and illness in, 143–163
   preventive strategies for, 332
   safety of, 302
Yukon, Aboriginal population of, 197